Didache and Judaism

Jewish
Roots
of an
Ancient
Christian-
Jewish
Work

MARCELLO DEL VERME

t&t clark

Copyright © 2004 by Marcello Del Verme

T & T Clark International
Madison Square Park, 15 East 26th Street, New York, NY 10010

T & T Clark International
The Tower Building, 11 York Road, London SE1 7NX

T & T Clark International is a Continuum imprint.

Cover design: Lee Singer

Library of Congress Cataloging-in-Publication Data

Del Verme, Marcello.
  Didache and Judaism : Jewish roots of an ancient Christian-Jewish work / Marcello Del Verme.
      p. cm.
  Includes bibliographical references and index.
  ISBN 0-567-02531-4 (hardcover) — ISBN 0-567-02541-1 (pbk.)
  1. Didache. 2. Judaism—Relations—Christianity. 3. Christianity and other reli-gions—Judaism. I. Title.
  BS2940.T5D45 2004
  270.1—dc22

                                    2004017561

Printed in the United States of America

04 05 06 07 08 09   10 9 8 7 6 5 4 3 2 1

To my sons
Francesco and Emanuele
and to the memory
of my parents

CONTENTS

ACKNOWLEDGMENTS

My educational journey over the past thirty years has followed a complex trajectory of different but complementary studies and methodologies: philosophical sciences (specialisation in historical-religious studies) at the University of Naples 'Federico II'; biblical and theological sciences (specialisation in Biblical Theology, Ancient languages, Exegesis of the OT and NT) in Rome (Antonianum and Pontifical Biblical Institute) and in Jerusalem (Studium Biblicum Franciscanum), and courses on the Judaisms of the Biblical Graeco-Roman period and on Rabbinics in Jerusalem and at the Oriental Institute of Oxford. The studies undertaken always focused on the so-called 'religions of the Book' (in particular Judaism and Christianity) which emerged in the ancient Eastern Mediterranean basin and developed up to late antiquity in both the East and the West.

This *opus parvum* on the Judaism(s) of the *Didache* consequently provides me with the occasion to express my immense gratitude to the numerous *magistri* whom I had the good fortune to encounter and whose lessons, lectures and expertise I had the privilege of experiencing during my studies in Rome, Jerusalem, Naples and Oxford, and to the Schools for the diversity in methodology and knowledge which they provided. This study is the outcome of longstanding research on the *Didache* initiated at the University of Lecce and concluded at the University of Naples. Should the patient reader find something of benefit in it, a great part of its merits are attributable to my *magistri,* many of whom have already departed this world. In memory of them: *Requiescant...*

The present work was concluded some time ago in Italian. A number of my noteworthy friends and colleagues, both here and abroad, urged me to publish it in English (I duly take the opportunity to thank them, below chap. 1 n. 6). In fact the work was lying idle in my *scriptorium,* just like a saddled and bridled horse ready for the race but waiting for its jockey. The final and decisive spur for its publication in English came from Prof. James Hamilton Charlesworth of the

Princeton Theological Seminary, a visiting fellow invited as a very distinguished foreign professor by the University of Naples 'Federico II' in the period March-June 2003. Prof. Charlesworth, who is the author of the Preface, presented my work with competence and enthusiasm to the editorial team of the JSPS Series, and they accepted it. Dr. Henry Carrigan of T. & T. Clark International has demonstrated concern and understanding during the entire publishing process. While I do not know him personally, I would very much like to meet him one day, in Naples I hope, to express my gratitude. Consequently, *in primis*, my most sincere thanks are due to Prof. Charlesworth, 'mentor' of this work, and then to Dr. Carrigan.

And now I pass on to the four white horses of what I refer to as 'my *quadriga*', recalling an image recurring in ancient Latin authors (see, for example, Q. Ennius, *Ann.* 513; M. Tullius Cicero, *Epist. Ad Q. fr.* 2, 13, 2; Q. Horatius Flaccus, *Epist.* 1, 11, 29; P. Vergilius Maro, *Georg.*, 1, 512; T. Livius, 1, 28, 10; T. Maccius Plautus, *Amph.* 422), because of its symbolic and positive meaning. These four have worked hard, especially in the final stages of the race, to reach the finishing post of publishing this book. In particular I thank Dr. Susanna Grazia Rizzo, currently tutor in history at the School of History and Politics of the University of Wollongong (Australia), a gifted former student of the University of Naples 'Federico II', who has along with Dr. Helen Brock of Oxford (Great Britain) translated the Italian text into English and reviewed some of the parts which had already been translated. I also thank two PhD Candidates whom I am currently supervising, Luca Arcari and Lara Guglielmo; they have collaborated in the research effort in particular in regard to the updating of the bibliographical record and the drawing up of the Indexes. Even at this final state, they prompted me to reflect on a series of issues and findings that I outlined and discussed in the book with pertinent and, I would say, rather perspicacious questions. Mr. Arcari is at the final stage of his PhD work in Ancient History and Miss Guglielmo is at the beginning of her long PhD journey. However to both of them I wish: *Fausta omina vobis*!

Finally I warmly thank my family for the serene atmosphere I experienced at home and for the patience and understanding demonstrated by my wife Antonia and two sons Francesco and Emanuele during the hard and long phases of this research, which at times led me to complete isolation and, often, to set aside family commitments.

To the few or many patient readers: *Valete et Shalom*.

Preface

The need to develop categories is essential in organizing data in scientific research, as Aristotle demonstrated. Such categories, however, can also tend to separate what fundamentally belongs together. For example, "Early Judaism" and "Early Christianity," as well as "Jewish" and "Christian," appear frequently in most publications by scholars and journalists who are discussing the origins of documents like the *Didache*. Sometimes scholars talk about "the parting of the ways," which denotes the categorical separation of Judaism and Christianity. Assuming a categorical separation between Jews and Christians, especially before the defeat of Bar Kokhba in 135 or 136 CE, removes Jesus, Paul, and the Evangelists from the context that alone provides the framework for understanding them.

Even worse are the prevalent tendencies to divorce the "New Testament" from Judaism, and to isolate the so-called "Patristics" texts from the New Testament and Judaism. When exposed for critical review, such boundaries are usually denied by authors who have perpetuated them, yet these rigid boundaries tend to define many books that introduce and portray the Mediterranean world that existed prior to Constantine the Great.

As many of us scholars have tried to demonstrate, we must not label Jesus as if he belongs outside of Judaism. Jesus belongs within Judaism. We should also avoid such terms as "Christianity" and "the church," when discussing first-century sociological and theological phenomena and thought. These terms are patently anachronistic before 135/6 CE.

It is clear that when the *Didache* was composed we might envision a community like the church with administrators called "deacons," "presbyters," and "bishops." Such institutional organization seems warranted from studying texts that originated sometime after 100 CE, notably in the Pastoral Epistles attributed to Paul in the New Testament. The danger then might be to forget that the origin of "the ecclesia" is fundamentally tied to Jewish institutions, groups, and even the synagogue, which was taking a more definite shape after the destruction of Jerusalem in 70 CE.

Professor M. Del Verme's studies, focused on first and second-century groups and texts, clarify correctly the antecedents of such works as the

Didache. Looking at this text, remembering what we have learned about the Jewishness of Matthew and John, and especially the continuing desire of Jesus' followers after 70 CE to attend synagogal services, we can agree that it is impossible and misleading to talk about "Jews" as paradigmatically distinct from "Christians." Many in the groups behind the *Didache* might well have thought, as did Paul, that they belonged within Israel and continued to be faithful "Jews."

What labels should be used to describe such groups? Work over the past four decades proves that "Jewish-Christianity" has not been easy to define or comprehend. Many "Jewish Christians"—or to use Professor Del Verme's judicious term "Christian Jews"—should not be evaluated as heretical. Indeed, the mere use of such terms as "orthodoxy" and "heresy" is anachronistic when studying documents and groups prior to the edicts of the Councils that were first convened in 325 at Nicea.

The *Didache* mirrors institutions and preserves ideas that have, in some way, been inherited from Judaism. Most prominently, among the ideas, is the concept of "Two Ways." One of the possible antecedents of this dualistic paradigm may be found in the concept of two warring spirits that is found in early Jewish documents, such as *The Rule of the Community*, which was certainly determinative for the Qumranites. It seems clear that while the Community at Qumran ceased to exist after 68 CE, the Essene Movement, to which it was related, did not vanish at that time.

Many questions are raised by such early texts as the *Didache*. Did Essenes join the Palestinian Jesus Movement and help shape the terminology that we find in the Gospel of John, the *Didache*, and in other early texts that have been traditionally studied only within the "history of the church"?

Texts like the *Didache* and their formative contexts are not lucidly portrayed for us to view if we continue to use old labels that misrepresent the world in which they originated. If we could ask the author (or compiler) of the *Didache* what were the most influential traditions or documents for him, what would his answers reveal? What categories would he have assumed were appropriate? If we are insensitive to his categories, then how can we discern his perspectives?

I salute Professor Del Verme for his pioneering insights and clarifying focus. He has shown possible ways to move ahead in studying early texts within a more enlightened perception of contexts.

J.H. Charlesworth
Princeton Theological Seminary
July 4, 2004

Abbreviations*

ANRW = Aufstieg und Niedergang der römischen Welt, Berlin-New York
ArbLGHJ = Arbeiten zur Literatur und Geschichte des hellenistischen Judentums, Leiden
ASE = *Annali di storia dell'esegesi*, Bologna
ASNU = Acta Seminarii Neotestamentici Upsaliensis, Stockholm-Lund-Uppsala-Copenhagen.
BBB = Bonner biblische Beiträge, Bonn
BCR = Biblioteca di cultura religiosa, Brescia
BeO = *Bibbia e Oriente*, Genova-Bornato (BS)
BEThL = Bibliotheca Ephemeridum Theologicarum Lovaniensium, Louvain-Gembloux
Bib = *Biblica*, Roma
BiblT = Biblioteca Teologica, Brescia
BJRL = *Bulletin of the John Rylands Library*, Manchester
BPat = Biblioteca Patristica, Firenze-Bologna
BZ = *Biblische Zeitschrift*, Paderborn
BZAW = Beihefte zur Zeitschrift für die alttestamentliche Wissenschaft, Berlin-New York
BZNW = Beihefte zur Zeitschrift für die neutestamentliche Wissenschaft und die Kunde der älteren Kirche, Berlin-New York
CBQ = *Catholic Biblical Quarterly*, Washington (D.C.)
CBQ.MS = The Catholic Biblical Quarterly - Monograph Series, Washington (D.C.)
CRINT = Compendia Rerum Iudaicarum ad Novum Testamentum, Assen/Maastricht-Philadelphia-Minneapolis
CrSt = *Cristianesimo nella storia*. Ricerche storiche esegetiche e teologiche, Bologna
CSCO = Corpus Scriptorum Christianorum Orientalium, Louvain
CSEL = Corpus Scriptorum Ecclesiasticorum Latinorum, Vindobonae
DACL = *Dictionnaire d'archéologie chrétienne et de liturgie*, Paris
DBS = *Dictionnaire de la Bible. Supplément*, Paris
DJD = Discoveries in the Judean Desert, Oxford
DPAC = *Dizionario Patristico e di Antichità Cristiane*, Casale Monferrato-Genova

* In addition see infra, chap. 1 n. 1.

Marcello Del Verme

DSSD = *Dead Sea Scrolls Discoveries*, Leiden
EncJud = *Encyclopaedia Judaica*, Jerusalem
ExpTim = *The Expository Times*, Edinburgh
FRLANT = Forschungen zur Religion und Literatur des Alten und Neuen Testaments, Göttingen
GCS = Die griechischen christlichen Schriftsteller der ersten drei Jahrhunderte, Leipzig-Berlin
Henoch = *Henoch*. Studi storicofilologici sull'Ebraismo, Università di Torino
HThK = Herders theologischer Kommentar zum Neuen Testament, Freiburg i. Br.
HThR = *Harvard Theological Review*, Cambridge (Mass.)
HSM = Harvard Semitic Monographs, Cambridge (Mass.)
IEJ = *Israel Exploration Journal*, Jerusalem
Int = *Interpretation*, Richmond (Virg.)
JBL = *Journal of Biblical Literature*, Philadelphia (Pa.)
JBL.MS = Journal of Biblical Literature Monograph Series, Philadelphia (Pa.)
JJS = *Journal of Jewish Studies*, Oxford
JSJ = *Journal for the Study of Judaism in the Persian, Hellenistic and Roman Period*, Leiden
JSJ.S = Supplements to Journal for the Study of Judaism, Leiden
JSNT = *Journal for the Study of the New Testament*, Sheffield
JSNT.S = Journal for the Study of the New Testament. Supplement Series, Sheffield
JSP = *Journal for the study of the pseudepigrapha and related Literature*, Sheffield
JSP.S = Journal for the study of the pseudepigrapha. Supplement Series, Sheffield
JSS = *Journal of Semitic Studies*, Manchester
JThS = *Journal of Theological Studies*, Oxford-London
KlP = *Der Kleine Pauly. Lexikon der Antike*, München.
Lat. = *Lateranum*, Roma
Materia giudaica = *Materia giudaica*. Rivista dell'Associazione italiana per lo studio del giudaismo, Firenze
Neotest. = *Neotestamentica*, Pretoria
NGS = New Gospel Studies, Macon (GA)
NHC = Nag Hammadi Codex
NT = *Novum Testamentum*, Leiden
NT.S = Supplements to Novum Testamentum, Leiden
NTS = *New Testament Studies*, Cambridge (UK)
NTS.MS = Society for New Testament Studies Monograph Series, Cambridge (UK)
PG = *Patrologiae Graecae* cursus completus, accurante et recognoscente J.-P. Migne, Parisiis
PL = *Patrologiae Latinae* cursus completus, accurante et recognoscente J.-P. Migne, Parisiis
PO = Patrologia Orientalis, Paris

PVTG = Pseudepigrapha Veteris Testamenti Graece, Leiden
PW = Pauly-Wissowa, *Real-Encyclopädie der classischen Altertumswissenschaft*, Stuttgart
PWSup = Supplement to PW, Stuttgart
QChr = *Qumran Chronicle*, Kraków
QHenoch = Quaderni di Henoch, Torino
RAC = *Reallexicon für Antike und Christentum*, Stuttgart
RB = *Revue biblique*, Paris
RdQ = *Revue de Qumrân*, Paris
RdT = *Rassegna di Teologia*, Napoli
RechSR = *Recherches de science religieuse*, Paris
RHPhR = *Revue d'histoire et de philosophie religieuses*, Strasbourg
RivBib = *Rivista biblica italiana*, Brescia-Bologna
RStB = *Ricerche storico-bibliche*, Bologna
Salm. = *Salmanticensis*, Salamanca
SBFLA = *Studii Biblici Franciscani Liber Annuus*, Jerusalem
SBL.SP = Society of Biblical Literature Seminar Papers, Atlanta
SC = Sources Chrétiennes, Paris
SNTS.MS= Society for New Testament Studies Monograph Series, Cambridge (UK)
SOCr = Scritti delle origini cristiane, Bologna
SPMed = Studia Patristica Mediolanensia, Milano
StBi = Studi biblici, Brescia
STDJ = Studies on the Texts of the Desert of Judah, Leiden
NT.S = Supplements to Novum Testamentum, Leiden
SVTP = Studia in Veteris Testamenti Pseudepigrapha, Leiden
TDNT = *Theological Dictionary of the New Testament*, Grand Rapids (Mich.)
TWAT = *Theologisches Wörterbuch zum Alten Testament*, Stuttgart
TWNT = *Theologisches Wörterbuch zum Neuen Testament*, Stuttgart
VetChr = *Vetera Christianorum*, Bari
VigChr = *Vigiliae Christianae*, Leiden
VT = *Vetus Testamentum*, Leiden
VT.S = Supplements to Vetus Testamentum, Leiden
WUNT = Wissenschaftliche Untersuchungen zum Neuen Testament, Tübingen
ZKG = *Zeitschrift für Kirchengeschichte*, Stuttgart
ZNW = *Zeitschrift für die neutestamentliche Wissenschaft und die Kunde des Urchristentums*, Berlin

INTRODUCTION

This research on the Judaism(s) of the *Didache* must be cast in a wider debate, which has become particularly lively in recent decades. Traditionally the relationship between Judaism and Christianity has been considered in terms of a contraposition between different religions since the predication of Jesus. Thus, for instance, in the erroneous although influential vision of a W. Bousset, Jesus appeared to be "a divine miracle" in relation to the surrounding Jewish *milieu*. Many factors, occurring in the last century, however, have contributed to change this narrow and historically groundless exegetical perspective. I recall just a few: the impact that the *Shoah* has had on the Western conscience and, consequently, the rise of a 'spirit of dialogue' fostering new relations among the Christian Churches, in particular between the Roman Catholic and the non-Christian religions, above all the so-called Abrahamic religions (Hebraism, Christianity and Islam). The new 'spirit of dialogue' among cultures and peoples has prompted the foundation on a new contextual (philological and historical) basis of the relations between Hebraism and Christianity, which are no longer considered separately but as two entities stemming from a common matrix,[1] that is two branches of the same tree (Rom 11:16; see also Eph 2:11-18, in particular v 14). This new atmosphere has produced – on the occasion of the Ecumenical Council Vatican II (in its documents and in those which followed: see Pesce 1994) – one of the most significant and prominent moments through the Council Declaration "Nostra Aetate" (October 28, 1965) and indirectly – however, not to be underestimated – with the successive Declaration "Dignitatis Humanae" (December 7, 1965) regarding religious freedom. Furthermore the earlier constitution of the State of Israel (1948), which brought about not only an autonomous re-definition of the Jewish identity – and not only in

---

1. A.H. Becker-A. Yoshiko Reed (eds.), *The Ways that Never Parted. Jews and Christians in Late Antiquity and the Early Middle Ages* (Tübingen: Mohr Siebeck, 2003). For other bibliographic references see infra, chap. 1.

political-territorial terms – in relation to Christianity, but has simultaneously created a dialectics of encounter/clash with the other two Abrahamic religions present in *Terra Sancta*: Christianity and Islam.

In methodological and historical-cultural terms, it was the discovery of the Dead Sea Scrolls (beginning from 1948) that has revealed and proven the existence of a pre-Christian Judaism(s) more variegated than what had been previously supposed. This has gradually brought about discarding the widespread, but erroneous, belief of a monolithic Palestinian Judaism, legalistic in character and substantially coinciding with the Pharisaism contemporary to Jesus and Jesus' movement, when the first 'Christian-Jewish' communities began to emerge in Palestine and in Syria, and which later became more distinctly 'Christian' in the oriental and occidental diaspora. The picture that one has today both of the Judaism(s) of the time of Jesus and of the formation of the first Christian communities – for obvious reasons – appears to be in fact richer and more articulated and complex than was previously thought.

The exploration and appreciation of the plurality of orientations/movements and the multiple identities within the Judaism of the Second Temple – in particular that of the final phase which is better documented – has induced rejecting the idea of a Jewish orthodoxy (the so-called 'common Judaism') of Pharisaic origin and in recent years some scholars have begun to refer to 'Judaisms' (see Neusner-Green-Frerichs 1987). Analogously a re-definition of the Judaism of the Diaspora and of its relations with the Greek *milieu*-context has become necessary, if not essential: in particular, scholars have felt the necessity to abandon the idea of a Diaspora Judaism as a 'minor' reality in relation to the Palestinian one, on the sole basis that it had been mitigated by its contact with Greek culture (see Hengel 1988[3]). On the contrary, Diaspora Judaism represents a social (and not only religious) phenomenon extremely variegated and widespread, and for some aspects even influential upon Greek *milieu* (see Barclay 1988).

The new perspectives on Judaism(s) also induce re-considering the beginnings of the movement of Jesus and casting the birth and successive expansion in a new light. Consequently the controversies between Jesus and the Pharisees, for instance, along with the critical statements of Paul in regard to his Pharisaic past and the Law, and even more the distancing of the Christian communities from Jewish practices and institutions, or the anti-Jewish polemics of some proto-Christian texts (see Sanders 1977.1985.1990a.1992) are no longer perceived as a 'conflict between different religions', but as a dialectic within Judaism itself. This means that it is possible to consider Christianity in its initial phase as one of the many Jewish orientations or movements (see, for example, Segal 1986; Boccaccini 1991; Barclay-Sweet 1996; Troiani 1993a.1993b. 1996. 1999a). In fact, as has happened with Judaism, scholars have also begun to use the plural 'Christianities' in the study of Ancient Christianity (see Norelli 1994).

This newly emerged framework has revealed the methodological and historical inadequacy of some of the traditional labels as that of 'Judaeo-Christianity' – a modern historical and historiographical invention – that do not appear to pertain to early Christianity, which is itself an intra-Judaic phenomenon (cf. Mimouni 1992. 1998a). This has favoured the flourishing of numerous studies of single proto-Christian (canonical and non-canonical) texts and of the Christian communities that produced them, considered in their relation with – or as part of – coeval Judaism (see Bibliography in Del Verme 2001a.2001b.2003b; and infra, in particular chap. 1).

This new perspective in the study of Judaism and Christianity has imposed the necessity to re-consider *ab imis* the chronology and the causes that brought to the separation between Jews and Christians: some scholars have considered the interpretation of the Law as the profound cause of the "split" (see for example Marguerat 1996); by contrast others have identified it in the Messianic question (Dunn 1991 and 1992). The general tendency today, which in my opinion appears to be also supported by the sources, shifts the chronology of the birth of Christianity, as a 'religion distinct' from Judaism, to the years following the First Jewish Revolt (66-73 [74?] CE) – although some scholars propose even a later date, that is after the Second Jewish Revolt against Rome led by Bar Kokhba in 132-135 CE (see Pesce 2003b. 2004).

The present study of the *Didache* is certainly neither new nor innovative in pointing out the presence and richness of borrowings from and references to Judaism (see in this regard the recent monograph by van de Sandt-Flusser 2002) prior or coeval to this ancient Christian-Jewish text, which still remains, for certain aspects, enigmatic. However I would like to indicate 'new paths' of reading that – through an analysis focusing on some institutions and rituals or doctrinal beliefs typically Jewish 'sedimented' in the text and reformulated for a Christian-Jewish *milieu* – redeem the interpretation of the

Didache from an unjust 'New Testament mortgage' or from the 'generic reference' to Judaism. In my opinion, the fecundity of the text appears to be richer if the research – certainly problematic – is limited to the exploration of historical questions regarding the definition of the identity of the various groups/currents/movements present in the *Didache*, which often institutionally and, at times, even doctrinally interact with antecedent or coeval Judaism(s). The identities of these groups/currents/movements however must be continuously defined and not merely evoked.

This perspective, by avoiding the danger of 'generically' referring to the Jewish origins/roots of the *Didache*, could lead to the identification – in some parts or *strata* of the text which has survived – of groups/factions within the Christian-Jewish community which shares the same (Jewish) institutions and re-proposes the same dialectics among different (Jewish) groups. At the same time – yet in a broader sense – such perspective might allow my research on the *Didache* to enter into the rich and fruitful stream of recent studies that aim at exploring the many identities existing in the Ancient Near East,[2] in particular among Jews and Christians with their inner dialectics (groups/movements/factions).[3]

Naples, October 2003.

---

2. On these trajectories of research see in general J. Assmann, *Das kulturelle Gedächtnis: Schrift, Erinnerung und politische Identität in frühen Hochkulturen* (München: C.H. Beck, 1992); Id., *Fünf Stufen auf dem Wege zum Kanon: Tradition und Schriftkultur im frühen Judentum und seiner Umwelt* (Münster: Lit: 1999); Id., *Religion und kulturelles Gedächtnis: zehn Studien* (Zürich-München: Artemis Verlag, 2000); and B. Lewis, *The Multiple Identities of the Middle East* (London: Weidenfield & Nicolson [also New York: Schocken Books], 1998), in particular the Introduction and chap. VIII; Id., *Cultures in Conflict: Christians, Muslims, and Jews in the Age of Discovery* (New York: Oxford University Press, 1995).

3. *A propos*, I mention two initiatives: firstly, the next IOQS meeting – to be held in Groningen July 27-28, 2004 – will deal with this very topic within Judaism/s of the Graeco-Roman Period (in particular that from the Essene-Qumranic *milieu*: "Defining identities: who is the other? We, you, and the others in the Dead Sea Scrolls". Therefore, new insights are to be expected and welcome on our subject. Secondly, an Italian team which – after two decades of studies devoted to the interpretation and the varied use of the sacred texts of Judaism and Christianity – is now moving towards a deeper study of Christian identities in both East and West in the first seven centuries of the Christian era. See the recent study by Pesce 2003b, pp. 39-56, as well as those of other scholars, in particular G. Filoramo, H. Moxnes, and E. Lupieri ("La costruzione dell'identità cristiana [I-VII secolo]", *ASE* 20/1, 2003).

Chapter 1

STATUS QUAESTIONIS: DEFINING TERMS AND PERSPECTIVES STARTING FROM AN ANNOTATED BIBLIOGRAPHY[1]

Introduction

In this chapter I will survey the existing studies on the *Didache* following previously published articles,[2] which are herein reviewed and updated. I aim to collect and comment on the most noteworthy works in order to facilitate an objective study of the *Didache* (second half of the 1st century CE)[3] in its original context, that is the 'Christian Judaism',[4] here understood as one of the many Judaisms active in the late phase of the so-called "Judaism of the Second Temple" or "Judaism of the Hellenistic and Roman Period".[5] In the course of this introductory chapter, I will also highlight some of the many questions and perspectives concerning the origins of Christianity and of the *Didache* itself while at the same time clarifying the meaning of both the concepts and the terminology used in this volume, since I believe that only a philological and historical study of the *Didache*, appropriately inserted in its Christian-Jewish context, could allow for its interpretation without falling into repetition.

---

1. Periodicals, reference works and serials abbreviations are those indicated in *TRE* (= *Theologische Realenzyklopädie, Abkürzungsverzeichnis*, 2., überarbeitete und erweiterte Auflage, zusammengestellt von S.M. Schwertner [Berlin-New York: W. de Gruyter, 1994]). Ancient Sources (Jewish, Christian, Pagan Greek and Roman Literature) are according to the Instructions for contributors to *JBL* (= *Journal of Biblical Literature*).

2. *VetChr* 38/1, 2001, pp. 5-39; 38/2, 2001, pp. 223-245; and *ASE* 20/2, 2003, pp. 495-584.

3. "Le dernier tiers du Ier siècle apparaît comme la date la plus probable à la majorité des critiques", argue Rordorf-Tuilier 1998[2], in the *Annexe*, pp. 232-233.

4. For this terminology, infra, III. Judaism and Christian Origins, and IV. Studies on the *Didache* and on the Judaism/s of the *Didache*.

5. As to the terminology "Middle Judaism" (300 BCE-200 CE), proposed by Boccaccini, infra, III.

Since the Metropolitan Philotheos Bryennios in 1872 reported the existence of the Codex *Hierosolymitanus* 54 (abbr. H), which includes the text of the *Didache* – though Bryennios did not realise that at first sight – and ten years later in 1883 published the *editio princeps* of H in Constantinople, our *Didache* (hereafter *Did.*) has constantly drawn the attention of scholars, who have prompted and produced both partial studies and sometimes specific monographs as well (see, for example, Taylor 1886; Seeberg 1908, and more recently Draper 1983, Jefford 1995a [passim], Manns 1977b.2000, and van de Sandt-Flusser 2002) (infra, IV.) searching for its Hebrew-Jewish *substratum* or roots. Although the *Didache* is a very short text – only 204 lines and fewer than five folios (76r-80v) of a Greek Codex [H] dated 1056 – in the 121 years since its publication this pseudonymous work has revealed itself as one of the most studied and debated books of the literary *corpus* (canonical and non-canonical) on which many studies of early Christianity are based.

The *Didache* is in fact a text of major interest since, according to some scholars (infra, II.: eg Audet 1958; Rordorf-Tuilier 1998[2] and others including myself [infra, IV.]), several of its sections appear to cast light on sources and traditions (customs, beliefs, institutions and rituals) of a time antecedent to the writing of the New Testament. Consequently, before considering the *Didache* a proto-Christian writing casting light on early Christianity (it would be more appropriate to say on 'Christian Judaism') I would regard it as a document recording the 'Jewish Prehistory' of 'Christian origins'.

This bibliography is the outcome of more than ten years of studies concerning the Hebrew-Jewish 'roots' of the *Didache*. This research commitment, which has led to the consultation and reading of scores of commentaries, monographs and articles regarding the *Didache,* was inspired by the wish to identify an approach – or at least initiate a process – which, taking into consideration the existing hypotheses, recent findings (i.e. the fragments of the mss. of Qumrân, in particular those of 4Q) and the new historiographical and methodological perspectives regarding proto-Christian literature in general, could provide a solution to persisting questions regarding the interpretation of such an enigmatic text.

Some scholars and colleagues, both Italian and foreign,[6] who have

---

6.   Just to remember some and also to take the opportunity to thank them for their suggestions and comments: G. Boccaccini, S.P. Brock, J.H. Charlesworth, C. del Valle,

read and have commented positively on some of my Didachean contributions (infra, IV.: Del Verme 1991. 1993.1995.1999.2001a.2001b. 2001c.2003), have also contributed to my decision to publish (and now update) the bibliography of my *scriptorium* as a useful *vademecum* for other scholars interested in the *Didache*, in order both to facilitate their research and, eventually, to prompt a productive debate. Thus this bibliography should serve a practical scholarly purpose. It is here presented divided into four parts (I-IV) only because of the need to arrange the numerous works in useful groupings, although it should be understood and read as a *totum*, a whole, or as a *continuum* for use as a research tool for further work on Judaism/s underlying the *Didache*.

The four parts are introduced by notes illustrating the various currents of research represented in the works listed, although in some cases I will dwell on single works which in my opinion deserve particular consideration.

I. *Main Bibliographical Aids*

In this part are listed the main bibliographical aids which, as from the first years following the discovery and publication of the Greek ms. H54, provide useful information regarding existing works on the *Didache*. For this section I single out in particular *KS* 1924ff.; *RAMBI* 1969ff., and in addition Draper 1996a and Harder-Jefford 1995, two extensive surveys of studies on the *Didache* which, apart from reprinting some of the most influential contributions in the history of past and recent studies of the *Didache*, indicate new research trajectories and currents emerging more recently (Draper 1996a, p. 42). Also useful are the *Annexe* by Rordorf-Tuilier 1998[2], pp. 211-246; and the *Bibliographies* by K.J. Harder-C.N. Jefford in Draper 1996a, pp. 1-42; and by van de Sandt in Id-Flusser 2002, pp. 374-404.

AnPh 1928ff. = J. Marouzeau-J. Ernst et alii (eds.), *L'Année Philologique. Bibliographie Critique et Analytique de l'Antiquité Gréco-Latine* (Paris:

N. Fernández Marcos, F. García Martinez, G. Gasparro, C. Grottanelli, I. Grünwald, P.C. Ioly Zorattini, G. Jossa, E. Lupieri, B.J. Malina, F. Manns, F. Michelini Tocci, A. Milano, H. Moxnes, A.V. Nazzaro, G. Otranto, M. Pesce, G.L. Prato, S. Pricoco, E. Prinzivalli, M. Raveri, P. Sacchi, G. Stemberger, Sh. Talmon, L. Troiani, G. Vermes and G. Visonà.

Les Belles Lettres), s.v. *Didache siue Didascalia* or *Didache* and references, t. Iff.

BiblAC 1951 = S. Lambrino (ed.), *Bibliographie de l'Antiquité Classique 1896-1914*. Première Partie: *Auteurs et Textes* (Paris: Les Belles Lettres), s.v. *Didache siue Didascalia*, pp. 173f. and references.

BPatr 1956ff. = W. Schneemelcher-K. Schäferdiek et alii (eds.), *Bibliographia Patristica. Internationale Patristische Bibliographie*, vol. I (Berlin-New York: Principat).

BiblASE 1990ff. = A. Camplani-L. Perrone et alii (eds.), *Bibliografia Generale di Storia dell'Interpretazione Biblica. Esegesi, ermeneutica, usi della Bibbia* (Engl.: *A General Bibliography on the History of Biblical Interpretation. Exegesis, Hermeneutics, Uses of the Bible*; Bologna: EDB), in *ASE* 7/1ff.

Draper 1996 = J.A. Draper, "The Didache in Modern Research: An Overview", in Draper 1996a, pp. 1-42 (infra, IV.).

Ehrhard 1900 = A. Ehrhard, *Die Altchristliche Literatur und ihre Erforschung von 1884-1900*. I: *Die Vornicänische Literatur* (Freiburg i. Br.: Herder), pp. 37-68.

Harder-Jefford 1995 = K.J. Harder-C.N. Jefford, "A Bibliography of Literature on the Didache", in Jefford 1995a, pp. 368-382 (infra, IV.).

KS 1924ff. = G. Scholem et alii (eds.), *Kiryat Sefer. Bibliography of All the Publications in Israel and of Judaica from Abroad* (Jerusalem: Bet Hasefarim), particularly the Sections 6.00: *Post-Biblical Literature and Early Christianity*; 6.01: *Apocrypha and Pseudepigrapha, Jewish-Hellenistic Literature, Dead Sea scrolls*; 6.02: *Early Christianity in Connection with Judaism*.

Marouzeau 1927 = J. Marouzeau (ed.), *Dix Années de Bibliographie Classique. Bibliographie Critique et Analitique de l'Antiquité Gréco-Latine pour la période 1914-1924*. Première partie: *Auteurs et Textes* (Paris: Les Belles Lettres, 1969 [repr.]), s.v. *Apostolica*, p. 23 and references.

Niederwimmer 1989 = K. Niederwimmer, "Literaturverzeichnis", in Niederwimmer 1989b, pp. 273-294 (infra, II.).

Pinnick 2001 = A. Pinnick, *The Orion Center Bibliography of the Dead Sea Scrolls (1995-2000)* (Leiden: Brill) [with many items regarding the Dead Sea Scrolls and Christian Origins].

RAMBI 1969ss. = *Index of Articles on Jewish Studies (and the Study of Eretz Israel)*, compiled and edited by the Editorial Board of "Kiryat Sefer" (Jerusalem: Bibliographical Quarterly of the Jewish National and University Library), especially the section 4. *Apocrypha. Dead Sea scrolls. Early Christianity*. See also 3. *Post-Biblical Literature and Early Christianity*.

Rordorf-Tuilier 1998[2] = W. Rordorf-A. Tuilier, "Bibliographie depuis 1976", pp. 213-220 (infra, II.).

Sieben 1980 = J.H. Sieben, *Voces. Eine Bibliographie zu Wörtern und Be-griffen aus der Patristik (1918-1978)* (BPatr.S 1; Berlin-New York: Principat).

van de Sandt-Flusser 2002 = H. van de Sandt-D. Flusser, "Bibliography", in van de Sandt-Flusser 2002, pp. 374-404 (infra, IV.).

Vokes 1993 = F.E. Vokes, "Life and Order in an Early Church: The Dida-che", in *ANRW* II.27.1; Berlin-New York: Principat), pp. 209-233, with an analytical *status quaestionis*.

II. *Editions, Versions, Translations and Commentaries of the Didache (and of Other Correlated Texts)*

Among contemporary scholars of early Christianity W. Rordorf – following a tendency which emerged in the 1950s, in particular after the publication of the outstanding commentary by Audet in 1958 – undoubtedly plays a foremost part in pointing out and enphasising the Jewish context of the *Didache*. Rordorf identifies in the *Didache* the presence not only of ancient oral traditions but also of written traditions, some of which may have preceded the final compilation of the New Testament. See Rordorf-Tuilier 1998[2] (already 1978 [SC 248]); and infra, IV., in particular 1972b.1981a.1991.

Several indications – although somewhat general – regarding the Judaism (or Judaisms) anterior to or contemporary with the *Didache*, which would have left traces in the text, can also be found in other modern commentaries, i.e. Giet 1970; Kraft 1965; Schöllgen 1991 and Niederwimmer 1989. The last-named is probably the most learned commentary among those written in the last fifty years, second only to the commentary by J.-P. Audet published in 1958. Niederwimmer always records (passim) the theses and/or hypotheses of those scholars who favour a 'Jewish reading' of the *Didache* and himself indeed draws attention in the *Prolegomena* (pp. 11-80) and in particular at § 7 (= *Rekonstruction der Entstehung der Didache*, pp. 64ff.) to the Judaism (as to both context and contents) underlying the *Didache*. In the course of his commentary however, the author tends to 'sway', contradicting what he had previously stated in the *Prolegomena*.[7]

---

7.   As to the hypothesis of a *Vorlage* or *Grund-Muster* of a Jewish *Zwei-Wege-Traktat* as source of *Did.* 1-6, I have already expressed in an article my criticism regarding Niederwimmer' 'swayings' (Del Verme 1995 [infra, IV.], in particular pp. 310f.).

As to the Italian commentaries of the *Didache*, the most influential and widely read by scholars of early Christianity or Patristics in general are Bosio 1958[2]; Mattioli 1986 (V ed.) and Quacquarelli 1998 (IX ed.). In particular Mattioli, whose commentary is more accurate, and Quacquarelli have nourished the latest generation of Italian readers of *Did.* Mattioli's commentary is more useful for its treatment of the Jewish context than that by Quacquarelli, whose translation of the the the so-called "Apostolic Fathers" appears at times to be somewhat inaccurate. I would further draw attention to Mattioli's concise introductory notes to the history (ibid., pp.17ff.), theology (ibid., pp. 47ff.), origins and style of the *Didache* (ibid., pp. 96ff.). However, notwithstanding its methodological and analytical accuracy, this excellent short commentary is heavily burdened by the author's frequent tendency (not adequately explained, and almost taken for granted) postulated to assume the presence of NT influences as well as to see Hellenistic rather than Jewish borrowings in the *Didache*.[8] By contrast the recent volume by Visonà published in 2000 can be considered exemplary and comes to replace authoritatively all previous Italian commentaries. The author modestly presents his work as one which "non intende soppiantare quello...pubblicato da Mattioli nella precedente serie della Collana Patristica di questa Editrice (i.e. Città Nuova, Roma), lavoro che rimane un apprezzato e autonomo contributo alla ricerca sulla Didachè".[9] In my opinion the accuracy of the translation, the comprehensive introduction and the concise and rigorous commentary make Visonà's the most complete commentary to have been published in Italy since the discovery of the Greek ms. H54. The thoroughness and mastery of the author in reporting and discussing the findings of other scholars, along with his carefully gauged ability to suggest personal opinions on the many controversial questions stemming from the analysis of the *Didache*, supported by an extensive bibliography, are impressive. Because of the scope of this bibliography, I draw attention to *Part One* of the Introduction, in particular point II: Genre, Structure, Formation of *Did.* (ibid., pp. 25ff.) containing a concise paragraph entitled "A «Jewish» *Didache*" (ibid., pp. 43-52), which testifies to the bibliographical accuracy of the work. Analogous richness of information and detail is

8. Cf. Del Verme, ibid., p. 306, for *Did.* 4:8 (the community of goods), and the biweekly fasting of the ὑποκριταί and that of "the others" of *Did.* 8:1 (Del Verme 1999.2003 [infra, IV.]).

9. Visonà 2000, p. 23 n. 30.

found in *Part Two* where Visonà expounds the contents of the *Didache*: in this section the cross-references to Judaism (either anterior to or contemporary with the *Did.*) are numerous, although it appears that the author is unaware of the multiplicity of the Judaism/s (the plural is preferable) which could have influenced the *Didache*. As to the identity or identities of the groups which "cohabit" and/or oppose each other within Christian Judaism – of which the *Didache* represents the best evidence – there is no particular note in this commentary. I will need to return later to this aspect of the *Didache* (infra, IV.) since I believe that it is of great importance to a contextualised study of the text.

Apart from some minor disagreement with Visonà concerning the interpretation of single passages (for example *a propos* of *Did.* 4:8 [the community of goods], 8:1 [the fasting of the *Hypocrites*] and 13:3-7 [the ἀπαρχή),[10] I believe that this commentary is coherent both as to its general outline and as to the organisation of the single parts. Well documented and judicious in its handling of controversial questions contained in the *Didache*, this work demonstrates a marked degree of rigour in argument and moreover will be found to be pleasant to read. In conclusion, I would like to point out that, in contrast with some Italian and foreign scholars of early Christian literature, who confine themselves to a more or less one-sided attention to philological and rhetorical aspects of Patristic texts (including the *Did.*), Visonà combines philological rigour with attention to the history of Christianity (or the Christianities) underlying the *Didache*. This is a point where there are some gaps to be filled and I will return to it more fully later (infra, IV.).

Altaner 1952 = B. Altaner, "Zum Problem der lateinischen Doctrina Apostolorum", *VigChr* 6, 160-167 (now in Id., *Kleine patristische Schriften* [TU 83; Berlin: De Gruyter & Co., 1967], pp. 335-342, under the title: *Die lateinische Doctrina Apostolorum und die griechische Grundschrift der Didache*).

Amélineau 1888 = E. Amélineau, "Vie de Schnoudi", in *Mémoires publiés par les membres de la Mission archéologique française au Caire, 1885-1886. Tome IV: Monuments pour servir à l'histoire de l'Égypte chrétienne aux IVe et Ve siècles* (Paris: Leroux), Chap. VI, pp. 289-478 (Arabic Text with French Translation).

---

10.   Del Verme 1993.1995.1999 (infra, IV.).

12   *Marcello Del Verme*

(Ps.) Athanasius, *Fides CCCXVIII Patrum*, in *PG* 28, 1637A-1644B.
(Ps.) Athanasius, *Syntagma doctrinae*, in *PG* 28, 836A-845B.
Attridge 2002 = H.W. Attridge (ed.), *The Apostolic Tradition. A Commentary* by P.F. Bradshow-M.E. Johnson -L.E. Phillips (Hermeneia; Minneapolis: Fortress Press).
Audet 1958 = J.-P. Audet (ed.), *La Didachè. Instructions des Apôtres* (EtB; Paris: Gabalda).
Ayán Calvo 1992 = J.J. Ayán Calvo (ed.), *Didaché. Doctrina Apostolorum. Epístola del Pseudo-Bernabé. Introducción, Traducción y Notas* (FP 3; Madrid: Ciudad Nueva).
Bosio 1958² = G. Bosio, *Dottrina dei Dodici Apostoli*, in Id., *I Padri Apostolici*, vol. I (Torino: SEI), pp. 1-63.
Botte 1984² = B. Botte (ed.), *Hippolyte de Rome. La Tradition Apostolic d'après les anciennes versions, Introduction, traduction et notes*. Deuxième édition revue (SC 11bis; Paris: Cerf, 1968 [I ed., SC 11]).
Botte 1989 (V Ed.) = Id., *La Tradition apostolic de Saint Hippolyte. Essai de reconstitution* (LQF 39; Münster: Aschendorff).
Bryennios 1883 = Ph. Bryennios, Διδαχὴ τῶν δώδεκα ἀποστόλων ἐκ τοῦ ἱεροσολυμιτικοῦ χειρογράφου νῦν πρῶτον ἐκδιδομένη μετὰ προλεγομένων καὶ σημειώσεως ἐν οἷς καὶ τῆς Συνόψεως τῆς Π.Δ., τῆς ὑπὸ Ἰωάνν. τοῦ Χρυσοστόμου, σύγκρισις καὶ μέρος ἀνέκδοτον ἀπὸ τοῦ αὐτοῦ χειρογράφου (Εν Κωνσταντινουπόλει: S.I. Voutyra; Engl. tr., New York: Scribner's Sons, 1885).
Cattaneo 2003 = E. Cattaneo, "Un 'nuovo' passo della Prima Clementis. La 'grande ammonizione' di 58,2-59,2A"; and "La Prima Clementis come un caso di correptio fraterna", in Ph. Luisier (ed.), *Studi su Clemente Romano* – Atti degli Incontri di Roma (29 marzo e 22 novembre 2001) (Roma: Herder), pp. 57-82; 83-105.
Chialà 1999 = S. Chialà (ed.), *Padri Apostolici. Agli inizi della chiesa. Didaché* (Magnano [Bi]: Qiqayon), pp. 5-28.
Cives-Moscatelli 1999 = S. Cives-F. Moscatelli, *Didaché. Dottrina dei Dodici Apostoli* (Cinisello Balsamo [Mi]: San Paolo).
Connolly 1924 = R.H. Connolly, "New Fragments of the Didache", *JThS* 25, pp. 151-153.
Coquin 1966² = R.G. Coquin, *Les Canons d'Hippolyte* (PO 31/2; Paris: Firmin-Didot).
Dix 1992² = G. Dix, *The Treatise on "The Apostolic Tradition" of St Hippolytus of Rome, Bishop and Martyr*, Reissued with Corrections, Preface and Bibliography by H. Chadwick (London: Alban-Press).
Durante Mangoni 2003 = M.B. Durante Mangoni (ed.), *Erma. Il Pastore. Introduzione, versione, commento* (SOCr 27; Bologna: EDB).
Elgvin 1996 = T. Elgvin, "4Q The Two Ways", in G. Brooke, J.Collins, T. Elgvin, P. Flint, J. Greenfield, E. Larsson, C. Newson, E. Puech, L. H.

Schiffman, M. Stone, and J. Trebolle Barrera, in consultation with J. Vanderkam (eds.), *Qumran Cave 4. XVII: Parabiblical Texts*, Part 3 (DJD 22; Oxford: Clarendon), pp. 289-294, pl. XXVI.

Funk 1905-1906 = F.X. Funk, *Didascalia et Constitutiones Apostolorum*, vols. I-II (Paderbornae: F. Schöningh; anastatic repr. Torino 1964).

Funk-Bihlmeyer 1970[3] = Id.-K. Bihlmeyer, *Die Apostolischen Väter. Neubearbeitung der Funkschen Ausgabe*. Dritte Auflage...mit einem Nachtrag von W. Schneemelcher. Erster Teil: *Didache, Barnabas, Klemens I und II, Ignatius, Polykarp, Papias, Quadratus, Diognetbrief* (Tübingen: Mohr, 1924 [I Ed.]), pp. 1-9.

Gero 1977 = S. Gero, "The So-called Ointment Prayer in the Coptic Version of the Didache: A Re-Evaluation", *HThR* 70, pp. 67-84.

Giet 1970 = St. Giet, *L'énigme de la Didachè* (PFLUS 149; Paris: Les Editions Orphrys).

Goodspeed 1945 = E.J. Goodspeed, "The Didache, Barnabas and the Doctrina", *AthR* 27, pp. 228-247.

Grenfell-Hunt 1922 = B.P. Grenfell-A.S. Hunt (eds.), *The Oxyrhyncus Papyri*, vol. 15 (London: Egyptian Exploration Society).

Harnack 1884 = A. Harnack, *Die Lehre der zwölf Apostel nebst Untersuchungen zur ältesten Geschichte der Kirchenfassung und des Kirchenrechts* (TU 2,1-2; Leipzig: Hinrichs [repr. 1893]).

Harris 1887 = J.R. Harris, *The Teaching of the Apostles (Didaché ton apostolon)*. Newly edited, with Facsimile Text and a Commentary (Baltimore: J. Hopkins University Press; London: Clay).

Horner 1904 = G. Horner, *The Statutes of the Apostles or Canones Ecclesiastici* (London: Williams & Norgate).

Horner 1924 = Id., "A New Fragment of the Didache in Coptic", *JThS* 25, pp. 225-231.

Jefford-Patterson 1989-90 = C.N. Jefford-S.J. Patterson, "A Note on Didache 12.2a (Coptic)", *SecCen* 7, pp. 65-75.

Joly 1958 = R. Joly (ed.), *Hermas. Le Pasteur. Introduction, texte critique, traduction et notes* (SC 53; Paris: Cerf).

Jones-Mirecki 1995 = F.S. Jones-P.A. Mirecki, "Considerations on the Coptic Papyrus of the Didache (British Library Oriental Manuscript 9271)", in Jefford 1995a, pp. 47-87 (infra, IV.).

Kmosko 1926 = M. Kmosko (ed.), *Liber graduum* (PS I/3; Paris: Firmin-Didot).

Knopf 1920 = R. Knopf, *Die Lehre der zwölf Apostel. Die Zwei Clemensbriefe* (Die apostolischen Väter, I, HNT ErgBd.; Tübingen: Mohr).

Kraft 1965 = R.A. Kraft, *Barnabas and the Didache* (ApF[T] 3; Toronto-New York-London: Nelson & Sons).

Lefort 1952 = L.-T. Lefort (ed.), *Les Pères Apostoliques en copte* (CSCO.C 17 [Text] and 18 [Translation]; Louvain: Durbecq).

Lightfoot-Harmer 1989[2] = J.B. Lightfoot-J.R. Harmer, *The Apostolic Fathers,* Second Edition, Translated by..., Edited and revised by M.W. Holmes (Leicester: Apollos), pp. 145-158 (= The Didache).

Lona 1998 = H.E. Lona, *Der erste Clemensbrief* (KAV 2; Göttingen: Vandenhoeck & Ruprecht).

Massebieau 1884 = L. Massebieau, "L'enseignement des Douze Apôtres", *RHR* 10, pp. 129-160.

Mattioli 1986 (V ed.) = U. Mattioli, *Didachè. Dottrina dei dodici apostoli. Introduzione, traduzione e note* (LCO 5; Milano: Paoline).

Metzger 1985-1987 = M. Metzger (ed.), *Les Constitutions Apostoliques. Introduction, texte critique, traduction et notes*, vol. I-III (SC 320.329.336; Paris: Cerf).

Milavec 1989 = A. Milavec, "The Pastoral Genius of the Didache: An Analytical Translation and Commentary", in J. Neusner-E.S. Frerichs-A.J. Levine (eds.), *Religious Writings and Religious Systems. Systemic Analysis of Holy Books in Christianity, Islam, Buddhism, Graeco-Roman Religions, Ancient Israel and Judaism* (BrSR 2), Vol. 2: Christianity (Atlanta: Scholars Press), pp. 89-125.

Milavec 2004 = Id., *The First Analytic, Gender-Inclusive Translation of the Didache with a Brief Commentary and Flow Charts* (Collegeville: forthcoming).

Niederwimmer 1979 = K. Niederwimmer, "Doctrina apostolorum (Cod. Mellic. 597)", in *Theologia Scientia eminens practica. F. Zerbst zum 70. Geburtstag,* ed. H.C. Schmidt-Lauber (Wien-Freiburg-Basel: Herder), pp. 266-272.

Niederwimmer 1989 = Id., *Die Didache* (KAV 1; Göttingen: Vandenhoeck & Ruprecht [repr. 1993]).

Niederwimmer 1995 = Id., "Der Didachist und seine Quellen", in Jefford 1995a, pp. 15-36 (infra, IV.).

Norelli 1995 = E. Norelli et alii, *Ascensio Isaiae. I. Textus. II. Commentarius* (CChr.SA 7-8; Turnhout: Brepols).

Peretto 1996 = E. Peretto (ed.), *Pseudo-Ippolito, Tradizione apostolica. Introduzione, traduzione e note* (CtePa 133; Roma: Città Nuova).

Peretto 1999 = Id. (ed.), *Clemente Romano. Lettera ai Corinzi* (SOCr 23; Bologna: EDB).

Peradse 1931 = G. Peradse, "Die Lehre der zwölf Apostel in der georgischen Überlieferung", *ZNW* 31, pp. 111-116.

Peterson 1951 = Id., "Über einige Probleme der Didache-Überlieferung", *RAC* 27, pp. 37-68 (now in *Frühkirche, Judentum und Gnosis. Studien und Untersuchungen* [Rom-Freiburg-Wien: Herder, 1959], pp. 146-182).

Preuschen 1900 = E. Preuschen, "Die lateinische Übersetzung der <Zwei Wege>", *ZNW* 1, p. 307.

Prigent-Kraft 1971 = P. Prigent-R.A. Kraft (eds.), *Épître de Barnabé, Intro-*

duction, traduction et notes (Prigent). *Texte grec établi et presenté* (Kraft) (SC 172; Paris: Cerf).

Quacquarelli 1998 (IX ed.) = A. Quacquarelli (ed.), *I Padri Apostolici. Traduzione, introduzione e note* (Ctepa 5; Roma: Città Nuova).

Quasten 1936 = J. Quasten (ed.), *Monumenta eucharistica et liturgica vetustissima* (FlorPatristicum, 7/I; Bonn: Hanstein).

Rehm-Paschke 1993[3] = B. Rehm-F. Paschke (hg. v.), *Die Pseudoklementinen,* I. *Homilien* (GCS 42; Berlin: Akademie Verlag).

Rehm-Strecker 1994[2] = Id.- G. Strecker (hg. v.), *Die Pseudoklementinen,* II. *Rekognitionen in Rufins Übersetzung,* 2 verbesserte Auflage (GCS 51; Berlin: Akademie Verlag).

Robinson 1934a = J.A. Robinson, "The Epistle of Barnabas and the Didache, ed. by R.H. Connolly", *JThS* 35, pp. 113-146.

Robinson 1934b = Id., "The Didache (continued)", *JThS* 35, pp. 225-248.

Rordorf-Tuilier 1998[2] = W. Rordorf-A. Tuilier (eds.), *La doctrine des douze apôtres (Didachè). Introduction, texte critique, traduction, notes, appendice, annexe et index,* Deuxième édition revue et augmentée (SC 248bis; Paris: Cerf, 1978 [I Ed. 1978, SC 248]).

Schermann 1903 = Th. Schermann (hg. v.), *Eine Elfapostelmoral oder die Christliche Rezension der "beiden Wege"* (VKHSM II/2; München: J.J. Lentneschern Buchhandlung), pp. 16-18.

Schermann 1914 = Id. (hg. v.), *Die allgemeine Kirchenordnung, frühchristliche Liturgien und kirchliche Überlieferung,* I. *Die allgemeine Kirchenordnung des zweiten Jahrhunderts* (Paderborn: F. Schöningh), pp. 12-34.

Schlecht 1901 = J. Schlecht, *Doctrina XII Apostolorum. Die Apostellehre in der Liturgie der katholischen Kirche* (Freiburg i. Br.: Herder).

Schmidt 1925 = C. Schmidt (ed.), "Das koptische Didache-Fragment des British Museum", *ZNW* 24, pp. 81-99.

Schöllgen 1991 = G. Schöllgen, *Didache. Zwölf-Apostel-Lehre,* in Id.-W. Geerlings (hg. v.), *Didache. Zwölf-Apostel-Lehre/Traditio Apostolica. Apostolische Überlieferung* (FC 1; Freiburg-Basel-Wien-Barcelona-Rom-New York: Herder), pp. 13-139.

Urbán 1993 = A. Urbán (ed.), *Concordantia in Patres Apostolicos.* Pars II: *Concondantia in Didachen (Doctrina duodecim Apostolorum)* (AlOm R.A 146; Hildesheim-Zürich-New York: Olms-Weidmann).

Visonà 2000 = G. Visonà, *Didachè. Insegnamento degli apostoli. Introduzione, testo, traduzione e note* (LCPM 30; Milano: Paoline).

Vööbus 1979 = A. Vööbus (ed.), *Die Didascalia Apostolorum in Syriac,* I (CSCO 401); II (CSCO 408; Louvain: University Press).

Walters 1991 = B.S. Walters, *Didachè, the Unknown Teaching of the Twelve Apostles* (with 3 adjusted reprints; San José: w.e.).

Wengst 1984 = K. Wengst (hg. v.), *Didache (Apostellehre), Barnabasbrief, Zweiter Klemensbrief, Schrift an Diognet. Eingeleitet, herausgegeben,*

übertragen und erlaütert (SUC 2; München-Darmstadt: Wissenschaftliche Buchgesellschaft), pp. 1-100.

Wohleb 1913 = L. Wohleb, *Die lateinische Übersetzung der Didache kritisch
und sprachlich untersucht* (SGKA 7/1; Paderborn: F. Schöningh [repr.
1967]).

III. *Judaism and Christian Origins*

In this section I list ca. 600 titles (although the list could and should
be extended) in order to indicate the works (monographs or thematic
issues of journals, articles from miscellanea and specialised journals)
which, recalling my initial image of the *scriptorium*, I would like to see
on the open shelves of any researcher interested in the *Didache*. Many
of the articles read or perused for my researches on the *Didache* in
recent years provide interesting propaedeutical, methodological or contextual cues for the study of the Hebrew-Jewish 'roots' of this enigmatic text.

A rapid glance at the list of works cited suggests that they are the
product of the ongoing historiographical debate regarding the study of
the Judaism of the Second Temple and its relation to the origins of
Christianity, initiated almost three decades ago and galvanised by new
methodological approaches. The study of Hellenistic Graeco-Roman
Judaism has been enriched, in fact, by new elements, which have
prompted researchers to review methodologically and conceptually
the interpretation of Judaism. The discovery of important material evidence and documents, in particular the Dead Sea Scrolls (*in primis*
those from Qumran, Wadi Murabba'at, Naḥal Ḥever and Masada)
and numerous papyrus fragments and ostraca from various sites in
the Judaea Desert, together with a renewed interest in apocryphal
and/or pseudoepigraphic literature of the OT and the contributions
derived from 'auxiliary sciences' (archaeology, geography, chronology,
numismatics and epigraphy), especially inscriptions, such as that from
Aphrodisias,[11] and important archaeological discoveries (such as the
synagogue[12] of Sardis), have triggered an impressive updating process
of the documents available on both Palestinian Judaism and the Jewish

---

11.   See, in particular, Reynolds-Tannenbaum 1987 and Feldman 1989.

12.   As to the synagogues in general see Gutmann 1981; Perrot-Contessa 2003
(for the archaeological study, in particular cols. 751ff.).

Diaspora. I refer for this section to the new edition of Schürer 1973-1987, which in the Italian translation of vol. III/2 (Brescia 1998) adds a detailed *Bibliographical Appendix* (pp. 1161-1287), edited by G. Firpo, C. Gianotto, C. Martone and G. Stemberger, which tends to compensate for some of the lacunae and corrects some of the inaccuracies of the English version.[13] See also Bickerman 1985.1988; Chiesa 1987; Davies-Finkelstein 1984-1989; Feldman 1996; Goodenough 1953-1968; Lieu-North-Rajak 1992; Momigliano 1975.1976; Prato 1989; Sacchi 1993.1999.2000; Safrai-Stern 1974-1976; Schäfer 1983; Smallwood 1976; VanderKam 2000.2001.

The vitality of Judaism between the 3rd century BCE and the 2nd century CE is documented by the presence of groups and/or movements reflecting different ideological, doctrinal and political tendencies, as well as different forms and degrees of religious devotion (some of them being tied to the Temple, others to schools and/or prophetic, sapiential and apocalyptic currents, and often grouped in particular communities or congregations such as the Essenes and some Pharisaic or Baptist groups). In some cases these groups went so far as to challenge the population by claiming to represent the sole 'Holy Rest' of Israel (as for instance the members of the community of Qumran). This information contributes to a picture of the Judaism of the time as a varied, multifarious and extremely dynamic reality. Furthermore it is possible to draw up a list, although incomplete and provisional, of the different 'species' of Judaism of the time: Ḥasidim, Jewish Hellenists, Enochians/Essenes, Qumranites (i.e. members of the Qumran community), Melchizedekians, Boethusians, Samaritans, Pharisees, Sadducees, Baptists, Zealots, Sicarii, and the 'Christian Judaism' groups of which traces can be found in the *Didache* (infra, IV.: Del Verme 1995.1999. 2001b.2001c.2003a). I will return later to this last point (infra, IV.).

For the documentation and description of the vitality and richness of the Judaism of this period – which is neither to be defined as 'late' (an attribute compromised by denominational uses) nor 'emergent' (an ideologically marked adjective and analogically derived from the label 'emergent Christianity') and which has also been defined as "Middle

---

13.   Cf. the learned review by M. Hengel (with an Appendix: *Inschriften*] by H. Bloedhorn), "Der alte und der neue 'Schürer' ", *JSSt* 35/1, 1990, pp. 19-72; and also G. Jossa, *RivBib* 47, 1999, pp. 248-252; ibid., 48, 2000, pp. 468-470.

Judaism"[14] – besides the works already cited above, I single out the following: Anderson 2002; Boccaccini 1991.1992. 1995a.1995b.1998a. 1998b.2002b; Charlesworth 1985.1988; Cirillo 1993; Deines 1997; Finkelstein 1962; García Martínez 1987; Grabbe 1989.2000; Gusella 2003; Hengel 1976.1988; Ibba 1986; Jossa 1980. 2001a.2001b; Kraft 1975; Lupieri 1987; Mason 1991; Meier 1991-2001; Neusner 1971.1973. 1983; Nickelsburg 1981. 1983. 1986.2003; Noja 1987; Pesce 1986; Rofé-Roifer 1987; Sacchi 1997b; Saldarini 1988; Sanders 1977.1992; Schremer 1997; Seidensticker 1959; Simon 1960; Smith 1971b; Stegemann 1990; Stemberger 1991.1993; Stone 1980.1983.1988; Talmon 1972; Troiani 1993a.1993b.2000.2001a; VanderKam 2001; Vivian 1993.[15]

The current research orientation on early Christianity, notwithstanding persisting uncertainties and the partial reservations of some scholars (I will deal with these later and in particular in the context of Italian research), has benefited from the so-called 'turning point' (in Italian 'svolta') which has appeared in the studies regarding the internal developments of Judaism between the 3rd century BCE and the 2nd century CE, and in particular in the 1st century CE, a period which coincides with the origins of Christianity. The positive 'fall-out' of this new direction in the field of NT studies and, more generally, in the history of early Christianity – beginning from the inquiry about Jesus and his first disciples with all its implications for the first Palestinian community (or communities) and the spread of Christia-

---

14.   Boccaccini 1993a, pp. 40-48. The terminological choice by Boccaccini should not be categorically refused. Well aware of the 'terminological relativism', I believe it is both useful and functional since it groups the various literary corpora which appeared in the period under examination as well as including the numerous groups/ movements which produced those texts. By contrast M. Pesce (and in particular non-Italian scholars) who instead of "medio giudaismo" prefers the terminology "ebraismo di età ellenistico-romana" since he believes that Boccaccini's terminology presupposes (but I believe unmotivatedly) a concept of "medietà" which "comporta l'idea di provvisorietà quasi che gli ebraismi dell'età 'media' non valessero di per sè e dovessero sfociare in qualcosa di definitivo". Pesce, an excellent historian of Ancient Christianity, gave me prior notice (for which I am deeply grateful) of his (partly critical) point of view in an e-mail dated 20.10.01, to which he attached some pages of his publication on the *lemma* "Ebraismo", now published in G. Barbaglio-G. Bof-S. Dianich (eds.), *Teologia* (I Dizionari San Paolo; Cinisello Balsamo, Mi: San Paolo, 2002), pp. 474-501, with a rich and useful Bibliography, pp. 499-501.

15.   For the Pharisees, in particular from the time of Herod the Great to 70 CE, see Vitelli 2004.

nity outside Palestine – are numerous, although complex in character. Firstly, the terminology used to define – either to distinguish or to connect or align – Jesus and his movement, as well as other groups active within the Palestinian Judaism of the 1st century CE, finds scholars, exegetes and historians taking various positions. See, for example, Boccaccini 1993b; Brown 1983; Charlesworth 1991a; Cohen 1971; Crotty 1999; Del Verme 1989; Downing 1999.2000; Georgi 1995; Lindeskog 1986; Malina 1976; Mimouni 1992; Perelmuter 1989; Pesce 1994; Quispel 1968; Riegel 1978; Rudolph 1991; Sacchi 1993; Sanders 1980.1985. 1992.1993; Stegemann 1990; Strecker 1993; Taylor 1990; Vermes 1983.2003.2004.

In view of these fundamental problems, it appears that proto-Christian literature as a whole, from the NT onwards – setting aside prejudices and distinctions in the historical perspectives informing the various *corpora* (both of those defined as 'canonical' and of the 'apocryphal/pseudepigrahical') – should be placed and studied in the context of the rich historical-literary phenomenon of the Judaism not only of the 1st century CE but also of the previous three centuries. Therefore in the footsteps of, and along with, other researchers (among whom are G. Boccaccini, J.H. Charlesworth, S.J.D. Cohen, J.D. Crossan, J.D.G. Dunn, D. Flusser, I. Grüenwald-Sh. Shaked-G.G. Stroumsa, R.A. Kraft, J. Neusner, G.W.E. Nickelsburg, M. Pesce, C. Rowland, P. Sacchi, A.S. Segal, M. Stone, VanderKam and G. Vermes – whose specific approaches and arguments can be found in the works listed below) I believe that the Christian movement in its initial phase and probably also after the year 70 CE, should be considered, from an historical point of view, as part of contemporary Judaism.[16] "The separation" – Boccaccini argues[17] – "between 'early Judaism' and early Christianity appears more and more disturbing; both the New Testament scholar (i.e., J.D.G. Dunn) and the specialist in Judaism (i.e. J. Maier) call for a more comprehensive approach to this period. Christianity and Rabbinism are finally being seen as fresh and twin deve-

---

16.   Del Verme 1989, in particular pp. 15-20; and Del Verme 2001a.2001b.2003 (infra, IV.). The literary and historical interpretation of the period between the III cent. BCE and the I cent. CE as an embryonic phase of (Rabbinic) Judaism, which coexisted with and confronted early Christianity, is strongly defended by J.H. Charlesworth, R.A. Kraft, G.W.E. Nickelsburg et al. See Boccaccini 1992 (*Introduction*, pp. IX-XXIX) and 1993b.

17.   1992, XXV-XXVI.

lopments of ancient Judaism (see S. Sandmel, J. Neusner, A. F. Segal, H.G. Perelmuter)".

In this part of the bibliography, notwithstanding the selective criteria adopted,[18] I have made a point of listing those works which have marked important research currents or directions, in particular in regard to the relations between Judaism and Christianity. Some of these directions have been interrupted or are currently being neglected, but most of them are still current and are continuously being reiterated by modern researchers, by applying a methodology to the study of the sources in line with the above-mentioned 'turning point'. Among the many contributions[19] on the so-called Judaistic-Christianity I point out Cullmann 1954; Daniélou 1958.1964; Fitzmyer 1971; Klijn 1973-1974; Klijn-Reinink 1973; Sabourin 1976; Schoeps 1949.1964; Simon 1962a.1964.1965.1975; Strecker 1964; and more recently: Blanchetière-Herr 1993; Buchanan 1979-1980; Grego 1982; Kaestli 1996; Lüdemann 1983; Pixner 1991; Trevijano 1995 and Vidal Manzanares 1995. The numerous studies of scholars and/or archaeologists of the Studium Biblicum Franciscanum in Jerusalem concerning the so-called Palestinian 'Church of the Circumcision',[20] must also be considered, in particular those by Bagatti 1970.1981; Mancini 1968.1977; Randellini 1968; Testa 1962. These scholars find their loyal (and 'prolific') successor in particular in F. Manns (see Id.1977.1979. 1984.1988.1998.2000 [infra, IV.])[21] who – in contrast with his predecessors – adopts a more critical approach[22] to the selection and evaluation of literary sources (both Christian and Jewish) and of material evidence,[23] appropriately considering also the available apo-

---

18. The list, however, can be further integrated with other titles noted by Malina 1973, Manns 1979; Boccaccini 1992.1993b; Blanchetière 2001; and Filoramo-Gianotto 2001.

19. For these and other studies see the *Introduzione* by L. Cirillo (pp. V-LXV) to the edition of Daniélou 1958, and to the *Bibliografia* (pp. 549-562); also Filoramo-Gianotto 2001.

20. As regards the archaeological findings by Bagatti and Testa as well as the interpretations provided by the two scholars (and their followers), Joan E. Taylor is very critical (Ead. 1990.1993).

21. In this regard see Dauphin's 1993 review.

22. Review by Saunders 1983.

23. For both I point out the three important volumes representing various research tendencies, regarding post-Biblical Palestine, in particular in archaeology, which have been published in the last decade by the Franciscan Printing Press of the "Custody of

cryphal/ pseudepigraphical texts and Rabbinic literature. For a general outline of early Judaistic-Christianity and an updated definition of the historical-literary 'phenomenon', I refer the reader to Mimouni 1998a (Id. 1992.1998b. 2000.2001), to integrate with Crossan 1998; Blanchetière 2001; Filoramo-Gianotto 2001; Penna 1999a; Pesce in Pitta 2003, pp. 21-44; Taylor 2003; and Tomson-Lambers-Petry 2003.[24]

Another noteworthy field of inquiry is that regarding the relations between Essenism, the community of Qumran and early Christianity (see, e.g., Cullmann 1955.1971; Daniélou 1955.1974; Keck 1966, Parente 1962.1964, et al.). This area of research, which in the 1950s drew the attention of many scholars,[25] – although often victims of an exasperated 'panqumranism' – is currently being taken up and more cautiously explored in the sources (in particular the Dead Sea Scrolls, the Hellenistic Graeco-Roman and Christian documentary evidences), by operating the necessary distinction between Essenism, as a group or movement widely spread throughout Judaea, and the Essene community of Qumran located on the north-western shores of the Dead Sea (i.e. Khirbet Qumran), a community characterised by peculiar doctrinal, institutional and sectarian traits (see Charlesworth 1988; Cansdale 1996.1997; Davies 1997; Davila 2002; García Martínez 1987.1988. 1991; Id.-Trebolle Barrera 1993; Jokirante 2001; Schiffman 1994. 1995; Schmitt 1978; Ulrich-VanderKam 1994; VanderKam 1992.

Terra Sancta": Bottini-Di Segni-Alliata 1990; Manns-Alliata 1993, and recently Bottini-Di Segni-Chrupcafa 2003.

24.   Other contributions to the topic have recently been added by the IX Conference of New Testament and Ancient Christian Studies held in Naples (September 13-15, 2001) on the theme: "Il giudeocristianesimo nel I e II sec. d. C." (cf. *RStB* 15/2, 2003, with studies by L. Cirillo, R. Fabris, C. Gianotto, P. Grech, E. Manicardi, F. Manns, G. Marconi, R. Penna, M. Pesce and A. Pitta). The conference was very successful and attracted the attention of many, giving rise to a productive debate among the participants (about thirty scholars) from State and Pontifical Universities. For a preliminary presentation of the works of the conference, see M. Vitelli, "Il giudeocristianesimo nel I e II sec. d. C. Nota sul IX Convegno Neotestamentario ABI", *RdT* 43/3, 2002, pp. 411-424. For the literary and historical material concerning the Judaeo-Christians (sic) both in Ancient Jewish and Christian Literature, see Tomson – Lambers-Petry 2003.

25.   For more complete bibliographical references (including reviews and annotations), cf. *RdQ* 1/1, 1958-1959ff.; *KS* 1924ff.; *RAMBI* 1969ff., and Pinnick 2001. A useful *status quaestionis*, including an evaluation of the latest Essene-Qumranic researches, is that produced by Jucci 1995.

1994, and others).[26] Nodet-Taylor's work (1998), advancing the thesis of the 'proximity' (with the necessary distinctions)[27] of early Christianity and Essenism, is to be placed in this specific area of research. For the question of Essenism, I refer also to Boccaccini 1998a.[28] In this

26.   In the subsequent paragraph I will discuss the 'Enochic-Essene' hypothesis advanced by Boccaccini 1998a. Here I want to stress the usefulness of this study, since the author refers to and discusses the main contributions which have characterised Essene-Qumranic research in recent decades. With a 'pinch' of forgetfulness: the author does not mention Del Verme 1977, who had already expressed reservations in regard to the supposed equation between Essenes and Qumranites (at the time a dominant thesis, ibid., pp. 73-74, and passim), although acknowledging a common matrix for *both* movements, which could be defined, as Boccaccini suggests, either as Enochic Essenism or as Enochism and Qumranic Essenism.

27.   See review by Harrington 1999.

28.   For the sake of completeness I must also cite the hypothesis formulated by Norman Golb, which maintains that Qumran could have been a military stronghold and the scrolls would have been brought there by people fleeing a besieged Jerusalem during the Jewish war of 66-73 AD [*A propos*, I would mention Greg Doudna's recent thesis questioning the traditional date 68 CE for the deposit of the scrolls at Qumran caves. He would suggest an earlier period, i.e. the 1st century BCE: "The Legacy of an Error in Archaeological Interpretation: the Dating of the Qumran Cave Scroll Deposits", in Galor-Zangenburg 2004; visit also http://www. bibleinterp.com/articles/Doudna_Scroll_Deposits_1.2.3.4.htm, with Bibliography]. Ph. R. Davies in *Currents in Research: Biblical Studies* 3, 1995, pp. 9-35, summarises – along with that proposed by Golb 1985.1995 – the main counter-hypotheses, i.e. by Rengstorf 1963; Cansdale 1997; Crown-Cansdale 1994; Donceel and Donceel-Voûte 1994; Cook 1996; Stegemann 1993; Humbert-Chambon 1994) regarding the identification of the Qumranites with the Essenes and the connections (and lack of them) between the site of Qumran and the caves 1-11. An excellent synthesis of the various positions in this regard can be found in Boccaccini 1998a, pp. 1-17. Generally one can accept G. Garbini's perspective (*Cantico dei cantici. Testo ebraico, traduzione, introduzione e commento* [Biblica 2; Brescia: Paideia, 1992], p. 135 and n. 1), who describes as "provocatorio ma salutare" Golb's work, whose radical position "ridimensionata, forse non è lontana dal vero". In my opinion, however, Golb's 'reading' neglects or underestimates many of the existing data (archaeological-monumental, documentary and literary), which contribute to make more veridical and better documents the hypothesis of a (close) connection between Khirbet Qumran and the documents and other finds from 1-11Q. Of course, the question must not be considered as solved (and Capelli's 'caution' is noteworthy [see his *Postfazione* to Sanders 1992, 691-693]), but I am more confident than he is (in contrast with Golb and others) in identifying/finding connections between the Essene–Qumranic community settled in Khirbet Qumran and the manuscripts and other things found in the Caves 1-11. This stance is in line with the theses proposed by learned Qumranologists, in particular É. Puech and F. García Martínez, whose theories I had a chance to consider during the conference held in Modena on September 26-30, 2001, on the theme: "Qumran. La più grande avventura biblica del XX secolo pre-

monograph Boccaccini reproposes and discusses the hypothesis (only partially new) based on the assumption that the Essenes mentioned in the Hellenistic Graeco-Roman (*in primis* Philo and Flavius Josephus but not Pliny the Elder and Dio of Prusa) and Christian sources are those Enochians whose activity is connected with the production of Enochic literature (in particular *1 Enoch* and *Jubilees*) and who continued to exist after the destruction of the community of Qumran in 68 CE.[29] Qumranic Essenism or Enochism was consequently a transitional

---

sentata dai suoi protagonisti", the Proceedings of which I hope will be published soon. The same topic has been dealt with during the *Enoch Seminar II,* held in Venice (The University of Michigan's Second Enoch Seminar, Venice, Italy [July 1-5, 2003]), which had on the agenda – among the other things – the re-discussion of both the so-called "Groningen Hypothesis" by F. García Martínez and the "Enochic-Essene Hypothesis" by Boccaccini, with a conclusive "Public session" on "The Dead Sea Scrolls: New Light on Early Judaism and Christian Origins". The Proceedings of the Venice Conference are forthcoming (see Boccaccini 2004). *A propos* I also wish to mention an unpublished thesis of a talented student of mine, Dr. Lara Guglielmo, under the title: "Manoscritti di Qumran ed Essenismo. Verso una nuova ipotesi" (University of Naples 'Federico II', December 2002). L. Guglielmo maintains that the centuries-old religious movement which has its point of reference in Qumran cannot be represented under a single label as Essene/Sadducean/Pharisaic/Zealot. Stemberger's careful analysis of the information provided by Hellenistic and Roman sources regarding the Jewish *hairesis* has revealed that such information is often unreliable, because contradictory (Stemberger 1991). Consequently it is believed that it would be methodologically more appropriate to explain the 'Qumran phenomenon' only in the light of its textual and archaeological heritage, respecting the temporal limits imposed by both palaeography and archaeology and valuing above all the historical elements transmitted by the Qumran *Pesharim* and the *Damascus Rule* (see Ead. 2003).

   29.   Boccaccini 1998a, in particular: (f) *The decline of the Essene movement* e (g) *The Essene legacy* (pp. 189-191). I refer the reader to three precise reviews of the Enochic-Essene hypothesis by Boccaccini: the first, generally descriptive, by Van Peursen 2001 (supra, III.); the second, very critical, is that by J.J. Collins (*ASE* 19/2, 2002, pp. 503-506), which I partially accept; the third is that by L. Arcari (in *Materia giudaica* 8/2, 2003, 407-413, containing good observations and some criticism in particular in regard to the 'rather broad definition' of Enochism proposed by Boccaccini ("...è possible" – Dr. Arcari argues – "ritenere tutti i movimenti antisadociti come enochici? L'opposizione antisadocita è un elemento che assicura l'appartenenza di un testo al movimento enochico?" [ibid., p. 412]), exposing Boccaccini to a risk of "oversimplification" as Collins wrote in his review. See also Gianotto 2004, who reports the reviews of the book by W. Adler, J.C. VanderKam, B.G. Wright, and the answer by Boccaccini, during the "Italian Evenings" at the Annual Meeting SBL 1998, held at Orlando (Florida). C. Martone ("Beyond *Beyond the Essene Hypothesis?* Some Observations on the Qumran Zadokite Priesthood", *Henoch* 25/3, 2003, pp. 267-275) has recently revisited some previous studies on the Zadokite Priesthod at Qumran by

phenomenon, isolated and marginal as well as extremist and sectarian. To prove the peculiar character of the community it suffices to consider the Qumranic doctrine of individual predestination (1QS and 1QHᵃ), the socio-economic model of the community of goods, the rule of celibacy imposed on the postulant once he became a permanent member of the community: the last two characteristics greatly impressed a contemporary pagan writer, the polygraph, historian and naturalist Pliny the Elder (23/24-79 CE), thirsty as he was for 'exotic curiosities' (cf. *Nat. Hist.* 5.17). In the year 68 the community was completely wiped out and the settlement of Qumran was partially destroyed but the Enochic-Essene movement did not cease to exist. The Enochic-Essene legacy,[30] somewhat present already in the activity of John the Baptist, in the movement led by Jesus of Nazareth and in the early Jerusalemite community as well as in Paul of Tarsus, will have survived in some groups and/or communities of that 'Christian Judaism' characteristic of the *Didache*, in which it is possible to find references to groups or factions within the community and to which the *Didache* appears to be addressed (infra, IV. Del Verme 1995. 1999.2001b. 2001c.2003a).

Recently the current of studies focusing on pagan anti-semitism and Christian anti-Judaism has drawn the attention of numerous scholars of ancient history. As to the works reflecting pagan perceptions, which are of very limited importance for our purposes, I list only a few titles.[31] I will be more selective in the perusal of those regarding the anti-Judaism characterising the Christian environment (in both the NT and Patristic texts).

I also record several general studies regarding the spread of Judaism in the eastern quarter of the Mediterranean region, in particular in the

---

singling out a trajectory of research initiated by P. Sacchi and carryed on by F. García Martínez and G. Boccaccini. He also adds new material on the topic, in particular from 4QS [4Q *256* and 4Q *258*] which – in his opinion – would be older than 1QS. *Contra*, L. Guglielmo, "*Micae Qumranicae*. I Manoscritti di Qumran a quasi sessant'anni dalla scoperta", in *Papyrologica Lupiensia* 12, 2003, pp. 99-114.

30.   Two conclusive observations by Boccaccini are rather interesting and more convincing: "The clear distinction between mainstream Essenism and Qumran calls for an urgent reassesment of the Essene contribution to Christian origins", and Enochic/ Essene (Apocalyptic) epistemology survived the decline of the organised movement. "The Christian claim to be the «new Israel» against the parallel claim of Rabbinic Judaism to be the «one eternal Israel» outshone even the memory of the pluralistic environment from which both the Church and the Synagogue emerged" (ibid., p. 189).

31.   Exemplary is the volume by Schäfer 1997.

Roman province of Syria and more precisely in the area surrounding the capital Antioch where, according to some eminent scholars, the final edition of the *Didache* was brought to completion. In particular, the enquiry into the Hebrew-Jewish roots of the *Didache* could and should greatly benefit from these studies since they provide specific information and details regarding the context in which the text was produced, a factor that could help to define the identity of the groups/movements underlying the *Didache*.

As to the anti-Judaism of the New Testament and of the ancient Christian literature, it must be clearly stated that these writings, besides expressing doctrinal, denominational and, probably, inter-communal controversies between the Judaism of the synagogue and the Christian community or communities, can prove to be an important source of information. Such information could help to identify the presence of particular groups within 'Christian Judaism' sympathetic towards contemporary Judaism, which appear to have continued to frequent the synagogues and observe Jewish rituals and practices. It will be for this very reason that the 'Great Church' will later brand them as 'heretics'. It is significant, in fact, that as late as the time of John Chrysostom, that is in the 4th century CE and in the region of Antioch, some groups, belonging to 'Christian Judaism',[32] will have to be reprimanded by Chrysostom, an 'eloquent' speaker,[33] because they continue to frequent the synagogues and participate to Jewish festivities[34] while showing no visible sign of doctrinal/confessional and communal (or sociological) ambivalence about it.[35]

---

32.   I prefer this term to the more widespread and common "Judaeo-Christians and/or Judaising Christians", which appears to be theologically charged – if not biased – because of doctrinal preoccupations typical of Christian apologists (Greek, Latin and Syrian), and recurring in heresiological texts (i.e., Justin, Origen, Irenaeus, Epiphanius of Salamis, Jerome and, above all, Eusebius of Caesarea).

33.   See in particular the eight homilies *Against the Jews* which he gave during the Jewish festivities in autumn and at Easter.

34.   As to 'Gentile Christians' observing 'Jewish festivals' of autumn (the fast of *Yom Kippur*), see D. Stöckl Ben Ezra, in Tomson - Lambers-Petry 2003, pp. 66-70 (Id., *The Impact of Yom Kippur on Early Christianity. The Day of Atonement from Second Temple Judaism to the Fifth Century*; Tübingen: Mohr Siebeck, 2003). On *Yom Kippur* in general see the short essay by Hruby 1965, and the lemma *Ro'sh ha-Shanah* and *Yom Kippur* by L. Jacobs in Eliade 1986, pp. 612-514 (with bibliography).

35.   Chrysostom's Homilies play an important part in the 'demonisation' of the Jews in the Christian context. The aggressive tone of the preacher's words are, in

I refer the reader to the bibliography below containing works which deal with the currents of research previously mentioned. I will group the titles of various currents into distinct blocks in order both to facilitate consultation and to direct the reader in selecting those works pertinent to his/her field of study.

For the spread of Judaism in the Mediterranean region see Adams 1988; Alexander 1992; van Amersfoort-van Oort 1990; Bickerman 1976-1986.1985.1988; Boccaccini 2001b; Barcklay-Sweet 1996; Boschi 1987; Charlesworth 1993; Cohn-Sherbok-Court 2001; Davies-Finkelstein 1984-1989; Feldman 1996; Gager 1983; Goodman 1996; Juster 1914; Leon 1960; Lieu 1996; Lieu-North-Rajak 1992; MacLennan 1990; Mélèze Modrzejewski 1993; Millar 1992; Neusner-Frerichs 1985; Rutgers 1998; Safrai-Stern 1974-1976; Schreckenberg-Schubert 1992; Schröer 1992; Schürer 1973-1987; Segal 1986; Sigal 1980; Simon 1964; Simon-Benoît 1985; Smallwood 1976.1999; Stemberger 1996; Stern 1974-1984; Stone 1980; Troiani 1993a.1993b. In particular for the Judaism in the Syrian province and in the area of Antiochia cf. Barrett 1995; Freyne 1994b; Gnilka 2000; Grant 1972; Hahn 1987; Kraeling 1932; Meeks-Wilken 1978; Sanders (J.T.) 1992; Simon 1962b; Verseput 1993; Wilson 1995a; Zetterholm 2003; for Asia Minor, Egypt and Rome, apart from the works listed above, see also Collins (J.J.) 2000 and now Garribba 2004.

For the anti-Judaism[36] (in some cases it may be also referred to as 'anti-semitism') found in ancient Christian sources, in the NT and, above all, in the Patristic texts, among the many works available I single out the following titles: *ASE* 1997.1999b; Bori 1983; Brockway

---

reality, proportional to the challenge which particular Christian groups represented within (and not external to) the community of Antioch... The relations with synagogual Judaism were, therefore, different from thoses wished by the pastor for his followers. As Monaci Castagno rightly believes, there is a diffuse perception in the speeches *Against the Jews* by the presbyter John that the relations between the Christian groups (which that scholar likes to define as 'judaising') and the Jews of the synagogue were stronger than the divisions the preacher attempted to inculcate: what unified them, in fact, was a common religious tradition and the common social setting of the city. "...la lotta contro il giudaismo non poteva essere vinta con le armi dei decreti dei concili e delle leggi imperiali, ma prosciugando il consenso, implicito ed esplicito, di cui godeva" (Ead. 1997, p. 152). A contrary perspective is proposed by Norelli 2001, who discusses the Judaising Christians in Ignatius of Antioch; cf. also Simon 1962b.

36.   For the anti-semitism of the pagan world, I refer the reader to Cracco Ruggini 1980a; Feldman 1993; Gager 1983; Rokeah 1982; and Stern 1976-1984.

2000; Conzelmann 1981; Cracco Ruggini 1980; de Lange 1976; Donahue 1975; Gardenal 2001; Hvalvik 1996; Limor-Stroumsa 1996; Mannucci 1993; Monaci Castagno 1997; Pesce 1997; Sanders 1993; Sandmel 1969.1977.1978; Schreckenberg 1982; Segal 1991; Simon 1962b; Stanton 1985.1996; Stroumsa 1993.1996b; Taylor 1995; Tyson 1992.1995; Wilson 1986.1995a.

In Italy the historiographical and methodological development which followed the 'turning point' in the study of Hellenistic and Roman Judaism and to which the problem regarding Christian origins is directly connected, have had a positive influence on historians (of Hellenistic and Roman Judaism and early Christianity) as well as on NT scholars and, to a certain extent, those interested in Ancient Christian literature. The scholar who could be considered the 'Coryphaeus' of the 'Italian School' and, in a certain sense, the co-author of the 'turning point' in the international arena, is Paolo Sacchi. Since the early 1980s, Sacchi has contributed much to the studies of post-exilic Judaism, including the Judaism contemporary with the Christian movement of Jesus and his disciples, with original research regarding Jewish apocalypticism and the Apocrypha/Pseudepigrapha of the OT. In this connection I refer the reader to Sacchi 1981-2000.1984. 1987.1993.1997b.1999.2000. Several researchers who have adopted Sacchi's historiographical, methodological and historical perspective – although borrowing from non-Italian scholarship too[37] – have greatly contributed to the analysis and study of texts, themes and personalities of the period in question. In this regard see Arcari 2001.2002.2003; Boccaccini 1992.1993a.1993b.1998a. 2001a. 2001b; Chiesa 1987a; Del Verme 1999.2001c.2003 (infra, IV.); Gianotto 1984; Lupieri 1993. 1997; Manzi 1997; Norelli 1980.1994; Pesce 1979.1994.2003b; Rosso Ubigli 1978. 1979.1983; Troiani 1993a.1993b, and others).[38]

At the 'XVI Meeting of Scholars of Christian Antiquity' held in Rome on the 7-9 May 1987, the trend towards analysis and understanding of Christian origins in the context of Judaism had already begun to appear among Italian scholars.[39] Since then, during the last fifteen

37.   Among these I cite: Collins 1998.1999a.1999b.2000; Stone 1980; Stone-Chazon 1998; VanderKam 1992.2000.2001; VanderKam-Adler 1996.

38.   Several important contributions are in the Proceedings of the annual and biennial seminars (see the following paragraph).

39.   Cf. AA. VV. 1988, in particular the contributions by M. Pesce (pp. 7-21) and P. Sacchi (pp. 23-50).

years, new positive signals have appeared on the horizon of Italian studies of early Christianity, as is evident from the recent publication of a number of excellent works. Consequently it appears that the new trends following on from the above-mentioned 'turning point' are well established in Italy. One need only peruse the *Proceedings* of the 'Conference of Studies of the New Testament and Early Christianity' which are held every two years in Italy since 1987 (cf. Penna 1989. 1993. 1995. 1997.1999.2001.2003), in particular on themes of historical, literary and doctrinal importance such as anti-Paulinism, Johannism, Prophetism, Apocalyptic, Qumran, Phariseism, the Acts of the Apostles and Judaistic Christianity which have been studied in the context of the Judaism coeval to the origins of Christianity and/or of the first three centuries of the Christian era.[40] The reader is referred to the bibliography below for those works dealing with some of these specific issues. Besides the numerous studies recorded in the Proceedings of annual research seminars on the 'Studies of Christian and Ancient Jewish Exegetical Literature', published in *ASE* 1/1984ff., I particularly draw the reader's attention to some of the monograph issues of *ASE*: "Logos of God and modern Sophia" (ibid. 11/1, 1994); "The Cult in Spirit and Truth" (ibid. 12/1, 1995); "Purity and Cult in Leviticus" (ibid. 13/1, 1996); "Paradise on Earth" (ibid. 13/2, 1996); "The Bible in the Anti-Hebrew Controversy" (ibid. 14/1, 1997); "Christian Millenarianism and its Scriptural Foundations" (ibid. 15/1, 1998); "The End of Time" (ibid. 16/1,1999); "Judaism and Anti-Judaism" (ibid. 16/2,1999); "Eschatology and Scripture" (ibid. 17/1, 2000); "Representations of Judaism and a Controversy on the Interpretation of the Koran" (ibid. 17/2, 2000); "Sacrifice in Judaism and in Christianity" (ibid. 18/1, 2001); "Jews and Christians in the Cities. Reciprocal Influences and Conflicts" (ibid. 18/2, 2001), "Christians and Pagan and Biblical Sacrifice" (ibid. 19/1, 2002);

---

40.   The X Conference of New Testament and Ancient Christian Studies (Foligno, September 11-13, 2003), on the topic "Il Gesù storico nelle fonti del I-II sec. d.C.", has produced new contributions to the study of Christian origins. I cite in particular those by G. Jossa ("Quadro storico, sociale, archeologico della Palestina al tempo di Gesù"), E. Manicardi ("I criteri applicabili alle fonti per giungere alla storia di Gesù"), M. Pesce ("Il Gesù degli *agrapha*"), L. Troiani ("Il Gesù di Flavio Giuseppe"), C. Gianotto ("Il Gesù della storia e il *Vangelo di Tommaso*), E. Norelli ("La presenza di Gesù nella letteratura gentile dei primi due secoli"), and M.P. Scanu ("I testi rabbinici su Gesù"). The *Proceedings* of the conference will be published in *RStB* 17/2, 2005.

"The Construction of Christian Identity (I-VII cent. AD)" (ibid. 20/1, 2003); and other themes already cited.

At this stage I can only hint at a question of historical and cultural importance which has been recently reconsidered in new terms,[41] that regarding the 'old question' of the spread of the Christian message outside Jerusalem both in Palestine and in the Jewish Diaspora and among the pagan populations inhabiting the western and eastern Mediterranean regions, in particular through the missionary activity and preaching of Paul of Tarsus. In the past two decades several researchers[42] have focused on the topic and recently[43] in Italy two scholars, L. Troiani and G. Jossa (Troiani 1993b.1996.1999a.1999b.2001; Jossa 1991 [revised edition, Rome 2000].2001a.2001b.2001c). The question still remains on the agenda, fuelling academic debates.[44] For Troiani the development and spread of Christianity, as outlined in the *Acts of the Apostles* by Luke, needs to be reconsidered and critically re-analysed. The historical and historiographical perspective of Jossa[45] appears to

41. Since the classical work by A. von Harnack, *Die Mission und Ausbreitung des Christentums in den drei ersten Jahrhunderten,* vols. I-II (Leipzig: Hinrichs, 1924 [IV ed.]).

42. I refer the reader, in particular, to Filoramo-Roda 1992; Frend 1984; Geoltrain 2000; Grant 1977; MacMullen 1984; Mayeur-Pietri-Vauchez-Venard 2000; Siniscalco 1983; Smith 1990; Sordi 1984; Stark 1996; and Vouga 1997.

43. But new perspectives should also emerge for the renewed project of an Italian team which – after two decades of studies devoted to the interpretation and the varied use of the sacred texts of Judaism and Christianity – is now moving towards a deeper study of Christian identity in both East and West in the first seven centuries of the Christian era. See in this regard the recent study by M. Pesce, "Quando nasce il cristianesimo? Aspetti dell'attuale dibattito storiografico e uso delle fonti", in *ASE* 20/1, 2003, pp. 39-56, as well as those of other scholars, in particular G. Filoramo, H. Moxnes, and E. Lupieri (ibid.).

44. *A propos*, "there is a growing number of scholars in the U.S. that does not us the word "Jew" or the word "Christian" for anything before Constantine. The reason for this is that the meaning of words comes from social systems, and in pre-Constantinian social systems there was nothing that looks like Judaism and Christianity as understood today. The words "Jew" and "Christian" are not universal constants. The English word "Jew" dates from the 13th century AD and all forms of Judaism today are post-Talmudic – just like all forms of Christianity are post-Nicean" (from an e-mail of B.J. Malina dated July 13, 2004).

45. In its 2004 editorial programme Paideia (Brescia, Italy) has just published a short monograph by G. Jossa, entitled *Giudei o cristiani? I seguaci di Gesù in cerca di una propria identità* (StBi 142), which might confirm (or at least 'dilute', I would hope) the position of my revered colleague and historian of Ancient Christianity. See

be more sympathetic towards the hypothesis claiming that the *opus Lucanum* contains reliable references to the origins of Christianity. Consequently, Jossa is more inclined to give prominence to the use of sources (and related literature) which support the theory of a 'precocious' autonomy of the Christian movement from Judaism. According to Troiani, the categories of the 'Hellenists', the 'God-fearers', the 'Proselytes' alone are insufficient to justify the passage-conversion of the Gentiles to Christianity. How indeed could the Scriptural passages quoted by Paul and other apostles be understood by the Gentiles? And what sense would it have made to proclaim "to the Gentiles", as Paul does, that the Law had been abrogated and had lost its saving effects? For this reason the author suggests a contextualised and historical interpretation of the noun "Gentiles/pagans" (Gr. τὰ ἔθνη) in the writings of Luke and Paul. This interpretation, which considers the philological – cultural *data* derived from Jewish-Hellenistic and pagan literature, can be seen to be more complex and problematical than that proposed by exegetes and historians of the NT. The ἔθνη of Paul and Luke are not *necessarily* the Gentiles *tout court* or, at least, they are not the only people who might be so designated. The ἔθνη may possibly include "il mondo delle famiglie ebraiche trapiantate da generazioni nelle città e nei paesi dell'ecumene greco-romana. Dal seno di queste famiglie, a Roma come a Beroea, nasce in buona misura, il movimento cristiano?".[46] Working from Graeco-Roman, pagan and Jewish sources, Troiani does not adopt an apodeictic tone,[47] but discusses his hypothesis with reference to several Christian, Jewish and pagan texts. His argument runs that "la via di Damasco (= the conversion) puo' aprirsi a chi frequenta da tempo le Scritture. La liberazione dalla legge, predicata da Paolo, sembra implicare familiarità, da generazioni, con i testi della Torah e dei profeti; questa familiarità, come è ovvio, avrà conosciuto fasi alterne

---

also Id., "Giudei e Cristiani visti dai Romani", in U. M. Criscuolo (ed.), *Societas studiorum. Per Salvatore D'Elia* (Napoli: Giannini, 2004), pp. 465-477, which – lightly amplified – is included in Id., *Giudei o cristiani?*, cit., pp. 173-198.

46.   Troiani 1999a, p. 12.

47.   "Vorrei aggiungere – he writes – che non v'è proprio nulla di apodittico in questi ragionamenti; nessuna (assurda) pretesa di dire una parola decisiva... Per esemplificare, non voglio sostituire alla perentoria, corrente definizione di Paolo 'apostolo dei gentili' quella di 'apostolo delle pecore che si sono perdute della casa d'Israele'. Vorrei però che si esplorasse anche questa possibilità" (ibid., p. 12).

di osservanza".[48] Among the Jews outside the Synagogue, and rather lukewarm in their observance of the prescriptions of the Torah, Paul and his companions might have found fertile grounds for their mission. In this regard Acts 19:9-10 relates a significant episode regarding the "school of one Tyrannus", where Paul, after leaving the Synagogue, resided for the following two years, during which he continued his elaboration of the "new doctrine". Such an episode could testify to the presence in Ephesus of Jews outside the Synagogue.[49] These Jews might have become followers of the "Word of the Lord". "Noi possiamo ritenere" – argues Troiani – "che, quando il cristianesimo tagliò definitivamente i ponti con il giudaismo, anche la storia precedente ne sia stata condizionata. Nell'età di Eusebio, gli *ethne* dei testi di Luca e di Paolo potevano essere ancora intesi come parte dell' ebraismo?". Certainly not. It happened that "l'identità dei primi destinatari del kerygma (= the Jews) presto si confuse con quella dei successivi (= the Gentiles/Pagans)".[50] In my opinion the problem of the spread of Christianity as understood by Troiani[51] could add new *tesserae* – found in the Hellenistic and cosmopolitan Judaism of the Diaspora – to the mosaic of Christian origins analysed in the context of 1st century Palestinian Judaism.

Before concluding this Part III. I want briefly to consider other two important questions. The first concerns the possible connections between Christian origins and Rabbinism, an area of research which in the first decades of 20th century[52] drew the attention of Christian exegetes and historians. This area is currently being explored – although repetitiously – and applied to the analysis of NT commentaries. The second

---

48.   Ibid.

49.   In an e-mail dated October 23, 2000, L. Troiani informed me that he believed to find perfectly congruent the extra-Synagogal *milieux* I had identified in some passages of the *Didache* (for example 4:8; 8:1-2; 13:3-7) with the narration of Acts 19:9-10 (= the "school of one Tyrannus" and so on).

50.   Troiani, ibid., pp. 74-75; and 2001a.

51.   His interpretative perspective has been also confirmed in a learned and detailed review (Troiani 2002) in which he presents – in mainly eulogistic tones, interspersed with some criticisms – the revised edition (Roma: Carocci, 2000) of Jossa 1991. Cf. *RivBib* 49, 2001, pp. 362-370. As to the identity of the 'Jew' and the 'Gentile' in *Acts*, cf. also Sanders 1991.

52.   In the wake of researches which have had a long tradition, such as J. Lightfoot's, *Horae Hebraicae et Talmudicae* (Lipsiae: w.e., 1658-1674) (with postumous Supplements on *Acts* and *Rom*, published by R. Kidder in 1678).

question concerns the use of the social sciences (sociology, cultural anthropology, psychology, psychanalysis and related disciplines) in the study of Ancient Christianity. It is a methodology of recent vintage and its possible application in the field of studies on Early Christianity is still being tested.[53] Consequently it has not yet been able to consolidate any remarkable findings or results. Although it would have deserved a wider discussion in this bibliography, I will cite only some of the most prominent works in this area.

For the study of the origins of Christianity and in particular of the fundamental Christian writings, both canonical and non-canonical, and their relation with Rabbinism (= the Rabbinic literature *in toto*: *Mishnah, Tosefta, Talmud, Midrashim* and *Targumim*) I refer the reader to the monumental work by (H.L. Strack-) P. Billerbeck, *Kommentar zum Neuen Testament aus Talmud und Midrasch*, vols. I-IV (München: Beck, 1922-1928), and the two Supplements: *Rabbinischer Index* and *Verzeichnis der Schriftgelehrten, Geographisches Register*, hrsg. von J. Jeremias in Verbindung mit K. Adolph, vols. V-VI (München: Beck), 1956-1961, a work which, although it has educated generations of Christian exegetes, in my opinion has had negative influences,[54] because of the 'indiscriminate' use and the 'magmatic' accumulation of citations derived from Post-Biblical Jewish texts, not only on the development of NT exegesis in general, but also on the compilation of the *lemmas* contained in the first volumes by G. Kittel-G. Friederich (hrsg. von), *Theologisches Wörterbuch zum Neuen Testament*, vols. I-X/1-2 (Stuttgart: W. Kohlhammer Verlag, 1933-1979). Besides these monu-

---

53.   This 'lacuna' in the studies of Ancient Christianity (in particular in Italy), is concisely dealt with by Destro-Pesce 1997[2], *Prefazione*, pp. VII-XV, in which immediately following the acknowledgement that "l'antropologia delle origini cristiane è uno degli esiti dell'applicazione alle società antiche dell'antropologia culturale" – and that great progress has been made in the study of the ancient world, as e.g. from the studies regarding ritual sacrifices by M. Mauss (Durkheim's school) up to more recent researches focusing on themes of Ancient Jewish anthropology (in particolar some of the works by M. Douglas) – the authors argue that "l'attenzione allo studio delle forme e degli intrecci culturali del primissimo cristianesimo è rimasta molto limitata...Sembra quasi che gli studi antropologici esitino a entrare nel campo del I secolo cristiano" (ibid., pp. XII-XIII). The essay by Destro-Pesce is useful and exemplary both for its bibliographical references on the topic and because – in the 'meagre' panorama of Italian studies devoted to this genre – their study represents a successful achievement.

54.   Del Verme 1989, in particular the *Premessa*, pp. 15-20, with bibliographical references interspersed in the footnotes.

mental works, one must also refer to somewhat similar works by G. Foot Moore, *Judaism in the First Centuries of the Christian Era. The Age of the Tannaim*, vols. I-III (Cambridge, MA: Harvard University Press, 1927-1930; in two volumes, New York: Shocken Books, 1971); G.C. Montefiore, *Rabbinic Literature and Gospel Teachings* (London: Macmillan & Co., 1930); and M. Smith, *Tannaitic Parallels to the Gospels* (JBL.MS, 6; Philadelphia, PA.: Fortress Press, 1951). As to the last named work, however, I would point out that the author appears to distance himself in a sense from (and indeed criticises) what I have defined as a "magmatic and indiscriminate accumulation" of Rabbinic citations as in Billerbeck. Later studies – critically more mature and methodologically more attentive to the relation text-context-chronology of Rabbinic sources – have tried to correct the unilateral and 'ancillary' perspective of the works cited above, which delved in Post-Biblical Judaism with the sole intention of finding either a support for or confirmation of (hence the 'ancillary' function) the New Testament.[55] In contrast to past tendencies, some Hebraists in the last three decades have also begun to turn to Christian sources (beginning with the New Testament) for a more comprehensive understanding of Hellenistic Graeco-Roman Judaism.[56] Among the few contemporary authors[57] who have deepened the knowledge of some of the aspects of Christian

---

55.   See the 'pioneering' essay by R. Bloch, "Note méthodologique pour l'étude de la littérature rabbinique", *RSR* 43, 1955, pp. 194-227; and those by G.Vermes, "Jewish Literature and New Testament Exegesis: Reflections on Methodology", *JJS* 33, 1982, pp. 361-376, who develops and establishes in methodological terms ideas already expressed in previous contributions published in the same journal (ibid., 27, 1976, pp. 107-116; 31, 1980, pp. 1-17). Prior to Vermes another scholar was writing on the same topic: J. Neusner, "Judaism 'after Moor: A Programmatic Statement", *JJS* 31, 1980, pp. 141-156. Cf. also Sanders 1977.1985.1992; McNamara 1983; Stemberger 1991 (exemplary his review of *Einleitung in Talmud und Midrasch* by H.L. Strack del 1982 [VII Ed.], a work which in the VIII Ed., München 1992, bears the signature of Stemberger only); Penna 1999; and in particular the more recent and copious scientific production by J. Neusner (and his team). It appears, however, that Neusner 1988a, pp. 391-419 strongly criticises 'other' readings of Rabbinic sources (i.e. differing from his), in particular those by Urbach and by Sanders. In reply to Neusner, A. Goldberg ("The Mishna – A Study Book of Halakha", in Safrai 1987-1991, First Part , p. 250) labels as "unfounded pretension" and "dilettantism" Neusner's critique of previous scholars of the *Mishnah*. These are examples from an ongoing debate which is far from being 'peaceful' and indeed is extremely complex in this particular context.
56.   Cf. Safrai 1987-1991; Safrai-Stern 1974-1976; and Stone 1984.
57.   Noteworthy is also the old contribution by Gavin 1929.

origins in relation to Rabbinism I single out Del Verme 1989[58]; Fisher 1988.1990; Pesce 1979. 1997; Sanders 1977.1980-1981.1985.1990a. 1992;[59] Shanks 1992b; Sigal 1984; Tomson 1990. 2001; and in some pages also Destro 1989.1992.1993; and Destro-Pesce 1992. I will discuss later the specific works on the *Didache* and its relation to Rabbinic literature (infra, IV.).

As to the second question, that concerning the application of socio-anthropological sciences to the study of Christian origins, a field of inquiry which I have labelled as "of recent vintage" and poorly explored by Italian scholars, this field needs further clarification to avoid engendering misunderstandings and consequent, often unjustified, criticisms. As a matter of fact, cultural anthropological studies of the ancient world – in particular Greece (I refer to the classic works by L. Gernet, J.-P. Vernant, M. Detienne and his school) – have been well received in Italy and can count many followers. In this regard it suffices to mention such scholars as M. Bettini, C. Cantarella, R. Di Donato and C. Grottanelli, attentive also – in particular the last-named – to the ancient Hebrew-Biblical world.[60] Since the late 1980s, Rabbinic Judaism itself has been explored by recourse to the methodology derived from the social sciences, in particular from cultural anthropology, as is seen in the works by Boyarin 1993.1999; Destro 1987.1989.1992.1993; Destro-Pesce 1992; and Eilberg-Schwartz 1990.[61]

In Italy, however, the study of early Christianity based on methodologies derived from social sciences is limited to a minority or *élite* of

---

58. In particular, the *Parte seconda* (= La storia delle decime nel Giudaismo del Secondo Tempio e di epoca tannaitica), pp. 117-249.

59. J. Neusner (*Jewish Law from Jesus to the Mishnah. A Systematic Reply to Prof. E.P. Sanders* [SFlaJud 84; Atlanta: Scholars Press, 1993]; see also Id., in *JSJ* 24/ 2, 1993, pp. 317-323) appears to be very critical of this and of other works by Sanders.

60. See *Prefazione* and *Bibliografia* by Destro-Pesce 2001, pp. VII-XV, and pp. 185-217.

61. It must be pointed out that these (and other) scholars base their studies on the 'systemic' analysis by which J. Neusner in the last twenty five years – obviously changing his previous reading perspective (i.e. Neusner 1971. 1972.1973) has reviewed the entire corpus of Rabbinic literature in what can be described as a 'continuous dialogue' with literary analysis, structuralism, system theory, comparative studies of religion and cultural anthropology. M. Pesce and his wife, who appear to be the most dedicated followers of Neusner's theories and writings among Italian scholars, are constantly bringing to colleagues' attention the numerous researches by this excellent and original American scholar, in particular those in the field of cultural anthropology. Cf. Destro-Pesce 2001, pp. 205f.

qualified researchers among whom, *in primis,* are M. Pesce and A. Destro, who have produced valuable works: Destro-Pesce 1992.1995. 1996.1997.2000.2001. This 'new season' for Italian research, although late, is part of a wider 'climate' of studies which from the late 1970s has experienced remarkable developments abroad especially in the English speaking world. Actually the best work using social science interpretation comes from the U.S., and to a lesser degree from Canada, Germany, Norway, Scotland, South Africa, and Spain.[62] There are several bibliographical reviews which provide thorough information on the state of this particular research perspective: see Barbaglio 1998; Elliott 1995, pp.138-174; Hanson 1994; Harrington 1988; Holmberg 1990, pp.158-170; May 1991; Norelli 1987; Stegemann-Stegemann 1995, pp. 689-728; Theissen 1983, pp. 331-348; 1988b. 1989. 2000. Among the many contributions I would single out: Barton 1989; Elliott 1986.1995; Grabbe 1989; Holmberg1990; Judge 1960; Malherbe 1983; Malina 1981.1982.1986.1991.1995; Malina-Neyrey 1988.1996; Malina-Rohrbaugh 1992; Meeks 1983.1986; Neyrey 1991; Osiek 1992; Pilch 1991.1992; Pilch-Malina 1993; Rohrbaugh 1997; Sim 1995; Stambaugh-Balch 1986; Zetterholm 2003. And among those from Germany: Kümmel 1985; Stegemann-Stegemann 1995; Theissen 1977. 1983.1988b.1989.2000; from Norway: Moxnes 1988.1991; from Scotland: Esler 1987.1994.1995; and from Spain: Aguirre 1987.1991.

In a comment on a PCB (= Pontifical Biblical Commission) Document:[63] "The Interpretation of the Bible in the Church" (dated April 15, 1993),[64] Pesce (1998) describes, with rich documentation,[65] and critically evaluates the humanistic approach to the reading and interpretation of the Bible. In general, however, I must point out that except for the NT other proto-Christian writings have been either only touched upon or considered only partially by the interpretative methodology of social sciences. As to the *Didache* there are only a few contributions

---

62.   I refer the reader to the concise but precise "I. Introduction to Social Scientific Criticism" by May 1991, pp. 1-11.

63.   Ed. by G. Ghiberti and F. Mosetto (Leumann [To]: Elle di ci, 1998).

64.   The original French text can be found in *Biblica* 74, 1993, pp. 451-528. The nos. 1343-1359 of the Document deal with "Approches par les sciences humaines".

65.   The article is extremely useful since the numerous bibliographical references are selected and discussed in relation to the individual areas which form the 'map' of the social sciences, in particular sociology, cultural anthropology, psychology and psychoanalysis.

(infra, IV.). Therefore it is desirable that the methodology derived from social sciences – providing it remains firmly committed to the fundamental aim of exploring the complexity of historical realities[66] – should play a part in uncovering and definiting the authentic value and meaning of the religious phenomena present in ancient texts.

AA. VV. 1972 = *Judéo-Christianisme. Recherches historiques et théologiques offertes en hommage au Cardinal J. Daniélou, RSR* 60.

AA.VV. 1974 = *Cristiani e ebrei,* a cura della sezione 'Ecumenismo' diretta da H. Küng e W. Kasper, *Conc*(I) 10/8.

AA. VV. 1977 = *Economia e società nei Padri: proprietà, lavoro, famiglia.* – V Incontro di studiosi dell'Antichità cristiana (Roma, maggio 1976), *Aug.* 17, pp. 1-282.

AA. VV. 1978 = *Studi sull'escatologia.* – VI Incontro di studiosi dell'Antichità cristiana (Roma, maggio 1977), ibid. 18, pp. 1-282.

AA. VV. 1982 = *L'Antico Testamento nei primi secoli della Chiesa.* – X Incontro di studiosi dell'Antichità cristiana (Roma, maggio 1981), ibid. 22, pp. 5-363.

AA. VV. 1983 = *Gli apocrifi cristiani e cristianizzati.* – XI Incontro di studiosi dell'Antichità cristiana (Roma, maggio 1982), ibid. 23, pp. 19-378.

AA. VV. 1985 = *Eresia ed eresiologia nella Chiesa antica.* – XIII Incontro di studiosi dell'Antichità cristiana (Roma, maggio 1984), ibid. 25, pp. 581-903.

AA. VV. 1988 = *Cristianesimo e giudaismo: eredità e confronti.* – XVI Incontro di studiosi dell'Antichità cristiana (Roma, maggio 1987), ibid. 28, pp. 5-460, especially the articles by M. Pesce (pp. 7-21) and P. Sacchi (pp. 23-50), which are general and introductory chapters.

AA. VV. 1989 = *Sogni, visioni e profezie nel cristianesimo antico.* – XVII Incontro di studiosi dell'Antichità cristiana (Roma, maggio 1988), ibid. 29.

Acquaviva 1994 = G. Acquaviva, *La Chiesa-madre di Gerusalemme: storia e risurrezione del giudeocristianesimo* (Casale Monferrato: Piemme, 1994).

Adams 1988 = W.S. Adams, "Christian Liturgy, scripture and the Jews. A Problematic in Jewish-Christian Relations", *JES* 25, pp. 39-55.

Aguirre 1987 = R. Aguirre, *Del movimiento de Jesús y la Iglesia cristiana. Ensayo de exégesis sociológica del cristianismo primitivo* (Bilbao: Desclée de Brouwer; II Ed., Estille 1998).

---

66. It appears that Pesce 1998, p. 206, also moves in this direction by quoting some of Esler's statements (1994, p. 2). In this regard see also the Document of the P.C.B., in particular no. 1348.

Aguirre 1991 = Id., *La Sagrada Escritura y el método sociológico*, in *La Palabra de Dios y la hermenéutica a los 25 años de la Constitución Dei Verbum del Concilio Vaticano II* (Valencia: Facultad de Teología S. Vicente Ferrer), pp. 89-109.

Alexander 1992 = Ph. S. Alexander, *The Parting of the Ways from the Perspective of Rabbinic Judaism*, in Dunn 1992, pp. 1-25.

Anderson 2002 = J.S. Anderson, *The Internal Diversification of Second Temple Judaism* (Lanham: University Press of America).

Amersfoort van-Oort van 1990 = J. van Amersfoort-J. van Oort (hg. V.), *Juden und Christen in der Antike* (Kampen: Kok).

Andrei 2001 = O. Andrei, "Il provvedimento anticristiano di Settimio Severo (SHA, Sev. 17,1): una tappa della 'divisione delle vie' fra giudaismo e cristianesimo", *Henoch* 23, pp. 43-79.

Arcari 2001 = L. Arcari, "La titolatura dell'Apocalisse di Giovanni: 'apocalisse' o 'profezia'? Appunti per una ri-definizione del 'genere apocalittico' sulla scorta di quello 'profetico' ", *Henoch* 23, pp. 243-265.

Arcari 2002 = Id., "Apocalisse di Giovanni ed apocalittica 'danielico-storica' del I sec. E.v.: prospettive per una 'nuova' ipotesi", *VetChr* 39, pp. 115-132.

Arcari 2003 = Id., "Il vocabolario della conoscenza nel testo greco del Libro dei Vigilanti. Per una definizione del *Sitz im Leben* della versione greca di 1Enoc", *Materia giudaica* 8/1, pp. 95-104.

ASE 1996 = *La purità e il culto nel* Levitico. *Interpretazioni ebraiche e cristiane*, 13/1.

ASE 1997 = *La Bibbia nella polemica antiebraica*, 14/1.

ASE 1998 = *Il millenarismo cristiano e i suoi fondamenti scritturistici*, 15/1.

ASE 1999a = *La fine dei tempi.* "L'escatologia giudaica e cristiana antica", 16/1.

ASE 1999b = *Giudaismo e antigiudaismo*, 16/2.

ASE 2000a = *Escatologia e scrittura*, 17/1.

ASE 2000b = *Rappresentazioni del giudaismo e una polemica sull'interpretazione del Corano*, 17/2.

ASE 2001a = *Il sacrificio nel Giudaismo e nel Cristianesimo*, 18/1.

ASE 2001b = *Ebrei e Cristiani nelle città. Influssi reciproci*, 18/2

ASE 2002 = *I Cristiani e il sacrificio pagano e biblico*,19/1.

ASE 2003 = *La costruzione dell'identità cristiana (I-VII secolo)*, 20/1.

Avi-Yonah 1984 = M. Avi-Yonah, *The Jews under Roman and Byzantine Rule. A Political History of Palestine from the Bar Kokhba War to the Arab Conquest* (Jerusalem: IES).

Bagatti 1970 = B. Bagatti, *The Church of the Circumcision. History and Archaeology of the Judaeo-Christians* (PSBF; Jerusalem: Franciscan Printing Press).

Bagatti 1981 = Id., *Alle origini della chiesa* (Storia e Attualità 5; Città del Vaticano: Libreria editrice vaticana).

Bar-Asher - Dimant 2003 = M. Bar-Asher - D. Dimant (eds.), *Meghillot-Studies in the Dead Sea Scrolls*, vol. One (Jerusalem: The Bialik Institute). Hebrew (pp. 1-246) and Abstracts (pp. I-II).

Barbaglio 1988 = G. Barbaglio, "Rassegna di studi di storia sociale e di ricerche sociologiche sulle origini cristiane", I e II, *RivBib* 36, pp. 377-410; 495-520.

Barclay 1988 = J.M.G. Barclay, *The Jews in the Mediterranean Diaspora from Alexander to Trajan (323 B.C.E.-117 C.E.)* (Edinburgh: T. & T. Clark).

Barclay-Sweet 1996 = J. Barclay-J. Sweet (eds.), *Early Christian Thought in Its Jewish Context* (Cambridge: Cambridge University Press).

Barrett 1995 = Ch.K. Barrett, "What Minorities?", *StTh* 49,1, pp. 1-10.

Barton 1989 = J. Barton, *Theology and the Social sciences*, in R. Morgan-J. Barton, *Biblical Interpretation* (Oxford: Oxford University Press), pp. 133-166.

Baslez 1998 = M.F Baslez, *Bible et histoire. Judaïsme, Hellenisme, Christianisme* (Paris: La Fayard).

Bauckham 1993 = R.J. Bauckham, "The Parting of the Ways: What Happened and Why", *StTh* 47,2, pp. 135-151.

Becker-Yoshiko Reed 2003 = A.H. Becker- A. Yoshiko Reed (eds.), *The Ways that Never Parted. Jews and Christians in Late Antiquity and the Early Middle Ages* (Tübingen: Mohr Siebeck).

Betz 1994 = H.D. Betz, "The Birth of Christianity as a Hellenistic Religion: Three Theories of Origin", *JR* 74,1, pp. 1-25.

Bickerman 1976-1986 = E.J. Bickerman, *Studies in Jewish and Christian History*, voll. I-III (Leiden: Brill).

Bickerman 1985 = Id., *Religions and Politics in the Hellenistic and Roman Periods*, ed. By E. Gabba and M. Smith, (Como: New Press).

Bickerman 1988 = Id., *The Jews in the Greek Age* (Cambridge Mass.-London: Harvard University Press).

Bieringer-Pollefeyt-Vandecasteele Vanneuville 2001 = R. Bieringer, D. Pollefeyt, F. Vandecasteele-Vanneuville (eds.), *Anti-Judaism and the Fourth Gospel* – Papers of the Leuven Colloquium, 2000 (Jewish and Christian Heritage Series 1; Assen: Royal Van Gorkum).

Biguzzi 2004 = G. Biguzzi, *L'Apocalisse e i suoi enigmi* (StBi 143; Brescia: Paideia).

Blanchetière 1973 = F. Blanchetière, "Aux sources de l'antijudaïsme chrétien", *RHPhR* 53, pp. 353-393.

Blanchetière 1993 = Id., "La «secte des Nazaréens» ou les débuts du christianisme", in Blanchetière-Herr 1993, pp. 72-78.

Blanchetière 1997 = Id., "Comment «le même» est-il devenue «l'autre»? Ou comment juifs et nazeréens se sont-ils séparés", *RSR* 71, pp. 9-32.

Blanchetière 2001 = Id., *Enquête sur les racines juives du mouvement chrétien (30-135)* (Initiations; Paris: Cerf).

Blanchetière-Herr 1993 = Id.-M.D. Herr (eds.), *Aux origines juives du christianisme* (Jérusalem: IES).
Boccaccini 1991 = G. Boccaccini, *Middle Judaism: Jewish Thought, 300 BCE-200 CE* (Minneapolis: Fortress Press).
Boccaccini 1992 = Id., *Portraits of Middle Judaism in Scholarship and Arts. A Multimedia Catalog from Flavius Josephus to 1991* (QHenoch 6; Torino: Zamorani).
Boccaccini 1993a = Id., *Il medio giudaismo. Per una storia del pensiero giudaico tra il terzo secolo a.e.v. e il secondo secolo e.v.* (Radici 14; Genova: Marietti).
Boccaccini 1993b = Id., "Middle Judaism and Its Contemporary Interpreters (1986-1992): Methodological Foundations for the Study of Judaism, 300 BCE to 200 CE", *Henoch* 15, pp. 207-234.
Boccaccini 1995a = Id., "History of Judaisms: Its Periods in Antiquity", in Neusner 1995, Vol. 2, pp. 285-308.
Boccaccini 1995b= Id., "Multiple Judaisms", *BiRe* 11/1, pp. 38-41,46.
Boccaccini 1998a = Id., *Beyond the Essene Hypothesis: The Parting of the Ways between Qumran and Enochic Judaism* (Grand Rapids Mi.-Cambridge U.K.: Eerdmans). Rev. by J.J. Collins, *ASE* 19/2, 2002, 503-5069; see also rev. of the new Italian edition (Brescia: Morcelliana, 2003) by L. Arcari, *Materia giudaica* 8/2, 2003, 407-413.
Boccaccini 1998b, Id., "Middle Judaism and Its Contemporary Interpreters (1993-1997): What makes any Judaism a Judaism?", *Henoch* 20, pp. 349-356.
Boccaccini 2001 = Id. "The Solar Calendars of Daniel and Enoch", in J.J. Collins-P.W. Flint (eds.), *The Book of Daniel: Composition and Reception*, Vol. 2 (Leiden: Brill), pp. 311-328.
Boccaccini 2002a = Id., *Roots of Rabbinic Judaism. An Intellectual History from Ezekiel to Daniel* (Grand Rapids Mi.: Eerdmans).
Boccaccini 2002b = Id. (ed.), *The Origins of Enochic Judaism* – Proceedings of the First Enoch Seminar (University of Michigan, Sesto Fiorentino, Italy, June 19-23, 2001) (Torino: Zamorani [= *Henoch* 24/1-2, 2002]). Cf. rev. by L. Arcari, in *Materia giudaica* 8/1, 2003, pp. 231-235, and G. Ibba, in *RivBib* 52, 2004, pp. 199-205.
Boccaccini 2004 = Id. (ed.), *Enoch and Qumran Origins: New Light on a Forgotten Connection* (Grand Rapids Mi.- Cambridge U.K.: Eerdmans Publishing Company), forthcoming.
Bockmühl 2000 = M.N.A. Bockmühl, *Jewish Law in Gentile Churches. Halakhah and the Beginning of Christian Public Ethics* (Edinburgh: T. & T. Clark).
Bolgiani 2001 = F. Bolgiani, "Erik Peterson e il giudeocristianesimo", in Filoramo-Gianotto 2001, pp. 339-374.
Bori 1983 = P.C. Bori, *Il vitello d'oro. Le radici della controversia antigiudaica* (Torino: Boringhieri).

Bori 1989 = Id., *L'estasi del profeta ed altri saggi tra Ebraismo e Cristianesimo* (Bologna: EDB).

Boschi 1987 = G.L. Boschi, *Alle radici del Giudaismo*, in Chiesa 1987, pp. 9-23.

Botte 1963 = B. Botte, *La tradition apostolique de Saint Hippolyte. Essai de reconstruction* (Münster: Aschendorff).

Bottini-Di Segni-Alliata 1990 = G.C. Bottini-L. Di Segni- E. Alliata (eds), *Christian Archaeology in the Holy Land. New Discoveries.* – Archaeological Essays in Honour of V. C. Corbo (SBF.Cma 36; Jerusalem: Franciscan Printing Press).

Bottini-Di Segni-Chrupcafa 2003 = Id.-Id.-L.D. Chrupcafa (eds.), *One Land – Many Cultures.* – Archaelogical Studies in Honour of St. Loffreda (SBF.Cma 41; Jerusalem: Franciscan Printing Press).

Boyarin 1993 = D. Boyarin (ed.), *Carnal Israel. Reading Sex in Talmudic Culture* (Berkeley: University of California Press).

Boyarin 1999 = Id., *Dying for God. Martyrdom and the Making of Christianity and Judaism* (Stanford: Stanford University Press).

Brandon 1968 = S.G.F. Brandon, *The Fall of Jerusalem and the Christian Church* (London: S.P.C.K.).

Brockway 2000 = A.R. Brockway, "Christianity on Judaism in Ancient and Medieval Times", in J. Neusner-A.J. Avery-Peck-W.S. Green (eds.), *The Encyclopaedia of Judaism,* Vol. I (Leiden-Boston-Köln: Brill), pp. 63-77.

Brooke 1998 = G.J. Brooke, "Shared Intertextual Interpretations in the Dead Sea Scrolls and the New Testament", in Stone-Chazon 1998, pp. 35-57.

Brown 1983 = R.E. Brown, "Not Jewish Christianity and Gentile Christianity but Types of Jewish/Gentile Christianity", *CBQ* 45, pp. 74-79.

Buchanan 1979-1980 = G.W. Buchanan, "Worship, Feasts and Ceremonies in the Early Jewish-Christian Church", *NTS* 26, pp. 279-297.

Campenhausen 1963[2] = H.F. von Campenhausen, *Kirchliches Amt und geistliche Vollmacht in den ersten drei Jahrhunderten* (Tübingen: Mohr).

Cansdale 1996 = L. Cansdale, "Have the Dead Sea Scrolls Any Direct Connection with Early Christianity?", *QChr* 6, pp. 65-92.

Cansdale 1997 = Ead., *Qumran and the Essenes: A Re-Evaluation of the Evidence* (TSAJ 60; Tübingen: Mohr). Rev. by E. Puech, *RdQ* 18, 1998, pp. 437-441.

Chadwick 1969 = H. Chadwick, *The Early Church* (London: Harmondsworth Penguin Books, 1993[2]) .

Charlesworth 1985 = J.H. Charlesworth, *The Old Testament Pseudepigrapha and the New Testament. Prolegomena for the Study of the Christian Origins* (Cambridge: Cambridge University Press).

Charlesworth 1988 = Id. (ed.), *Jesus Within Judaism. New Light from Exiting Archaelogical Discoveries* (New York: Doubleday).

Charlesworth 1990a = Id. (ed.), *John and the Dead Sea Scrolls* (New York:

Doubleday; extended version of *John and Qumran* [London: Chapman, 1972]).

Charlesworth 1990b = Id. (ed.), *Jews and Christians. Exploring the Past, Present, and Future* (New York: The Crossroad Publishing Company).

Charlesworth 1991a = Id. (ed.), *Jesus' Jewishness: Exploring the Place of Jesus Within Early Judaism* (Philadelphia: Fortress Press).

Charlesworth 1991b = Id., "Qumran in Relation to the Apocrypha, Rabbinic Judaism and Nascent Christianity. Impacts on University Teaching of Jewish Civilization in the Hellenistic-Roman Period", in Talmon 1991, pp. 168-180.

Charlesworth 1992a = Id. (ed.), *Jesus and the Dead Sea Scrolls* (New York: Doubleday).

Charlesworth 1992b = Id., *The Messiah. Developments in Earliest Judaism and Christianity* – First Princeton Symposium on Judaism and Christian Origins 1987 (Minneapolis: Fortress Press).

Charlesworth 1993 = Id., "Christians and Jews in the First Six Centuries", in H. Shanks (ed. By), *Christianity and Rabbinic Judaism. A Parallel History of Their Origins and Early Development* (London-Washington D.C.: Biblical Archaelogy Society), pp. 305-325.

Charlesworth 1996 = Id., *The Jewish Apocaliptic Heritage in Early Christianity* (Minneapolis: Fortress Press).

Charlesworth 2001 = Id., "The Gospel of John: Exclusivism Caused by a Social Setting Different from That of Jesus (John 11:54 and 14:6)", in Bieringer-Pollefeyt-Vandecasteele-Vanneuville 2001, pp. 479-513.

Chazon-Stone-Pinnick 1999 = E.G. Chazon-M.E. Stone-A. Pinnick (eds.), *Pseudepigraphic Perspectives: The Apocrypha and Pseudepigrapha in Light of the Dead Sea Scrolls* (Leiden: Brill).

Chiat 1981 = M.J.S. Chiat, "First Century Synagogues: Methodological Problems", in Gutmann 1981, pp. 49-60.

Chiesa 1987a = B. Chiesa (ed.), *Correnti culturali e movimenti religiosi del Giudaismo* – Atti del V Congresso Internazionale dell'AISG (S. Miniato, 12-15 novembre 1984) (TSAISG 5; Roma: Carucci).

Chiesa 1987b = Id., "Il giudaismo caraita", in Chiesa 1987a, pp. 151-173.

Chilton 1986 = B. Chilton, *Targumic Approaches to the Gospels. Essays in the Mutual Definition of Judaism and Christianity* (Lanham-London: University Press of America).

Chilton-Neusner 1995 = Id.-J.Neusner (eds.), *Judaism in the New Testament. Practices and Beliefs* (London-New York: Routledge).

Chilton-Neusner 2002 = Id.-Id. (ed.), *The Brother of Jesus. James the Just and His Mission* (Louisville KY: Westminster John Knox Press).

Chouraqui 1981 = A. Chouraqui, *Retour aux racines* (Paris: Laffont).

Cirillo 1993 = L. Cirillo, "Fenomeni battisti", in Sacchi 1993, pp. 19-57 (repr. in *RSLR* 29, pp. 269-303).

Cirillo 2000 = Id., "Courants judéo-chrétiens", in Mayer-Pietri-Vauchez-Venard 2000, pp. 273-330.

Cohen 1971 = A. Cohen, *The Mith of the Judeo-Christian Tradition* (New York: Doubleday).

Cohen 1989 = S.J.D. Cohen, "Crossing the Boundary and Becoming a Jew", *HThR* 82, pp. 13-33.

Cohen 1999 = Id., *The Beginnings of Jewishness. Boundaries, Varieties, Uncertainties* (Berkeley-Los Angeles-London: University of California).

Cohn-Sherbok 1988 = D. Cohn-Sherbok, *The Jewish Heritage* (Oxford-New York: Oxford University Press).

Cohn-Sherbok-Court 2001 = Id.-J.M. Court (eds.), *Religious Diversity in the Graeco-Roman World. A Century of scholarship* (Sheffield: Academic Press).

Collins 1989 = J.J. Collins, "Judaism as *Praeparatio Evangelica* in the Work of Martin Hengel", *RStR* 15, pp. 226-228.

Collins 1997 = *Apocalypticism in the Dead Sea Scrolls* (London-New York: Routledge).

Collins 1998 = J.J. Collins, *Seers, Sybils and Sages in Hellenistic-Roman Judaism* (JSJ.S 54; Leiden-New York-Köln: Brill).

Collins 1999 = J.J. Collins, "Pseudepigraphy and Group Formation in Second Temple Judaism", in Chazon-Stone-Pinnick 1999, pp. 43-58.

Collins 2000² = Id., *Between Athens and Jerusalem. Jewish Identity in the Hellenistic Diaspora* (Grand Rapids MI-Cambridge U.K.: Eerdmans).

Collins 1993 = R.F. Collins, *The Birth of the New Testament: The Origin and Development of the First Christian Generation* (New York: Doubleday).

Colpe 1993 = C. Colpe, "The Oldest Jewish-Christian Community", in J. Becker (ed.), *Christian Beginnings. Word and Community from Jesus to Post-Apostolic Times* (Louisville KY: Westminster John Knox), pp. 75-102,

Conzelmann 1981 = H. Conzelmann, *Heiden-Juden-Christen. Auseinendersetzungen in der Literatur der hellenistisch-römischen Zeit* (Tübingen: Mohr).

Conzelmann 1987² = Id., *Geschichte der Urchristentums* (GNT, Erg. Reihe zu NTD 5; Göttingen: Vandenhoeck & Ruprecht).

Cook 1996 = E.M. Cook, "Qumran: A Ritual Purification Center", *BarR* 22/6, p. 39; pp. 48-51; pp. 73-75.

Cracco Ruggini 1980a = L. Cracco Ruggini, "Pagani, ebrei, cristiani: odio sociologico e odio teologico nel mondo antico", in AA.VV., *Gli ebrei nell'Alto Medioevo* – XXVI Settimana di Studi sull'Alto Medioevo (Spoleto: w.e.), t. I, pp. 15-101.

Cracco Ruggini 1980b = Ead., "Nuclei immigrati e forze indigene in tre grandi centri commerciali dell'impero", *MAAR*, pp. 55-76.

Cross 1995³ = F.M. Cross, *The Ancient Library of Qumran* (Sheffield: Academic Press; I Ed., Garden City NY: Doubleday, 1958).

Crossan 1995 = J.D. Crossan, *Who Killed Jesus? Exposing the Roots of Antisemitism in the Gospel Story of the Death of Jesus* (San Francisco: Harper).

Crossan 1998 = Id., *The Birth of Christianity. Discovering What Happened in the Years Immediately After the Execution of Jesus* (San Francisco: Harper).

Crotty 1999 = R. Crotty, "Method in the Study of Early Christianity as a Jewish Sect", *WCJS* 12, A, pp. 235-242.

Crow 1993 = A.D. Crow, "The Parting of the Ways", *AJJS* 7/2, pp. 62-81.

Crown-Cansdale 1994 = A.D. Crown-L. Cansdale, "Qumran: Was It an Essene Settlement?", *BarR* 20/5, pp. 24-35; pp. 73-78.

Cullmann 1954 = O. Cullmann, "Die neuentdeckten Qumrantexte und das Judenchristentum der Pseudo-Klementinen", in *Neutestamentliche Studien für R. Bultmann* (BZNTW 21; Berlin: Töpelmann), pp. 33-51.

Cullmann 1955 = Id., "The Significance of the Qumran Texts for Research into the Beginnings of Christianity", *JBL* 74, pp. 213-226.

Cullmann 1971 = Id., "I testi di Qumrân e lo studio delle origini del cristianesimo", in Id., *Dalle fonti dell'Evangelo alla teologia cristiana* (Teologia oggi 15), Presentazione di E. Lanne (Roma: AVE; original Edition., Neuchâtel: Delachaux, 1969), pp. 9-28.

Daniélou 1955 = J. Daniélou, "La Communauté de Qumrân et l'organisation de l'Église ancienne", *RHPhR* 35, pp. 104-116.

Daniélou 1958 = Id., *Théologie du Judéo-Christianisme. Histoire des doctrines chrétiennes avant Nicée*, I (BT 1), (Tournai-Paris: Desclée).

Daniélou 1967 = Id., "Une vision nouvelle des origines chrétiennes, le judéo-christianisme", in *Études*, pp. 595-608.

Daniélou 1974[2] = Id., *Les Manuscripts de la Mer Morte et les Origines du Christianisme* (Paris: L'Orante).

Daniélou 1985 = Id., s.v. "Judéo-Christianisme", in Encyclopaedia Universalis X.

Dauphin 1993 = C. Dauphin, "De l' Église de la circoncision à l' Église de la gentilité. Sour une nouvelle voie hors de l'impasse", *SBFLA* 43, pp. 223-242.

Davies 1995 = Ph.R. Davies, *Currents of Research in Biblical Studies* 3, 1995, pp. 9-35.

Davies 1996 = Id., *Sects and Scrolls. Essays on Qumran and Related Topics* (Atlanta: Scholars Press).

Davies 1997 = Id., "Qumran and the Quest for the Historical Judaism", in Porter-Evans 1997, pp. 24-42.

Davies-Finkelstein 1984-1989 = W.D. Davies-L. Finkelstein (eds.), *The Cambridge History of Judaism*. Vol. 1: *Introduction; The Persian Period.* Vol 2: *The Hellenistic Age* (Cambridge-London-New York-Melbourne-Sidney: Cambridge University Press).

Davies-White 1990 = Ph.R. Davies-R.T. White (eds.), *A Tribute to Geza Vermes. Essays on Jewish and Christian Literature and History* (JSOT.S 100; Sheffield: Sheffield Academic Press).
Davila 2002 = J.R. Davila (ed.), *The Dead Sea Scrolls as Background to Postbiblical Judaism and Early Christianity.* – Papers from an International Conference at St. Andrews in 2001 (StTDJ 46; Leiden: Brill).
Deines 1997 = R. Deines, *Die Pharisäer. Ihr Verständnis im Spiegel der christlichen und jüdischen Forschung seit Wellhausen und Graetz* (Tübingen: Publisher).
de Lange 1976 = N. de Lange, *Origen and the Jews. Studies in Jewish-Christian Relations in Third-Century Palestine*, (Cambridge: Cambridge University Press).
Delcor 1978 = M. Delcor (ed.), *Qumrân. Sa piété, sa théologie et son milieu* (BEThL 46; Paris-Gembloux-Leuven: Duculot).
Del Verme 1977 = M. Del Verme, *Comunione e condivisione dei beni. Chiesa primitiva e giudaismo esseno-qumranico a confronto* (Brescia: Morcelliana).
Del Verme 1978 = Id., "Povertà e aiuto del povero nella Chiesa primitiva (Atti)", in AA.VV., *Evangelizare pauperibus.* Atti della XXIV Settimana Biblica dell'A.B.I. (Brescia: Paideia), pp. 405-427.
Del Verme 1984 = Id., "Le decime del fariseo orante (Lc 18, 11-12). Filologia e storia", *VetChr* 21, pp. 253-283.
Del Verme 1989 = Id., *Giudaismo e Nuovo Testamento. Il caso delle decime* (Studi sul Giudaismo e sul Cristianesimo antico 1; Napoli: D'Auria).
Denis 2000 = A.-M. Denis et collaborateurs avec le concours de J.-C. Haelewyck, *Introduction à la littérature religieuse judéo-hellénistique* (Pseudépigraphes de l'Ancien Testament), 2 vols. (Turnhout: Brepols).
de Sainte Croix 1981 = G.E.M. de Sainte Croix, *The Class Struggle in the Ancient Greek World from the Archaic Age to the Arab Conquests* (Ithaca: Cornell University Press).
Destro 1966² = A. Destro, *Le vie dell'antropologia. Dalle culture alle scritture* (Bologna: EDB).
Destro 1987 = Ead., "Parah e 'Eglah 'Arufah. Richiami ad alcuni riti ebraici antichi", *Studi Orientali e Linguistici* 4, pp. 21-40.
Destro 1989 = Ead., *In caso di gelosia. Antropologia del rituale di Sotah* (Bologna: EDB).
Destro 1992 = Ead., *Antropologia del giudaismo rabbinico* (Letture I/2 – CISEC; Bologna: EDB).
Destro 1993 = Ead., *Le sembianze dello straniero. La condizione del ger nel progetto sociale rabbinico* (Letture II/4 – CISEC; Bologna: EDB).
Destro-Pesce 1992 = Ead.-M. Pesce, "Il rito ebraico di Kippur. Il sangue nel tempio; il peccato nel deserto", in G. Galli (a cura di), *Interpretazione e perdono* (Genova: Marietti), pp. 47-73.

Destro-Pesce 1995 = Ead.-Id., "Kinship, Discipleship, and Movement. An Anthropological Study of the Gospel of John", *Biblical Interpretation* 3/ 3, pp. 266-284.

Destro-Pesce 1996 = Ead.-Id., "Identità nella comunità paolina: santi e fratelli", in L. Padovese (a cura di), *Atti del IV Simposio di Tarso su S. Paolo apostolo* (Turchia: La Chiesa e la sua storia X; Roma: PAA), pp. 107-124.

Destro-Pesce 1997[2] = Ead.-Id., *Antropologia delle origini cristiane* (Quadrante 78; Roma-Bari: Laterza, 1995 [I ed.]).

Destro-Pesce 2000 = Ead.-Id., *Come nasce una religione. Antropologia ed esegesi del* Vangelo di Giovanni (Roma-Bari: Laterza).

Destro-Pesce 2001 = Ead.-Id., "Un confronto di sistemi. Il Vangelo di Giovanni e la Regola della Comunità di Qumran", in L. Padovese (a cura di), *Atti dell'VIII Simposio di Efeso su S. Giovanni Apostolo* (Roma: PAA), pp. 81-107.

Di Berardino 2001 = A. Di Berardino, "Percorsi di koinônía nei primi secoli cristiani", *Concilium* 37/3, pp. 67-85.

Díez Merino = L. Díez Merino, "Ideologías del Targum", in Sacchi 1993, pp. 59-105.

Dimant-Rappaport 1992 = D. Dimant-U. Rappaport (eds.), *The Dead Sea Scrolls: Forty Years of Research* (StTDJ 10; Leiden: Brill).

Donahue 1973 = P.J. Donahue, *Jewish Christian Controversy in the Second-Century. A Study in the «Dialogue» of Justin Martyr* (Diss. Yale).

Donceel-Donceel Voûte 1994 = R. Donceel-P. Donceel Voûte, "The Archaeology of Khirbet Qumran", in M.O. Wise et al. (eds.), *Methods of Investigation of the Dead Sea Scrolls and the Khirbet Qumran Site. Present Realities and Future Prospects* (New York: Doubleday), pp. 1-38.

Downing 1999 = F.G. Downing, *Making Sense in (and of) the First Christian Century* (JSNT.S 197; Sheffield: Sheffield Academic Press).

Downing 2000 = Id., *Doing Things with Words in the First Christian Century* (JSNT.S 198; Sheffield: Sheffield Academic Press).

Dunn 1990[2] = J.D.G. Dunn, *Unity and Diversity in the New Testament. An Inquiry into the Character of Earliest Christianity* (London: SCM, 2nd ed.).

Dunn 1991 = Id, *The Parting of the Ways between Christianity and Judaism and Their Significance for the Character of Christianity* (London-Philadelphia: Fortress Press).

Dunn 1992 = Id. (ed.), *Jews and Christians. The Parting of the Ways A.D. 70 to 135* (WUNT 66; Tübingen: Mohr).

Dunn 1996 = Id., "Two Covenants or One? The Interdependence of Jewish and Christian Identity", in H. Lichtenberger (ed.), *Geschichte-Tradition-Reflexion. Fs. für M. Hengel zum 70. Geburtstag.* Bd. III: *Frühes Christentum* (Tübingen: Mohr), pp. 97-122.

Eilberg-Schwartz 1990 = H. Eilberg-Schwartz, *The Savage in Judaism. An Anthropology of Israelite Religion and Ancient Judaism* (Bloomington-Indianapolis: Indiana University Press).

Eliade 1986 = M. Eliade (ed.), *The Encyclopedia of Religion: A Comprehensive Guide to the History, Beliefs, Concepts, Practices, and Major Figures of Religious Past and Present*, vol 6: *Hebraism* (New York: Macmillan Publishing Company).

Elliott 1986 = J.H. Elliott (ed.), *Social-scientific Criticism of the New Testament and Its Social World*, Semeia 35.

Elliott 1995[2] = Id., *Social-scientific Criticism of the New Testament. An Introduction* (London: S.P.C.K., 1993 [I Ed.]).

Esler 1987 = Ph. F. Esler, *Community and Gospel in Luke-Acts. The Social and Political Motivation of Lukan Theology* (MSSNTS 57; Cambridge: Cambridge University Press).

Esler 1994 = Id., *The First Christians in Their Social World* (London-New York: Routledge).

Esler 1995 = Id. (ed.), *Modelling Early Christianity. Social-scientific Studies of the New Testament in Its Context* (London: Routledge).

Fabris 1981 = R. Fabris (ed.), *Problemi e prospettive di scienze bibliche* (Brescia: Queriniana), especially the articles by L. Moraldi about "La letteratura intertestamentaria, apocrifi e scrittori giudaici" (pp. 41-66), and by M. McNamara about "Letteratura rabbinica e i targumim" (pp. 67-109).

Fabris 2001 = Id., "La comunità di Gerusalemme", *RStB* 13/2, pp. 65-82.

Feldman 1989 = L.H. Feldman, "Proselytes and «Sympathizers» in the Light of the New Inscriptions from Aphrodisias", *REJ* 148, pp. 265-305.

Feldman 1993 = Id., *Jew and Gentile in the Ancient World. Attitudes and Interactions from Alexander to Justinian* (Princeton: Princeton University Press).

Feldman 1996 = Id., *Studies in Hellenistic Judaism* (AGJU 30; Leiden-New York-Köln: Brill).

Feldman-Reinhold 1996 = Id.-M. Reinhold (eds.), *Jewish Life and Thought Among Greeks and Romans: Primary Readings* (Minneapolis: Fortress Press).

Ferguson 1987 = E. Ferguson, *Backgrounds of Early Christianity* (Grand Rapids: Eerdmans).

Fernández Marcos = N. Fernández Marcos, "Exégesis y ideología en el Judaísmo del siglo primero. Héroes, Heroínas y mujeres", in Sacchi 1993, pp. 107-122.

Filoramo-Gianotto 2001 = G. Filoramo-C. Gianotto (eds.), *Verus Israel. Nuove prospettive sul giudeocristianesimo. – Atti del Colloquio di Torino* (4-5 novembre 1999) (BCR 65; Brescia: Paideia).

Filoramo-Roda 1992 = Id.-S. Roda, *Cristianesimo e società antica* (Storia e società; Bari: Laterza).

Finkelstein 1962³ = L. Finkelstein, *The Pharisees. The Sociological Background of Their Faith*, Vols. I-II (Philadelphia: Fortress Press).

Fisher 1988 = E.J. Fisher, "Judaísmo bíblico, judaísmo rabínico y cristianismo naciente", *El Olivo* 28, pp. 127-174.

Fisher 1990 = Id. (ed.), *The Jewish Roots of Christian Liturgy* (New York: Paulist Press).

Fisher-Kleinicki 1990 = Id.-L.Kleinicki (eds.), *In Our Time. The Flowering of Jewish-Catholic Dialog* (New York: Crossroad).

Fitzmyer 1971 = J.A. Fitzmyer, "The Qumran scrolls, the Ebionites and their Literature", in Id., *Essays in the Semitic Background of the New Testament* (London: Chapman), pp. 435-480.

Fitzmyer 1992 = Id., *Responses to 101 Questions on the Dead Sea scrolls* (New York-Mahwah NJ: Chapman).

Flothkötter-Nacke 1990 = H. Flothkötter-B. Nacke (hg. v.), *Das Judentum – eine Wurzel des Christlichen. Neue Perspektiven des Miteinanders* (Würzburg: Echter).

Flusser 1968 = D. Flusser, *Jesus in Selbstzeugnissen und Bilddokumenten* (Hamburg: Rowohlt).

Flusser 1988 = Id., *Judaism and the Origins of Christianity* (Jerusalem: The Magnes Press).

Flusser 1991-1992 = "Miqṣat ma'aśe ha-tora e Birkat ha-minim", *Tarb.* 61, pp. 333-374.

Foraboschi 1993 = D. Foraboschi, "Tra guerra, sfruttamento e sviluppo: l'economia della Palestina (I a.c.- I d.C.)", in Sacchi 1993, pp. 123-136.

Frankemölle 1998 = H. Frankemölle, *Jüdische Wurzeln christlichen Theologie* (BBB 116; Bodenheim: Philo).

Frankfurter 2001 = D. Frankfurter, "Jews or Not? Reconstructing the 'Other' in Rev 2:9 and 3:9", *HThR* 94, pp. 403-425.

Frend 1984 = W.H.C. Frend, *The Rise of Christianity* (London: Longman & Todd).

Freyne 1994a = S.V. Freyne, "Christians in a Jewish World. The First Century", in V.A. McInnes (ed.), *New Visions. Historical and Theological Perspectives on the Jewish-Christian Dialogue* (New York: Doubleday), pp. 11-30.

Freyne 1994b = Id., *Jews in a Christian World. The Fourth Century*, ibid., pp. 31-53.

Fusco 1997 = V. Fusco, *Le prime comunità cristiane. Tradizioni e tendenze nel cristianesimo delle origini* (La Bibbia nella storia 8; Bologna: EDB).

Gager 1983 = J.G. Gager, *The Origins of Anti-Semitism. Attitudes towards Judaism in Pagan and Christian Antiquity* (New York-Oxford: Oxford University Press).

Gager 1992 = Id., "Jews, Christians and the Dangerous Ones in Between", in Sh. Biberman-A. Scharfstein (eds.), *Interpretation in Religion* (Leiden: Brill), pp. 249-257.

Galor-Zangenburg 2004 = K. Galor and J. Zangenburg (eds.), *Qumran. The Site of the Dead Sea Scrolls. Archaeological Interpretation and Debate* (Volume of papers of Brown University Conference, November 2002; Leiden: Brill). Forthcoming.

García Martínez 1987 = F. García Martínez, "Essénisme qumranien: Origines, caractéristiques, héritage", in Chiesa 1987, pp. 38-57.

García Martínez 1988 = Id., "Les limites de la Communauté: pureté et impureté à Qumran et dans le Nouveau Testament", in T. Baarda et alii (eds.), *Text and Testimony. Essays on New Testament and Apocryphal Literature in Honour of A.F.J. Klijn* (Kampen: Uitgeversmaatsschapij J.H. Kok), pp. 111-122.

García Martínez 1991 = Id., "La apocaliptica judía como matriz de la teología cristiana?", in A. Piñero (ed.), *Orígines del Cristianismo: Antecedentes y primeros pasos* (Cordoba-Madrid: Ediciones El Almendro), pp. 177-199.

García Martínez 1996 = Id. (a cura di), *Testi di Qumran*. Traduzione italiana dai testi originali con note di C. Martone (Biblica 4; Brescia: Paideia).

García Martínez-Parry 1996 = Id.-D.W. Parry, *A Bibliography of the Finds in the Desert of Judah 1970-1995. Arranged by Author with Subject and Citation Indexes* (STDJ 19; Leiden: Brill). Continued by Id- E.J.C. Tigchelaar, *RdQ* 18, 1998, pp. 459-490.

García Martínez-Trebolle Barrera 1993 = Id.-J. Trebolle Barrera, *Los hombres de Qumran. Literatura, estructura social y concepciones religiosas* (Madrid: Trotta).

Gardenal 2001 = G. Gardenal, *L'antigiudaismo nella letteratura cristiana antica e medievale* (Brescia: Morcelliana).

Garribba 2004 = D. Garribba, *L'identità giudaica nella diaspora del I secolo d.C.* (Unpublished PhD Diss. in Ancient History – Università degli Studi "Federico II" of Naples: Dipartimento di discipline storiche "E. Lepore").

Gasparro 2002 = G. Gasparro, *Profeti Oracoli Sibille* (Roma: LAS).

Gavin 1929 = F. Gavin, "Rabbinic Parallels in Early Church Orders", *HUCA* 6, pp. 55-67 (now also in Petuchowski 1970, pp. 305-317).

Geftman 1985 = R. Geftman, *L'Église primitive de Jerusalem* (Jerusalem: w.e.).

Genot-Bismuth 1986 = J. Genot-Bismuth, *Un homme nommé salut. Genèse d'une "hérésie" à Jérusalem* (Paris: w.e.).

Geoltrain 1980-1981 = P. Geoltrain, *Origines du christianisme* (AEPHE Ve Sect. SR; Paris: Gallimard), pp. 433-439.

Geoltrain 2000 = Id. (ed.), *Aux origines du christianisme* (Paris: Gallimard).

Georgi 1995 = D. Georgi, "The Early Church: Internal Migration or New Religion?", *HThR* 88/1, pp. 36-68.

Gianotto 1984 = C. Gianotto, *Melchisedek e la sua tipologia. Tradizioni giudaiche, cristiane e gnostiche (sec. II a. C.- sec. III d. C.)* (SrivBib 12; Brescia: Paideia).

Gianotto 2001a = Id., "Giacomo e la comunità cristiana di Gerusalemme", *RStB* 13/2, pp. 83-101.

Gianotto 2001b = Id., "Giacomo e il giudeocristianesimo antico", in Filoramo-Id. 2001, pp. 108-119.

Gianotto 2002 = Id. (ed.), "Il giudeocristianesimo", *Primi secoli* 5/13.

Gianotto 2004 = Id., " «Enoch e le origini qumraniche». Dibattito attorno a un libro", *RivBib* 52, 2004, 183-194.

Gillet-Didier 2001 = Véronique Gillet-Didier, "Calendrier lunaire, calendrier solaire et gardes sacerdotales: recherches sur 4Q 321", *RdQ* 20/78, pp. 171-205.

Gnilka 2000 = J. Gnilka, *I primi cristiani. Origini e inizio della Chiesa* (Suppl. CTNT 9; Brescia: Paideia) (Orig. Edition, Freiburg i. B.: Herder, 1999). Especially chap. V.10: "Chiesa e sinagoga. Giudaismo e cristianesimo", pp. 399-415.

Goff 2002 = M. J. Goff, *The Worldly and Heavenly Wisdom of 4QInstruction* (PhD Diss.: University of Chicago).

Golb 1985 = N. Golb, "Les manuscrits de la Mer Morte: une nouvelle approche du problème de leur origine", *Annales* 40, pp. 1133-1149.

Golb 1995 = Id., *Who Wrote the Dead Sea Scrolls? The Search for the Secret of Qumran* (New York: Scribner).

Goodenough 1953-1968 = E.R. Goodenough, *Jewish Symbols in the Greco-Roman Period*, voll. I-XIII (New York: Pantheon Books).

Goodman 1990 = M. Goodman, "Identity and Authority in Ancient Judaism", *Jdm* 39, pp. 192-201.

Goodman 1994 = Id., *Mission and Conversions. Proselyticing in the Religious History of the Roman Empire* (Oxford: Clarendon).

Goodman 1996 = Id. (ed.), *Jews in a Graeco-Roman World* (Oxford: Clarendon).

Goppelt 1954 = L. Goppelt, *Christentum und Judentum im ersten und zweiten Jahrhundert* (Gütersloh: Bertelsmann).

Goppelt 1964 = Id., *Jesus, Paul and Judaism* (New York: T. Nelson).

Goppelt 1966² = Id., *Die apostolische und nachapostolische Zeit* (KIG Bd. 1/ A), *Zweite durchgesehene Auflage*, (Göttingen: Vandenhoeck & Ruprecht, 1962 [I Ed.]).

Grabbe 1989 = L.L. Grabbe, "The Social Setting of Ancient Apocalypticism", *JSPE* 4, pp. 27-47.

Grabbe 2000 = Id., *Judaic Religion in the Second Temple Period* (London: Routledge).

Grässer 1985 = E. Grässer, *Der Alte Bund im Neuen. Exegetische Studien zur Israelfrage im Neuen Testament* (WUNT 35; Tübingen: Mohr).

Grant 1972 = R.M. Grant, "Jewish Christianity at Antioch in the Second Century", *RSR* 60, pp. 97-108.

Grant 1977 = Id., *Early Christianity and Society. Seven Studies* (San Francisco: Harper & Row).

Grappe 1992 = C. Grappe, *D'un temple à l' autre. Pierre et l'Eglise de Jéusalem* (Paris: Presses Universitaires de France).

Grappe 2001 = Id., *Le Royaume de Dieu. Avant, avec et après Jésus* (Genève: Labor et Fides).

Grappe 2002 = Id., "L'apport de l'essénisme à la compréhénsion du Christianisme naissant; une perspective historique", in *Etudes Théologiques et Religieuses* 77/4, pp. 517-536.

Gray 1973 = B.C. Gray, "Movements of the Jerusalem Church During the First Jewish War", *JEH* 24, pp. 1-7.

Grego 1982 = I. Grego, *I giudeo-cristiani nel IV secolo* (Gerusalemme: Franciscan Printing Press).

Grünwald-Shaked-Stroumsa 1992 = I. Grünwald-Sh. Shaked-G.G. Stroumsa (eds.), *Messiah and Christos. Studies in the Jewish Origins of Christianity Presented to D. Flusser on the Occasion of His Seventy-Fifth Birthday* (TSAJ 32; Tübingen: Mohr).

Guglielmo 2002 = L. Guglielmo, *Manoscritti di Qumran ed Essenismo. Verso una nuova ipotesi* (Tesi di laurea in Storia religiosa dell'Oriente cristiano, Università degli Studi "Federico II" of Naples: Dipartimento di discipline storiche "E. Lepore").

Guglielmo 2003 = Ead., "*Micae Qumranicae*. I Manoscritti di Qumran a quasi sessant'anni dalla scoperta", in *Papyrologica Lupiensia* 12, 2003, 99-114.

Gusella 2003 = L. Gusella, *Esperienze di comunità nel giudaismo antico. Esseni, Terapeuti, Qumran* (Firenze: Nerbini).

Gutmann 1981 = J. Gutmann (ed.), *Ancient Sinagogues* (Chico: Scholars Press).

Hahn 1988 = F. Hahn, "Die Verwurzelung des Christentums im Judentum", *KuD* 34/3, pp. 193-209.

Hall 1991 = S.G. Hall, *Doctrine and Practice in the Early Church* (Grand Rapids: Eerdmans).

Hamel 1990 = G. Hamel, *Poverty and Charity in Roman Palestine, First Three Centuries CE* (Berkeley: University of California Press).

Hann 1987 = R.R. Hann, "Judaism and Jewish Christianity in Antioch: Charisma and Conflict in the First Century", *JRH* 14, pp. 341-360.

Hanson 1994 = H.C. Hanson, "Graeco-Roman Studies and the Social-scientific Study of the Bible: A Classified Periodical Literature (1970-1994)", *Forum* 9, pp. 63-119.

Harrington 1988 = D. Harrington, "Second Testament Exegesis and the Social Sciences: A Bibliography", *BTB* 18, pp. 77-85.

Harrington 1999 = D.J. Harrington, rev. to Nodet-Taylor 1998, in *Bib.* 80, pp. 443-447.

Hauser 1996 = H. Hauser, *L'Église à l'âge apostolique* (Paris: Cerf).

Heid 1992-93 = St. Heid, "Das Heilige Land: Herkunft und Zukunft der Judenchristen", *Kairos* 34-35, pp. 1-26.

Hellholm 1983 = D. Hellholm (ed.), *Apocalypticism in the Mediterranean World and the Near East* – Proceedings of the International Colloquium on Apocalypticism (Uppsala, August 12-17, 1979; Tübingen: Mohr).

Hellholm-Moxnes-Karlsen Seim 1995 = Id.-H. Moxnes- T. Karlsen Seim (eds.), *Mighty Minorities? Minorities in Early Christianity – Positions and Strategies. Essays in honour of J. Jervell on his 70th Birthday (21 May 1995)* (Oslo-Copenhagen-Stockholm-Boston: Scandinavian University Press).

Hemer 1989 = C.H. Hemer, *The Book of Acts in the Setting of Hellenistic History* (Tübingen: Mohr).

Hempel-Lange-Lichtenberger 2002 = C. Hempel-A. Lange-H. Lichtenberger (eds.), *The Wisdom Texts from Qumran and the Development of Sapiential Thought: Studies in Wisdom at Qumran and its Relationship to Sapiential Thought in the Ancient Near East, the Hebrew Bible, Ancient Judaism, and the New Testament* (BEThL 159; Leuven: Peeters-Leuven University Press).

Hengel 1975 = M. Hengel, "Zwischen Jesus und Paulus. Die "Hellenisten", die "Sieben" und Stephanus (Apg 6,1-15; 7,54-8,3)", *ZThK* 72, pp. 151-206.

Hengel 1976 = Id., *Juden, Griechen und Barbaren. Aspekte der Hellenisierung des Judentums in vorchristlicher Zeit* (Stuttgart: KBW Verlag).

Hengel 1979 = Id., *Zur urchristlichen Geschichtsschreibung* (Stuttgart: Calwer Verlag).

Hengel 1988³ = Id., *Judentum und Hellenismus. Studien zu ihrer Begegnung unter besonderer Berücksichtigung Palästinas bis zur Mitte des 2. Jh.s. v. Chr.* (WUNT 10; Tübingen: Mohr).

Hengel 1990 = Id. With a contribution by H. Bloedhorn, "Der alte und der neue 'Schürer' ", *JSS* 35/1, pp. 19-72.

Hengel 1991 = Id. in coll. Con Ch. Markschies, *L'<ellenizzazione> della Giudea nel I secolo d.C.* Edizione italiana a cura di G. Firpo (StBi 104; Brescia: Paideia) (Original Edition., Tübingen: Mohr, 1991).

Hengel-Deines 1995 = Id.- R. Deines, "E.P. Sanders' 'Common Judaism', Jesus and the Pharisees", *JThS* 46, pp. 1-70.

Hengel-Schwemer 1997 = Id.-A.M. Schwemer, *Paul Between Damascus and Antioch. The Unknown Years* (London: SCM).

Herford 1924 = R.T. Herford, *The Pharisees* (London: Allen & Unwind).

Holmberg 1990 = B. Holmberg, *Sociology and the New Testament: An Appraisal* (Minneapolis: Fortress Press).

Hvalvik 1996 = R. Hvalvik, *The Struggle for Scripture and Covenant. The Purpose of the Epistle of Barnabas and Jewish-Christian Competition in the Second Century* (WUNT 2, R. 82; Tübingen: Mohr).

Humbert-Chambon 1994 = J.-B. Humbert-A. Chambon, *Fouilles de Khirbet Qumran et de Ain Feshkha*, 1 (Göttingen-Fribourg: Vandenhoeck & Ruprecht).

Hurtado 1988 = L.W. Hurtado, *One God, One Lord. Early Jewish Christian Devotion and Ancient Jewish Monotheism* (Philadelphia: Fortress Press).

Ibba 1996 = G. Ibba, "Considerazioni sull'importanza delle scoperte qumraniche per la conoscenza del pensiero ebraico e delle origini cristiane", *Nuova Umanità* 18, pp. 213-232.

Jefferies 2002 = D.F. Jefferies, *Wisdom at Qumran: A Form-Critical Analysis of the Admonitions in 4QInstruction* (Gorgias Dissertations: Near Eastern Studies 3) (Piscataway, NJ: Gorgias Press).

Jeremias 1962³ = J. Jeremias, *Jerusalem zur Zeit Jesu. Eine kulturgeschichtliche Untersuchung zur neutestamentlichen Zeitgeschichte* (Göttingen: Vandenhoeck & Ruprecht).

Jokiranta 2001 = J.M. Jokiranta, " 'Sectarianism' of the Qumran 'Sect': Sociological Notes", *RdQ* 20/78, pp. 223-239.

Jones 1995 = F.S. Jones, *An Ancient Jewish-Christian Source on the History of Christianity. Pseudo-Clementine Recognitions 1, 27-71* (Atlanta GE: Scholars Press).

Jones 1998 = S. Jones, "Identities in Practice: Towards an Archaeological Perspective on Jewish Identity in Antiquity", in Jones-Pearce 1998, pp. 29-49.

Jones-Pearse 1998 = S. Jones-S. Pearse (eds.), *Jewish Local Patriotism and Self-Identification in the Graeco-Roman Period* (Sheffield: Academic Press).

Jossa 1977 = G. Jossa, *Giudei, pagani, cristiani. Quattro saggi sulla spiritualità del mondo antico* (KOINΩNIA 1; Napoli: D'Auria).

Jossa 1980 = Id., *Gesù e i movimenti di liberazione della Palestina* (BCR 37; Brescia: Paideia).

Jossa 1991 = Id., *I cristiani e l'impero romano. Da Tiberio a Marco Aurelio* (Studi sul giudaismo e sul cristianesimo antico 2; Napoli: D'Auria) (rev. Edition, Roma: Carocci, 2000).

Jossa 2001a = Id., "Giudei e greci nel primo secolo dell'era cristiana. Osservazioni in margine al volume di L. Troiani, *Il perdono cristiano*, Paideia, Brescia 1999", *RivBib* 49, pp. 83-89.

Jossa 2001b = Id., "Sul problema dell'identità giudaica nell'impero romano", in Id., *I gruppi giudaici ai tempi di Gesù* (BCR 66; Brescia: Paideia, 2001), pp. 176-191.

Jossa 2001c = Id., "Gli ellenisti e i timorati di Dio", *RStB* 13/2, pp. 103-122.

Jossa 2004a = Id., *Giudei o cristiani? I seguaci di Gesù in cerca di una propria identità* (StBi 142; Brescia: Paideia).

Jossa 2004b = Id. "Giudei e cristiani visti dai Romani", in U.M. Criscuolo (ed.), *Societas studiorum. Per Salvatore D'Elia* (Napoli: Giannini), pp. 465-477.

Jucci 1995 = E. Jucci, "I manoscritti ebraici di Qumran: a che punto siamo?", *RIL.L* 129/1, pp. 243-273.

Jucci 2000 = Id., "Nuovi manoscitti del Mar Morto? Annotazioni sul cosiddetto 'Rotolo dell'Angelo' ovvero 'Il Libro delle Visioni di Yeshua ben Padiah'", *BeO* 42/1, pp. 41-48.

Judge 1960 = E.A. Judge, *The Social Pattern of Christian Groups in the First Century* (London: Tyndale Press).

Juster 1914 = J. Juster, *Les Juifs dans l'empire romain: leur condition juridique, économique et sociale*, vols. I-II (Paris: Geuthner).

Kaestli 1996 = J.-D. Kaestli, "Où en est le débat sur le judéo-christianisme?", in Marguerat (ed.), *Le déchirement. Juifs et Chrétiens au premier siècle* (MoBi 32; Genève: Labor et Fides), pp. 243-272.

Kaufmann 1970 = K. Kaufmann, "The Origin and Composition of the Eighteen Benedictions", in Petuchowsky 1970, pp. 52-90.

Kaufmann 1973 = Id., *Origins of the Synagogue and the Church*, ed. By H.G. Enelow (New York: Doubleday).

Keck 1966 = L.E. Keck, "The Poor among the Saints in Jewish Christianity and Qumran", *ZNW* 57, pp. 54-78.

Kelly 1995 = J.N.D. Kelley, *Golden Mouth. The Story of John Chrysostom, ascetic, preacher, bishop* (London: Duckworth).

Kimelman 1981 = R. Kimelman, "Birkat ha-minim and the Lack of Evidence for an Anti-Christian Jewish Prayer in Late Antiquity", in Sanders-Baumgarten-Mendelson 1981, pp. 226-244.

Klijn 1973-74 = A.F.J. Klijn, "The Study of Jewish Christianity", *NTS* 20, pp. 419-431.

Klijn-Reinink 1973 = Id.-G.J. Reinink, *Patristic Evidence for Jewish-Christian Sects* (Leiden: Brill).

Knibb 2002 = M.A. Knibb, "Interpreting the Book of Enoch: Reflections on a Recent Published Commentary", *JSJ* 33/4, pp. 437-450.

Koch-Lichtenberger 1993 = D.-A. Koch-H. Lichtenberger, *Begegnungen zwischen Christentum und Judentum in Antike und Mittelalter*, Fs. H. Schreckenberg (Göttingen: Vandenhoeck & Ruprecht).

Köster 1965 = H. Köster, "ΓΝΟΜΑΙ ΔΙΑΦΟΡΟΙ. The Origin and Nature of Diversification in the History of Early Christianity", *HThR* 58, pp. 279-318.

Kraabel 1981 = A.T. Kraabel, "Social Systems of Six Diaspora Synagogues", in Gutmann 1981, pp. 79-121.

Kraabel 1992 = Id., "The Disappearance of the God-fearers", and "The Roman Diaspora: Six Questionable Assumptions", in Overman-MacLennan 1992, pp. 1-20; 119-130.

Kraeling 1932 = C.H. Kraeling, "The Jewish Community at Antioch", *JBL* 51, pp. 130-160.

Kraemer 1992 = R.S. Kraemer, "On the Meaning of the Term 'Jew' in Greco-Roman Inscriptions", in Overman-MacLennan 1992, pp. 311-329.

Kraft 1975 = R.A. Kraft, "The Multiform Jewish Heritage of Early Christianity", in J. Neusner (ed.), *Christianity, Judaism and Other Graeco-Roman Cults*, vol. 3 (Leiden: Brill), pp. 175-199.

Kraft-Nickelsburg 1986 = Id.-G.W.E. Nickelsburg (eds.), *Early Judaism and Its Modern Interpreters* (Philadelphia: Fortress Press).

Kümmel 1985 = W. Kümmel, "Zur Sozialgeschichte und Soziologie der Urkirche", *ThR* 50, pp. 327-363.

Laperrousaz 1976 = E.-M. Laperrousaz, *Qoumrân. L'établissement essénien des bords de la Mer Morte. Histoire et archéologie du site* (Paris: Publisher).

Larsson 1987 = E. Larsson, "Die Hellenisten und die Urgemeinde", *NTS* 33, pp. 205-225.

Larsson 1995 = Id., "How Mighty was the Mighty Minorities?", *StTh* 49/1, pp. 67-77.

Leaney 1984 = A.R.C. Leaney, *The Jewish and the Christian World 200 BC to AD 200* (Cambridge: Cambridge University Press).

Le Moyne 1972 = J. Le Moyne, *Les Sadducéens* (Paris: Gabalda).

Leon 1960 = H.J. Leon, *The Jews of Ancient Rome* (Philadelphia: Fortress Press).

Levine 1987 = L.I. Levine (ed.), *The Synagogue in Late Antiquity* (Philadelphia: Fortress Press).

Lewin 2001 = A. Lewin (ed.), *Gli ebrei nell'impero romano* (Firenze: Giuntina).

Lieu 1995 = J.M. Lieu, "The Race of God-fearers", *JThS* 46, pp. 483-501.

Lieu 1996 = Id., *Image and Reality. The Jews in the World of the Christians in the Second Century* (Edinburgh: T. & T. Clark).

Lieu-North-Rajak 1992 = J. Lieu-J. North-T. Rajak (eds.), *The Jews Among Pagans and Christians in the Roman Empire* (London-New York: Routledge).

Limor-Stroumsa 1996 = O. Limor-G.G. Stroumsa (eds.), *Contra Iudaeos. Ancient and Medieval Polemics between Christians and Jews* (TSMJ 10; Tübingen: Mohr).

Lindeskog 1986 = G. Lindeskog, *Das jüdisch-christliche Problem* (Stockholm: Almqvist och Wiksell).

Liverani 2003 = M. Liverani, *Oltre la Bibbia. Storia antica di Israele* (Bari: Laterza). Rev. by A. Rofé, *Henoch* 25/3, pp. 361-371.

Lohse 1977³ = E. Lohse, *Umwelt des Neuen Testaments* (Göttingen: Vandenhoeck & Ruprecht).

Long 1989 = W.R. Long, "Martin Hengel on Early Christianity", *RStR* 15, pp. 230-234.

Lüdemann 1980 = G. Lüdemann, "The Successors of Pre-70 Jerusalem Christianity: A Critical Evaluation of the Pella-Tradition", in Sanders 1980, pp. 161-173.

Lüdemann 1983 = Id., *Paulus, der Heidenapostel,* II. *Antipaulismus im frü-hen Christentum* (Göttingen: Vandenhoeck & Ruprecht).

Lüdemann 2000 = Id., "Das Urchristentum I. und II.", *ThR* 65.

Lupieri 1991 = E. Lupieri, *Giovanni e Gesù, storia di un antagonismo* (Milano: Mondadori).

Lupieri 1993 = Id., "Dalla storia al mito. La distruzione di Gerusalemme in alcune apocalissi degli anni 70-135", in Sacchi 1993, pp. 137-155.

Lupieri 1997 = Id., "Fra Gerusalemme e Roma", in G. Filoramo-D. Menozzi (a cura di), *Storia del Cristianesimo. I. L'Antichità* (Roma-Bari: Laterza), pp. 5-137.

Lupieri 2002 = E. Lupieri, "Apocalisse giovannea e Millennio cristiano", in Uglione 2002, pp. 27-42.

Luz 1993 = U. Luz, "L'antigiudaismo nel vangelo di Matteo come problema storico e teologico: uno schizzo", *Gr.* 74/3, pp. 425-445.

Luz 1999 = Id., "Das ‚Auseinandergehen der Wege': über die Trennung des Christentums von Judentum", in W. Dietrich et alii (eds.), *Antijudaismus-christliche Erblast* (Stuttgart: Kohlhammer), pp. 56-73.

Maccoby 1991 = H. Maccoby, *Judaism in the First Century* (London: Sheldon).

Maccoby 1993 = Id., *Judaism on the Trial. Jewish-Christian Disputations in the Middle Ages* (London: The Littman Library of Jewish Civilization).

Mach 1994 = M. Mach, "Verus Israel. Towards the Clarification of a Jewish Factor in Early Christian Self-Definition", *IOS* 14, pp. 143-171.

MacLennan 1990 = R.S. MacLennan, *Early Christian Texts on Jews and Judaism* (BJSt 194; Atlanta: Scholars Press).

MacMullen 1984 = R. MacMullen, *Christianizing the Roman Empire (A.D. 100-400)* (New Haven-London: Yale University Press).

Maier 1989 = J. Maier, *Geschichte des Judentums im Altertum. Grundzüge* (Darmstadt: Wissenschaftliche Buchgesellschaft).

Maier 1990 = Id., *Zwischen den Testamenten. Geschichte und Religion in der Zeit des zweiten Tempels* (Würzburg: Echter).

Maier 1993 = Id., "Der Messias", in Sacchi 1993, pp. 157-186.

Maier 1994 = Id., *Gesù Cristo e il cristianesimo nella tradizione giudaica antica* (StBi 106), Italian Ed. by M. Zonta (Brescia: Paideia) (Orig. German Edition in EdF 82 and 177, Darmstadt: Wissenschaftliche Buchgesellschaft., 1978 and 1982).

Malherbe 1983[2] = A. Malherbe, *Social Aspects of Early Christianity,* Second Edition Enlarged (Philadelphia: Fortress Press, 1977 [I Ed.]).

Malina 1973 = B.J. Malina, "Jewish Christianity: A Select Bibliography", *AJBA* 6, pp. 60-65.

Malina 1976 = Id., "Jewish Christianity or Christian Judaism: Toward a Hypothetical Definition", *JSJ* 7, pp. 46-57.

Malina 1981 = Id., *The New Testament World: Insights from Cultural Anthropology* (Louisville Ke: J. Knox).

Malina 1982 = Id., "The Social Sciences and Biblical Interpretation", *Interp.* 37, pp. 229-242.

Malina 1986 = Id., "Normative Dissonance and Christian Origins", *Semeia* 3, pp. 35-59.

Malina 1991 = Id., "Scienze sociali e interpretazione. La questione della retrodizione", *RivBib* 39, pp. 305-323.

Malina 1995 = Id., "Early Christian Groups: Using Small Group Formation Theory to Explain Christian Organizations", in Esler 1995, pp. 96-113.

Malina-Neyrey 1988 = Id.-J.H. Neyrey, *Calling Jesus Names. The Social Value of Labels in Matthew* (Sonoma Ca.: Polebridge).

Malina-Neyrey 1996 = Id.-Id., *Portraits of Paul. An Archaeology of Ancient Personality* (Louisville KY: J. Knox).

Malina-Rohrbaugh 1992 = Id.-R.L. Rohrbaugh, *Social-Science Commentary on the Synoptic Gospels* (Minneapolis Mn: Fortress Press).

Mancini 1968 = I. Mancini, *Le scoperte archeologiche sui Giudeo-cristiani. Note storiche* (Gerusalemme: Franciscan Printing Press).

Mancini 1977 = Id., *L'Archéologie judéo-chrétienne. Notices historiques* (Jérusalem: Franciscan Printing Press) (= English Edition, Jerusalem 1970). The Book is an enlarged edition of *Le scoperte archeologiche sui Giudeo-cristiani. Note storiche* (Gerusalemme: Franciscan Printing Press, 1968).

Manns 1977 = F. Manns, *Essais sur le Judéo-Christianisme* (ASBF 12; Jérusalem: Franciscan Printing Press).

Manns 1979 = Id., *Bibliographie du Judéo-Christianisme* (ASBF 13; Jérusalem: Franciscan Printing Press).

Manns 1984 = Id., "Une nouvelle source littéraire pour l'étude du Judéo-Christianisme", *Henoch* 6, pp. 165-179.

Manns 1988 = Id., "Une tradition judéo-chrétienne mentionnée par Egérie", *Henoch* 10, pp. 283-291.

Manns 1991 = Id., "L'Evangile de Jean, réponse chrétienne aux décisions de Jabne", in Id., *L'Evangile de Jean à la lumière du Judaïsme* (Jerusalem: Franciscan Printing Press).

Manns 1998 = *L'Israele di Dio. Sinagoga e Chiesa alle origini cristiane* (Bologna: Dehoniane).

Manns-Alliata 1993 = Id.-E. Alliata (eds), *Early Christianity in Context. Monuments and Documents. – In Honour of E. Testa* (SBF.Cma 38; Jerusalem: Franciscan Printing Press).

Mannucci 1993 = C. Mannucci, *L'odio antico. L'antisemitismo cristiano e le sue radici* (Milano: Mondadori).

Manzi 1997 = F. Manzi, *Melchisedek e l'angelologia nell'Epistola agli Ebrei e a Qumran* (Analecta Biblica 136; Roma: PIB Editrice).

Marguerat 1994 = D. Marguerat, "Juden und Christen im lukanischen Doppelwerk", *EvTh* 54/3, pp. 241-264.

Marguerat 1995 = Id., "Le Nouveau Testament est-il anti-juif? L'exemple de Matthieu et du livre des Actes", *RTL* 26, pp.145-164.

Marguerat 1996 = Id. (ed.), *Le déchirement. Juifs et chrétiens au premier siècle* (Genève: Labor et Fides).

Marguerat-Norelli-Poffet 1998 = Id.- E. Norelli- J.-M. Poffet (eds.), *Jésus de Nazareth. Nouvelles approches d' une énigme* (Le Monde de la Bible 38; Genève: Labor et Fides).

Marmorstein 1950 = A. Marmorstein, "Judaism and Christianity in the Middle of the Third Century", in J. Rabbinowitz-M.S. Lew (eds.), *Studies in Jewish Theology* (London: Cumberledge [Freeport 1972²]), pp. 179-224.

Marrassini 1987 = P. Marrassini, "Sul problema del giudaismo in Etiopia", in Chiesa 1987a, pp. 175-183.

Mason 1991 = S. Mason, *Flavius Josephus and the Pharisees. A Composition-Critical Study* (Leiden: Brill).

Mazza 1978 = M. Mazza, *Ritorno alle scienze umane. Problemi e tendenze della recente storiografia sul mondo antico, Studi Storici* 19, pp. 469-507.

May 1991 = D.M. May, *Social Scientific Criticism of the New Testament: A Bibliography* (NABPRBibliogr.Ser. 4; Macon GE: Mercer University Press).

Mayeur-Pietri-Vauchez-Venard 2000 = J-M. Mayeur-Ch. et L. Pietri-A. Vauchez-M. Venard, *Histoire du Christianisme*, Tome 1: *Le nouveau peuple (des origines à 250)* (Paris: Desclée).

McNamara 1983 = M. McNamara, *Palestinian Judaism and the New Testament* (Wilmington DE: M. Glazier).

Meeks 1983 = W.A. Meeks, *The First Urban Christians. The Social World of the Apostle Paul* (New Haven-London: Yale University Press).

Meeks 1985 = Id., "Breaking Away: Three New Testament Pictures of Christianity's Separation from the Jewish Community", in Neusner-Frerichs 1985, pp. 93-115.

Meeks 1986 = Id., *The Moral World of the First Christians* (Philadelphia: Fortress Press), espec. Chap. 3: "The Great Traditions: Israel", pp. 65-96.

Meeks-Wilken 1978 = Id.-R.L. Wilken, *Jews and Christians in Antioch in the First Four Centuries of the Common Era* (SBL.MS 13; Missoula Mont: SBL Press).

Meier 1991-2001 = J.P. Meier, *A Marginal Jew. Rethinking the Historical Jesus. Vol. I: The Roots of the Problem and the Person*; Vol. 2: *Mentor, Message and Miracles*; Vol. 3: *Companions and Competitors* (New York: Doubleday, 1991.1994.2001).

Mélèze Modrzejewski 1993 = J. Mélèze Modrzejewski, "Les juifs dans le monde greco-romain. Racines et antécédents d' une pensée juive du christianisme", *Les Nouveaux Cahiers* XXVIII/113, pp. 5-13.

Millar 1992 = F. Millar, "The Jews of the Graeco-Roman Diaspora between Paganism and Christianity, AD 312-348", in AA.VV. 1992, pp. 97-123.

Mimouni 1992 = S.C. Mimouni, "Pour une définition nouvelle du judéochristianisme ancien", *NTS* 38, pp. 161-186.

Mimouni 1998a = Id., *Le Judéo-christianisme ancien. Essais historiques* (Paris: Cerf).

Mimouni 1998b = Id., "Les Nazoréens. Recherche étymologique et historique", *RB* 105, pp. 208-262.

Mimouni 2001 = Id., "I nazorei a partire dalla notizia 29 del Panarion di Epifanio di Salamina", in Filoramo-Gianotto 2001, pp. 120-146.

Mimouni-Stanley Jones 2000 = Id.- F. Stanley Jones (eds.), *Le judéo-christianisme dans tous ses états* – Actes du Colloque de Jérusalem (6-10 juillet 1998) (Paris: Cerf).

Momigliano 1975 = A. Momigliano, *Alien Wisdom: The Limits of Hellenization* (Cambridge: Cambridge University Press).

Momigliano 1976 = A. Momigliano, "Ebrei e greci", repr. in *Pagine ebraiche* (Torino: Einaudi, 1987), pp. 13-32.

Monaci Castagno 1997 = A. Monaci Castagno, "Ridefinire il confine: ebrei, giudaizzanti, cristiani nell'Adversus Iudaeos di Giovanni Crisostomo", *ASE* 14/1, pp. 135-152.

Monaci Castagno 2001 = Ead., "I giudaizzanti di Antiochia: bilancio e nuove prospettive di ricerca", in Filoramo-Gianotto 2001, pp. 304-338.

Moxnes 1988 = H. Moxnes, *The Economy of the Kingdom. Social Conflict and Economic Relations in Luke's Gospel* (Philadelphia: Fortress Press).

Moxnes 1991 = Id., "Social Relations and Economic Interaction in Luke's Gospel", in P. Luomanen (ed.), *Luke-Acts. Scandinavian Perspectives* (SESJ 54; Göttingen: Vandenhoeck & Ruprecht), pp. 58-75.

Muddiman 1991 = J. Muddiman, "The First-Century Crisis: Christian Origins", in L. Houlden (ed.), *Judaism and Christianity* (London: SCM Press), pp. 29-48.

Mulder 1988 = M.J. Mulder (ed.), *Mikra. Text, Translation, Reading and Interpretation of the Hebrew Bible in Ancient Judaism and Early Christianity* (CRINT II/1; Assen/Maastricht-Philadelphia: Fortress Press).

Müller 1976 = U.B. Müller, *Zur frühchristlichen Theologiegeschichte. Judenchristentum und Paulinismus in Kleinasien an den Wende vom ersten zum zweiten Jahrhundert n. Chr.* (Gütersloh: Mohn).

Munck 1959-60 = J. Munck, "Jewish Christianity in Post-Apostolic Times", *NTS* 6, pp. 102-116.

Munck 1965 = Id., "Primitive Christianity and Later Jewish Christianity: Continuation or Rupture?", in *Aspects du Judéo-Christianisme* (infra, Simon 1965), pp. 77-93.

Musella 2001 = L. Musella, "Esseni, comunità di Qumran, terapeuti", *Materia giudaica* VI/2, pp. 223-247.

Neusner 1971 = J. Neusner, *The Rabbinic Traditions about the Pharisees Before 70*, Vols. I-III (Leiden: Brill).

Neusner 1972 = Id., "Judaism in a Time of Crisis: Four Responses to the Destruction of the Second Temple", *Jdm* 21, pp. 314-327.

Neusner 1973 = Id., *From Politics to Piety. The Emergence of Pharisaic Judaism* (Englewood Cliffs NJ: Prentice-Hall) (repr. New York, 1979).

Neusner 1983 = Id., "Josephus's Pharisees: A Complete Repertoire", in *Formative Judaism*, s. III (Chico CA: Scholars Press), pp. 61-82.

Neusner 1984 = Id., *Judaism in the Beginning of Christianity* (Philadelphia: Fortress Press).

Neusner 1987 = Id., "L'idea della storia nel periodo di formazione del giudaismo (200-600 ca.)", in Chiesa 1987a, pp. 121-137.

Neusner 1988a[2] = Id., *Judaism: The Evidence of the Mishnah* ("BJSt" 129; Atlanta Ge.: Scholars Press).

Neusner 1988b = Id., *From Testament to Torah. An Introduction to Judaism in Its Formative Period* (Englewood Cliffs NJ: Prentice-Hall).

Neusner 1990 = Id., "Judaism and Christianity in the First Century: How Shall We Perceive their Relationship?", in Id. (ed.), *Lectures in Judaism in the History of Religions* (Atlanta: Scholars Press), pp. 33-44.

Neusner 1995, = Id., *Judaism in Late Antiquity*, Voll. 1-2 (Leiden: Brill).

Neusner – Avery-Peck – Green 2000 = Id. – A.J. Avery-Peck – W.S. Green (eds.), *The Encyclopaedia of Judaism*, vol. I (A-I) (Leiden-Boston-Köln: Brill), pp. 63-77 (*Christianity on Judaism in Ancient and Medieval Times*).

Neusner-Borgen-Frerichs-Horsley 1988 = Id.-P. Borgen-E.S. Frerichs-R. Horsley (eds.), *The Social World of Formative Christianity and Judaism. Essays in Tribute to H. Cl. Kee* (Philadelphia: Fortress Press).

Neusner-Chilton 1996 = Id.- B.D. Chilton, *The Body of Faith. Israel and the Church: Christianity and Judaism – The Formative Categories* (Valley Forge PA: Trinity Press International).

Neusner-Frerichs 1985 = Id.-E.S.Frerichs (eds.), *To See Ourselves as Others See Us. Christians, Jews "Others" in Late Antiquity* (Chico CA: Fortress Press).

Neusner-Green-Frerichs 1987 = J. Neusner-W.S. Green-E.S. Frerichs (eds.), *Judaisms and Their Messiahs at the Turn of the Christian Era* (Cambridge: Cambridge University Press).

Neyrey 1991 = J.H. Neyrey, *The Social World of Luke-Acts. Models for Interpretation* (Peabody Mass.: Hendrickson).

Newman-Davila-Lewis 1999 = C.C. Newman-J.R. Davila-G.S. Lewis (eds.), *The Jewish Roots of Christological Monotheism. Papers from the St. Andrews Conference on the Historical Origins of the Worship of Jesus* (Leiden-Boston-Köln: Brill).

Nickelsburg 1981 = G.W.E. Nickelsburg, *Jewish Literature Between the Bible and the Mishnah. A Historical and Literary Introduction* (Philadelphia: Fortress Press).

Nickelsburg 2001 = Id., *1 Enoch: A Commentary on the Book of 1 Enoch, Chapters 1-36; 81-108* (Hermeneia; Minneapolis: Fortress Press). Cf. rev. by S. Chialà, *Bibl.* 85, 2004, pp. 143ff.

Nickelsburg 2003 = Id., *Ancient Judaism and Christian origins: Diversity, Continuity, and Transformation* (Minneapolis: Fortress Press).

Nickelsburg-Stone 1983 = Id.-M.E. Stone, *Faith and Piety in Early Judaism. Text and Documents* (Philadelphia: Fortress Press).

Nock 1972 = A.D. Nock, *Essays on Religion and the Ancient World*, Vols. I-II (Oxford: Clarendon Press).

Nodet-Taylor 1998 = É. Nodet-J. Taylor, *Essai sur les origines du christianisme. Une secte éclatée* (Initiations; Paris: Cerf).

Noja 1987 = S. Noja, *Gli ultimi dieci anni di studi sui Samaritani*, in Chiesa 1987a, pp. 139-149.

Norelli 1980 = E. Norelli, "Il martirio di Isaia come 'testimonium' anti-giudaico?", *Henoch* 2, pp. 37-57.

Norelli 1987 = Id., "Sociologia del cristianesimo primitivo. Qualche osservazione a partire dall'opera di Gerd Theissen", *Henoch* 9, pp. 97-123.

Norelli 1993 = Id. (a cura di), *La Bibbia nell'antichità cristiana. I. Da Gesù a Origene* (La Bibbia nella storia 15/1; Bologna: EDB).

Norelli 1994 = Id., *L'Ascensione di Isaia. Studi su un apocrifo al crocevia dei cristianesimi* (Origini 3; Bologna: EDB).

Norelli 2001 = Id., "Ignazio di Antiochia combatte veramente dei cristiani giudaizzanti?", in Filoramo-Gianotto 2001, pp. 220-264.

North 1955 = R. North, "The Qumran Sadducees", *CBQ* 17, pp. 164-188.

Novak 1983 = D. Novak, *The Image of the Non-Jew in Judaism. An Historical and Constructive Study of the Noahide Laws* (Lewiston: The Edwin Mellen Press).

Osiek 1992[2] = C. Osiek, *What Are They Saying About the Social Setting of the New Testament*, Revised and Expanded Edition (New York: Paulist Press, 1984 [I Ed.]).

Overman 1990 = J.A. Overman, *Matthew's Gospel and Formative Judaism: The Social World of the Matthean Community* (Minneapolis: Fortress Press).

Overman-MacLennan 1992 = J.O. Overman-R.S. MacLennan (eds.), *Diaspora Jews and Judaism. Essays in Honor, and in dialogue with Thomas Kraabel* (Atlanta Ge.: Scholars Press).

Parente 1962 = F. Parente, "Il problema storico dei rapporti tra essenismo e cristianesimo prima della scoperta dei Rotoli del Mar Morto", *ParPass* 86, pp. 333-370.

Parente 1964 = Id., "Il problema storico dei rapporti fra essenismo e giudeo-cristianesimo prima della scoperta dei Rotoli del Mar Morto", *ParPass* 100, pp. 81-124.

Parente 1993 = Id., "Gerusalemme", in G. Cambiano-L. Canfora-D. Lanza (eds.), *Lo spazio letterario della Grecia antica* I/2 (Roma: Salerno Ed.), pp. 553-624.

Parente 2001 = Id., "Verus Israel di Marcel Simon a cinquant'anni dalla pubblicazione", in Filoramo-Gianotto 2001, pp. 19-46.

Patte 1975 = D. Patte, *Early Jewish Hermeneutic in Palestine* (Missoula Mont.: Fortress Press).

Pearson-Kraabel-Nickelsburg-Petersen 1991 = B.A. Pearson-A. Thomas Kraabel-G.W.E. Nickelsburg-N.R. Petersen (eds.), *The Future of Early Christianity. Essays in Honor of H. Koester* (Minneapolis: Fortress Press).

Pedersen 1995 = S. Pedersen, "Israel als integrierter Teil der christlichen Hoffnung (Matth. 23)", *StTh* 49/1, pp. 133-149.

Penna 1989 = Id. (ed.), *Antipaolinismo: reazioni a Paolo tra il I e il II secolo* – Atti del II Convegno nazionale di Studi Neotestamentari (Bressanone, 10-12 settembre 1987), *RStB* 1/2.

Penna 1991³ = Id., *L'ambiente storico-culturale delle origini cristiane. Una documentazione ragionata* (La Bibbia nella storia 7; Bologna: EDB).

Penna 1993 = Id. (ed.), *Il profetismo da Gesù di Nazaret al montanismo* – Atti del IV Congresso di Studi Neotestamentari (Perugia, 12-14 settembre 1991), *RStB* 5/1.

Penna 1995 = Id. (ed.), *Apocalittica e origini cristiane* – Atti del V Convegno di Studi Neotestamentari (Seiano, 15-18 settembre 1993), *RStB* 7/2.

Penna 1997 = Id. (ed.), *Qumran e le origini cristiane* – Atti del VI Convegno di Studi Neotestamentari (L'Aquila, 14-17 settembre 1995), *RStB* 9/2.

Penna 1999 = Id. (ed.), *Fariseismo e origini cristiane* – Atti del VII Convegno di Studi Neotestamentari (Rocca di Papa, 12-15 settembre 1997), *RStB* 11/2.

Penna 2001 = "Cristologia senza morte redentrice: un filone di pensiero del giudeocristianesimo più antico", in Filoramo-Gianotto 2001, pp. 68-94.

Perelmuter 1989 = H.G. Perelmuter, *Siblings. Rabbinic Judaism and Early Christianity at Their Beginnings* (New York: Doubleday).

Pesce 1979 = M. Pesce, *Dio senza mediatori. Una tradizione teologica dal giudaismo al cristianesimo* (TRSR 16; Brescia: Paideia).

Pesce 1986 = Id., "Movimenti e istituzioni nel Giudaismo dai Maccabei a Bar Kokhbah (167 a.C.-135 d.C.)", in *L'Ebraismo* (Quaderni della Fondazione S. Carlo, 4/1986).

Pesce 1994 = Id., *Il cristianesimo e la sua radice ebraica. Con una raccolta di testi sul dialogo ebraico-cristiano* (Bologna: EDB).

Pesce 1997 = Id., "Antigiudaismo nel Nuovo Testamento e nella sua utilizzazione. Riflessioni metodologiche", *ASE* 14/1, pp. 11-38.

Pesce 1998 = Id., "L'approccio secondo le scienze umane", in *L'interpretazione della Bibbia nella Chiesa. Commento a cura di G. Ghiberti e F. Mosetto* (Torino: Leumann), pp. 195-221.

Pesce 2001 = Id., "Il Vangelo di Giovanni e le fasi giudaiche del giovannismo. Alcuni aspetti", in Filoramo-Gianotto 2001, pp. 47-67.

Pesce 2003a = Id., "Il 'sacrificio' in prospettiva interdisciplinare e comparatista. Osservazioni in margine a una recente pubblicazione di G. Grottanelli" (*Il sacrificio* [BEL] [Bari-Roma: Laterza, 1999]), *RivBib* 51, pp. 193-202.

Pesce 2003b = Id., "Quando nasce il cristianesimo? Aspetti dell'attuale dibattito storiografico e uso delle fonti", in *ASE* 20/1, pp. 39-56

Pesce 2003c = Id. "Sul concetto di giudeocristianesimo", in Pitta 2003, pp. 21-44.

Pesce 2004 = Id. (ed.), *Come è nato il cristianesimo*, Brescia, Morcelliana, forthcoming.

Peterson 1959 = E. Peterson, *Frühkirche, Judentum und Gnosis. Studien und Untersuchungen* (Rom-Freiburg-Wien: Herder).

Petuchowski 1970 = J.J. Petuchowski (ed.), *Contributions to the Scientific Study of Jewish Liturgy* (New York: Doubleday).

Pilch 1991 = J.J. Pilch (ed.), *Introducing the Cultural Context of the New Testament* (New York-Mahwah: Paulist Press).

Pilch 1992 = Id., "Lying and Deceit in the Letters to the Seven Churches: Perspectives from Cultural Anthropology", *BTB* 22, pp. 126-135.

Pilch-Malina 1993 = Id.-B.J. Malina, *Biblical Social Values and Their Meanings. A Handbook* (Peabody Mass.: Hendrickson).

Pitta 2001 = A. Pitta (ed.), *Gli Atti degli apostoli: storiografia e biografia –* Atti dell'VIII Convegno di Studi Neotestamentari (Torreglia, 8-11 settembre 1999), *RStB* 13/2.

Pitta 2003 = Id., Il giudeo-cristianesimo nel I e II sec. D.C. – Atti del IX Convegno di Studi Neotestamentari (Napoli, 13-15 settembre 2001), *RStB* 15/2.

Pixner 1991 = B. Pixner, *Wege des Messiasund Stätten der Urkirche. Jesus und das Judenchristentum im Licht neuer archäologischer Erkenntnisse.* Herausgegeben von R. Riesner, Giessen-Bâle.

Pixner 2000 = Id., "Nazoreans on the Mount Sion (Jerusalem)", in Mimouni-Stanley Jones 2000.

Porter-Evans 1997 = S.E. Porter-C.A. Evans (eds.), *The Scrolls and the Scriptures Fifty Years After* (JSPE.S 26; Sheffield: Academic Press).

Prato 1989 = G.L. Prato (ed.), *Israele alla ricerca di identità tra il III sec. A.C. e il I sec. D.C. –* Atti del V Convegno di Studi Veterotestamentari (Bressanone, 7-9 settembre 1987), *RStB* 1/1.

Prete 1987 = B. Prete, "I giudei nei dati del quarto vangelo", in Chiesa 1987a, pp. 79-104.

Pritz 1988 = R.A. Pritz, *Nazarene Jewish Christianity. From the End of the New Testament Period until its Disappearance* (Jerusalem-Leiden: Publisher).

Quispel 1968 = G. Quispel, "The Discussion of Judaic Christianity", *VigChr* 22, pp. 81-93.

Randellini 1968 = L. Randellini, *La Chiesa dei Giudeo-cristiani* (StBi 1; Brescia: Paideia).

Rengstorf 1963 = K.H. Rengstorf, *Hirbet Qumrân and the Problem of the Library of the Dead Sea Caves* (Leiden: Brill).

Reynolds-Tannenbaum 1987 = J. Reynolds-R. Tannenbaum, *Jews and God-fearers at Aphrodisias. Greek Inscriptions with Commentary* (Camdridge: Cambridge University Press).

Richardson 1969 = P. Richardson, *Israel in the Apostolic Church* (Cambridge: Cambridge University Press).

Riegel 1978 = S.K. Riegel, "Jewish Christianity: Definitions and Terminology", *NTS* 24, pp. 410-415.

Riesner 1998² = R. Riesner, *Essener und Urgemeinde in Jerusalem. Neue Funde und Quellen* (Giessen: Brunnen Verlag).

Rofé-Roifer 1987 = A. Rofé-Roifer, "Gli albori delle sette nel giudaismo postesilico (Notizie inedite dai Settanta, Trito-Isaia, Siracide e Malachia)", in Chiesa 1987a, pp. 25-35.

Rohrbaugh 1997 = R. Rohrbaugh (ed.), *The Social Sciences and the New Testament Interpretation* (Peabody MA: Hendrickson).

Rokeah 1982 = D. Rokeah, *Jews, Pagans and Christians in Conflict* (Jerusalem-Leiden: Brill).

Rosso Ubigli 1978 = L. Rosso Ubigli, "Il Documento di Damasco e la halakhah settaria: Rassegna di studi", *RdQ* 9, pp. 357-399.

Rosso Ubigli 1979 = Ead., "Alcuni aspetti della concezione della 'porneia' nel tardo giudaismo", *Henoch* 1, pp. 201-245.

Rosso Ubigli 1983 = Ead., "Qohelet di fronte all'apocalittica", *Henoch* 5, pp. 209-234.

Rowland 1995 = Ch. Rowland, "Moses and Patmos. Reflections on the Jewish Background of Early Christianity", in J. Davies-G. Harvey-W.G.E. Watson (eds.), *Words Remembered. Texts Renewed*, Essays in Honour of J.F.A. Sawyer, (Sheffield: Sheffield Academic Press), pp. 280-299.

Rudolph 1991 = K. Rudolph, "Early Christianity as a Religious-historical Phenomenon", in *The Future of Early Christianity*, pp. 16-34.

Russel 1986 = D.S. Russel, *From Early Judaism to Early Church* (London-Philadelphia: SCM).

Rutgers 1998 = L.V. Rutgers, *A Hidden Heritage of Diaspora* (Leuven: Peeters).

Sabourin 1976 = L. Sabourin, "Jewish Christianity of the First Centuries", *BTB* 6, pp. 5-26.

Sacchi 1981-2000 = P. Sacchi (a cura di), *Apocrifi dell'Antico Testamento*, voll. I-II (Torino: UTET, 1981-1989); III-V (Biblica 5.7-8; Brescia: Paideia, 1997-2000).

Sacchi 1984 = Id., "Gesù l'ebreo", *Henoch* 6, pp. 347-368.

Sacchi 1987 = Id., "L'apocalittica del I sec.: peccato e giudizio", in Chiesa 1987a, pp. 59-77.

Sacchi 1992 = Id., "Recovering Jesus' Formative Background", in Charlesworth 1992a, pp. 123-139.

Sacchi 1993 = Id. (ed.), *Il Giudaismo palestinese: dal 1 secolo a.C. al 1 secolo d.C.* – Atti dell'VIII Congresso Internazionale dell' AISG (San Miniato 5-6-7 novembre 1990) ("TSAISG" 8; Bologna: AISG).

Sacchi 1995 = Id., "Qumran e le origini cristiane", in Strus 1995, pp. 61-86.

Sacchi 1997a = Id., "A New Step toward a Deeper Knowledge of the Jewish Second Temple Thought", *Henoch* 19, pp. 367-377.

Sacchi 1997b = Id., *Jewish Apocalyptic and Its History* (JSPE.S 20; Sheffield: Sheffield Academic Press).

Sacchi 1999 = Id., "Introduzione", in Sacchi 1999, pp. 9-51.

Sacchi 2000 = Id., *The History of the Second Temple History* (JSOT.S 285; Sheffield: Sheffield Academic Press).

Sacchi 2002a = Id., "Origini dell'enochismo e apocalittica", *Materia giudaica* 7/1, 2002, 7-13.

Sacchi 2002b = Id., "The Theology of Early Enochism: The Problem of the Relation between Form and Content of the Apocalypses; the Worldview of Apocalypses", in Boccaccini 2002b, pp. 77-86.

Sachot 1985 = M. Sachot, "Comment le christianisme est-il devenue 'religio'?", *RSR* 59, pp. 95-118.

Sachot 1998 = Id., *L'invention du Christ. Genèse d'une religion* (Paris: Cerf).

Safrai 1987-1991 = S. Safrai (ed.), *The Literature of the Sages*. First Part: *Oral Tora, Halakha, Mishna, Tosefta, Talmud, External Tractates* (CRINT II/3a). Second Part: *Midrash, Aggada, Midrash Collections, Targum, Prayer* (CRINT II/3b; Assen/Maastricht-Philadelphia: Fortress Press).

Safrai-Stern 1974-76 = S. Safrai-M. Stern (eds.), *The Jewish People in the First Century. Historical Geography, Political History, Social, Cultural and Religious Life and Institutions*, in co-operation with D. Flusser and W.C. van Unnik (CRINT I/1-2; Assen/Amsterdam: Fortress Press).

Saldarini 1988 = A.J. Saldarini, *Pharisees, Scribes and Sadducees in Palestinian Society. A Sociological Approach* (Wilmington DE: M. Glazier).

Saldarini 1992 = Id., "Jews and Christians in the First Two Centuries. The Changing Paradigm", *Shafar* 10/2, pp. 16-34.

Saldarini 1994 = Id., *Matthew's Christian-Jewish Community* (Chicago: University of Chicago Press).

Sanders 1977 = E.P. Sanders, *Paul and Palestinian Judaism. A Comparison of Patterns of Religion* (Philadelphia-London: SCM Press, 1984[2]).

Sanders 1980-1981 = Id. (ed.), *Jewish and Christian Self-Definition*, Vol. I. *The Shaping of Christianity in the Second and Third Centuries*; Vol. II. *Aspects of Judaism in the Greco-Roman Period* (London-Philadelphia: Fortress Press).

Sanders 1985 = Id., *Jesus and Judaism* (London: SCM Press).

Sanders 1990a = Id., *Jewish Law from Jesus to the Mishnah. Five Studies* (London-Philadelphia: SCM Press).

Sanders 1990b = Id., "Jewish Association with Gentiles and Galatians 2,11-14", in R. Fortna-B. Gaventa (ed.), *The Conversation Continues. Studies in Paul and John in Honor of J.L. Martin* (Nashville: Abingdon Press), pp. 170-188.

Sanders 1991 = Id., "Who is a Jew and Who is a Gentile in the Book of Acts?", *NTS* 37, pp. 434-455.

Sanders 1992 = Id., *Judaism. Practice and Belief 63 BCE-66 CE* (London-Philadelphia: SCM Press (Italian tr.: *Il Giudaismo. Fede e prassi [63 a.C.-66 d.C.]*, ed. by P. Capelli, with *Postfazione*, pp. 675-694; Brescia: Morcelliana, 1999).

Sanders-Baumgarten-Mendelson 1981 = Id.-A.I. Baumgarten-A. Mendelson (eds.), *Jewish and Christian Self-Definition, II. Aspects of Judaism in the Graeco-Roman Period* (London: Fortress Press).

Sanders 1992 = J.T. Sanders, "Jewish Christianity in Antioch before the Time of Hadrian: Where Does the Identity Lie?", in E.H. Lovering (ed.), *SBL.SP 31* (Atlanta: Scholars Press), pp. 346-361.

Sanders 1993 = Id., *Schismatics, Sectarians, Dissidents, Deviants. The First One Hundred Years of Jewish-Christian Relations* (Valley Forge PA: SCM Press).

Sandmel 1969 = S. Sandmel, *The First Christian Century in Judaism and Christianity. Certainties and Uncertainties* (New York: University Press).

Sandmel 1977 = Id., *A Jewish Understanding of the New Testament*, Augmented Ed. (London: Ktav Publishing House; I Ed., New York 1956).

Sandmel 1978 = Id., *Judaism and Christian Beginnings* (New York: Oxford University Press).

Saulnier 1993 = Ch. Saulnier, "Le cadre politico-religieux en Palestine de la révolte des Maccabées à l' intervention romaine", in Sacchi 1993, pp. 199-211.

Saunders 1983 = E.W. Saunders (rev.), "Jewish Christianity and Palestinian Archeology", *RStR* 9, pp. 201-205.

Schäfer 1983 = P. Schäfer, *Geschichte der Juden in der Antike. Die Juden Palästinas von Alexander dem Grossen bis zur arabischen Eroberung* (Stuttgart: Verlag Katholisches Bibelwerk).

Schäfer 1997 = Id., *Judeophobia. Attitudes toward the Jews in the Ancient World* (Cambridge: Cambridge University Press).

Schiffman 1984 = L.H. Schiffman, *Who was a Jew? Rabbinic and Halakhic Perspectives on the Jewish-Christian Schism* (Haboken NJ: Ktav Publishing House).

Schiffman 1994 = Id., "Judaism and Early Christianity in the Light of the Dead Sea Scrolls", in M. Perry-Fr. M. Schweitzer (eds.), *Jewish-Christian Encounters over the Centuries. Symbiosis, Prejudice, Holocaust, Dialogue* (New York: Doubleday), pp. 27-44.

Schiffman 1995 = Id., *Reclaiming the Dead Sea Scrolls. The History of*

Judaism, the Background of Christianity, the Lost Library of Qumran (New York: Doubleday).

Schiffman 2002 = Id., Les manuscrits de la mer Morte et le judaïsme: l'apport de Qumrân à l'histoire (Québec Fides: Saint Laurent).

Schirmann 1953-54 = J. Schirmann, "Hebrew Liturgical Poetry and Christian Hymnology", JQR 44, pp. 123-161.

Schmitt 1978 = J. Schmitt, "Qumrân et la première génération Judéo-chrétienne", in Delcor 1978, pp. 385-440

Schneemelcher 1981 = W. Schneemelcher, Das Urchristentum (Stuttgart: Kohlhammer).

Schoeps 1949 = H.J. Schoeps, Theologie und Geschichte des Judenchristentums (Tübingen: Mohr).

Schoeps 1964 = Id., Das Judenchristentum (Bern: Francke).

Schreckenberg 1982-1988 = H. Schreckenberg, Die christlichen Adversus-Judaeos-Texte und ihr literarisches und historisches Umfeld (1-11 Jh.), Vol. I-II (Frankfurt a. M.-Bern-New York-Paris: Peter Lang).

Schreckenberg-Schubert 1992 = Id.-K. Schubert (eds.), Jewish Historiography and Iconography in Early and Medieval Christianity. I. Josephus in Early Christian Literature and Medieval Christian Art – II. Jewish Pictorial Traditions in Early Christian Art, with an Introduction by D. Flusser (CRINT III/2; Assen/Maastricht-Minneapolis: Fortress Press).

Schremer 1997 = A. Schremer, "The Name of the Boethusians. A Reconsideration of Suggested Explanations and Another One", JJS 48, pp. 290-299.

Schröer 1992a = S. Schröer (ed.), Christen und Juden. Voraussetzungen für ein erneuteres Verhältnis, mit Beiträgen von E. Brocke et al. (Altenberge: w.e.).

Schürer 1973-1987 = E. Schürer, The History of the Jewish People in the Age of Jesus Christ (175 B.C-A.D. 135), a New English Version rev. and ed. by G. Vermes, F. Millar, M. Black and M. Goodman, Literary Editor P. Vermes, Organizing Editor M. Black, Vols. I-III/1.2 (Edinburgh: T. & T. Clark) (Italian translation: Storia del popolo giudaico al tempo di Gesù Cristo [175 a.C.-135 d.C.], a cura di O. Soffritti, B. Chiesa e C. Gianotto, voll. I-III/1.2 [BSSTB 1.6.12.13; Brescia: Paideia, 1985-1998]).

Schwartz 1992 = D.R. Schwartz, Studies in the Jewish Background of Christianity (WUNT 60; Tübingen: Mohr).

Segal 1986 = A.F. Segal, Rebecca's Children. Judaism and Christianity in the Roman World (Cambridge MA: Harvard University Press).

Segal 1987 = Id., The Other Judaisms of Late Antiquity (Atlanta: Scholars Press).

Segal 1991 = Id., "Studying Judaism with Christian Sources", USQR 44, pp. 267-286.

Seidensticker 1959 = P. Seidensticker, "Die Gemeinschaftsform der religiösen Gruppen des Spätjudentums und der Urkirche", SBFLA 9, pp. 94-198.

Setzer 1994 = C. Setzer, *Jewish Responses to Early Christians* (Minneapolis: Fortress Press).

Sevenster 1975 = J.N. Sevenster, *The Roots of Pagan Antisemitism in the Ancient World* (NT.S 41; Leiden: Brill).

Shanks 1992a = H. Shanks (ed.), *Understanding the Dead Sea Scrolls. A Reader from the BarR* (New York: Random House).

Shanks 1992b = Id., *Christianity and Rabbinic Judaism. A Parallel History of their Origins and Early Development* (Washington D.C.: Biblical Archaelogy Society).

Sherwin-White 1967 = A.N. Sherwin-White, *Racial Prejudice in Imperial Rome* (Cambridge: Cambridge University Press).

Sigal 1980 = Ph. Sigal, *The Foundations of Judaism from Biblical Origins to the Sixth Century A. D.*, Vol. I/1: *From the Origins to the Separation of Christianity* (PThMS 29; Pittsburgh: w.e.).

Sigal 1984 = Id., "Early Christian and Rabbinic Liturgical Affinities: Exploring Liturgical Acculturation", *NTS* 30, pp. 63-90.

Sim 1995 = D.C. Sim, "The Social Setting of Ancient Apocalypticism: A Question of Method", *JSPE* 13, pp. 5-16.

Sim 1998 = Id., *The Gospel of Matthew and Christian Judaism. The Historical and Social Setting of the Matthean Community* (Stud. in the NT and Its World; Edimburgh: T. & T. Clark).

Simon 1960a = M. Simon, *Les sectes juives au temps de Jésus* (Paris: Presses Universitaires de France).

Simon 1960b= Id., *Les premiers chretiens* (Que sais-je? 551; Paris: Presses Universitaires de France).

Simon 1962a = Id., *Recherches d'Histoire Judéo-Chrétienne* (EtJ 6; Paris: Mouton).

Simon 1962b = Id., "La polémique antijuive de s. Jean Chrysostome et le mouvement judaïsant d'Antioche", in Simon 1962a, pp. 140-153.

Simon 1964[2] = Id., *Verus Israel. Étude sur les relations entre Chrétiens et Juifs dans l'Empire romain (135-425)* (Paris: De Boccard; revised Edition with a «Post-scriptum» from the I Ed. of 1948), espec. pp. 165-213.

Simon 1965 = Id., "Problèmes du Judéo-Christianisme", in AA.VV., *Aspects du Judéo-Christianisme* – Colloque de Strasbourg, 23-25 avril 1964 (Paris: Presses Universitaires de France), pp. 1-17.181-185 (Conclusion générale).

Simon 1975 = Id., "Réflexions sur le Judéo-Christianisme", in J. Neusner (ed.), *Christianity, Judaism and Other Graeco-Roman Cults. Fs. Morton Smith* (Leiden: Brill), pp. 53-76.

Simon 1981a = Id., *Le Christianisme antique et son contexte religieux. Scripta varia*, voll. I-II (Tübingen: Mohr).

Simon 1981b = Id., "Le christianisme: naissance d'une catégorie historique", in Id. 1981a, vol. I, pp. 312-335.

Simon 1982 = Id., "La diaspora ebraica in età ellenistico-romana e la diffusione del cristianesimo nelle regioni dell'impero", in *Mondo classico e cristianesimo* (Roma: Istituto della Enciclopedia italiana), pp. 9-16.

Simon-Benoît 1985[2] = Id.-A. Benoît, *Le judaïsme et le christianisme antique d'Antiochus Epiphane à Constantin* (Paris: Presses Universitarie de France, 1968 [I Ed.]).

Simonetti 1994 = M. Simonetti, *Ortodossia ed eresia tra I e II secolo* (Soveria Mannelli: Rubbettino).

Simonetti 1995 = Id., "Il giudeocristianesimo nella tradizione patristica dal II secolo al IV secolo", in Strus 1995, pp. 117-130.

Siniscalco 1983 = P. Siniscalco, *Il cammino di Cristo nell'Impero romano* (Roma-Bari: Laterza).

Smallwood 1976 = E.M. Smallwood, *The Jews under Roman Rule from Pompey to Diocletian. A Study in Political Relation* (Leiden: Brill, 1981 [repr.]).

Smallwood 1999 = Id., "The diaspora in the Roman period before CE 70", in W.Horbury-W.D. Davies-J.Sturdy (eds.), *The Cambridge History of Judaism* (Cambridge: Cambridge University Press), Vol. III, pp. 168-191.

Smith 1990 = J.Z. Smith, *Drudgery Divine. On the Comparison of Early Christianities and the Religions of Late Antiquity* (Chicago: Chicago University Press).

Smith 1956 = M. Smith, "Palestinian Judaism in the First Century", in M. Davies (ed.), *Israel: Its Role in Civilization* (New York: The Jewish Theological Seminary of America).

Smith 1971a = Id., *Palestinian Parties and Politics that Shaped the Old Testament* (New York-London: Columbia University Press).

Smith 1971b = Id., "Zealots and Sicarii: Their Origins and Relations", *HThR* 64, pp. 1-19.

Sordi 1984 = M. Sordi, *I cristiani e l'impero romano* (Milano: Jaca Book).

Stanton 1985 = G.N. Stanton, "Aspects of Early Christian-Jewish Polemic and Apologetic", in *NTS* 31, pp. 377-392.

Stanton 1996 = Id., "Other Early Christian Writings: 'Didache', Ignatius, Barnabas, Justin Martyr", in Barclay-Sweet 1996, pp. 174-190.

Stark 1996 = R. Stark, *The Rise of Christianity. How the Obscure, Marginal Jesus Movement Became the Dominant Religious Force in the Western World in a Few Centuries* (Princeton N.J.: Princeton University Press).

Stauffer 1952 = E. Stauffer, "Zum Kalifat des Jacobus", *ZRGG* 4/3, pp. 193-214.

Stambaugh-Balch 1986 = J.E. Stambaugh-D. Balch, *The New Testament in Its Social Environment* (Philadelphia: The Westminster Press).

Stegemann 1990 = D. Stegemann, *Jüdische Wurzeln des Christentums. Grundstrukturen des alttestamentlichen und nachtestamentlichen Glaubens bis zur Zeit Jesu* (RPBE 2; Essen: Verlag Die Blaue Eule).

Stegemann 1994 = E.W. Stegemann, "Zwischen Juden und Heiden, aber "mehr" als Juden und Heiden? Neutestamentliche Anmerkungen zur Identitätsproblematik des frühen Christentums", *KuI* 9/1, pp. 53-69.

Stegemann-Stegemann 1995 = Id.-W. Stegemann, *Urchristliche Sozialgeschichte. Die Anfänge im Judentum und die Christusgemeinden in der mediterranen Welt* (Stuttgart-Berlin-Köln: Kohlhammer).

Stegemann 1992 = H. Stegemann, "The Qumran Essenes: Local Members of Main Jewish Union in Late Second Temple Times", in J. Trebolle Barrera-L. Vegas Montaner (eds.), *The Madrid Congress* – Proceedings of the International Congress on the Dead Sea Scrolls (Madrid, 18-21 March, 1991) (StTDJ 11/1-2; Leiden: Brill), Vol. 1, pp. 83-166.

Stegemann 1993 = Id., *Die Essener, Qumran, Johannes der Täufer und Jesus. Ein Sachbuch* (Freiburg i. Br.: Herder).

Stegner 1995 = W.R. Stegner, "Breaking Away: The Conflict with Formative Judaism", *BR* 40, pp. 7-36.

Stemberger 1979 = G. Stemberger, *Das klassische Judentum* (München: Beck).

Stemberger 1991 = Id., *Pharisäer, Sadduzäer, Essener* (Stuttgart: Katholisches Bibelwerk).

Stemberger 1993 = Id., "Il contributo delle Baraitot babilonesi alla conoscenza storica della Palestina prima del 70 d. C. (Shabbat, 13b-17b: le diciotto halakot e tradizioni connesse)", in Sacchi 1993, pp. 213-229.

Stemberger 1996 = Id., "Exegetical Contacts between Christian and Jews in the Roman Empire", in C. Brekelmans-M. Haran-M. Sæbø (eds.), *Hebrew Bible/Old Testament. The History of its Interpretation. 1. From the Beginnings to the Middle Ages (Until 1300). Part I: Antiquity* (Göttingen: Vandenhoeck & Ruprecht), pp. 569-586.

Stern 1974-1984 = M. Stern, *Greek and Latin Authors on Jews and Judaism*, Vols. I-III (Jerusalem: The Israel Academy of Sciences and Humanities).

Stone 1980 = M.E. Stone, *Scriptures, Sects, and Visions. A Profile of Judaism from Ezra to the Jewish Revolts* (Philadelphia: Fortress Press).

Stone 1984 = Id. (ed.), *Jewish Writings of the Second Temple Period. Apocrypha, Pseudepigrapha, Qumran Sectarian Writings, Philo, Josephus* (CRINT II/2; Assen-Philadelphia: Fortress Press).

Stone 1996 = Id., *The Dead Sea Scrolls and the Pseudepigrapha, DSSD* 3, pp. 270-295.

Stone-Chazon 1998 = Id.-E.G. Chazon (eds.), *Biblical Perspectives: Early Use and Interpretation of the Bible in Light of the Dead Sea Scrolls* – Proceedings of the First International Symposium of the Orion Center for the Study of the Dead Sea Scrolls and Associated Literature (12-14 May 1996) (STDJ 28; Leiden: Brill).

Strecker 1964[2] = G. Strecker, "Nachtrag I. Zum Problem des Judenchristentums", in W. Bauer (ed.), *Rechtgläubigkeit und Ketzerei im ältesten Christentum* (BHTh 10; Tübingen: Mohr), pp. 245-287.

Strecker 1993 = Id., "On the Problem of Jewish Christianity", in E. Ferguson (ed.), *Early Christianity and Judaism* (New York: Garland Publishing), pp. 31-75.

Strecker-Maier 1988 = Id.-J. Maier, *Neues Testament – Antikes Judentum* (Stuttgart: Kohlhammer).

Stroker 1989 = W.D. Stroker, *Extracanonical Sayings of Jesus* (SBLRBS 18; Atlanta, G.A.: Scholars Press).

Stroumsa 1993 = G.G. Stroumsa, "Le radicalisme religieux du premier christianisme: contexte et implications", in É. Patlagean-A. Le Boulluec (eds.), *Les retours aux Écritures. Fondamentalismes présents et passés* (BEHE.R 99; Louvain-Paris: Peeters), pp. 357-381.

Stroumsa 1996a = Id., *Hidden Wisdom. Esoteric Traditions and the Roots of Christian Mysticism* (Numen Book Series 70; Leiden-New York-Köln: Brill).

Stroumsa 1996b = Id., "Dall'antigiudaismo all'antisemitismo nel cristianesimo primitivo?", *CrSt* 17, pp. 13-45 (Italian translation by L. Perrone).

Stroumsa 1999a = Id., *Barbarian Philosophy. The Religious Revolution of Early Christianity* (WUAT 112; Tübingen: Mohr).

Stroumsa 1999b = Id., *La formazione dell'identità cristiana*, a cura di P. Capelli, Introduzione di G. Filoramo, (Brescia: Morcelliana).

Strus 1995 = A. Strus, *Tra giudaismo e cristianesimo. Qumran – Giudeocristiani* (Ieri oggi domani 17; Roma: LAS).

Swetnam 1993 = J. Swetnam, "Reflections on Luke's Treatment of Jews in Luke-Acts", *Bib.* 74/4, pp. 529-555.

Talmon 1965[2] = Sh. Talmon, *The Calendar reckoning of the Sect from the Judaean Desert*, *ScrHie* IV, pp. 162-199.

Talmon 1991 = Id. (ed.), *Jewish Civilization in the Hellenistic-Roman Period* (Philadelphia: Fortress Press).

Talmon 1994 = Id., "The Community of the Renewed Covenant: Between Judaism and Christianity", in Ulrich-VanderKam 1994, pp. 3-24.

Taylor 1990 = Joan E. Taylor, "The Phenomenon of Early Jewish-Christianity: Reality or Scholarly Invention?", *VigChr* 44, pp. 313-334.

Taylor 1993 = Ead., *Christians and the Holy Places. The Mith of Jewish-Christian Origins* (Oxford: Clarendon Press).

Taylor 2003 = J. Taylor, *D'où vient le christianisme* (Paris: Cerf).

Taylor 1995 = M.S. Taylor, *Anti-Judaism and Early Christian Identity. A Critique of the Scholarly Consensus* ("StPB" 46; Leiden: Brill).

Tcherikover 1961 = V. Tcherikover, *Hellenistic Civilization and the Jews* (Philadelphia: Fortress Press).

Testa 1962 = E. Testa, *Il simbolismo dei Giudeo-cristiani* (CMSBF 14; Jerusalem: Franciscan Printing Press, 1982 [repr.]).

Theissen 1977 = G. Theissen, *Soziologie des Jesusbewegung. Ein Beitrag zur Entstehungsgeschichte des Urchristentums* (TEH 194; München: Kaiser).

Theissen 1983[2] = Id., *Studien zur Soziologie des Urchristentums* (Tübingen: Mohr).

Theissen 1988a = Id., "Zur Entstehung des Christentums aus dem Judentum. Bemerkungen zu David Flussers Thesen", *KuI* 3, pp. 179-189.

Theissen 1988b = Id., "Vers une théorie de l'histoire sociale du Christianisme primitif", *ETR* 63, pp. 199-225.

Theissen 1989 = Id., *Lokalkolorit und Zeitgeschichte in den Evangelien* (Freiburg: Universitätverlag).

Theissen 2000 = Id., *Die Religion der ersten Christen. Eine Theorie des Urchristentums* (Gütersloh: Gütersloher Verlagshaus Gerd Mohn).

Tomson 1990 = P.J. Tomson, *Paul and the Jewish Law. Halakha in the Letters of the Apostle to the Gentiles* (CRINT III/1; Assen/Maastricht-Minneapolis: Fortress Press).

Tomson 2001 = Id., *'If this be from Heaven...'. Jesus and the New Testament Authors in their Relationship to Judaism* (Sheffield: Sheffield Academic Press).

Tomson - Lambers-Petry 2003 = Id. - Doris Lambers-Petry (eds.), *The Image of the Judaeo-Christians in Ancient Jewish and Christian Literature* (WUNT 158; Tübingen: Mohr Siebeck)

Toombs 1960 = L.E. Toombs, *The Threshhold of Christianity: Between the Testament* (Philadelphia: Fortress Press).

Trevijano 1995 = R. Trevijano, *Orígenes del Cristianismo. El trasfondo judío del cristianismo primitivo* (Plenitudo Temporis. Estudios sobre los orígines y la antigüedad cristiana 3; Salamanca: Universidad Pontificia).

Trevijano Etcheverría 2001 = R. Trevijano Etcheverría, *La Biblia en el cristianismo antiguo. Prenicenos. Gnosticos. Apócrifos* (Estella: Editorial Verbo Divino)

Trocmé 1997 = E. Trocmé, *L'enfance du christianisme* (Paris: Noêsis).

Troiani 1993a = L. Troiani, "Osservazioni sopra il quadro storico-politico del giudaismo del I secolo d.C.", in Sacchi 1993, pp. 231-243.

Troiani 1993b = Id., "Giudaismo ellenistico e cristianesimo", in G. Busi (ed.), וזאת לאנג'לו. *We-Zòt le-Angelo. Raccolta di studi giudaici in memoria di Angelo Vivian* (Testi e studi 10; Bologna: Fattoadarte), pp. 555-571.

Troiani 1996 = Id., "A proposito delle origini del cristianesimo", *At.NS* 84, pp. 7-22.

Troiani 1999a = Id., *Il perdono cristiano e altri studi sul cristianesimo delle origini* (StBi 123; Brescia: Paideia).

Troiani 1999b = Id., "Osservazioni sopra la diffusione del cristianesimo", in L. Cagni (ed.), *Biblica et Semitica*. Studi in memoria di F. Vattioni (IUO. Dip. di Studi Asiatici. Series Minor 59; Napoli: IUO), pp. 667-674.

Troiani 2000 = Id., "Il giudaismo negli autori greci e latini dei primi secoli d.C.", *ASE* 17/2, pp. 341-353.

Troiani 2001a = Id., "Gli Atti degli Apostoli e il mondo ebraico-ellenistico", *RStB* 13/2, pp. 15-24.

Troiani 2001b = Id., "La circoncisione nel Nuovo Testamento e la testimonianza degli autori greci e latini", in Filoramo-Gianotto 2001, pp. 95-107.

Troiani 2001c = Id., rev. of Jossa 1991 (revised Edition, Roma: Carocci, 2000), *RivBib* 49, pp. 362-370.

Troiani 2002 = Id., rev. of Jossa 2001b, *Henoch* 24/3, pp. 355-365.

Tyson 1992 = J.B. Tyson, *Images of Judaism in Luke-Acts* (Columbia S.C.: University of South Carolina Press).

Tyson 1995 = Id., "Jews and Judaism in Luke-Acts: Reading as a Godfearer", *NTS* 41/1, pp. 19-38.

Uglione 2002 = R. Uglione (ed.), *"Millennium": L'attesa della fine nei primi secoli cristiani* – Atti delle III Giornate Patristiche Torinesi, Torino 23-24 ottobre 2000 (Torino: Celid).

Ulrich-VanderKam 1994 = E.C. Ulrich-J.C. VanderKam (eds.), *The Community of the Renewed Covenant* – The Notre Dame Symposium on the Dead Sea scrolls (Notre Dame: Notre Dame Press).

Urbach 1975 = E.E. Urbach, *The Sages. Their Concepts and Beliefs*, transl. from Hebrew by I. Abrahams (Jerusalem: The Magnes Press).

Vana 2001 = L. Vana, "La birkat ha-minim è una preghiera contro i cristiani?", in Filoramo-Gianotto 2001, pp. 147-189.

VanderKam 1984 = J.C. VanderKam, *Enoch and the Growth of an Apocalyptic Tradition* (CBQ.MS 16; Washington: University Press).

VanderKam 1992 = J.C. Vanderkam, "Implications for the History of Judaism and Christianity", in AA.VV., *The Dead Sea Scrolls After Forty Years* – Symposium at the Smithsonian Institution, October 1990 (Washington D.C.: Biblical Archaelogy Society), pp. 19-36.

VanderKam 1994 = Id., *The Dead Sea scrolls Today* (Grand Rapids Mi.: Eerdmans).

VanderKam 1996 = Id., *Enoch: A Man for All Generations* (Columbia: University Press).

VanderKam 2000 = Id., *From Revelation to Canon: Studies in Hebrew Bible and Second Temple Literature* (JSJ.S 62; Leiden: Brill).

VanderKam 2001 = Id., *An Introduction to Early Judaism* (Grand Rapids: Eerdmans).

VanderKam-Adler 1996 = Id.-W. Adler (eds.), *Jewish Apocalyptic Heritage in Early Christianity* (CRINT III/4; Assen-Minneapolis: Van Gorkum-Fortress Press).

van der Ploeg 1959 = J. van der Ploeg (ed.), *La Secte de Qumrân et les origines du Christianisme* (Paris: Desclée de Brouwer).

van Peursen 2001 = van Peursen, "Qumran Origins: Some Remarks on the Enochic/Essene Hypothesis", *RdQ* 20/78, pp. 241-253.

van Voorst 1989 = R.E. van Voorst, *The Ascents of James. History and Theology of a Jewish-Christian Community* (SBL.DS 112; Atlanta GA: Scholars Press).

Vermes 1973 = G. Vermes, *Jesus the Jew. A Historian's Reading of the Gospels* (London: Collins).

Vermes 1983 = Id., *Jesus and the World of Judaism* (London: SCM; Philadelphia: Fortress Press, 1984).

Vermes 1994³ = *The Dead Sea Scrolls: Qumran in Perspective* (London: SCM).

Vermes 2003 = Id., *The Authentic Gospel of Jesus* (Harmondsworth [Middlesex]: Penguin).

Vermes 2004 = Id., *Who Was Who in the Age of Jesus* (Harmondsworth [Middlesex]: Penguin, forthcoming).

Vidal Manzanares 1995 = C. Vidal Manzanares, *El judeo-cristianismo palestino en el siglo I* (Madrid: Trotta).

Vitelli 2004 = M. Vitelli, *I farisei dall'età di Erode al 70 d.C.: influenza, popolarità e diffusione* (Unpublished PhD Diss. in Ancient History - Università degli Studi "Federico II" of Naples: Dipartimento di discipline storiche "E. Lepore").

Vivian 1993 = A. Vivian, "I movimenti che si oppongono al Tempio. Il problema del sacerdozio di Melchisedeq", in Sacchi 1993, pp. 245-259 (Original Ed.: *Henoch* 14, 1992, pp. 97-112).

Vouga 1997 = F. Vouga, *Les premiers pas du Christiamisme. Les écrits, les acteurs, les débats* (Genève: Labor et Fides).

Wacholder 1983 = B.Z. Wacholder, *The Dawn of Qumran. The Sectarian Torah and the Teacher of Righteousness*, (Cincinnati: HUC Press).

Wacholder 1992 = Id., "Ezekiel and Ezekielianism as Progenitors of Essenianism", in Dimant-Rappaport 1992, pp. 186-196.

Wacholder 2001 = Id., "Calendars Wars between the 364 and 365-Day Year", *RdQ* 20/78, pp. 207-222.

Wehnert 1997 = J. Wehnert, *Die Reinheit des "christlichen Gottesvolkes" aus Juden und Heiden. Studien zum historischen und theologischen Hintergrund des sogennanten Aposteldekrets* (FRLANT 173; Göttingen: Vandenhoeck & Ruprecht).

Werner 1970 = E. Werner, "The Doxology in Synagogue and Church", in Petuchowsky 1970, pp. 318-370.

Whitelocke 1976 = L.T. Whitelocke, *The Development of Jewish Religious Thought in the Intertestamental Period* (New York: Vantage Press).

Wilken 1971 = R.L. Wilken, *Judaism and the Early Christian Mind* (New Haven-London: Yale University Press).

Wilken 1980 = Id., "The Christians as the Romans (and Greek) Saw Them", in Sanders 1980 = Id. (ed.), *Jewish and Christian Self-Definition*, Vol. I. *The Shaping of Christianity in the Second and Third Centuries*, pp. 100-125.

Wilken 1983 = Id., *John Chrysostom and the Jews. Rhetoric and Reality in the Late 4ᵗʰ Century* (Berkeley-Los Angeles-London: University of California Press).

Williams 1997 = M.H. Williams, "The Meaning and Function of Ioudaios in Graeco-Roman Inscriptions", *ZPE* 116, pp. 249-262.

Will-Orrieux 1992 = E. Will-C. Orrieux, *«Proselytisme juif»? Histoire d'une erreur* (Histoire; Paris: Les Belles Lettres).

Wilson 1986 = S.G. Wilson (ed.), *Anti-Judaism in Early Christianity*, Vols. I-II (Waterloo, Ontario [Canada]: Wilfried Laurier University Press).

Wilson 1995a = Id., *Related Strangers. Jews and Christians 70-170 C.E.* (Minneapolis: Fortress Press).

Wilson 1995b = Id., "The Apostate Minority", *StTh* 49/1, pp. 201-211.

Wylen 1996 = S.M. Wylen, *The Jews in the Time of Jesus: An Introduction* (New York: Paulist Press).

Yadin 1957 = Y. Yadin, *The Message of the Scrolls* (London: Weidenfeld and Nicolson, 1991 [repr.], with an Introduction by J.H. Charlesworth).

Yarbro Collins 1996 = Adela Yarbro Collins, *Cosmology and Eschatology in Jewish and Christian Apocalypticism* (Leiden-New York-Köln: Brill).

Zeitlin 1973-1978 = S. Zeitlin, *Studies in the Early History of Judaism*, voll. I-IV (New York: KTAV).

Zetterholm 2003 = M. Zetterholm, *The Formation of Christianity in Antioch. A social-scientific approach to the separation between Judaism and Christianity* (London-New York: Routledge).

Zwi Werblowsky 1971 = R.J. Zwi Werblowsky, s.v. "Christianity", *EJ* 5, cols. 505-515.

IV. *Studies on the* Didache *and on the Judaism/s of the* Didache

In this section I list more than 400 titles, which are far from exhausting the entire production of studies regarding the *Didache* and the Judaism(s) of the *Didache*. Despite its incompleteness, the following list includes those studies I believe to be valuable and those which have marked the beginning of significant currents of research and still represent a key position or a seminal advance on some aspect of research into the *Didache*.[67] For a complete list of works on the *Didache*, I refer the reader to the bibliographical aids discussed in Part I. (supra, pp. 7-9).

Lack of space and editorial requirements do not allow for the introduction and extensive comment on the titles of this Part IV. which I would see as desirable and in some cases necessary. Consequently I limit the discussion to some fundamental and preliminary observations

---

67. Concisely pointed out by Draper 1996a, pp. 1-42.

regarding the assumptions which underlie my (and some others scholars') understanding of the *Didache* in the context of 'Christian Judaism'. The latter should be envisaged as a movement emerging and developing within and alongside other Judaisms or Jewish currents in the 1st century CE and only later assuming those characteristic doctrinal and institutional traits which will contribute to distinguishing it from Judaism and to defining it as 'Early Christianity'.

In my opinion, the phase of 'cohabitation' of Christian Judaism with other contemporary Judaisms is well documented by the *Didache*, in particular by the earlier *strata* of the work, which may be dated before 70 CE.[68] In later *strata*, by contrast, those written around the end of the 1st century (or according to some, probably at the beginning of the 2nd century), there emerges a community situation that could be already defined as 'Early Christianity', as the presence of peculiar rituals and institutions seems to suggest.[69] But there is no trace yet of the Church-Synagogue controversy,[70] which will come to mark, in the second half of 2nd CE, the birth of two distinct religions, Christianity and Rabbinism (or Rabbinic Judaism). As a matter of fact some institutions present in the *Didache* appear to be a mere adaptation or transposition

68. For instance the catechetic and moral section of chapters 1-6, which recalls a previous Jewish 'treatise' on the "Two Ways" (excluding the evangelical interpolation of *Did.* 1:3b-2:1)

69. For instance the Eucharist (κυριακὴ κυρίου of *Did.* 14 (if compared with the *berakhot* of chaps. 9-10), or the ministerial situation of the community with a hierarchy of resident bishops and deacons in *Did.* 15 (if compared with the situation of itinerant charismatic ministers, apostles and prophets found in *Did.* 11-13).

70. "La separazione tra quelle che si chiamano comunemente 'la sinagoga' e 'la chiesa' è avvenuta al termine di un processo assai lungo e non fu il risultato di una decisione presa nel corso di una riunione o di un presunto 'sinodo' a proposito di una presunta maledizione", writes Vana 2001, p. 189 (cf. also Stemberger 1977 and 1990, pp. 375-389 [supra III.]), concluding a precise and well documented study in which she attempts to demolish a widespread conviction (almost a commonplace) which maintains that the separation between the two communities would have been the result of the insertion, between 85 and 100 CE, of the *birkat ha-minim* in the *Shemoneh 'Esreh* to Yavneh. For the French scholar Liliane Vana the insertion of the *birkat ha-minim* in the daily prayer of the *Eighteen Benedictions* not only helps to clarify the relations between the Jews and the Christians in the first centuries of the Christian era but also to cast a light on the developments which brought Christianity to become the official religion of the Roman Empire from the IV cent. (Ead., ibid., with reference to some passages from Epiphanius, *Pan.* 29.9.1-2). See also Tomson 2003, in Id.- Lambers-Petry 2003, pp. 8-24.

to the new Christian environment of institutions typically Jewish,[71] which are not yet perceived as either competing against or opposed to those of Christianity. If at times a contrast does arise – as in the case of the fasting of the "hypocrites" compared to those of the "others" (*Did.* 8:1) – this appears to concern distinct Jewish groups or factions, which by adhering to the Christian movement have transferred to this new environment the 'open debate' regarding the calendar (luni-solar for those of Pharisaic origin; solar for the Enochic and/or Essene-Qumranic members).[72] However there is no sign of a clear-cut division yet between the community (or communities) of the *Didache* and the other coeval Jewish groups and movements.

I deliberately avoid assuming a Judaeo-Christian context for the *Didache* because I believe that this "historical-literary phenomenon" or "historical category" is a modern invention to counteract a tendency (found in particular among early 20th century German scholars) "to consider the doctrinal development of early Christianity as completely influenced by Hellenistic culture to a point that any Jewish contribution disappears".[73] Moreover the emerging of historical and archaeological studies in the aftermath of the Second World War have proved the existence of a Judaeo-Christian phenomenon which is currently being denied by some illustrious scholars.[74] The latter observation explains why a distinguished scholar of early Christianity, M. Simonetti, excludes the *Didache* from his study of the theme of Judaeo-Christianity in the developments of the Patristic tradition between the 2nd and 4th centuries CE.[75] By contrast, J. Daniélou, animated by a 'hypertrophic' tendency to consider Judaeo-Christianity as a complex of beliefs and doctrinal elaborations, that is "as a form of Christian thought which, although not necessarily implying a link

---

71. See my studies on the community of goods in *Did.* 4:8 (Del Verme 1995), the fasting (and prayer) of the "hypocrites" in *Did.* 8:1 (Del Verme 1999), the ἀπαρχή of *Did.* 13:3-7 (Del Verme 1993.1995), now reviewed and updated in this volume.

72. Del Verme 1999.

73. Simonetti 1995, p. 117.

74. Taylor 1990 (supra, III.); Ead., *Christians and the Holy Places. The Myth of Jewish-Christian Origins* (Oxford: University Press, 1993). According to this scholar, the Nazorei were merely one of the groups described in the Christian literature as belonging to early Judaistic Christianity (Ead. 1990, p. 326). The most important documents regarding the Nazorei are those collected by Klijn-Reinink 1973 (supra, III.).

75. Simonetti, ibid.

with the Jewish community, expresses itself within the conceptual frameworks of Judaism",[76] has greatly emphasised the importance of the *Didache* in that specific context. A contemporary scholar of Judaeo-Christianity, F. Manns, can even dare to assume that the *Didache* can be regarded as a treatise of Judaeo-Christian *halakhot*.[77] In my opinion the hypothesis elaborated by M. Simon, who suggests that the most reliable criterion to define Judaeo-Christianity is the presence of a strict observance of Mosaic prescriptions – although he does not exclude references to doctrinal contents[78] – does not authorise the use of the *Didache* to document or map the reality of the Judaeo-Christian phenomenon. This historical reality – if indeed real – has to be traced in the Christian primary and secondary sources of the second half of the 2nd century CE, for instance the fragments of the Judaeo-Christian Gospels, the Pseudo-Clementine *corpus*, the Jewish and Patristic evidences and, above all, the Christian heresiological tradition (Justin, Origen, Irenaeus, Epiphanius of Salamis, Jerome and Eusebius of Caesarea).[79]

I assume that the expression 'Christian Judaism' indicates the years in which Jesus' followers still 'cohabit' with Judaism (understood as a plurality of groups and movements) and gradually and in different ways begin to move away from those institutions, practices, doctrinal concepts and organisational structure that can be defined as Jewish,[80] transferring

76. Filoramo-Gianotto 2001, p. 12.

77. Manns 2000, pp. 335-350, which further develops a study already published in 1977 (supra, III.).

78. This position is already present in two classic monographs by F.J.A. Hort, *Judaistic Christianity* (London: SPCK, 1984) and G. Hoennicke, *Das Judenchristentum im ersten und zweiten Jahrhundert* (Berlin: Akademie Verlag, 1908), to the conclusions of which M. Simon (supra, III.; Id., 1964.1965 and Simon-Benoît 1968) reiterated fifty years later to define Judaistic Christianity in particular on the basis of the criterion of observance of Mosaic prescriptions and ritual norms. I refer the reader for these and other studies to L. Cirillo, *Introduzione* to the edition by Daniélou 1958 (supra, III.), pp. V-LXV, and to the *Bibliografia* (ibid., pp. 549-562); also Filoramo-Gianotto 2001.

79. Other contributions to the topic have emerged from the IX Conference of Neo-Testamentary and Ancient Christian Studies, held in Naples on the 13-15 September 2001, on the theme: "Il giudeo-cristianesimo nel I e II sec. d. C." Cf. supra, p. 21, n. 24.

80. I agree with M. Pesce ("Il *Vangelo di Giovanni* e le fasi giudaiche del giovannismo. Alcuni aspetti", in Filoramo-Gianotto 2001, p. 48), although he prefers avoiding the adjective 'Christian' for this period, since he believes it is tied to a form of religion which establishes itself only after the second half of the 2nd century CE. Pesce

and adapting them to a new community environment.[81] Mimouni also argues that "for the period before 135 CE ...it appears unnecessary to attempt to formulate a definition of Judaeo-Christianity, because Christianity is still nothing but a current within Judaism".[82] Crossan shares the same opinion and warns his readers: "Every time I use the terms Christian or Christianity in this book,[83] I intend a sect within Judaism. I refer to Christian Judaism in the same sense as I refer to Pharisaic Judaism, Sadducean Judaism, Essene Judaism, Apocalyptic Judaism or any of the other sects and factions of the Hebrew land in the 1st century CE".

The documents available to describe 'Christian Judaism' are those writings or literary genres which constitute the earlier *strata* of the synoptic traditions and of other either coeval or immediately antecedent or subsequent canonical and non-canonical writings. Often exegetes and historians erect a barrier separating canonical books – the 'New Testament' – from other contemporary writings, labelling the latter as either 'Apostolic Fathers' or 'Apocrypha and/or Pseudepigrapha of the Old and New Testament', although the traditions present in the New Testament and in other writings belong to and represent the same historical period.[84] The *Didache* has been traditionally placed in the category of the 'Apostolic Fathers' although it is contemporary with works such as *4 Ezra* and *2 Baruch*[85] composed at more or less the same

---

delimits this intra-Judaistic phase of emerging Christianity (which I would prefer to define as 'Christian Judaism') as a period "che inizia subito dopo la morte di Gesù e *che non sappiamo quando finisca,* ma che certamente finisce in tempi diversi, a seconda delle diverse situazioni religiose e geografiche. Solo alla fine di questo periodo si può parlare di cristianesimo e comunque non prima della metà del II secolo" (ibid.).

81. Supra, n. 69. The *berākhôth* of *Did.* 9-10, some elements of the Christian baptism in *Did.* 7, and many traits of Jewish apocalyptic flown into *Did.* 16 (see Del Verme 2001c, and Chap. 5 of this volume) may be interpreted in this sense.

82. Mimouni 1998a (supra, III.), p. 40.

83. Crossan 1998, p. XXXIII.

84. For this historical-literary perspective, see Del Verme 1989 (supra, III.), in particular pp. 15-20, with *Bibliografia.* More generally, Charlesworth 1985 (supra, III.); Id., "A History of Pseudepigrapha Research: The Reemerging Importance of the Pseudepigrapha", in *ANRW* 19.1 (Berlin-New York: W. de Gruyter, 1979), pp. 54-88; and M. Pesce, "Orientamenti e problemi dell'attuale rinascita di studi sugli scritti «pseudepigrafi» dell'Antico Testamento", in *Gesù Apostolo e Sommo Sacerdote. Studi biblici in memoria di P. Teodorico Ballarini* (Casale Monferrato [Al]: Marietti, 1984), pp. 3-22.

85. M. Del Verme, "Sui rapporti tra *2Baruc* e *4Ezra.* Per un'analisi dell'apocalittica 'danielico-storica' del I sec. e.v.", *Orph. N.S.* 24/1-2, 2003, pp. 30-54.

time as John's *Apocalypse*. Unfortunately this group of texts comes to be divided into distinct categories as though it were possible to operate a clear-cut distinction between 'Jewish' and 'Christian' writings.[86] Exemplary in this regard is the case of the *Apocalypse,* which the majority of exegetes regard as 'originally' Christian and very few as 'originally' Jewish.[87] These debates induce us to conclude that the supposed Jewish and Christian texts should be studied and discussed together, since they share and represent a common ideological and institutional context.[88] That Acts 11:26 reports that Jesus'disciples began to be called *christianoi* in Antioch (the capital of the Roman province of Syria, the region where according to a great number of scholars the *Didache* was written), does not mean that Christianity began there and then, since the term does not denote an institutional-doctrinal reality and a religious praxis in the sense that we understand Christianity today.[89] The passage from the *Acts* merely tells of a group of Christ's followers (consisting of Jewish and Gentile converts), that is belonging to the movement of Christ, just as the Greek term *christianos,* formed with the Latin suffix *-ianus* attached to the name *Christos,* suggests.[90]

---

86.   G. Boccaccini, along with other scholars, strongly opposes this historiographical perspective in the reading of the literary *corpora* of Middle Judaism (300 BCE-200 CE): Id., 1991.1993b.1998b (supra, III.) which he believes is inappropriate.

87.   For instance, Adela Yarbro Collins (*The Combat Myth in the Book of Revelation*, Harvard University Press, 1976) identifies in John's text Jewish and non- Jewish material (pp. 101-116). For a history of the literary problem posed by the *Apocalypse*, besides the first commentaries until 1980, cf. U. Vanni, *La struttura letteraria dell'Apocalisse* (Brescia: Queriniana, 1980²), pp. 1-104; 255-311. See also the hypothesis regarding the existence of a first edition of the *Gospel according to John* (between 68 and 70 CE, and therefore prior to the Synoptics: hypothesis already proposed by D.F. Schleiermacher in 1819), with attention to the Essene traditions identifiable in the work, now re-proposed by J.H. Charlesworth, "The Priority of John? Reflections on the Essenes and the First Edition of John", in P.L. Hofrichter (hrsg. von), *Für und wider die Priorität des Johannesevangeliums. –* Symposion in Salzburg am 10. März 2000 (Hildesheim-Zürich-New York: G. Olms Verlag, 2002), pp. 73-114.

88.   See *Appendix*, in Charlesworth 1985. The 'turning point' previously referred to (supra, III.) in the study of the Judaism of the Hellenistic-Roman period – which has also had a positive influence on the 'Italian School' – is to a certain extent the outcome of this new historiographical perspective, directly informing the problem of 'Christian origins'.

89.   Pesce 2001, p. 48, n. 3 (supra, III.).

90.   The Greek term *christianoi* in this period is quite rare. It is confirmed only by analogous Latin adjectives used as nouns, i.e *kaisarianoi* and *herodianoi,* namely Caesar's (the Caesarians) or Herod's followers (the Herodians) (cf. G. Jossa, *Il cri-*

These brief reflections, added to complete the previous sections II. and III., aim at helping the reader and student of the *Didache* profitably to peruse the rich bibliography presented below, in particular those works on the Judaism/s of the *Didache*, and to compare the results achieved by the researchers whilst inaugurating new studies on the *Didache*.

I also add a few *desiderata* or suggestions which could, at first sight, appear propaedeutical but which in the long run could prove to be extremely important both for a profitable consultation of the numerous titles listed below and for future developments in the study of the *Didache*.

1. It is important not merely to identify the presence of 'generic' Jewish influences or contributions in the text of the *Didache* but also to ask continuously probe to which Jewish group or current the institutions, rituals, norms and doctrines present in the text can be referred.[91]

2. As to the problem of determining the aspect of the 'Christian Judaism' of the *Didache*, it must be pointed out that both past[92] and recent[93] studies, which either concentrate on or make indiscriminate use of Rabbinic literature, appear to be inconclusive and insufficient compared to those which explore the problem by resorting to the use of Jewish sources of the Hellenistic and Roman period, with attention to the various Judaisms, in particular of sapiential, apocalyptic and/or Enochic-Essene *milieux*. Consequently Palestinian apocryphal and pseudepigraphical literature[94] as well as the Greek texts of the Ju-

---

stianesimo antico. Dalle origini al concilio di Nicea [Roma: Carrocci, 1997], pp. 37-38 and n. 5, who sees in the epithet of 'Christians' in Acts 11:26 a stronger self-designation of the group "che tende a contrapporsi in maniera radicale a tutto il resto della popolazione"). Probably this excellent scholar tends to overestimate the interpretation of the term *christianoi*, useful – without doubt – to support his (and others') thesis of a 'precocious' separation between Christianity and Judaism as early as the time of the mission of the "Hellenists" outside Judaea, that is in Phoenicia, in Cyprus and in Antioch of Syria (ca. 34/38 CE). Cf. Hengel 1979, chap. 2; Id. 1975 (supra, III.).

91. This methodological and historical 'preoccupation' has guided myself in writing some contributions on the *Didache* (Del Verme 1991.1993.1995.1999.2001c. 2003).

92. For example, Taylor 1886 and Alon 1958.

93. Manns 1977.2000; and, in some parts, also van de Sandt-Flusser 2002, pp. 172-179 (= Derekh Erets Materials) and passim.

94. See Charlesworth 1985 and, more in general, Chazon-Stone-Pinnick 1999 (supra, III.).

daism(s) of the Hellenistic Diaspora – in particular the gnomic, sapiential, ethical and liturgical writings – appear to be important for clarifying the identity of groups, the institutions and doctrinal beliefs[95] of the community/ies of the *Didache*.

3. As to the use of the NT literature, in order either to clarify or to interpret rituals, institutions, doctrines or even only expressions and *lexemes* present in the *Didache* – in particular if one intends to maintain the direct (literary) dependence of the *Didache* on the New Testament – I believe this must be *exclusively* limited to the later *strata* of the text, as for instance to the interpolation of the so-called "sectio evangelica" of *Did.* 1,3b-2,1 and 15,3-4. Such interpolations reveal, in fact, a clear intent of the editor of the *Didache* – second half of the 1st century[96] (or around the end of the 1st century or beginning of the 2nd century CE) to 'christianise' an earlier Jewish moral teaching regarding the 'Two Ways'.[97] More often, however, it appears that in those passages of the

---

95.   In particular, the Christology of the *Didache* still remains an unexplored and unchartered territory (E. Cattaneo already noticed, reviewing Visonà 2000, in *RdT* 42, 2001, pp. 621-625, in particular p. 624), considering however also the Christological 'poverty' of the work itself (cf. Vokes 1993). A conference has recently been held in Brescia on the 28-29 October 2003, on the theme "Vincitori e vinti nel cristianesimo delle origini", including, among the others, a speech by G. Visonà on "Una cristologia 'debole': la *Didachè*". This appears to be a good indication that scholars are starting to devote more attention to the Christological issue of the *Didache*. In this regard, I refer the reader to some former studies: Bammel 1961; Draper 1997a; and Stommel 1953, with reference to *Did.* 16. But on this eschatological-apocalyptic chapter of the *Didache* and its references (or, better, non-references) to Jesus' resurrection, see Del Verme 2001c (including a detailed bibliography); and infra, chap. 5. See also J. Verheyden, "Eschatology in the Didache and the Gospel of Matthew", in *Proceedings of the Tilburg Conference...*

96.   As to this chronology see Rordorf-Tuilier 1998², pp. 91-97. The author states that it is impossible to be more precise regarding the chronology of the *Didache* at this stage (ibid., p. 96, n. 2); cf. also Vokes 1993, pp. 209-233 (supra, I.), in particular pp. 230-231.

97.   *Sic* Visonà 2000, p. 91, referring to Nautin 1959a, pp. 191-214. As to the question of a pre-existing 'document/treatise' on the 'Duae viae' (abbr. DVD), either incorporating or underlying chaps. 1-6 of the *Didache*, there is an extensive bibliography: all the commentaries deal with the question *in extenso* and a number of studies have covered it since the discovery and publication of the Greek manuscript H54. Recently van de Sandt-Flusser 2002 has devoted four chapters to this question (see in particular chap. 5, pp. 140-190). For the different stages which have led scholars of ancient Christianity to an almost general consensus regarding the antiquity of the Jewish source underlying *Did.* 1-6, I refer the reader to Rordorf 1972b and Suggs

Didache referring to communitarian situations or to institutions known also from the NT, the religious system of the author (confronted by

1972. In the context of this historical-literary hypothesis, Brock 1990, pp. 139-152, expounds with greater precision and in a philological (but also partially historical) perspective the importance of the *Pal. Tgs.* (i.e. *Tg. Neof.*, *Tg. Ps.-J.*, and *Frg. Tg.*) in identifying and following the formation of the tradition of the 'Two Ways' as from inter-connecting the texts of Jer 21:8 and Deut 30:15,19 and those of the Old Testament (in particular *Psalms* and *Proverbs*). The learned Oxford Aramaicist is certainly not the first to point out the importance of the texts of the OT in the genesis and development of the theme of the 'Two Ways'(already before him, J.-P. Audet, G. Klein, J. Daniélou, Kl. Balzer, A. Orbe and others had discussed it), but he appears to be more attentive and precise in observing both the nuances in the formulation ("details of wording") of the various sources and the probable diachronic organisation of the motif of the 'Two Ways': from the OT context to the Judaism of the Second Temple (and Rabbinic Judaism as well) up to the NT and proto-Christian (canonical and non-canonical) literature. See, in particular, his summaries (pp. 146-148). Furthermore it appears that the solution of the *vexata quaestio* regarding the literary relations between *Did.* 1-6; *Doctr.* 1-6 and *Barn.* 18:1-21:9 is to be found in supposing, behind the three Christian texts, a multifarious Jewish tradition of the 'Two Ways', which had already had a previous revising phase with variants and particular forms documented by the many evidences which have survived in other texts (cf. W. Michaelis, *s.v. hodos*, in *TWNT* V, cols. 47-56), among which particular attention deserves 1QS (see the 'pioneering' article by Audet 1952 and Id. 1958 [supra, II.], pp. 159-161; 255ff.); *1-2 Enoch*; *Tg. Neof.*, *Tg. Ps.-J.*, *Frg. Tg.*, *T. Asher* and *T. Abr.* (discussion of the texts in Michaelis, ibid.); Fil., *Plant.*; *Vit. Mos.* (citations and other texts, ibid., cols. 59-65, in particular cols. 61ff.). This solution had already been advanced by Rordorf-Tuilier 1998[2] (I ed. 1978), pp. 22-23 and 28, and pp. 221-223; and earlier by J.-P. Audet, P. Prigent-R.A. Kraft, and St. Giet. In line with this perspective are the recent commentaries by K. Niederwimmer (1989), G. Schöllgen (1991) and J.J. Ayán Calvo (1992). It is known that the image of the 'Two Ways' and, more generally, the metaphorical use of the term 'way' appears early among the Greeks (cf., i.e. Theogn. 220.231; Pind., *Nem.* 1.25; Heracl., frg. 135 [I 181.1f., ed. H. Diels]; Pind., *Olymp.* 8.13f.; Thuc. I.122.1; Democr., frg. 230 [II 191,11f., ed. H. Diels]; Plat., *resp.* 10.600a). The image was also widespread outside the specific historical-religious context, as for instance, the eight branches of the Buddhist Way and the Chinese Tao (other citations in Michaelis, ibid., cols. 42-47). As to the famous fable by the Sophist Prodicus, portraying the image of Hercules at the crossroads (recorded by Xenoph., *Mem.* 2.1.21-34 with references also to Hes., *op.* 287-292 [in Xenoph., *Mem.* 2.1.20], to which many commentaries of the *Didache* refer in order to support the hypothesis of the universality of the motif of the 'Two Ways', that is the 'Way of Good' and the 'Way of Evil', others with the probable intention of nuancing or denying the Jewish specificity of the 'Two Ways' of the *Didache* (i.e., Quacquarelli 1998, pp. 27; Mattioli 1986, pp. 29 and 35, 61ff. [supra, II.]; also E. Norelli, "Risonanze qumraniche nella letteratura cristiana tra I e II secolo. Questioni di metodo ed esempi", in Penna 1997 [supra, III.], pp. 265-293;

common contemporary problems) induces him to propose either variant or altogether different solutions from those present in the NT.[98]

4. Consequently, the parallel often drawn between *Matthew-Luke* (and the New Testament in general) and the *Didache* in order either to clarify the nature and origins of some of the institutions present in the two sources (i.e. fasting and prayer, cf. *Did.* 8:1-3) or to determine the identity of the groups (such as 'the Perfect Ones' of *Did.* 6:1-2a or the 'ordinary' members of the community of 6:2b-3,[99] or the *hypokritai* of *Did.* 8:1-2), referring to the tithes and fasting (and prayer) of the "hypocrite Pharisees" of Matt 23:23 (par. Luke 11:42) and Luke 18:11-12 [and to Matt 5-7 in general[100]]) – along with the community of goods'

Palla 1998 and in a sense also Giannantoni 1998) – the conclusive remark by Michaelis appears to be acceptable: "This is not to say – he writes – that the fable, and esp. its introduction, is not an important instance of the metaphor of the two ways. Nevertheless, in the secular Gk. of the following period the passages which apply this figure of speech to the ethical decisions of man cannot all be regarded as under the influence of the Prodicus fable. The metaphor is older than the fable and has its own life alongside and after it. Similarly, there is no methodological justification for jumping to the conclusion that the fable influenced the use of the metaphor in Jewish and Christian writings" (tr. from *TDNT*, *s.v. hodos*, vol. V, p. 46 [in the original German edition, cit., col. 46]). A rich documentation on the *topos* of the 'Two Ways' can be found also in Niederwimmer 1989b, pp. 83-87 [supra, II.). For a parallel between Matt 5-7 and the "Two Ways" of *Did.* 1-6, see also K. Syreeni, "The Sermon on the Mount and the Teaching of the Two Ways", in *Proceedings of the Tilburg Conference...*

98.   I quote one case. The traumatic vicissitudes of the early communities of Jerusalem and of Antioch of Syria documented in Acts 15 and Gal 2, appear to be well known, as can be inferred from some passages of the *Didache*, i.e. 6:2-3. The observance of the Law in the Didachean community appears vacillate between Pharisaic rigorism, visible in the group led by James who believed in the strict observance of Mosaic prescriptions including the circumcision (see 2a: "If you can bear the entire yoke of the Lord, you will be perfect") and the more relaxed and less demanding approach of others, who limited themselves to the observance of some dietary prescriptions in order to avoid impurity and the dangers of idolatry (vv 2b-3: "but if you cannot, do what you can. As for food, bear what you can, but be very much on your guard against food offered to idols, for it is [related to] worship of dead gods"). However in the text of the *Didache* the climate of tension which, by contrast, weighs upon the struggle between Peter and Paul in Antioch (Gal 2:11-14) because of the arrival in the city of "some from James" (v 12), is absent. Nevertheless the stakes were somewhat similar.

99.   Analogously it is possible to establish a parallel with Paul's 'opponents', who appear to share some of the characteristics of the group known as 'the Perfect Ones' in *Did.* 6:1-2a (Draper 1991b).

100.   Recently Syreeni, "The Sermon on the Mount", and two decades ago Montagnini 1983.

of *Did.* 4:8, the '*aparche*' of 13:3-7 or doctrinal sections as the (escha-
tological-) apocalyptic section of *Did.* 16,[101] should not aim at stating a
direct dependence of the *Didache* on *Matthew*[102] or the New Testament.
In my opinion,[103] an opinion shared also by other scholars,[104] the *Didache* – at least in its earlier *strata*[105] – precedes the final compilation of

101. Del Verme 1993.1995.2001c. For *Did.* 16, see also J. Verheyden, "Eschatology in the Didache...", ibid.
102. Massaux 1949.1950. has been a strong supporter of the hypothesis regarding
the dependency of the *Didache* on Matthew. An excellent synthesis of the problem
regarding the relations between the NT and the *Didache* and of the various hypotheses
advanced by scholars is provided by Visonà 2000, pp. 90-121; see also Rordorf-Tuilier
1998², pp. 83-91 and 231-232, with further bibliographical references.
103. The *Didache* cannot depend entirely on the NT because the collection of the
neo-testamentary books had not yet been completed when the *Didache* was written. It is
known that the traditions which formed the NT remained 'fluid' during and after the
writing of *Matthew* and *Luke* (after ca. 70 CE), as can be inferred for instance from
Papias and Tatian. Papias (ca. 130 CE) wrote, in fact, "Logiôn kyriakôn exêgêseôs" in
five books (Eusebius, *Hist. eccl.* 3.39.1-8, 14-17), fragments of which remain regarding
an Asian tradition, resumed and re-formulated by Irenaeus, characterised by millenna-
rian accents, a widely spread current at the time of the emergence of Christianity (see
ASE 1998 [supra, III.]); and the Syrian Tatian, who was a disciple of the martyr Justin,
composed the *Diatessaron*, a sort of 'evangelical harmony'. In my opinion (also shared
by other scholars), in an historical context or perspective, the books of the NT, of the
'Apostolic Fathers' and other proto-Christian texts (contained, for instance, in the
agrapha, in the apocrypha and/or pseudepigrapha of both Old and New Testament)
either Jewish or Christian (contemporary or immediately preceding or following the
edition of the NT) should be neither considered separately nor incapsulated in distinct
compartments. I refer the reader also – besides the Manuscripts of Qumran – to the
importance of the codex of Nag Hammadi, in particular the *Gospel according to
Thomas* (NHC II,2) but also the *Gospel according to Truth* (NHC I, 3), the *Gospel
according to Philip* (NHC II, 3), and the *Gospel according to the Egyptians* (NHC III,
2; IV, 2); also to the various apocryphal *Apocalypses* and other exegetical texts found
in that settlement. As to *Matthew*'s dependence on the *Didache*, see Garrow 2003.
104. As to the question regarding the independence of the *Didache* on the existing text of Matthew Tuilier 1995, pp. 110-130, corroborates the theory with new
arguments, concluding that it is necessary to suppose "une source commune qu'il
convient de situer dans l'histoire" (ibid., p. 117). Consequently it appears that one is
not far, in the field of literary criticism (of *Matthew* and *Didache*), from the extremist
positions advanced by Massaux 1950, pp. 647-655, who envisaged the *Didache* as "un
résumé catéchétique du premier évangile". Uncertainties however still persist for some
scholars. Cf. Vokes 1964 and 1993 (supra, I.)
105. The *Didache* is a complex and stratified text which is classified as belonging
to the genre (Germ. *Gattung*) of "evolved literature" (according to Kraft 1965; see also
Draper 1996a, pp. 19-22), indicating a writing of an active and traditionalist commu-

the Gospels by Matthew and Luke. However the traditions from *Matthew* and *Luke* regarding the fasting, tithes and the prayer of the Pharisees (*Matthew* and *Luke*) and the 'hypocrites' (only in *Matthew*) could help to define the identity of the *hypokritai* of *Did.* 8:1-2 vis-à-vis that of another community group (i.e. "the Others" or "true members of the community") which perceives itself as different from the "hypocrites" (= dissidents/wicked) but not separated.[106] The picture emerging from the *Didache* is that of a community internally marred by divisions but not yet broken off from the coeval Judaism(s).[107] I believe that

nity rather than a book of a sole author. Imaginatively the *Didache* could be described as a fluvial 'vertex' (a term used by Steimer 1992), where many waters mix: "in primis" the previous and ancient traditions (in particular Jewish), which are (more often) adapted to or (at times) contrasted with the ethical and cultural needs emerging in the 'new' communitarian situation which the writer lives in or writes of. And the development process will continue, even after, with the interpolation of synoptic sections (1:3b-2:1; 15:3-4), which represent the last editorial stage. *Contra*, A. Milavec ("When, Why, and for Whom Was the Didache Created? An Attempt to Gain Insights into the Social and Historical Setting of the Didache Communities") who maintains – in my opinion too obstinately – the unity of the *Didache*: "...the Didache has an intentional unity from beginning to end which, up to this point, has gone unnoticed" (from an outline of his lecture at *The Tilburg Conference on "The Didache and Matthew"* [Tilburg, 7-8 April, 2003], forthcoming publication by the Royal Van Gorkum-Fortress Press, Assen-Minneapolis). Draper 1996a in the conclusion of paragraph 8. (= *The "Didachist" as a Redactor of Tradition*) correctly observed: "We do not know what occasion led to this compilation, except that the author wishes to apply old tradition to new circumstances in a time of transition. It is not intended to be comprehensive" (p. 24).

106. I have further studied the question regarding this specific communitarian situation: Del Verme 1999 and 2003 (in the latter with references and specific parallels with several NT traditions, in particular from the synoptic Gospels and the Pauline Epistles). For the sake of correctness I must refer the reader also to Rordorf-Tuilier 1998², pp. 36-38 and 224, who already, in his introduction and comment to *Did.* 8, wrote: "...les commentateurs de la *Didachè* ont souvent pensé que les hypocrites en question devaient être les Juifs. Mais il serait surprenant qu'un écrit comme la *Didachè*, qui doit tant à la tradition judaïque, s'exprime d'une manière aussi violente à l'égard des Juifs...En fait, celle-ci (= l'appellation d'hypocrites) doit s'appliquer à un groupe de dissidents qui recommandaient de jeûner avec les Juifs et de prier à la manière de ces derniers" (ibid., pp. 36-37). In the "Annexe", moreover, he pursues the point further: "Il est donc clair que les hypocrites évoqués par le didachiste au ch. 8 désignent principalement certains judéo-chrétiens qui restaient attachés aux pratiques rituelles du judaïsme. Mais ce judaïsme devait être celui des Pharisiens et non celui des Esséniens, puisque la *Didachè* adopte la discipline de ces derniers pour le jeûne" (ibid., p. 224).

107. See also Tomson 2001, pp. 380-391 (supra, III.); and recently Id., "The

neither the meaning nor the identity of the rival parties present in *Did.*
8:1-3 can be defined by means of a *merely literary operation* based on
the identification of literary influences and dependences between *Matthew* and the *Didache*. By contrast, the parallel between the *Didache* on
one side and *Matthew* and *Luke* on the other could prove useful and
profitable if the study of the question regarding fasting and tithes is
directed towards an examination of the tradition of the hypocrisy of the
Pharisees in its pre-editorial stage (in both *Matthew* and *Luke*) in order
to verify what and which aspect of the Pharisaic hypocrisy Matthew
and Luke were criticising with the use of the epithet or *lemma* "Hypo-
crites/hypocrisy". The conclusions of this historical-formal or morpho-
critical operation appear to be extremely interesting and, to a certain
extent, original.[108]

Halakhic Evidence of Didache 8 and Matthew 6 and the Didache Community's Relationship to Judaism", and J.A. Draper, "Does the [Final?] Version of the *Didache* and
Matthew Reflect An 'Irrevocable Parting of the Ways' with Judaism?", both in *Proceedings of the Tilburg Conference*... It must be pointed out that Draper, an excellent
scholar of the *Didache*, has recently changed his opinion with regard to an hypothesis
advanced previously in 1992 ("Christian Self-Definition against the 'Hypocrites' in
Didache 8, in E.H. Lovering jr. [ed.], SBL 1992 Seminar Papers [Atlanta: Scholars
Press], pp. 362-377 [now in Draper 1996a, pp. 223-243]). *Contra*, I refer the reader to
Niederwimmer 1989b, pp. 165-173 ("In summa: der ganze Abschnitt 8,1-3 zeigt eine
judenchristliche Gemeinde in polemischer Abgrenzung gegenüber der sie umgebenden
jüdischen Umwelt. Die Absonderung vollzieht sich an dieser Stelle in der Ablehnung
bestimmter Kultsitten des Judentums, die durch eigene Kultsitten ersetzt werden",
ibid., p. 173); and van de Sandt-Flusser 2002, pp. 291-296 ("The whole section [i.e.
Did. 8], in sum, reflects an attitude of animosity to Jews and Judaism; the unsubstantiated disparagement of the 'hypocrites' does not seem to leave open any possibilities
of reconciliation", ibid., p. 296).

108.   For this specific argument I refer the reader to Del Verme 2003, in particular
to the last points 4.5. (= "Toward a conclusion") and 5. (= "Conclusion"), in which
some Enochic and/or Essene-Qumranic traditions are considered documenting the
importance of the solar calendar and therefore of the days of Wednesday and Friday
(and, of course, Sunday) to which the "others" of *Did.* 8:1-2 refer, and on the basis of
which they contrast the "hypocrites" (= the wicked/dissidents) who choose instead the
days of Monday and Thursday for the bi-weekly fastings. This line of research exploring the presence of specific Jewish groups and/or specific Jewish traditions in the
Didache – which I had already followed for the reading/interpretation of other passages
of the *Didache* (see Del Verme 1991.1993.1995.1999.2001c) – could induce scholars
of the *Didache* to consider insufficient and inappropriate the admission or postulate of
the existence of 'generic' influences or of the 'mere' presence of Jewish traditions on
and in the *Didache*, and, consequently, that it is necessary further to investigate which
Judaism/s one is dealing with in the various sections or passages examined of the

5. Consequently there is no reason to state that in the *Didache* there is a trace of an irreversible "parting of the ways"[109] between Christian community or communities and the Jews, namely of an already accomplished separation or distinction between Early Christianity and the Synagogue. The passage *Did.* 8:1-2, according to my interpretation of the Greek lemma *"hypokritai"* (corresponding to the Hebrew-Aramaic root חנף),[110] presents the scenario of two opposing groups within the same Christian-Jewish community. The Gospel according to Matthew,[111] by contrast, would record an incipient conflict with coeval Judaism, a Judaism which is developing towards what will come to be known a few decades later as "Rabbinism".[112]

6. A final annotation. I believe that the application of socio-anthro-

---

Didache. As to the presence of and problems stemming from the two (solar and lunar) calendars in the Judaism of the Second Temple, and for the solar calendar in Qumran and the Enoch literature (in particular *1 Enoch* and *Jubilees*), besides the studies already cited (Del Verme 2003), see also Gillet-Didier 2001 and Wacholder 2001 (supra, III.).

109. On this topic in general see now Becker-Yoshiko Reed 2003.

110. U. Wilkens, s.v. Ὑποκρίνομαι κτλ., in *TWNT* VIII, cols. 558-570; E. Zucchelli, *ΥΠΟΚΡΙΤΗΣ. Origine e storia del termine* (Brescia: Paideia, 1962); J. Barr, "The Hebrew/Aramaic Background of 'Hypocrisy' in the Gospels", in Davies-White 1990 (supra, III.), pp. 307-326; M. Gertner, "The Terms Pharisaioi, Gazarenoi, Hypokritai: Their Semantic Complexity and Conceptual Correlation", *BSO(A)S* 26, 1963, pp. 245-268; P. Joüon, "ΥΠΟΚΡΙΤΗΣ dans l'Évangile et l'Hébreu *Hanef*", *RechSR* 20, 1930, pp. 312-316; R. Knierim, "חנף pervertiert sein", in *THAT* I, cols. 597-599; D. Matheson, " 'Actors': Christ's Word of Scorn", *ExpTim* 41, 1929-1930, pp. 333-334; and the dictionaries by H.-G. Liddell-R. Scott-H. Stuart Jones, *A Greek-English Lexicon...* with a *Supplement*, s.v. ὑποκρίνομαι and ὑπόκρισις (Oxford: Clarendon Press, 1968); M. Jastrow, *A Dictionary of the Targumim, the Talmud Babli and Yerushalmi, and the Midrashic Literature*, I-II (New York-London: Pardes, 1886-1903), s.v. חנף (= I, pp. 484-485); J. Levy, *Neuhebräisches und Chaldäisches Wörterbuch über die Talmudim und Midrashim*, I-IV (Leipzig: Baumgärtner, 1876-1889, repr. Darmstadt: Wissenschaftliche Buchgessellschaft, 1962), s.v. חנף (= II, pp. 83-84); and K. Seybold, s.v. חנף etc., in G.J. Botterweck-H. Ringgren (eds.) in Verbindung mit G.W. Anderson, H. Cazelles, D.N. Freedman, Sh. Talmon und G. Wallis, *Theologisches Wörterbuch zum Alten Testament*, Band III (Stuttgart-Berlin-Köln-Mainz: W. Kohlhammer, 1982), cols. 41-48.

111. From the above-mentioned publication of the *Proceedings of the Tilburg Conference* on "The Didache and Matthew" additional arguments are expected.

112. Tomson and Draper move also in this direction (supra, n. 107). By contrast, Zetterholm 2003 – it seems to me – does not add new findings to this argument: in his monograph, in fact, there are not explicit references to the *Didache*, although he studies the Christianity of the area of Antioch.

pological methodologies – discussed above in Part III. – could inaugurate a new season in the study of the *Didache*.[113] Until now, as already stated, few studies taking up this new methodological perspective have been published (Ascough 1994; Draper 1992.1995b; Milavec 1995b;[114] and Riggs 1995). This 'new' research approach or trajectory could effectively address those persisting institutional and doctrinal problems associated with and stemming from the *Didache* by contextualising the groups referred to in the text and their specific doctrines, rituals and practices in their appropriate social and religious *milieux*.

Achtemeier 1990 = P.J. Achtemeier, "Omne verbum sonat: The New Testament and the Oral Environment of Late Western Antiquity", *JBL* 109/1, pp. 3-27.

Adam 1956 = A. Adam, "Erwägungen zur Herkunft der *Didache*", *ThLZ* 81, pp. 353-356.

Adam 1957 = Id., "Erwägungen zur Herkunft der *Didache*", *ZKG* 68, pp. 1-47.

Agnoletto 1959 = A. Agnoletto, "Motivi etico-escatologici nella Didachè", in AA.VV., *Convivium Dominicum. Studi sull'Eucarestia nei Padri della Chiesa antica* (Catania: Università di Catania), pp. 259-276.

Agnoletto 1968 = Id., *La «Didachè». Lettura di un testo cristiano antico* (Milano: La goliardica).

Aldridge 1999 = R.E. Aldridge, "The Lost Ending of the Didache", *VigChr* 53, pp. 2-4.

Alfonsi 1972 = L. Alfonsi, "Aspetti della struttura letteraria della Διδαχή", in AA.VV., *Studi classici in onore di Q. Cataudella* (Catania: Edigraf), Vol. 2, pp. 465-481.

Alfonsi 1977 = Id., "Proprietà, lavoro e famiglia nella Διδαχή. Premessa alla società dei Padri", *Aug.* 17, pp. 101-106.

Alon 1958 = G. Alon, "The Halakah in the Teaching of the Twelve Apostles (Didache)", in Id., *Studies in Jewish History in the Times of the Second Temple, The Mishnah and the Talmud*, vol. I (Tel Aviv: Tel Aviv University), pp. 274-294 (now in Draper 1996a, 165-194).

---

113.   Draper 1996a, also appears to look forward to that in "The Didache in Modern Research: An Overview" (ibid., pp. 1-42), when in the presentation of the, not many, sociological and anthropological studies on the *Didache* – along with the new findings of Jewish texts and new research methodologies – he talks of "New currents in Research... " (ibid., paragraphe 12, p. 42).

114.   See also his study "When, Why , and for Whom Was the Didache Created? An Attempt to Gain Insights into the Social and Historical Setting of the Didache Communities", in *Proceedings of the Tilburg Conference...*

Aron 1966 = R. Aron, "Les origines juives du Pater", *MD* 85, pp. 36-40.

Arranz 1973 = M. Arranz, "La 'sancta sanctis' dans la tradition liturgique des Églises", *ALW* 15, pp. 31-67.

scough 1994 = R.S. Ascough, "An Analysis of the Baptismal Ritual of the Didache", *StLi* 24, pp. 201-213.

Audet 1952 = J.P. Audet, "Affinités littéraires et doctrinales du 'Manuel de Disciplin '", *RB* 59, pp. 219-238 (now in Draper 1996a, pp. 129-147).

Audet 1958 = Id., "Esquisse historique du genre littéraire de la 'bénédiction' juive et de l'eucharistie chrétienne", *RB* 65, pp. 371-399.

Balabanski 1997 = V. Balabanski, *Eschatology in the Making: Mark, Matthew and the Didache* (MSSNTS 97; Cambridge: Cambridge University Press).

Baltzer 1964 = Kl. Baltzer, *Das Bundesformular* (WMANT 4; Neukirchen: Neukirchener Verlag).

Bammel 1961 = E. Bammel, "Schema und Vorlage von Didache 16", in F.L. Cross (ed.), *Studia Patristica*. Vol. IV – Papers Presented to the Third International Conference on Patristic Studies held at Christ Church, Oxford 1959. Part II: Biblica, Patres Apostolici, Historica (TU 79; Berlin: Akademie Verlag), pp. 253-262 (ora in Draper 1996b, pp. 364-372).

Barnard 1966 = L.W. Barnard, "The Dead Sea Scrolls, Barnabas, the Didache and the Later History of the 'Two Ways'", in Id., *Studies in the Apostolic Fathers and their Background* (Oxford: Oxford University Press), pp. 87-107.

Barnard 1993 = Id., "The 'Epistle of Barnabas' and its Contemporary Setting", in *ANRW* II.27.1 (Berlin-New York: Principat), pp. 159-207.

Barnikol 1936-37 = E. Barnikol, "Die triadische Taufformel: Ihr Fehlen in der Didache und im Matthäusevangelium und ihr altkatholischer Ursprung", *ThJ* 4-5, pp. 144-152.

Bartlet 1921 = J.V. Bartlet, "The Didache Reconsidered", *JThS* 22, pp. 239-249.

Batiffol 1899 = P. Batiffol, "Une découverte liturgique", *BLE* 1, pp. 69-81.

Batiffol 1905 = Id., "L'Eucharistie dans la Didaché", *RB* 14, pp. 58-67.

Bauckham 1993 = R. Bauckham, *The Climax of Prophecy. Studies on the Book of Revelation* (Edimburgh: T. & T. Clark).

Bauer 1961 = J.B. Bauer, "Variantes de traduction sur l'hébreu?", *Muséon* 74, pp. 435-439.

Beatrice 1979 = P.F. Beatrice, "Il sermone 'De centesima, sexagesima, tricesima' dello Ps. Cipriano e la teologia del martirio", *Aug.* 19, pp. 215-243.

Beckwitt 1981 = R.T. Beckwitt, "The Daily and Weekly Worship of the Primitive Church in Relation to its Jewish Antecedents", *QuLi* 62, pp. 5-20.83-105.

Beckwitt 1996 = Id., *Calendar and Chronology. Jewish and Christian Biblical, Intertestamental and Patristic Studies* (AGJU 33; Leiden-New York-Köln: Brill).

Beckwitt 1997 = Id., "The Temple Scroll and its Calendar: Their Character and Purpose", *RdQ* 69/18, pp. 3-19.

Beer 1914 = H. Beer, *Aparché und verwandte Ausdrücke in griechischen Weihinschriften* (Würzburg: w.e.).

Bellinzoni 1992 = A.J. Bellinzoni, "The Gospel of Matthew in the Second Century", *SecCen* 9, pp. 197-258.

Benoît 1953 = A. Benoît, *Le baptême chrétien au second siècle. La théologie des Pères* (Paris: Presses Universitaires de France), pp. 5-33.

Benoît 1959 = P. Benoît, rec. A Audet 1958, in *RB* 66, pp. 594-600.

Bergadá 1993 = M.M. Bergadá, "La doctrina de los dos caminos y los dos espíritus en sus etapas iniciales y en los dos primeros siglos cristianos", *PaMe* 14, pp. 63-79.

Berger 1984 = K. Berger, "Hellenistische Gattungen im Neuen Testament", in *ANRW* II.25.2 (Berlin-New York: Principat), pp. 1031-1432.

Bergman 1976-77 = J. Bergman, "Zum Zwei-Weg Motiv. Religionsgeschichtliche und exegetische Bemerkungen", *SEÅ* 41-42, pp. 27-56.

Betz 1969 = J. Betz, "Die Eucharistie in der Didache", *ALW* 11, pp. 10-39 (now – in English tr. – in Draper 1996a, pp. 244-275).

Bigg 1904-05 = C. Bigg, "Notes on the Didache", *JThS* 5, pp. 579-589; 6, pp. 411-415.

Blanchetière 2001 = F. Blanchetière, *Enquête sur les racines juives du mouvement chrétien (30-135)* (Initiations; Paris: Cerf).

Blanchetière-Herr 1993 = Id.-M.D. Herr (eds.), *Aux origines juives du christianisme* (Jerusalem: CRFJ Service de documentation; Louvain: Peeters).

Bligh 1958 = J. Bligh, "Compositio Didaches eiusque scendan ad Evangelium Scriptum", *VD* 36, pp. 350-356.

Blum 1966 = G.G. Blum, "Eucharistie und Opfer in der Alten Kirche. Eine problemgeschichtliche Skizze", *Oec.* 1, pp. 9-60.

Boccaccini 2002 = Id. (ed.), *The Origins of Enochic Judaism*. Proceedings of the First Enoch Seminar (University of Michigan, Sesto Fiorentino, Italy, June 19-23, 2001) (Torino: Silvio Zamorani) (= Enoch 24/1-2).

Bock 1909 = J.G. Bock, "Didache IX-X. Der eucharistische Charakter und die Gliederung in Wechselgebete der 'Propheten' (resp. 'Episkopen') und des Volkes vor der Konsekration und nach der Kommunion", *ZKTh* 33, pp. 417-437; 667-692.

Botte 1949 = B. Botte, "Liturgie chrétienne et liturgie juive", *Csion* 3, pp. 215-223.

Bousset 1915 = W. Bousset, "Eine jüdische Gebetssammlung im siebenten Buch der apostolischen Konstitutionen", in *NGWG*, Berlin, pp. 435-489.

Bradshaw 1992 = P.F. Bradshaw, *The Search for the Origins of Christian Worship: Sources and Methods for the Study of Early Liturgy* (London: SPCK).

Bradshaw 1997 = Id., "Introduction: The Early Anaphoras", in Id. (ed.),

Essays on Early Eastern Eucharistic Prayers (Collegeville, Minn.: The Liturgical Press), pp. 1-18.

Braun 1960 = F.-M. Braun, "Les Testaments des XII Patriarches et le problème de leurs origines", *RB* 67, pp. 516-549.

Bridge 1997 = S.L. Bridge, "To Give or Not to Give? Deciphering the Saying of Didache 1.6", *Journal of Early Christian Studies* 5, pp. 555-568.

Brock 1990 = S.P. Brock, "The Two Ways and the Palestinian Targum", in Davies-White 1990 (supra, III.).

Brock 1993 = Id., "Fire from Heaven: from Abel's Sacrifice to the Eucharist. A Theme in Syriac Christianity", in E.A. Livingstone (ed.), *Studia Patristica*. Vol. XXV – Papers Presented at the Eleventh International Conference on Patristic Studies held in Oxford 1991 (Leuven: Peeters Press), pp. 142-158.

Brown 1961-62 = J.P. Brown, "The Form of 'Q' Known to Matthew", *NTS* 8, pp. 27-42.

Bruno 1957 = A. Bruno, *Das Buch der Zwölf. Eine rhythmische und Textkritische Untersuchung* (Stockholm: Almqvist & Wiksell).

Burkitt 1932 = F.C. Burkitt, "Barnabas and the Didache", *JThS* 33, pp. 25-27.

Butler 1960 = B.C. Butler, "The Literary Relations of Didache, ch. XVI", *JThS* 11, pp. 265-283.

Butler 1961 = Id., "The 'Two Ways' in the Didache", *JThS* 12, pp. 27-38.

Cacitti 1994 = R. Cacitti, *Grande Sabato. Il contesto pasquale quartodecimano nella formazione della teologia del martirio* (SPMed 19; Milano: Vita e pensiero).

Campenhausen 1971 = H. von Campenhausen, "Taufen auf den Namen Jesu?", *VigChr* 25, pp. 1-16.

Carmignac 1969 = J. Carmignac, *Recherches sur le 'Notre Père'* (Paris: Letouzey).

Cattaneo 1995 = E. Cattaneo, "'Rendila perfetta nell'amore. Il tema del raduno della chiesa nella 'Didachè' (9-10). Antecedenti e prolungamenti", in Id., *Evangelo, chiesa e carità nei Padri* (Roma: AVE), pp. 13-48.

Cattaneo 1997 = Id., *I ministeri nella Chiesa antica. Testi patristici dei primi tre secoli* (LCPM 25; Milano: Paoline; Augm. Bibliogr., pp. 211-215).

Cattaneo 2001 = Id., rev. Visonà 2000, in *RdT* 42, pp. 621-625.

Cazelles 1975 = H. Cazelles, "Eucharistie, bénédiction et sacrifice dans l'Ancien Testament", *MD* 123, pp. 7-28.

Cerfaux 1959 = L. Cerfaux, "La multiplication des pains dans la liturgie de la Didachè (Did. 9,4)", *Bib.* 40, pp. 943-958.

Chase 1891 = F.H. Chase, "The Lord's Prayer in the Early Church", in J. Armitage Robinson (ed.), *Text and Studies*, (Cambridge: University Press; repr. Nendeen-Liechtenstein 1967).

Cirillo 1993 = L. Cirillo, "Fenomeni profetici in tre settori della chiesa antica: Siria-Palestina, Mesopotamia, Roma", in R. Penna (ed.), *Il profetismo da Gesù di Nazaret al montanismo* – Atti del IV convegno di Studi Neotestamentari (Perugia, 12-14 settembre 1991), *RStB* 5/1, pp. 111-122.

Cirillo 2001 = Id., "L'antipaolinismo nelle Pseudoclementine. Un riesame della questione", in Filoramo-Gianotto 2001, pp. 280-303.

Clark 1959-60 = K.W. Clark, "Worship in the Jerusalem Temple after A.D. 70", *NTS* 6, pp. 269-280.

Clerici 1966 = L. Clerici, *Einsammlung der Zerstreuten. Liturgiegeschichtliche Untersuchung zur Vor- und Nachgeschichte der Fürbitte für die Kirche in Didache 9,4 und 10,5* (LWQF 44; Münster: Aschendorff).

Connolly 1923 = R.H. Connolly, "The Use of Didache in the Didascalia", *JThS* 24, pp. 147-157.

Connolly 1932 = Id., "The Didache in Relation to the Epistle of Barnabas", *JThS* 33, pp. 237-253.

Connolly 1937a = Id., "Agape and Eucharist in the Didache", *DR* 55, pp. 477-489.

Connolly 1937b = Id., "Barnabas and the Didache", *JThS* 38, pp. 165-167.

Connolly 1937c = Id., "Canon Streeter on the Didache", *JThS* 38, pp. 364-379.

Connolly 1937d = Id., "The Didache and Montanism", *Drev* 55, pp. 339-347.

Court 1981 = J.M. Court, "The Didache and St. Matthew's Gospel", *SJTh* 34, pp. 109-120.

Crossan 1998 = Id., *The Birth of Christianity. Discovering What Happened in the Years Immediately After the Execution of Jesus* (San Francisco: Harper).

Dal Covolo 1994 = E. dal Covolo, *Chiesa, Società, Politica* (Ieri oggi domani 14; Roma: LAS).

Dal Covolo 1995 = Id., *Laici e laicità nei primi secoli della Chiesa* (LCPM 21; Milano: Paoline).

Daniélou 1950 = J. Daniélou, "Une antique liturgie judéo-chrétienne", *Csion* 4, pp. 293-303.

Daniélou 1968 = Id., *La catéchèse aux premieres siècles* (Paris: Fayard).

Davies 1995 = C. Davies, "The Didache and Early Monasticism in the East and West", in Jefford 1995, pp. 352-367.

De Clerck 1980 = P. de Clerck, "La Didachè", *MD* 142, pp. 107-112.

De Halleux 1980 = A. de Halleux, "Les ministères dans la Didachè", *Irén.* 53, pp. 5-29 (now in Draper 1996b, pp. 300-320).

Dehandschutter 1995 = B. Dehandschutter, "The Text of the 'Didach: Some Comments on the Edition of Klaus Wengst", in Jefford 1995a, pp. 37-46.

Delcor 1968 = M. Delcor, "Repas cultuels esséniens et thérapeutes, thiases et haburoth", *RdQ* 6,23, 401-425 (now in Id., *Religion d'Israel et Proche-*

Orient ancien. Des Phéniciens aux Esséniens [Leiden: Brill, 1976], pp. 320-344).

Del Verme 1991 = M. Del Verme, "Didaché e Giudaismo: la ἀπαρχή di *Did*. 13, 3-7", *VetCh* 28, pp. 253-265.

Del Verme 1993 = Id., "The Didache and Judaism: the ἀπαρχή of Didache 13: 3-7", in E.A.Livingstone (ed.), *Studia Patristica*. Vol. XXVI – Papers presented at the Eleventh International Conference on Patristic Studies held in Oxford 1991 (Leuven: Peeters Press), pp. 113-120.

Del Verme 1995 = Id., "Medio giudaismo e Didaché: il caso della comunione dei beni (*Did*. 4,8)", *VetChr* 32, pp. 293-320.

Del Verme 1999 = Id., "Il digiuno bisettimanale degli ΥΠΟΚΡΙΤΑΙ e quello degli 'altri' (*Did*. 8,1). Gruppi in cerca di identità", in G. Luongo (ed.), *Munera Parva. Studi in onore di B. Ulianich*, vol. I. *Età antica e medievale* (Napoli: FEU), pp. 93-123.

Del Verme 2001a = Id., "*Didaché* e origini cristiane. Una bibliografia per lo studio della *Didaché* nel contesto del giudaismo cristiano. I", *VetChr* 38/1, pp. 5-39.

Del Verme 2001b = Id. "*Didaché* e origini cristiane. Una bibliografia per lo studio della *Didaché* nel contesto del giudaismo cristiano. II", ibid., 38/2, pp. 223-245.

Del Verme 2001c = Id., "*Did*. 16 e la cosiddetta 'apocalittica giudaica' ", *Orph*. NS 22/1-2, pp. 39-76.

Del Verme 2003a = Id., "Who are the People Labelled as "Hypocrites" in Didache 8? *A propos* of Fasting and Tithing of the "Hypocrites": *Did*. 8:1(-2), Matt 23:23 (par. Luke 11:42), and Luke 18:11-12", *Henoch* 25/3, 321-360.

Del Verme 2003b = Id., "*Didaché* e origini cristiane. Aggiornamento bibliografico per lo studio della *Didaché* nel contesto del "Giudaismo cristiano", *ASE* 20/2, pp. 495-584.

Denaux 1982 = A. Denaux, "Der Spruch von den zwei Wege im Rahmen des Epilogs der Bergpredigt (Mt 7,13-14 par Lk 13,23-24). Tradition und Redaktion", in J. Delobel (ed.), *Logia* (Leuven: University Press), pp. 305-335.

Denis-Boulet 1966 = N.M. Denis-Boulet, "La place du Notre Père dans la liturgie", *MD* 85, pp. 67-91.

der Goltz 1905 = E. von der Goltz, *Tischgebete und Abendmahlsgebete in der altchristlichen und in der griechischen Kirche* (Leipzig: w.e.).

Deussen 1972 = G. Deussen, "Weisen der Bischofswahl im 1. Clemensbrief und in der Didache", *ThGl* 62, pp. 125-135.

Dibelius 1938 = M. Dibelius, "Die Mahl-Gebete der Didache", *ZNW* 37, pp. 32-41 (now in Id., *Botschaft und Geschichte. Gesammelte Aufsätze* II [Zürich: Evangelische Verlag, 1956], pp. 117-127).

Díez Macho 1980 = A. Díez Macho, "Qaddis y Padre nuestro", *El Olivo*.

Documentación y estudios para el diálogo entra judíos y cristianos 12, pp. 23-46.

Dihle 1962 = A. Dihle, *Die Goldene Regel. Eine Einführung in die Geschichte der antiken frühchristlichen Vulgarethik* (Göttingen: Vandenhoeck & Ruprecht).

Dockx 1984 = S. Dockx, *Date et origine de la doctrine des Apôtres aux gentils (Did. 7,1-10,7; 14,1-15,2)*, in *Cronologies néotestamentaries et vie de l'Église primitive* (Louvain: Peeters), pp. 363-392.

Draper 1983 = J.A. Draper, *A Commentary on the Didache in the Light of the Dead Sea Scrolls and Related Documents*, Unpublished PhD Diss. (Cambridge: St. John's College).

Draper 1985 = Id., "The Jesus Tradition in the Didache", in D. Wenham (ed.), *Jesus Tradition Outside the Gospels* (GoPe 5; Sheffield: Academic Press), pp. 269-287 (updated in Draper 1996b, pp. 72-91).

Draper 1989a = Id., "Lactantius and the Jesus Tradition in the Didache", *JThS* 40, pp. 112-116.

Draper 1989b = Id., *Weber, Theissen and the Wandering Charismatics of the Didache*. Unpublished Paper presented at the Annual Meeting of the SBL, Anaheim: November 1989.

Draper 1991a = Id., "The Development of the "Sign of the Son of Man" in the Jesus Tradition", *NTS* 39, pp. 1-21.

Draper 1991b = Id., "Torah and Troublesome Apostles in the Didache Community", *NT* 33/4, pp. 347-372 (ora in Draper 1996a, pp. 340-363).

Draper 1992 = Id., "Christian Self-Definition against the 'Hypocrites' in Didache 8", in E.H. Lovering jr. (ed.), *SBL 1992 Seminar Papers* (Atlanta: Scholars Press), pp. 362-377 (now in Draper 1996a, pp. 223-243).

Draper 1993 = Id., "The Development of 'The Sign of the Son of Man' in Jesus Tradition", *NTS* 39, pp. 1-21.

Draper 1995a = Id., "Barnabas and the Riddle of the Didache Revisited", *JSNT* 58, pp. 89-113.

Draper 1995b = Id., "Social Ambiguity and the Production of Text: Prophets, Theachers, Bishops, and Deacons and the Development of the Jesus Tradition in the Community of the Didache", in Jefford 1995, pp. 284-312.

Draper 1996a = Id. (ed.), *The Didache in Modern Research* (AGJU 37; Leiden-New York-Köln: Brill).

Draper 1996b = Id., "Confessional Western Text-Centred Biblical Interpretation and an Oral or Residual-Oral Context", *Semeia* 73, pp. 61-80.

Draper 1997a = Id., "Resurrection and Zechariah 14.5 in the Didache Apocalypse", *Journal of Early Christian Studies* 5, pp. 155-179.

Draper 1997b = Id., "The Role of Ritual in the Alternation of Social Universe: Jewish-Christian Initiation of Gentiles in the Didache", *Listening* 32, pp. 48-67.

Draper 1998 = Id., "Weber, Theissen, and 'Wandering Charismatics' in the Didache", *JECS* 6/4, pp. 541-576.

Draper 1999 = Id., "The Genesis and Narrative Thrust of the Paraenesis in the Sermon on the Mount", *JSNT* 75, pp. 25-48.

Draper 2000 = Id., "Ritual Process and Ritual Symbol in Didache 7-10", *VigChr* 54, pp. 121-158.

Draper 2003 = Id., "A Continuing enigma: the 'Yoke of the Lord' in Didache 6.2-3 and early Jewish-Christian Relations', in Tomson - Lambers-Petry (supra, III.), pp. 106-123.

Drews 1904 = P. Drews, "Untersuchungen zur Didache", *ZNW* 5, pp. 53-79.

Dugmore 1962 = C.W. Dugmore, "Lord's Day and Easter", in *Neotestamentica et Patristica* (Leiden: Brill), pp. 272-281.

Dunn 1983 = J.D.G. Dunn, "The Incident of Antioch (Gal. 2:11-18)", *JSNT* 18, pp. 3-57.

Dunn 1991 = Id., "What was the Issue between Paul and 'Those of the Circumcision'?", in M. Hengel-U. Heckel (eds.), *Paulus und das antike Judentum* – Tübingen-Durham-Symposium im Gedanken an den 50. Todestag A. Schlatters (Tübingen: Mohr), pp. 295-313.

Dupont 1966 = J. Dupont (en collab. avec P. Bonnard), "Le Notre Père. Notes exegetiques", *MD* 85, pp. 7-35.

Faivre 1980 = A. Faivre, "La documentation canonico-liturgique de l'Église ancienne", *RSR* 54, pp. 204-219.273-297.

Faivre 1981 = Id., "Le texte grec de la Constitution ecclésiastique des apôtres et ses sources", ibid., 55, pp. 31-42.

Felmy 1993 = K.C. Felmy, "Was unterscheidet diese Nacht von allen anderen Nächten? Die Funktion des Stiftungsberichtes in der urchristlichen Eucharistiefeier nach Didache 9f. und dem Zeugnis Justins", *JHL* 27, pp. 1-15.

Ferrua 1992 = V. Ferrua, "Dal battesimo cristologico a quello trinitario: una conferma nella Didachè?", *Sal.* 54, pp. 223-230.

Filoramo-Gianotto 2001 = G. Filoramo-C. Gianotto (eds.), *Verus Israel. Nuove prospettive sul giudeocristianesimo* – Atti del Colloquio di Torino (4-5 novembre 1999) (BCR 65; Brescia: Paideia).

Finkelstein 1928-29 = L. Finkelstein, "The Birkat Ha-Mazon", *JQR* 19, pp. 211-262.

Flusser 1979 = D. Flusser, "The Two Ways", in Id., *Jewish Sources in Early Christianity* (Tel Aviv: Tel Aviv University), pp. 235-252 (Hebrew); English version (New York: Adama Books, 1987).

Flusser-Safrai 1986 = Id.-S. Safrai, "Das Aposteldekret und die Noachitischen Gebote", in E. Brocke-H.-J. Barkenings (eds.), *Wer Torah vermehrt, mehrt Leben* (Neukirchen-Vluyn: Neukirchener Verlag), 173-192.

Flusser 1987 = Id., "Paul's Jewish-Christian Opponents in the Didache", in S. Shaked-D. Shulman-G.G. Stroumsa (eds.), *Gilgul. Essays on the Transformation, Revolution and Permanence in the History of Religions. De-*

dicated to *R.J. Zwi Werblowsky* (SHR 50; Leiden-New York-København-Köln: Brill), pp. 71-90 (now in Draper 1996b, pp. 195-211).

Flusser 1994 = Id., *Das essenische Abenteur. Die jüdische Gemeinde vom Toten Meer: Auffälligkeiten bei Jesus, Paulus, Didache und Martin Buber* (Winterthur: Cardun Verlag).

Fraigneau-Julien 1960 = B. Fraigneau-Julien, "Eléments de la structure fondamentale de l'eucharistie: I. Bénédiction, anamnèse et action de grâces", *RSR* 34, pp. 35-61.

Frank 1978 = K.S. Frank, "Maleachi 1,10ff. in der frühen Väterdeutung. Ein Beitrag zu Opferterminologie und Opferverständnis in der alten Kirche", *ThPh* 53, pp. 70-78.

Fredrikson 1991 = P. Fredrikson, "Judaism, the Circumcision of Gentiles, and Apocalyptic Hope: Another Look at Galatians 1 and 2", *JThS* 42.

Freudenberger 1968-69 = R. Freudenberger, "Zum Text der zweiten Vaterunserbitte", *NTS* 15, pp. 419-432.

Gamber 1987 = K. Gamber, "Die 'Eucharistia' der Didache", *EL* 101, pp. 3-32.

Garrow 2003 = A. Garrow, *The Gospel of Matthew's Dependence of Didache* (JSNT.S; Edinburgh: T. & T. Clark International).

Geoltrain 1960 = P. Geoltrain, "Le traité de la Vie Contemplative de Philon d'Alexandrie", *Sem.* 10, pp. 5-61.

Giannantoni 1988 = G. Giannantoni, "Le due 'vie' di Parmenide", *ParPass* 43, pp. 207-221.

Gianotto 2001 = C. Gianotto, "Giacomo e il giudeocristianesimo antico", in Filoramo-Gianotto 2001, pp. 108-119.

Gibbins 1935 = H.J. Gibbins, "The Problem of the Liturgical Section of the Didache", *JThS* 36, pp. 373-386.

Giet 1966 = St. Giet, "Coutume, évolution, droit canon. A propos de deux passages de la Didachè", *RDC* 16, pp. 118-132.

Giet 1967 = Id., "La Didachè: Enseignement des douze apôtres?", *Melto* 3, pp. 223-236.

Giordano 1964 = O. Giordano, "L'escatologia nella Didachè", in *Oikoumene. Studi paleocristiani in onore del Concilio Ecumenico Vaticano II* (Catania: Univ. Di Catania. Centro di studi sull'antico cristianesimo), pp. 121-139.

Giraudo 1981 = C. Giraudo, *La struttura letteraria della preghiera eucaristica. Saggio sulla genesi letteraria di una forma* (AnBib 92; Roma: PIB).

Glover 1958-59 = R. Glover, "The Didache's Quotations and the Synoptic Gospels", *NTS* 5, pp. 12-29.

Glover 1985 = Id., "Patristic Quotations and Gospel Sources", *NTS* 31, pp. 234-251.

Gordon 1974 = R.P. Gordon, "Targumic Parallels to Acts XIII 18 and Didache XIV 3", *NT* 16, pp. 285-289.

Grant 1962 = R.M. Grant, "The Apostolic Fathers' First Thousand Years", *ChH* 31, pp. 421-429.

Graziani 1999 = D. Graziani, "Marco 2,18-20: storia e interpretazione", in L. Cagni (ed.), *Biblica et Semitica...* (supra, III., vd. Troiani 1999b), pp. 281-301.

Gribomont 1960 = J. Gribomont, " 'Ecclesiam adunare'. Un écho de l'eucharistie africaine et de la Didachè", *RthAM* 27, pp. 20-28.

Griffe 1977 = E. Griffe, "De l'Église des Apôtres à l'Église des presbytres", *BLE* 78, pp. 81-102.

Grimonprez-Damm 1990 = B. Grimonprez-Damm, "Le sacrifice eucharistique dans la Didachè", *RevSR* 64, pp. 9-25.

Gundry 1996 = R.H. Gundry, "ΕΥΑΓΓΕΛΙΟΝ: How Soon a Book?", *JBL* 115, pp. 321-325.

Hadidian 1964 = D.Y. Hadidian, "The Background and Origin of the Christian Hours of Prayer", *TS* 25, pp. 59-69.

Hamman 1966 = A. Hamman, "Le Notre Père dans la catéchèse des Pères de l'Église", *MD* 85, pp. 41-68.

Harnack 1896 = Id., *Die Apostellehre und die jüdischen Beiden Wege. Zweite verbesserte und vermehrte Auflage der kleineren Ausgabe* (Leipzig: Hinrichs).

Harris 1890 = J.R. Harris, "On the Locality of Pseudo-Barnabas", *JBL* 9, pp. 60-70.

Hartmann 1973-74 = L. Hartmann, " 'Into the Name of Jesus'. A Suggestion Concerning the Earliest Meaning of the Phrase", *NTS* 20, pp. 432-440.

Harvey 1982 = A.E. Harvey, " 'The Workman is Worthy of his Hir. Fortunes of a Proverb in the Early Church", *NT* 24, pp. 209-221.

Heinemann 1977 = J. Heinemann, *Prayer in the Talmud. Forms and Patterns* (SJ 9; Berlin-New York: W. de Gruyter) (revised version from Hebrew).

Henderson 1992 = I.H. Henderson, "Didache and Orality in Synoptic Comparison", *JBL* 111, pp. 283-306.

Henderson 1995 = Id., "Style-Switching in the *Didache*: Fingerprint or Argument?", in Jefford 1995, pp. 177-209.

Hoermann 1957 = K. Hoermann, "Das Reden im Geiste nach der Didache und dem Pastor Hermae", *MyTh* 3, pp. 135-161.

Hoffman 1991 = L.A. Hoffman, "Reconstructing Ritual as Identity and Culture", in P.F. Bradshaw-Id. (eds.), *The Making of Jewish and Christian Worship* (Notre Dame: University of Notre Dame Press), pp. 22-41.

Hofrichter 1995 = P. Hofrichter, "L'anaphore d'Addai et Mari dans l'Église d'Orient. Une eucharistie sans récit d'institution", *Ist.* 40, pp. 95-105.

Holz 1986 = T. Holz, "Der antiochenische Zwischenfall (Galater 2:11-14)", *NTS* 32, pp. 321-343.

Horbury 1982 = W. Horbury, "The Benediction of the Minim and the Early Jewish-Christian Controversy", *JThS* 33, pp. 19-61.

Horbury 1998 = Id., *Jews and Christians in Contact and Controversy* (Edinburgh: T. & T. Clark).

Hruby 1965 = K. Hruby, "Le Yom ha-Kippurim du Jour de l'Expiation", *OrSyr* 10, 4, pp. 417-422.

Hruby 1978 = Id., "Le geste de la fraction du pain ou les gestes eucharistiques dans la tradition juive", in A.M. Triacca-A. Pistoia (eds.), *Gestes et paroles dans les diverses familles liturgiques* (BEL.S 14; Roma: Ed. Liturgiche), pp. 123-133.

Jay 1981 = E.G. Jay, "From Presbyter-Bishops to Bishops and Presbyters. Christian Ministry in the Second Century: A Survey", *SecCen* 1, pp. 125-162.

Jefford 1988 = C.N. Jefford, *An Analysis of the Sayings of Jesus in the Teaching of the Twelve Apostles. The Role of the Matthean Community* (Diss. Claremont CA: University Press).

Jefford 1989a = Id., "Presbyters in the Community of the Didache", in E.A. Livingstone (ed.), *Studia Patristica*. Vol. XXI (Leuven: Peeters), pp. 122-128.

Jefford 1989b = Id., *The Sayings of Jesus in the Teaching of the Twelve Apostles* (SVigChr 11; Leiden-New York-København-Köln: Brill).

Jefford 1990 = Id., "An Ancient Witness to the Apostolic Decree of Acts 15?", *Proceedings: Eastern Great Lakes and Midwest Biblical Societies* 10, pp. 204-213.

Jefford 1992 = Id., "Tradition and Witness in Antioch: Acts 15 and Didache 6", *PRSt* 19/4, pp. 409-419.

Jefford 1995a = Id. (ed.), *The Didache in Context. Essays on Its Text, History and Trasmission* (NT.S 77; Leiden-New York-Köln: Brill).

Jefford 1995b, = Id., "Did Ignatius of Antioch Know the Didache?", in Jefford 1995a, pp. 330-351.

Jefford 1997 = Id., "Household Codes and Conflict in the Early Church", *Studia Patristica* 31, pp. 121-127.

Jefford 2001a = Id., "Conflict at Antioch: Ignatius and the Didache at Odds", *Studia Patristica* 36, pp. 262-269.

Jefford 2001b = Id., s.v. "Didache", in *Eerdmans Dictionary of the Bible*, ed. By D.N. Freedman (Grand Rapids: Eerdmans), pp. 345a-346b.

Jones 1964 = B.H. Jones, "The Quest for the Origins of the Christian Liturgies", *AthR* 46, pp. 5-21.

Jungmann 1962 = J.A. Jungmann, *La liturgie des premiers siècles jusqu'à l'époque de Grégoire le Grand* (LO 33; Paris: Cerf).

Kaestli 1996 = J.-D. Kaestli, "Où en est le débat sur le judéo-christianisme?", in Marguerat 1996, pp. 243-272.

Kittel 1950-1951 = G. Kittel, "Der Jakobusbrief und die apostolischen Väter", *ZNW* 43, pp. 54-112.

Klauser 1939 = Th. Klauser, "'Taufet in lebendigem Wasser!'. Zum religions- und kulturgeschichtlichen Verständnis von Didache 7,1-3", in Id.-

A. Rükker (eds.), *Pisciculi. Studien zur Religion und Kultur des Alter- tums*. Fs. für F.G. Dölger zum 60. Geburtstag dargeboten von Freunden (Münster: Verehrern und Schülern), pp. 157-164 (now in E. Dassmann [ed.], *Gesammelte Arbeiten zur Liturgiegeschichte, Kirchengeschichte und christlichen Archäologie* [JAC.E 3] [Münster: Aschendorff, 1974], pp. 177-183).

Klein 1908 = G. Klein, "Die Gebete in der Didache", *ZNW* 9, pp. 132-146.

Klein 1909 = Id., *Der älteste christliche Katechismus und die jüdische Pro- paganda-Literatur* (Berlin: Akademie Verlag).

Kloppenborg 1976 = J.S. Kloppenborg, *The Sayings of Jesus in the Didache. A Redactional-Critical Approach* (St. Michael's College: Diss. University of St. Michael's College).

Kloppenborg 1979 = Id., "Didache 16,6-8 and Special Matthean Tradition", *ZNTW* 70, pp. 54-67.

Kloppenborg 1995 = Id., "The Transformation of Moral Exhortation in Didache 1-5", in Jefford 1995, pp. 88-109.

Knoch 1980 = O. Knoch, "Die Stellung der Apostolischen Väter zu Israel und zum Judentum. Eine Übersicht", in J. Zmijewski-E.Nellesen (eds.), *Begegnung mit dem Wort*. Fs. für H. Zimmermann (BBB 53; Bonn: Peter Hanstein), pp. 347-378.

Köhler 1987 = W.D. Köhler, *Die Rezeption des Matthäusevangeliums in der Zeit vor Irenäus* (WUNT 2, Series 24; Tübingen: Mohr).

Kollmann 1990 = B. Kollmann, *Ursprung und Gestalt der frühchristlichen Mahlfeier* (GTA 43; Göttingen: Vandenhoeck & Ruprecht).

Konidaris 1964 = G. Konidaris, "De la prétendue divergence des formes dans le régime du christianisme primitif. Ministres et ministères du temps des Apôtres à la mort de saint Polycarpe", *Ist.* 10, pp. 59-92.

Köster 1957 = H. Köster, *Synoptische Überlieferung bei den apostolischen Vätern* ("TU" 65; Berlin: Akademie Verlag).

Kraft 1992 = R.A. Kraft, "Didache", in *AncBDict* II, pp. 197-198.

Kretschmar 1964 = G. Kretschmar, "Ein Beitrag zur Frage nach dem Ur- sprung frühchristlicher Askese", *ZThK* 61, pp. 27-67.

Kuhn 1958 = K.G. Kuhn, "The Lord's Supper and the Communal Meal at Qumran", in K. Stendahl (ed.), *The Scrolls and the New Testament* (New York: Harper & Brothers), pp. 65-93.

Ladeuze 1902 = P. Ladeuze, "L'Eucharistie et les repas communs des fidèles dans la Didache", *ROC* 7, pp. 339-359.

Lake 1905 = K. Lake, "The Didache", in *The New Testament in the Apo- stolic Fathers by a Commitee of the Oxford Society of Historical Theo- logy* (Oxford: Clarendon), pp. 24-36.

Lanne 1977 = E. Lanne, "L'Église une dans la prière eucharistique", *Irén.* 50, pp. 46-58.

Layton 1968 = B. Layton, "The Sources, Date and Trasmission of Didache 1.3b-2.1", *HThR* 61, pp. 343-383.

Leloir 1991 = L. Leloir, "Et laissez les prophètes scend scend autant qu'ils voudront", in AA.VV., *Atti del IX Congresso Tomistico Internazionale*, Vol. V. *Problemi teologici alla luce dell'Aquinate* (StTom 44; Città del Vaticano: LEV), pp. 380-393.

Lemaire 1971 = A. Lemaire, *Les Ministères aux origines de l'Église* (LeDiv 68; Paris: Cerf).

Lietzmann 1926 = H. Lietzmann, *Messe und Herrenmahl. Studie zur Geschichte der Liturgie* (AKG 8; Bonn: Weber; Berlin 1955[3]).

Lods 1979 = M. Lods, "Préface eucharistique et confession de foi. Aperçu sur les premiers textes liturgiques chrétiens", *RHPhR* 59, pp. 121-142.

Logan 1998 = A.H.B. Logan, "Post-Baptismal Chrismation in Syria: The Evidence of Ignatius, the 'Didache' and the 'Apostolic Constitutions' ", *JThS* 49, pp. 92-108.

Lohmann 1989 = H. Lohmann, *Drohung und Verheissung. Exegetische Untersuchungen zur Eschatologie bei den Apostolischen Vätern* (BZNW 55; Berlin-New York: W. de Gruyter).

Loisy 1921 = A. Loisy, "La Didaché et les lettres des Pères apostoliques", *RHLR* 4, pp. 433-481.

Lupieri 1993 = E. Lupieri, "Il battesimo di Giovanni Battista e il movimento battistico", in *Battesimo-Purificazione-Rinascita*, from *Dizionario di spiritualità biblico-patristica* (Roma: Borla), VI, pp. 63-75.

Machielsen 1981 = J.J. Machielsen, "Le problème du mal selon les pères apostoliques", *EeT(O)* 12, pp. 195-222.

Magne 1974 = J. Magne, "Klasma, sperma, poimnion. Le voeu pour le rassemblement de Didachè IX,4", in *Mélanges d'histoire des religions offerts à H.-Ch. Puech*, Avant-propos de P. Lévy et E. Wolff (Paris: Cerf), pp. 197-208.

Manns 1977 = Fr. Manns, "Un recueil de halakot judéo-chrétiennes: la Didache", in Manns 1977 (supra, III.), pp. 117-129.

Manns 2000 = Id., *Le Judéo-christianisme, mémoire ou prophétie* (ThH 112; Paris: Beauchesne), espec. Chap. V (= "La Didachê. Traité de halakot judéo-chrétiennes"), pp. 335-350.

Marguerat 1996 = D. Marguerat (ed.), *Le déchirement. Juifs et Chrétiens au premier siècle* (MoBi 32; Genève: Labor et Fides).

Marty 1930 = J. Marty, "Études de textes cultuels de prière conservés par les 'Pères apostoliques' ", *RHPhR* 10, pp. 90-98.

Massaux 1949 = E. Massaux, "L'influence littéraire de l'évangile de saint Matthieu sur la Didachè", *EthL* 25, pp. 5-41.

Massaux 1950 = Id., *Influence de l'Évangile de saint Matthieu sur la littérature chrétienne avant saint Irénée* (Louvain-Gembloux: University Press).

Massebieau 1885 = Id., "Une nouvelle interprétation de la Didachè par M. Ménégoz", *RHR* 11, pp. 333-335.

Massyngberde Ford 1966 = J. Massyngberde Ford, "A Note on Didache IX-X: Reception of the Sacrament Reserved in the Home", *StLi* 5, pp. 55-56.

Mazza 1978 = E. Mazza, "Didachè IX-X: elementi per una interpretazione eucaristica", *EL* 92, pp. 393-419 (now in Draper 1996a, pp. 276-299).

Mazza 1986 = Id., "L'Eucaristia di 1 Corinzi 10:16-17 in rapporto a Didachè 9-10", in *EL* 100, pp. 193-223.

Mazza 1988 = Id., *Le odierne preghiere eucaristiche. 1. Struttura, teologia, fonti* (Liturgia e vita 1). 2. Testi e documenti editi e inediti (Liturgia e vita 2; Bologna: EDB, 1991[repr.]).

Mazza 1990 = Id., "Temi biblici dell'eucarestia", in B. Salvarani (ed.), *Eucaristia: tra memoria e attesa* (Brescia: Morcelliana), pp. 55-63.

Mazza 1992 = Id., *L'anafora eucaristica. Studi sulle origini* (BEL.S 62; Roma: Ed. Liturgiche) (rev. in *RevSR* 68/1[1994], p. 118).

Mazza 1994 = Id., "La structure des anaphores alexandrine et antiochienne", *Irén.* 67, pp. 5-40.

McDonald 1980 = J.I.H. McDonald, *Kerygma and Didache. The Articulation and Structure of the Earliest Christian Message* (SNTS Mon. 37; Cambridge: Cambridge University Press).

McGowann 1999 = A. McGowann, *Ascetic Eucharists* (Oxford: Oxford University Press).

McKenna 1981 = M.M. McKenna, *The Two Ways in Jewish and Christian Writings of the Greco-Roman Period. A Study in the Form of Repentance Parenesis*, PhD Diss. (Pennsylvania: University of Pennsylvania).

Mees 1971 = M. Mees, "Die Bedeutung der Sentenzen und ihrer auxesis für die Formung der Jesusworte nach Didaché 1,3b-2,1", *VetChr* 8, pp. 55-76.

Menestrina 1977 = G. Menestrina, "Citazioni e intertesti biblici nella Didaché", in Id., *Bibbia, liturgia e letteratura cristiana antica* (Brescia: Morcelliana), pp. 59-87.

Menestrina 1995 = Id., "L'immagine delle 'due vie nei Padri Apostolici'", in Id., *Tra il Nuovo Testamento e i Padri* (Brescia: Morcelliana), pp. 57-74.

Menestrina 1999 = Id., "Sul testo della 'Didaché'. Riflessioni e proposte critiche", in E. Curzel (ed.), *In factis mysterium legere*. Miscellanea di studi in onore di I. Rogger in occasione del suo ottantesimo compleanno (Bologna: EDB), pp. 383-401.

Menestrina 2001 = Id., rev. Visonà 2000, in *ASE* 18/2, pp. 682-686.

Metzger 1971 = M. Metzger, "Les deux prières eucharistiques des Constitutions apostoliques", *RevSR* 45, pp. 52-77.

Metzger 1992 = Id., "A propos des règlements ecclésiastiques et de la prétendue Tradition apostolique", *RevSR* 66, pp. 249-261.

Meyer 1989 = H.B. Meyer, *Eucharistie. Geschichte, Theologie, Pastoral* (GDK 4; Regensburg: F. Pustet).

Middleton 1935 = R.D. Middleton, "The Eucharistic Prayers of the Didache", *JTS* 36, pp. 259-267.

Milavec 1992 = A. Milavec, "The Didache", *JBL* 111, pp. 715-725.

Milavec 1994 = Id., "Distinguishing True and False Prophets: The Protective Wisdom of the Didache", *Journal of Early Christian Studies* 2/2, pp. 117-136.

Milavec 1995a = Id., "The Saving Efficacy of the Burning Process in Didache 16.5", in Jefford 1995a, pp. 131-155.

Milavec 1995b = Id., "The Social Setting of 'Turning the Other Cheek' and 'Loving Ons Enemies' in Light of the Didache", *BTB* 25, pp. 131-143.

Milavec 1996 = Id., "The Economic Safety Net in the Didache", in *Proceedings: Eastern Great Lakes and Midwest Biblical Societies* 16, pp. 73-84.

Milavec 1999 = Id., "How the Didache Attracted, Cooled Down, and Quenched Prophetic Fire", in *Proceedings: Eastern Great Lakes and Midwest Biblical Society* 19, pp. 103-117.

Milavec 2003a = Id., *The Didache: Faith, Hope, and Life of the Earliest Christian Communities, 50-70 C.E.* (Mahwah NJ: Paulist Press).

Milavec 2003b = Id., "Synoptic Tradition in the Didache Revisited", *JECS* 11/4, pp. 443-480.

Milavec 2003c = Id., "The Purifying Confession of Failings Required by the Didache's Eucharistic Sacrifice", *BTB* 33/2, 64-76.

Minnerath 1994 = R. Minnerath, *De Jérusalem à Rome. Pierre et l'unité de l'Église apostolique* (ThH 101; Paris: Beauchesne).

Mitchell 1995 = N. Mitchell, "Baptism in the Didache", in Jefford 1995a, pp. 226-255.

Moll 1975 = H. Moll, *Die Lehre von der Eucharistie als Opfer* (Köln: Hanstein).

Monaci Castagno 2001 = A. Monaci Castagno, "I giudaizzanti di Antiochia: bilancio e nuove prospettive di ricerca", in Filoramo-Gianotto 2001, pp. 304-338.

Montagnini 1983 = F. Montagnini, "Echi del discorso del monte nella Didaché", in *BeO* 25, pp. 137-145.

Moraw 1922 = W. Moraw, "Charismatic Ministry in the Primitive Church", *IthQ* 17, pp. 48-55.

Moule 1955 = C.F.D. Moule, "A Note on Didache IX.4", *JThS* 6, pp. 240-243.

Moule 1959-60 = Id., "A Reconsideration of the Context of Maranatha", *NTS* 6, pp. 307-310.

Moutsoulas 1964 = E.D. Moutsoulas, "ΑΠΑΡΧΗ. Ein kürzer Überlick über die wesentlichen Bedeutungen des Wortes in heidnischer, jüdischen und christlicher Literatur", *SE* 15, pp. 5-14.

Muilenburg 1929 = J. Muilenburg, *The Literary Relations of the Epistle of Barnabas and the Teaching of the Twelve Apostles* (Marburg: w.e.).

Nautin 1959a = P. Nautin, "La composition de la Didachê et son titre", *RHR* 155, pp. 191-214.

Nautin 1959b = Id., "Notes critiques sur la Didachê", *VigChr* 13, pp. 118-120.

Neymeyr 1989 = U. Neymeyr, *Die christlichen Lehrer im Zweiten Jahrhundert* (SVigChr 4; Leiden: Brill).

Neyrey 1991 = J.H. Neyrey, *Ceremonies in Luke-Acts: The Case of Meals and Table Fellowship*, in Id. (ed.), *The Social World of Luke-Acts: Models for Interpretation* (Peabody Mass.: Hendrickson), pp. 361-387.

Neyrey 1996 = Id., "Meals, Food, and Table Fellowship", in R. Rohrbaugh, *The Social Sciences and New Testament Interpretation* (Peabody Mass.: Hendrickson), pp. 159-182.

Niederwimmer 1977 = K. Niederwimmer, "Zur Entwicklungsgeschichte des Wanderradikalismus im Traditionsbereich der Didache", *WSt* 11, pp. 145-167 (now in Draper 1996b, pp. 321-339).

Niederwimmer 1982 = Id., "Textprobleme der Didache", *WSt* 16, pp. 114-130.

Niederwimmer 1995 = Id., "Der Didachist und seine Quellen", in Jefford 1995, pp. 15-36.

Norelli 1993 = E. Norelli, "L'Ascensione di Isaia nel quadro del profetismo cristiano", in R. Penna (ed.), *Il profetismo da Gesù di Nazaret al montanismo*, Atti del IV Convegno di Studi Neotestamentari (Perugia, 12-14 settembre 1991) (Bologna: EDB), pp. 123-148.

Norelli 1994 = Id., *L'Ascensione di Isaia. Studi su un apocrifo al crocevia dei cristianesimi* (Bologna: EDB).

Norelli 1997 = Id., "Risonanze qumraniche nella letteratura cristiana tra I e II secolo. Questioni di metodo ed esempi", in R. Penna (ed.), *Qumran e le origini cristiane*, *RStB* 9/2, pp. 265-293.

Novak 1983 = D. Novak, *The Image of the Non-Jew in Judaism: An Historical and Constructive Study of the Noahide Laws* (New York: The Edwin Mellen Press).

Offord 1904 = J. Offord, "The 'De duabus viis' Chapters", *PSBA* 26, pp. 105-108.

Ong 1967 = W. Ong, *The Presence of the Word* (New Haver: Yale University Press).

Otranto 1969 = G. Otranto, "Matteo 7,15-16a e gli ψευδοπροφῆται nell'esegesi patristica", *VetChr* 6, pp. 33-45.

Oulton 1940 = J.E.L. Oulton, "Clement of Alexandria and the Didache", *JThS* 41, pp. 177-179.

Palla 1998 = R. Palla, La parafrasi di Matth. 7,13-14 negli *Evangeliorum Libri* di Giovenco, in S. Lucà-L. Perria (eds.) 'Οπώρα. *Studi in onore di Mgr. P. Canart per il LXX compleanno*, II, *BBGG* 52, pp. 19-29.

Papa 1974 = B. Papa, "Profeti e dottori ad Antiochia di Siria", *Nicolaus* 2, pp. 231-254.

Pardee 1995 = N. Pardee, "The Curse that Saves (Didache 16.5)", in Jefford 1995a, pp. 156-176.

Paretsky 1997 = A. Paretsky, "The Two Ways and 'Dipsychia' in Early

Christian Literature. An Interesting Dead End in Moral Discourse'', *Ang.* 74, pp. 305-334.

Patterson 1995 = S.J. Patterson, "Didache 11-13: The Legacy of Radical Itinerancy in Early Christianity'', in Jefford 1995a, pp. 313-329.

Penna 1995 = R. Penna (ed.), *Apocalittica e origini cristiane* – Atti del V convegno di Studi Neotestamentari (Seiano, 15-18 settembre 1993), *RStB* 7/2 (in particular, *Introduzione* by R. Penna [*Apocalittica e origini cristiane: lineamenti storici*], pp. 5-17, and the article by E. Norelli [*Apocalittica: come pensarne lo sviluppo?*], pp. 163-200).

Penna 2001 = "Cristologia senza morte redentrice: un filone di pensiero del giudeocristianesimo più antico'', in Filoramo-Gianotto 2001, pp. 68-94.

Pera 1941-42-43 = C. Pera, "Eucharistia fidelium'', *Sal.* 3, pp. 81-117.4, pp. 145-172.5, pp. 1-46.

Peterson 1944 = E. Peterson, "Didachè cap. 9 e 10'', *EL* 58, pp. 3-13.

Peterson 1951 = Id., "Über einige Probleme der Didache-Überlieferung'', *RAC* 27, pp. 37-68 (now in *Frühkirche, Judentum und Gnosis. Studien und Untersuchungen* [Rom-Freiburg-Wien: Herder, 1959], pp. 146-182).

Pillinger 1975 = R. Pillinger, "Die Taufe nach der Didache. Philologisch-archäologische Untersuchung der Kapitel 7,9,10 u. 14'', *WSt* 9, pp. 152-162.

Pines 1971-76 = Sh. Pines, "The Oath of Asaph the Physician and Yohanan Ben Zabda. Its Relation to the Hippocratic Oath and the Doctrina duarum viarum of the Didache'', *PIASH* 5, pp. 223-264.

Ponthot 1959 = J. Ponthot, *La signification religieuse du "Nom" chez Clement de Rome et dans la Didache* (ALBO III. 14; Louvain: University Press).

Prigent 1960 = P. Prigent, "Une thèse nouvelle sur la Didachè'', *RThPh* 10, pp. 298-304.

Prigent 1972 = Id., "Une trace de liturgie judéo-chrétienne dans le chapitre XXI de l'Apocalypse de Jean'', *RecSR* 60, pp. 165-172.

Prostmeier 1995 = F.-R. Prostmeier, "Unterscheidendes Handeln: Fasten und Taufen gemäss Did 7,4 und 8,1'', in J.B. Bauer (ed.), *Φιλοφρόνεσις*. Fs. für N. Brox (Graz: Styria Verlag), pp. 55-75.

Puech 2001 = É. Puech, "Dieu le Père dans les écrits péritestamentaires et les manuscrits de la mer Morte'', *RdQ* 20/78, pp. 287-310.

Quaranta 1962 = P.M. Quaranta, "La comunità della nuova alleanza e la Didachè. Rapporti tra il tardo giudaismo e il cristianesimo delle origini'', *AFLF(N)* 8, pp. 49-68.

Rebell 1992 = W. Rebell, *Neutestamentliche Apokryphen und Apostolische Väter* (München: Christian Kaiser).

Reed 1995 = J. Reed, "The Hebrew Epic and the Didache'', in Jefford 1995a, pp. 213-225.

Reiff 1991 = S.C. Reiff, "The Early History of Jewish Worship'', in P.F. Bradshaw-L.A. Hoffman (eds.), *The Making of Jewish and Christian Worship* (Notre Dame: Notre Dame University Press), pp. 109-136.

Reiff 1993 = Id., *Judaism and Hebrew Prayer: New Perspective in Jewish Liturgical History* (Cambridge: Cambridge University Press).

Réveillaud 1966 = M. Réveillaud, "Pastorat et salariat au cours des premieres siècles de l'Église", *ETR* 41, pp. 27-41.

Riedmatten 1959 = H. de Riedmatten, "La Didachè: solution du problème ou étape décisive?", *Ang.* 36, pp. 410-429.

Riesenfeld 1956 = H. Riesenfeld, "Das Brot von den Bergen. Zu Did. 9,4", *Er.* 54, pp. 142-150.

Riggs 1984 = J.W. Riggs, "From Gracious Table to Sacramental Elements: The Tradition-History of Didache 9 and 10", *SecCen* 4, pp. 83-102.

Riggs 1995 = Id., "The Sacred Food of Didache 9-10 and Second-Century Ecclesiologies", in Jefford 1995a, pp. 256-283.

Robinson 1912 = J.A. Robinson, "The Problem of the Didache", *JThS* 13, pp. 339-356.

Robinson 1920 = Id., *Barnabas, Hermas and the Didache* (London: SPCK).

Robinson 1976 = J.A.T. Robinson, *Redating the New Testament* (London: SPCK).

Robles 1969 = L. Robles, "Jerarquía y carismas en la Iglesia naciente", *RET* 29, pp. 419-444.

Rordorf 1967 = W. Rordorf, "La confession de foi et son 'Sitz im Leben' dans l'Église ancienne", *NT* 9, pp. 225-238.

Rordorf 1969 = Id., "Le sacrifice eucharistique", *ThZ* 25, pp. 335-353.

Rordorf 1970 = Id., "Les prières eucharistiques de la Didachè", *FuOrOc* 1, pp. 65-82.

Rordorf 1971 = Id., "La vigne et le vin dans la tradition juive et chrétienne", *Annales de l'Université de Neuchâtel* 1969-1970, pp. 131-146.

Rordorf 1972a = Id., "Le baptême selon la Didachè", in AA.VV., *Mélanges liturgiques offerts au R.P.Dom. B. Botte (de l'Abbaye du Mont César, à l'occasion du 50e anniversaire de son ordination sacerdotale)* (Louvain: University Press), pp. 499-509 (now in Draper 1996, pp. 212-222).

Rordorf 1972b = Id., "Un chapitre d'éthique judéo-chrétienne: les deux voies", *RSR* 60, pp. 109-128 (English tr. in Draper 1996b, pp. 148-164).

Rordorf 1973 = Id., "La rémission des péchés selon la Didachè", *Irén.* 46, pp. 283-297.

Rordorf 1975 = Id., "Une nouvelle édition de la Didache", *Studia Patristica* 15/1, pp. 26-36.

Rordorf 1976 = Id., "L'eucharistie selon la Didachè", in AA.VV., *L'eucharistie des premiers chrétiens* ("PoTh" 17; Paris: Beauchesne), pp. 7-28 (now in Rordorf 1988, pp. 187-208).

Rordorf 1981a = Id., "Le problème de la transmission textuelle de Didachè 1.3b-2.1", in F. Paschke (ed.), *Überlieferungsgeschichtliche Untersuchungen* (TU 125; Berlin: Akademie Verlag), pp. 499-513.

Rordorf 1981b = Id., "The Lord's Prayer in the Light of its Liturgical Use in the Early Church", *StLi* 14, pp. 1-19, now in Id., *Lex orandi-lex credendi.*

Gesammelte Aufsätze zum 60. Geburtstag (Par. 11; Fribourg-Neuchâtel: Universitätsverlag, 1993), pp. 86-104.

Rordorf 1984a = Id., "Beobachtungen zum Gebrauch des Dekalogs in der vorkostantinischen Kirche", in *The New Testament Age. Essays in Honour of Bo Reicke*, II (Macon: Mercer University Press), pp. 431-442 (now in Id., *Lex orandi...*, cit. [see Rordorf 1981b], pp. 318-329).

Rordorf 1984b = Id., "Une nouvelle édition de la Didachè", in E.A. Livingstone (ed.), *Studia Patristica*. Vol XV. Part I – Papers Presented to the Seventh International Conference on Patristic Studies held in Oxford 1975 (TU 128; Berlin: Akademie Verlag), pp. 26-30.

Rordorf 1986 = Id., *Liturgie, foi et vie des premiers chrétiens. Études patristiques* (ThH 75; Paris: Beauchesne) (II Ed. 1988).

Rordorf 1991 = Id., "Does the Didache Contain Jesus Tradition Indipendently of the Synoptic Gospels?", in H. Wansbrough (ed.), *Jesus and the Oral Gospel Tradition* (JSNT.S 64; Sheffield: Sheffield Academic Press), pp. 394-423 (now in Id., *Lex orandi...*, cit., pp. 330-359).

Rordorf 1993 = Id., "Terra Incognita. Recent Research on Christian Apocryphal Literature especially on Some Acts of Apostles", in E.A. Livingstone (ed.), *Studia Patristica*. Vol. XXV – Papers Presented at the Eleventh Conference on Patristic Studies held in Oxford 1991 (Leuven: Peeters), pp. 142-158.

Rordorf 1996 = Id., "Le preghiere della cena in Didachè 9-10: un nuovo status quaestionis", in E. Manicardi-F. Ruggiero (eds.), *Liturgia ed evangelizzazione nell'epoca dei Padri e nella Chiesa del Vaticano II. Studi in onore di E. Lodi* (Bologna: EDB), pp. 55-76 (German tr., in *VigChr* 51/ 1997, pp. 229-246).

Rordorf 1997 = Id., "Die Mahlgebete in Didache Kap. 9-10", *VigChr* 51/3, pp. 229-246.

Rordorf 1999 = Id., "Ta agia tois agiois", *Irén.* 72/3-4, pp. 346-364.

Rordorf 2001 = Id., "La Didachè en 1999", in M.F. Wiles-E.J. Yarnold (eds.), *Papers Presented at the 13th International Conference on Patristic Studies in Oxford 1999, Studia Patristica* 36, pp. 293-299.

Rouwhorst 1980 = G.A.M. Rouwhorst, "Bénédiction, action des grâces, supplication. Les oraisons de la table dans le judaïsme et les célébrations de l'eucharistie des chrétiens syriaques", *QuLi* 61, pp. 211-240.

Rouwhorst 1993 = Id., "La célébration de l'Eucharistie dans l'Église primitive", *QuLi* 74, pp. 89-112.

Rufe 1994 = J.B. Rufe, *Early Christian Fasting: a Study of Creative Adaptation* (Charlottesville, Va.: Diss. University of Virginia).

Ruwet 1943 = J. Ruwet, "Les 'Antilegomena' dans les oeuvres d'Origene", *Bib.* 23, pp. 18-42.

Salvarani 1986 = B. Salvarani, "L'eucarestia di Didachè IX-X alla luce della teologia giovannea: un'ipotesi", *RivBib* 34, pp. 369-390.

Sandelin 1986 = K.-G. Sandelin, *Wisdom as Nourisher. A Study of an Old Testament Thema, its Development within Early Judaism and Its Impact on Early Christianity* (AAAbo Series A 64,3; Åbo: Åbo Akademi).

Sass 1951 = G. Sass, "Die Apostel in der Didache", in W. Schmauch (ed.), *In memoriam E. Lohmeyer* (Stuttgart: Evangelisches Verlagswerk), pp. 233-239.

Schiffman 1987 = L.H. Schiffman, "The Dead Sea Scrolls and the Early History of Jewish Liturgy", in L.I. Levine (ed.), *The Synagogue in Late Antiquity* (Philadelphia: Fortress Press), pp. 33-48.

Schille 1966 = G. Schille, "Das Recht der Propheten und Apostel – gemeinderechtliche Beobachtungen zu Didache Kapitel 11-13", in P. Wätzel-G. Schille (eds.), *Theologische Versuche*, Vol. 1 (Berlin: Evangelische Verlagsanstall), pp. 84-103.

Schöllgen 1985 = G. Schöllgen, "Die Didache, ein frühes Zeugnis für Landgemeinden", *ZNTW* 76, pp. 140-143.

Schöllgen 1986 = Id., "Die Didache als Kirchenordnung. Zur Frage des Abfassungszweckes und seinen Konsequenzen für die Interpretation", *JAC* 29, pp. 5-26 (now in Draper 1996b, pp. 43-71).

Schöllgen 1990 = Id., "Wandernde oder seßhafte Lehrer in der Didache?", *BN* 52, pp. 19-26.

Schöllgen 1995 = Id., "Balnea mixta: Entwicklungen der spätantiken Bademoral im Spiegel der Textüberlieferung der Syrischen Didaskalie", in M. Wacht (ed.), *Panchaia. Fs. K. Thraede* (JAC.E 22; Münster: Aschendorff), pp. 182-194.

Schöllgen 1996 = Id., "Pseudoapostolizität und Schriftgebrauch in den ersten Kirchenordnungen. Anmerkungen zur Begründung des frühen Kirchenrechts", in *Stimuli. Exegese und ihre Hermeneutik in Antike und Christentum. Fs. E. Dassmann* (Münster: Aschendorff), pp. 96-121.

Schöllgen 1997 = Id., "Der Abfassungszweck der frühchristlichen Kirchenordnungen. Ammerkungen zu den Thesen Bruno Steimers", *JAC* 40, pp. 55-78.

Schweitzer 1970 = E. Schweizer, "Observance of the Law and Charismatic Activity in Matthew", *NTS* 16, pp. 213-230.

Seeberg 1906 = A. Seeberg, *Die beiden Wege und das Aposteldekret* (Leipzig: A. Deichtertische Verlagsbuchhandlung Nachf).

Seeberg 1908 = Id., *Die Didache des Judentums und der Urchristenheit* (Leipzig: A. Deichertische Verlagsbuchhandlung Nachf).

Seeliger 1989 = H.R. Seeliger, "Erwägungen zur Hintergrund und Zweck des apokalyptischen Schlußkapitels der Didache", in E.A. Livingstone (ed.), *Studia Patristica*. Vol. XXI (Leuven: Peeters), pp. 185-192 (now in Draper 1996a, pp. 373-382).

Simonetti 1995 = M. Simonetti, "Il giudeocristianesimo nella tradizione patristica dal II secolo al IV secolo", in Strus 1995, pp. 117-130.

Skehan 1963 = P.W. Skehan, "Didache 1,6 and Sirach 12,1", in *Bib.* 44, pp. 533-536.

Smith 1996 = M.A. Smith, "Did Justin Know the Didache?", in F.L. Cross (ed.), *Studia Patristica*. Vol. VII (TU 92; Berlin: Akademie Verlag), pp. 287-290.

Sparks 1978 = J.N. Sparks, *The Apostolic Fathers* (Nashville: T. Nelson).

Speyer 1967 = W. Speyer, "Ein angebliches Zeugnis für die Doctrina Apostolorum oder Pelagius bei Pseudo-Hieronymus", *VigChr* 21, pp. 241-246.

Stegemann 1988 = H. Stegemann, "Zu Textbestand und Grundgedanken von 1QS III,13-IV,26", *RdQ* 13, pp. 95-131.

Steimer 1992 = B. Steimer, *Vertex Traditionis. Die Gattung der altchristlichen Kirchenordnungen* (BZNW 63; Berlin-New York: W. de Gruyter).

Stempel 1980 = H.-A. Stempel, "Der Lehrer in der 'Lehre der Zwölf Apostel' ", *VigChr* 34, pp. 209-217.

Stommel 1953 = E. Stommel, "Σημεῖον ἐκπετάσεως" (Didache 16,6)", *RQ* 48, pp. 21-41.

Streeter 1924 = B.H. Streeter, "Didache I 3-II 1", *JThS* 25, p. 78.

Streeter 1930 = Id., "Origin and Date of the Didache", in *The Primitive Church Studied with Special Reference to the Origins of the Christian Ministry* (London: MacMillan), pp. 279-287.

Streeter 1936 = Id., "The Much-Belaboured Didache", *JThS* 37, pp. 369-374.

Strus 1995 = A. Strus (ed.), *Tra giudaismo e cristianesimo. Qumran – Giudeocristiani* (Ieri oggi domani 17; Roma: LAS).

Stuiber 1961 = A. Stuiber, "Das ganze Joch des Herrn (Didache 6,2-3)", in F.L. Cross (ed.), *Studia Patristica*. Vol. IV/2 – Papers Presented to the 3rd International Conference on Patristic Studies at Christ Church, Oxford 21-26 September 1959 (Berlin: Akademie Verlag), pp. 323-329.

Suggs 1972 = M.J. Suggs, "The Christian Two Ways Tradition: Its Antiquity, Form, and Function", in D.E. Aune (ed.), *Studies in New Testament and Early Christian Literature. Essays in Honor of A.P. Wikgren* (Leiden: Brill), pp. 60-74.

Suso Frank 1978 = K. Suso Frank, "Maleachi I,10ff. in der frühen Väterdeutung. Ein Beitrag zu Opferterminologie und Opferverständnis in der alten Kirche", *ThPh* 53, pp. 70-78.

Talley 1976a = T.J. Talley, "De la 'berakah' à l'Eucharistie. Une question à réexaminer", *MD* 125, pp. 11-39.

Talley 1976b = Id., "The Eucharistic Prayer of the Ancient Church According to Recent Research: Results and Reflections", *StLi* 11, pp. 138-158.

Talley 1984 = Id., "The Literary Structure of the Eucharist Prayer", *Worship* 58, pp. 404-420.

Talley 1992 = Id., "Structures des anaphores anciennes et modernes", *MD* 191, pp. 15-43.

Talmon 1978 = Sh. Talmon, "The Emergence of Institutionalised Prayer in Israel in the Light of the Qumrân Literature", in Delcor 1978 (supra, III.).

Taylor 1886 = C. Taylor, *The Teaching of the Twelve Apostles with Illustrations from the Talmud*. Two Lectures on an Ancient Church Manual Discovered at Constantinople Given at the Royal Institution of Great Britain on May 29th and June 6th 1885 (Cambridge: Cambridge University Press).

Taylor 1890 = Id., "The Didache Compared with the Shepherd of Hermas", *JP* 18, p. 297s.

Taylor 1907 = Id., "Traces of a Saying of the Didache", *JThS* 8, pp. 115-117.

Taylor 1992 = N. Taylor, *Paul, Antioch and Jerusalem. A Study in Relationships and Authority in Earliest Christianity* (SNNTSup. 66; Sheffield: Sheffield Academic Press).

Telfer 1939 = W. Telfer, "The Didache and the Apostolic Synod of Antioch", *JThS* 40, pp. 133-146.258-271.

Telfer 1944 = Id., "The 'Plot' of the Didache", *JThS* 45, pp. 141-151.

Terzoli 1972 = R. Terzoli, "Didachè e S. Scrittura: un esame letterario", *SCC* 6, pp. 437-457.

Theissen 1975 = G. Theissen, "Legitimation und Lebensunterhalt. Ein Beitrag zur Soziologie urchristlichen Missionäre", *NTS* 21, pp. 199-221.

Theissen 1979 = Id., "Wanderradikalismus. Literatursoziologische Aspekte der Überlieferung von Worten Jesu im Urchristentum", in Id., *Studien zur Soziologie des Urchristentums* (WUNT 19; Tübingen: Mohr, 1983 [II Ed.]), pp. 79-105.

Thiering 1980-1981 = B.E. Thiering, "Qumran Imitation and New Testament Baptism", *NTS* 27, pp. 615-631.

Tidwell 1999 = N.L.A. Tidwell, "Didache XIV:1 (ΚΑΤΑ ΚΥΡΙΑΚΗΝ ΔΕ ΚΥΡΙΟΥ) Revisited", *VigChr* 53, pp. 197-207.

Trevett 1983 = C. Trevett, "Prophecy and Anti-Episcopal Activity: A Third Error Combatted by Ignatius?", *JEH* 34, pp. 1-18.

Trevett 1998 = Id., rev. of Draper 1996b, *JThS* 49/2, pp. 818-820.

Trevijano Etcheverria 1976 = R. Trevijano Etcheverria, "Discurso escatologico y relato apocaliptico en Didache 16", *Burg.* 17, pp. 365-393.

Trevijano Etcheverria 1993 = Id., "La valoracion de los dichos no canonicos: el caso de 1 Cor. 2.9 y Ev. Tom. Log. 17", in E.A. Livingstone (ed.), *Studia Patristica*. Vol. XXIV – Papers Presented at the Eleventh International Conference on Patristic Studies held in Oxford 1991 (Leuven: Peeters), pp. 406-414.

Tuckett 1989 = Ch. M. Tuckett, "Synoptic Tradition in the Didache", in J.-M. Sevrin (ed.), *The New Testament in Early Christianity. La réception des écrits neotestamentaires dans le Christianisme primitif* (BEThL 86; Leuven: University Press), pp. 197-230 (also in Draper 1996a, pp. 93-128).

Tugwell 1990 = S. Tugwell, *The Apostolic Fathers. Outstanding Christian Thinkers* (Harrisburg: Morehouse Publishing).

Tuilier 1981 = A. Tuilier, "Didache", *TRE* 8 (Berlin-New York: Akademie Verlag), pp. 731-736.

Tuilier 1989 = Id., "La Doctrine des Apôtres et la hiérarchie dans l'Église primitive", in E.A. Livingstone (ed.), *Studia Patristica*. Vol. XVIII, 3 – Papers of the 1983 Oxford Patristics Conference (Kalamazoo-Leuven: Peeters), pp. 229-262.

Tuilier 1993 = Id., "La liturgie dans la Didachè et l'essénisme", in E.A. Livingstone (ed.), *Studia Patristica*. Vol. XXVI – Papers Presented at the Eleventh International Conference on Patristic Studies held in Oxford 1991 (Leuven: Peeters Press), pp. 200-210.

Tuilier 1995 = Id., "La Didachè et le problème synoptique", in Jefford 1995a, pp. 110-130.

Turner 1906 = C.H. Turner, "Adversaria patristica", *JThS* 7, pp. 590-605.

Turner 1912 = Id., "The Early Christian Ministry and the Didache", Studies in Early Church History (Oxford: Clarendon Press), pp. 1-31.

Urbán 1993 = A. Urbán (ed.), *Concordantia in Patres Apostolicos. 2. Concordantia in Didachen (Doctrina duodecim Apostolorum)* (Hildesheim-Zürich-New York: Olms).

Vana 2001 = L. Vana, "La birkat ha-minim è una preghiera contro i giudeo-cristiani?", in Filoramo-Gianotto 2001, pp. 147-189.

van Cangh 1995 = J.-M. van Cangh, "Le déroulement primitif de la cène (Mc 14,18-26 et par.)", *RB* 102, pp. 193-225.

van de Sandt 1992 = H. van de Sandt, "Didache 3,1-6: A Transformation of an Existing Jewish Hortatory Pattern", *JSJ* 23, pp. 21-41.

van de Sandt-Flusser 2002 = Id.-D. Flusser (eds.), *The Didache. Its Jewish Sources and Its Place in Early Judaism and Christianity* (CRINT III/5; Assen-Minneapolis: Royal Van Gorkum-Fortress Press).

Verheul 1979 = A. Verheul, "La prière eucharistique dans la Didachè", *QuLi* 60, pp. 197-207.

Verheul 1983 = Id., *La prière eucharistique dans la Primitive Église* (TEL 6; Louvain: University Press).

Verseput 1993 = D.J. Verseput, "Paul's Gentile Mission and the Jewish Christian Community. A Study of the Narrative in Galatians 1 and 2", *NTS* 39, pp. 36-58.

Vielhauer-Strecker 1997 (VI ed.) = P. Vielhauer-G. Strecker, "Das Schlusskapitel der Didache", in W. Schneemelcher (ed.), *Neutestamenliche Apocryphen*, vol. II (Tübingen: Mohr), pp. 536-537.

Vokes 1938 = F.E. Vokes, *The Riddle of the Didache. Fact or Fiction, Heresy or Catholicism?* (London-New York: SPCK).

Vokes 1955 = Id., "The Didache Re-Examined", *Theol.* 58, pp. 12-16.

Vokes 1964 = Id., "The Didache and the Canon of the New Testament", Studia Evangelica 3/2 ("TU" 88; Berlin: Akademie Verlag), pp. 427-436.

Vokes 1970 = Id., "The Didache-Still Debated", *CQR* 3, pp. 57-62.

Vööbus 1951 = A. Vööbus, "Celibacy: A Requirement for Admission to Baptism in the Early Church", *ETSE* 1.

Vööbus 1958.1988 = Id., *History of Ascetism in the Syrian Orient* (CSCO. Sub 14.81; Louvain: University Press).

Vööbus 1968 = Id., *Liturgical Traditions in the Didache* (PETSE 16; Stockholm: Impr. Orientaliste).

Vööbus 1969 = Id., "Regarding the Background of the Liturgical Traditions in the Didache. The Question of Literary Relation between Didache IX,4 and the Fourth Gospel", *VigChr* 23, pp. 81-87.

Walker 1962 = J.H. Walker, "Terce, Sext and None. An Apostolic Custom?", in F.L. Cross (ed.), *Studia Patristica*. Vol. V – Papers Presented to the 3rd International Conference on Patristic Studies, Oxford 21-26 September 1959 (Berlin: Akademie Verlag), pp. 206-212.

Walker 1966 = Id., "An Argument from the Chinese for the Antiochene Origin of the Didache", in F.L. Cross (ed.), *Studia Patristica*. Vol. VIII – Papers Presented to the 4th International Conference on Patristic Studies held at Christ Church, Oxford 1963. Part II: Patres Apostolici, Historica, Liturgica, Ascetica et Monastica (TU 93; Berlin: Akademie Verlag), pp. 44-50.

Walker 1980 = Id., "A Pre-Markan Dating for the Didache. Further Thoughts of a Liturgist", in E.A. Livingstone (ed.), *Papers on the Gospels* – Sixth International Congress on Biblical Studies (Oxford 3-7 April 1978) (JSNT.S 2; Sheffield: Sheffield Academic Press), pp. 403-411.

Walker 1981 = Id., "Reflections on a New Edition of the Didache", *VigChr* 35, pp. 35-42.

Walker 1983 = Id., "Nouveaux aperçus sur la pratique de la réserve eucharistique et la dévotion à l'Eucharistie. L'apport de l'Église romaine ancienne", *MD* 154, pp. 167-184.

Wehnert 2001 = J. Wehnert, "'Falsi fratelli, attori, superapostoli'. Per una storia della missione giudeocristiana ai pagani nel I e II secolo", in Filoramo-Gianotto 2001, pp. 265-279.

Wengst 1971 = K. Wengst, *Tradition und Theologie des Barnabasbriefes* (AKG 42; Berlin-New York: W. de Gruyter).

Zizioulas 1983 = J.D. Zizioulas, "Épiskopè et Épiskopus dans l'Église primitive. Bref inventaire de la documentation", *Irén.* 56, pp. 484-502.

Zizioulas 1994 = Id., *L'Eucharistie, l'Évêque et l'Église durant les trois premiers siècles* (Paris: Desclée de Brouwer; Orig. Edition in Greek, Athens 1965).

Chapter 2

BENEFICENCE/CHARITY OR COMMUNITY OF GOODS? *A PROPOS* OF *DID.* 4:8

1. Introduction

As previously observed, among scholars of Ancient Christianity (and of "Middle Judaism")[1] there is a general consensus regarding the historical-literary hypothesis which assumes that the first six chapters of the *Didache* – commonly referred to as the "Two Ways"[2] – have a pre-historical existence in Jewish sources (probably already written) the nature of which was mainly ethical. This type of teaching was probably circulating in a Semitic and a Greek version,[3] a fact that would account for both the similarities and the differences to be found in the different editions and/or in Christian-Jewish or merely Christian readings of the Jewish 'Two Ways'.[4]

This chapter aims to re-examine one of the issues connected with the doctrine of the 'Two Ways', that is the community of goods of *Did.* 4:8, which appears to be one of the qualifying points of the doctrine of

---

1.   This terminology is useful but should not be used either in an absolute manner or as a substitute for other expressions such as "Judaism of the Second Temple" or "Judaism of the Hellenistic Graeco-Roman period" (supra, chap. 1, pp. 17-18 and n. 14).

2.   Since the first words of the writing: Ὁδοὶ δύο εἰσί κτλ. (*Did.* 1:1a). Cf. *Barn.* 18:1b: Ὁδοὶ δύο εἰσί κτλ., and *Doctr. Ap.* 1:1a: Viae duae sunt in saeculo etc. In Herm., *mand.* 6:1,2ff. the image of the two ways is present but not a specific terminology.

3.   Cf. Rordorf 1972b, pp. 114-115; R.A. Kraft, s.v. *Didache*, in D.N. Freedman et alii (eds.), *The Anchor Bible Dictionary*, II (New York-London-Toronto-Sidney-Auckland: Doubleday, 1992), p. 197; Tuilier 1981, p. 732; Id., s.v. *Didachè*, in *DPAC* I (Casale Monferrato [Al]: Marietti, 1983), cols. 947-948.

4.   For this type of re-readings, apart from the already cited article by Rordorf 1972b, I refer the reader to the commentaries by Audet 1958, pp. 120-186; Giet 1970, pp. 39-170; Rordorf-Tuilier 1998², pp. 22-34; and 102-128; Niederwimmer 1989, pp. 48-64. See in particular van de Sandt-Flusser 2002, pp. 55-139.

the "way of life" described in section 1:2-4:14, literarily bounded by and with an inclusion of the statement: 'Η μὲν οὖν ὁδὸς τῆς ζωῆς ἐστιν αὕτη at the beginning (1:2a), and Αὕτη ἐστίν ἡ ὁδός τῆς ζωῆς at the end (4:14c) of the section. *Did.* 4:8 is an extremely difficult text to interpret. I believe, however, that it would be reductive to consider it merely as a call to practice charity or almsgiving, as some commentators of the *Didache* maintain.[5] Besides the call for charity – and always in observance of the *regula aurea* "love thy neighbour" (*Did.* 1:2b) – the text appears to suggest a more radical form of giving, or even to refer to a precise institution: the practice of the community or sharing of goods among (some of) the members of the community.

As I have argued in the previous chapter, my reading perspective of the *Didache* is placed within the new historiographical and methodological perspectives emerging in the study of Christian origins: the NT and other proto-Christian writings (including the apocrypha/ pseudepigrapha) are considered and interpreted in the light of a literary, cultural and religious history which is extremely complex and multifarious and which is often referred to as "Middle Judaism" (300 BCE to 200 CE).[6] Middle Judaism, consequently, can be regarded as the common matrix

5. For instance, Mattioli 1986, p. 125, n. 35, writes: "A differenza del generico 1,5-6 questo passo 4,5-8 tratta della generosità da esercitare verso i fratelli della comunità", referring to the commentary by Rordorf-Tuilier, p. 160, n.1. However he appears to disregard what the authors (i.e. Rordorf-Tuilier) state on p. 161, n. 7, although acknowledging the problem of the community of goods underlying *Did.* 4:8 (ibid., pp. 61ff.). Kraft 1965, merely refers to "obligations toward the needy" (p. 155); Niederwimmer 1989, pp. 138-141, extensively comments on the passage 4:5-8, in which he identifies "typisch jüdische Forderung nach möglichst grosszügiger Wohltätigkeit (insofern also um das Verhalten gegenüber den Armen)" (p. 139). His comment on 4:8 is clearly articulated and I will need to come back later to it. In his opinion the dictation of the didachist – which refers to a previous Jewish text and considering what the writer reports in chaps. 12ff. – would not go beyond "eine – nun christlich motivierte – fast selbstverständliche Gebefreudigkeit und Opferbereitschaft innerhalb der Gruppe hin, eine Einstellung, durch die der einzelne sozial gesichert war" (p. 141); and earlier: "Damit – i.e. v 8 – hat das Gebot der Mildtätigkeit und Fürsorge für den Nächsten seine schärfste und consequenteste Ausformung erhalten" (p. 140). Schöllgen 1991, comments on *Did.* 4:8 as follows: "Der Rekurs auf das Ideal der Gütergemeinschaft dient hier – wie meist in der frühchristlicher Literatur (vgl. Schöllgen, Ecclesia 286-294) – nicht der Aufforderung zur gänzlichen Aufgabe des Vermögens, sondern lediglich der nachdrücklichen Ermahnung zum Almosengeben" (pp. 112-113, n. 70).

6. The reason for this 'new' terminology can be found in Boccaccini 1991; I believe however that the 'substance' of such a terminology was already in use in the

in which and from which two great religious and cultural 'innovations' (Christianity and Rabbinism) developed. This could also be regarded as the epistemological and spatio-temporal *locus* where the Orient and the Occident met and where our civilisation was forged.[7] According to this historical and methodological perspective, the *Didache* cannot be studied merely 'against the background' of contemporary Judaism since it represents an 'integral and revealing part' of what I (along with other scholars) have defined as 'Christian Judaism', that is one of the many Jewish systems and/or movements which form the constellation of "Middle Judaism".[8]

As we see – and as will be confirmed by the analysis of *Did.* 4:8 (and of other passages that will be examined in the following chapters) – this reading perspective not only produces terminological changes or corrections but, by consciously acknowledging the pluralism and the dynamism of the groups/movements characterising the period of Middle Judaism (or, if one prefers, Judaism of the Hellenistic Graeco-Roman period or Judaism of the Second Temple), could produce relevant results, in particular regarding the understanding of the function and existence of some religious and social institutions which appear to be still active and significant in the various Judaisms of the 1st (and 2nd) century CE, including therefore also the 'Christian Judaism' of the *Didache*.[9]

2. Text and Contexts of Did. 4:8

In an unstructured but thematically coherent text regarding a series of norms informing all aspects of social life (*Did.* 4:1-11),[10] the passage under examination (v 8) closes the central section of the text: that is the pericope centred on the idea of giving and property (vv 5-8).

I would point out that, as to literary genre, chap. 4 of the *Didache* is

United States (eg by J. Neusner, J.H. Charlesworth, and other scholars) and in Europe (in particular in studies by G. Vermes and J. Carmignac to mention only some).

7.   Boccaccini, ibid., Preface.

8.   For the many *species* which can be encompassed in the *genus* "Judaism", see Boccaccini, ibid. chap. I.

9.   This direction is also followed in the subsequent chaps. Three and Four of this book. See also my earlier monograph *Giudaismo e Nuovo Testamento* (= Del Verme 1989, supra, chap. 1, III.).

10.   Cf. Niederwimmer 1989, pp. 133-144 (134f.).

characterised by a marked degree of complexity and multifariousness. As a matter of fact although one finds in the prelude (v 1) the expression *teknon mou*, by which familiar sayings belonging to the gnomic or sapiential genre are introduced – referred to as "τέκνον-sayings" from the initial apostrophe "my son" or merely "son" – in reality the chapter includes different literary units, belonging to the didactic and normative genre.[11] It is possible to identify the following sections or thematic units: 1. *community norms* (vv 1-8);[12] 2. *domestic 'table'* (vv 9-11);[13] 3. *epilogue* (vv 12-14) of the first section of the DVD, that is the 'way of life'.

I refer the reader to the synopsis of *Did.* 4:8 below along with the other two ancient Christian-Jewish (or merely Christian) versions of the "Two Ways" (*Doctr.* and *Barn.*), in order to facilitate the identification of both their similarities and their differences. Furthermore it appears to be possible to identify behind these texts (born probably in the context of Christian Judaism) traces of an ancient tradition regarding the community of goods, already hypothesised as present in the *Urtext* or *Vorlage* of the Jewish DVD.

Did. 4:8	*Doctr.* 4:8	*Barn.* 19:8a
Οὐκ ἀποστραφήσῃ	Non auertes te ab	
τόν ἐνδεόμενον,	egente,	
συγκοινωνήσεις	communicabis	Κοινωνήσεις
δέ	autem	

11.   This morphocritical (Germ. *formgeschichtlich*) annotation is important since it helps to clarify the original *Sitz im Leben* of section *Did.* 4:5-8 on which could also depend the 'problematic' interpretation of the κοινωνία of v 8. I draw the reader's attention to the significant abandonment in the course of chap. 4 (except for v 5) of the use of the didactic imperative (as defined by Audet 1958, p. 305), which appears to characterise the 'τέκνον-sayings' as, for instance, those found in 3:1-6. As a matter of fact in the literary unit *Did.* 4:1-11 one can find a string of normative futures (as well as didactic), most often alone (vv 1, 2, 3, 4, 7, 9, 10a,11) but also at times in conjunction with hypothetical propositions (vv 6 and 8). The latter construct follows the Hebrew phraseology regarding hypothetical propositions with *im* – *kî* plus a verbal form, recurring in pericopes of the casuistic genre. Cf. *Did.* 13:3-7 (Del Verme 1993, pp. 253-265 [255], herein re-presented and reviewed in chap. 4).

12.   Distinguished in: a) norms regarding the attitude toward teachers or ministers of the word (vv 1-2); b) norms regulating the proper conduct of the members of the community; c) norms concerning charity toward the poor and property (vv 5-8).

13.   It consists in a family code regulating both the behaviour of parents toward their children (v 9) and the relations between slave and master (vv 10-11).

πάντα	omnia	ἐν πᾶσιν
τῷ ἀδελφῷ	σου cum fratribus tuis	τῷ πλησίον σου
καί οὐκ ἐρεῖς	nec dices	καί οὐκ ἐρεῖς
ἴδια εἶναι.	tua esse;	ἴδια εἶναι
εἰ γὰρ	si enim	εἰ γὰρ
ἐν τῷ ἀθανάτῳ	<in im>mortalibus	ἐν τῷ ἀφθάρτῳ
κοινωνοί ἐστε,	socii sumus,	κοινωινοί ἐστε,
πόσῳ μᾶλλον	quanto magis	πόσῳ μᾶλλον
ἐν τοῖς θνητοῖς;[14]		ἐν τοῖς φθαρτοῖς;[15]
	hinc initiantes	
	esse debemus?	
	Omnibus enim	
	dominus dare	
	uult de donis suis.[16]	

The call, directed to the members of the community, to practice the κοινωνία of material goods,[17] because of an already existing participa-

---

14. Critic text: Rordorf-Tuilier 1998², p. 160.

15. Critic text: Funk-Bihlmeyer 1970³, p. 32.

16. Critic text: Schlecht 1901, p. . The reading <in im>*mortalibus* is a conjecture, but codex F (= *Monacensis* lat. 6264 [olim *Frisingensis* 64] membr. saec. XI) records the reading: *mortalibus*, accepted for instance by Audet 1958 (see synopsis, ibid., p. 147). Giet 1967, p. 233, also maintains that ἐν τῷ θάνατῳ (see *Epit.[ome canonum sanctorum apostolorum]*) is the original reading, while Niederwimmer and others prefer the conjecture proposed by Schlecht (Niederwimmer, ibid., p. 141, n. 70). In my opinion the reading-conjecture *in immortalibus*, is to be preferred to *mortalibus* of cod. F, since it is possible to suppose that during the handwriting tradition *in im* may have been 'elided' from the archetype through haplography with the preceding *enim*. Furthermore the reading *hinc initiantes esse debemus? omnibus enim dominus dare uult de donis suis* (om. *Did.* and *Barn.*), remains obscure. It is, in fact, impossible to determine whether it is a Christian addition (as the evangelical interpolation of *Did.* 1:5) or a peculiarity of *Doctr.* If the latter case is true, Audet (cit., p. 134) believes that the text could refer to a previous Jewish tradition of the *Duae viae*.

17. The neutral plurals of *Did.* 4:8: πάντα and ἐν τοῖς θνητοῖς, and those of *Barn.* 4:8: ἐν πᾶσιν and ἐν τοῖς φθαρτοῖς indicate that the community of goods is total. It informs *all* the goods, which *Did.* qualifies as *mortal* or perishable while *Barn.* defines them as *corruptible*. Also *Doctr.* 4:8 insists on the totality (*omnia*) of the community of goods but motivates it by referring to the divine will, according to which everyone is recipient (*omnibus enim dominus dare uult*) of his material goods (*de donis suis*). Such a concept is typical of Jewish morality and spirituality: the 'theology of the land' considered God's property but entrusted to man (cf. Ps 24:1; Deut 10:14; Lev

tion in higher goods,[18] appears to be unquestionably present in the three texts. The prescription figures also as formulated in a sequence of synonymous or equivalent terms and constructions, which induce us to suppose a dependence on a previous (oral or written) source.

Of course the discussion will continue regarding which of the three texts reflects more directly the supposed source of reference (which I believe is Jewish), but the presence in *Did.* 4:8 (and parr.) of a tradition regarding the community or sharing of material (and spiritual) goods appears to be documented and confirmed.

The interpretation of the κοινωνία of *Did.* 4:8 depends also from the literary context of the pericope (vv 5-8) in which the line is inserted. As argued, *Did.* 4:5-8 represents the first section or thematic unit of chap. 4 (vv 1-8) in which different, although analogously formulated, community norms are prescribed.[19] I refer the reader to the text below.

Did. 4:5-8:[20]

v 5   Do not be (Μὴ γίνου) the sort of person who holds out his hands to receive but draws them back when it comes to giving.[21]

v 6   If you have ('Εὰν ἔχῃς) [something] through the work of your

---

25:23ff.; and in particular the motivations at the basis of the social institutions of Israel, such as the Jubilee, the Sabbatical Year and the tithes).

18.   Such a participation is uniformly expressed in *Did.*, *Barn.* and *Doctr.* (in particular if one is willing to accept the conjecture *<in im>mortalibus* by Schlecht). One must observed that the contrapposition of *Did.* ἀθάνατον-θνητόν, in Greek literature (cf. W. Bauer, *Griechisch-deutsches Wörterbuch zu den Schriften des Neuen Testaments und der übrigen urchristlichen Literatur* [Berlin: Verlag Alfred Töpelmann, 1952, repr.1971], s.v. θνητός) is more frequent than the ἄφθαρτον-φθαρτόν found in *Barn.* But Niederwimmer believes the latter to be "vielleicht ursprünglich" (cit.) without providing an adequate explanation. Furthermore in all the three texts the same process of reasoning can be found: εἰ γὰρ ... πόσῳ μᾶλλον (*Did.* and *Barn.*); si enim...quanto magis (*Doctr.*), that is the first of the seven *middôth* (= hermeneutic rules) by Hillel, that of *qal wa-homer* (= *a minori ad maius* or *a fortiori*). This represents a further indication of the probable reference to an earlier Jewish source. However, the reasoning *a minori ad maius* occurs also in both Classical and Hellenistic literature.

19.   Supra, nn. 11-13.

20.   Critical text: Rordorf-Tuilier 1998², p. 160; Engl. tr. by A. Cody, in Jefford 1995a, p. 7.

21.   Parr: *Doctr.* 4:5 and *Barn.* 19:9a. The verse, as both to content and form refers to a typical sapiential maxim (cf. Sir 4:31 and Deut 15:7f.).

hands, you shall give (δώσεις) [something as] redemption of your sins.[22]

v 7   You shall not hesitate (διστάσεις) to give, and when you give you shall not grumble (γογγύσεις), for you will know who the paymaster is who gives good wages.[23]

v 8   You shall not turn away (οὐκ ἀποστραφήσῃ) anyone who is in need; on the contrary, you shall hold everything in common (συγκοινωνήσεις) with your brother, and you shall not say that anything is your own (καί οὐκ ἐρεῖς ἴδια εἶναι), for if you are partners in what is immortal (εἰ γάρ ἐν τῷ ἀθανάτῳ κοινωνοί ἐστε), [should you not be so] all the more in things that perish (ἐν τοῖς θνητοῖς)?[24]

Students of *Didache,* who tend to dwell on a mere philological analysis of single lines (and terms) of the pericope 4:5-8,[25] appear to disregard two aspects of this passage, which I believe merit more attention.[26] The first aspect is the thematic progression identifiable in the context of the community norms listed in the passage. The second is the historical value and importance of the passage itself since – consi-

---

22.   Parallels: *Doctr.* 4:6 (om. δώσεις of the *Vorlage,* and links v 6 to v 7) and *Barn.* 19:10 in the final section. In *Barn.,* however, the material assistance to the poor in atonement for one's sins is considered as one of the options (the other is the 'ministry of the word') to which the members of the community are called to practice, cf. Prigent, in Id.-Kraft, ibid., pp. 208-209 and n.1. The expiatory value of charity is constant in both Hebrew literature and spirituality of ancient, middle and Rabbinical Judaism. I refer the reader to some Biblical passages: Tob 4:10; 12:9; Sir 3:30; Dan 4:27 (LXX). See also [Strack-] Billerbeck, cit., II, pp. 561f.; and IV/1, pp. 554f. As to Christian Judaism and Early Christianity, cf. 1 Pet 4:8; *2 Clem.* 16:4, and Pol., *Phil.* 10:2.

23.   Parr: *Doctr.* 4:7 and *Barn.* 19:11a. The ideas expressed in the text are not new: for the first part of the verse, cf. Prov 3:28; Ps. Phoc. 22 (vd. *Sib. Or.* 2.78 Y), Herm., *Sim.* 9:24.2; as to the second part, see Sir 12:2; Tob 4:14; *T. Zab.* 6:6; 8:1-3; Luke 14:14; *2 Clem.* 20:4.

24.   *Did.* 4:8a (par. *Doctr.* 4:8a), which resumes Sir 4:5 (cf. Prov 3:27), om. *Barn.* The remaining part of v 8 is common to the three texts. Peculiar to *Barn.* is τῷ πλησίον (= neighbour), while *Did.* and *Doctr.* have respectively brother (τῷ ἀδελφῷ) and brothers (cum fratribus).

25.   See in particular Niederwimmer, pp. 138-141, in a constant dialogue with previous commentators and with many references to the OT, Jewish and Christian (and pagan) literature. Also Mattioli, pp. 34-35; 60-63 and notes; Schöllgen, pp. 111-113.

26.   Cues in tune with my interpretative perspective can be found here and there in some commentaries mainly of the French school: Audet, cit., pp. 330-337; Giet, cit., pp. 59ff.; 76ff.; 163-166; Rordorf-Tuilier, cit, pp. 155 n. 6; 161 n. 7; Prigent, in Id.-Kraft 1971, p. 206 n. 1.

dered in conjunction with the information derived from *Barn.*, *Doctr.* and other related proto-Christian texts – it appears to be connected to the previous Jewish ethical tradition modelled on the *topos* of the "Two Ways".

Nonetheless the historiographical and methodological perspective which considers community norms reported by the *Didache* as an expression of a community different and separated from contemporary Judaism still appears to characterise the approach of many scholars. Furthermore the 'ancillary use' of Jewish sources, aimed at stressing the (supposed) specificity of the Christian phenomenon and the canonical and normative value of NT texts contribute to influence many commentators quick to read the norms and institutions present in non-canonical writings as subordinated to and in the light of similar realities reported by the New Testament. This approach produces questionable results from a historical point of view.

In my opinion, the historiographical perspective present in the 'historical-literary phenomenon' denoted as "Middle Judaism", cast in the mould of that 'turning point' referred to in the foregoing chapter of this monograph, calls for a re-examination of Christian origins in the context of the Jewish movements and/or currents, which, whether anterior or contemporary to the *Didache*, caution the modern reader against the above listed interpretative 'limits'.

2.1. The Thematic Progression of Did. 4:5-8

Scholars of the *Didache* tend to acknowledge the thematic unity of the passage 4:5-8[27] but neglect – except for some[28] – what I believe appears to be a distinct thematic progression in the passage, that is the

27. Niederwimmer, cit., p. 134, describes the literary unit *Did.* 4:1-11 as: "...eine gewisse, allerdings nur mässig strukturierte Einheit"; Giet, *ib.*, p. 76, states that "l'instruction sur l'aumône qu'on lit aux versets 4, 5-8 de la Didachè répond à une pensée très coherente ", and maintains that – for this section – *Did.* precedes *Barn.* which presents rewritings of the original Jewish source. Finally Kraft 1965, pp. 154f., with reference to *Barn.* 19:4c-12 and *Did.* 3:7-4:14, writes: "With respect to the materials shared by Barnabas and Didache here, the latter presents them in more organized fashion" (p. 155).

28. Among the few I cite Prigent (cit., p. 206 n. 1) who, as to the terminological differences between *Did./Doctr.* 4 :8 (brother/brothers) and *Barn.* 19:8a (neighbour), qualifies *en passant Did.* 4 :5-8 as "un paragraphe... bien composé et parfaitement centré sur l'idée du don et de la proprieté ". More explicit and detailed Audet (cit., pp. 330-337), whose arguments tend to coincide with what I will discuss next.

transition: a. from the prescriptions regarding gifts and alms, b. to the statements and norms regarding private property and the community of goods. Let us consider the most significant stages of this progression. Following the introductory exhortation modelled, as to form and content, on a typical sapiential saying (Sir 4:31) – caustically condemning both the impudence in asking and the stinginess in giving (v 5) – the pericope assumes legalistic tones.[29] It lists realistic situations regarding the practice of charity (vv 6-7), which is never separated from spiritual aims and motivations whether practiced in atonement of one's sins (v 6b) or in view of a future divine retribution (v 7b). Furthermore charity does not consist merely in giving what one has earned by working (v 6a), but includes also the necessary modes and intentions prompting the act of giving. The giver is advised to set aside any hesitation and to avoid complaining (v 7a).

The difficult and debated v 8, which from a formal and structural point of view continues the didactic-legalistic tones of the preceding vv 5-7, insists at the beginning on the same theme regarding general charity: "You shall not turn away anyone who is in need" (v 8a). But from v 8b the thematic horizon of the didachist comes to be enriched with new considerations regarding property, material and spiritual goods and the sharing of these among the members of the community. The aim is not of mere charity toward a poor man (including the foreigner) but it is possible to identify a thematic progression toward the κοινωνία among brothers, namely among the members (or 'some' members) of the community itself.

The transition from the εὐποΐα-ἐλεημοσύνη to the κοινωνία is expressed from a literary point of view by the adversative particle δέ.[30] Such a κοινωνία of material or mortal (i.e. perishable) goods is believed to be possible and practicable, since the members of the community

---

29. Supra, n. 11.

30. Audet correctly observes: "Toute aumone est un partage de biens, mais la κοινωνία est un partage qui s'établit suivant des formes plus particulières. Elle concerne d'abord le "frère", ἀδελφός, qui n'est pas tout à fait le même que l' ἐνδεόμενος" (p. 332). And before: "On remarquera, d'abord, que l'auteur avait bien conscience d'aborder ici un point que son instruction n'avait pas encore touché. La transition est soulignée par d. C'est le passage de l'εὐποΐα, ou ἐλεημοσύνη, à la κοινωνία. Les deux «charités» ne sont pas identiques" (p. 331).

already share the participation in a higher good, namely immortality (or immortal goods).

Furthermore there is a gradient/transition in the various situations of daily life, prompting various responses: 1. the situation of the occasional poor which assumes that anyone can lapse into a condition of having to ask or to receive. These are advised to exercise detachment and moderation (v 5); 2. the situation of one who earns by working and is invited to practice charity in atonement for his sins (v 6); 3. The situation of the wealthy members who must practice charity towards all the poor (v 8a); 4. finally, the particular situation of the κοινωνία or community of goods among all the brothers (or 'some groups' of brothers) of the same community (v 8b-c-d).

The acknowledgement of this thematic progression: the transition from general norms regarding charity and almsgiving to the particular situation of the community of goods among the members (or *some* members) of the community, does not recur in the commentaries of the *Didache*. By contrast the reductionist interpretation, according to which the κοινωνία of *Did.* 4:8b-c-d is nothing but a mere literary motif, an expediency adopted by the didachist to encourage charity or beneficence among the members of his community/ies, which would conduce to the community of goods,[31] appears to be widespread.

2.2. The Community of Goods of Did. 4:8b-c-d

If this exegesis of the passage examined is correct, *Did.* 4:5-8 would document the existence of two social arrangements or institutions, distinct but related, in the life of the community or communities to which the didachist addresses the community statute: almsgiving or charity towards all the needy alongside the community of goods among the members (or 'some members') of the community.

The association and the practicability of the two different institutions in a common social environment could appear somewhat problematic since the practice of the community of goods seems to exclude or overrule the prescription of almsgiving in the same community. The dilemma consequently requires deeper investigation of the question in

---

31. This exegetical trend was already present in Harnack 1884, who commented thus on *Did.* 4:5-8: "eine zweite Gruppe von Pflichten..., die sich auf die Bereitschaft des Christen beziehen, sein Vermögen im Hinblick auf Gott und im Dienste der Gemeinde zu verwalten" (p. 55).

order to identify the possible literary and historical motivations which could justify the 'co-existence'[32] of two institutions in this passage, which, as already pointed out, probably encompasses ethical material derived from a previous Jewish source (or *Vorlage*) centred on the doctrine of the "Two Ways".

I will dwell in particular on the motif of the κοινωνία of *Did.* 4:8b-c-d, since the charity norms of vv 5-8a do not present exegetical difficulties: these are formulated with explicit references to texts of the Old Testament – well documented in Judaism[33] – expressing the religious and social ideal of attention to the poor.[34] This ideal passed on directly to the Christian Judaism of the 1st century CE, of which the *Didache* remains an important testimony.

The statement: "on the contrary, you shall hold everything in common with your brother, and you shall not say that anything is your own" (*Did.* 4:8b-c), with the related argument *qal wa-ḥomer* "for if you are partners in what is immortal [should you not be] all the more in

---

32. A first reply: the impersonal, stratified and compound character of the *Didache*, as well as its specificity of "evolved literature" – that is the work of an active and traditional community rather than of a single author (Kraft 1965, pp. 1ff.) – favours the matching of different materials of different periods, neither always harmonised nor presented in a diachronic and systematic manner. This would justify the co-existence or juxtaposition within the same passage of forms and institutions, ministries and doctrines, liturgical practices and ethical and disciplinary norms deriving from different sources and contexts. To illustrate the situation one could use the image of the 'tesserae of a mosaic' (i.e., fragments of pre-existing mosaics) the historical meaning and value of which should be traced in the original environment of the re-used tesserae rather than in their current position within the text (that is the 'mosaic', represented by the *Didache*).

33. Supra, nn. 21-23. One could consider these norms as a Biblical inter-text, which the didachist either composes or takes on from the Jewish tradition, composed of explicit citations, allusions or imitations of the Old Testament. On the fertility of the inter-textual approach to the interpretation of complex texts of ancient Christian literature, see A.V. Nazzaro, "Intertestualità biblica e classica in testi cristiani antichi", in B. Amata (ed.), *Cultura e lingue classiche*: III Convegno di aggiornamento e di didattica. Palermo, 29 ottobre-1 novembre 1989 (Roma: LAS, 1993), 3, pp. 489-514; Id., "Intertestualità biblico-patristica e classica in testi poetici di Venanzio Fortunato", in *Venanzio Fortunato tra Italia e Francia*: Atti del convegno internazionale di studi. Valdobbiadene, 17 maggio 1990-Treviso 18-19 maggio 1990 (Treviso: Provincia di Treviso, 1993), pp. 99-135.

34. For a thorough investigation of theme in question I refer the reader to the studies cited by both Del Verme 1989, p. 176 n. 167, and A. George, s.v. "Pauvre", in *DBS* VII (Paris: Letouzey & Ané, 1966), cols. 387-406.

things that perish?" (v 8d), is interpreted by many scholars in the light
of analogous NT texts (eg Acts 2:44f.; 4:32ff.; Gal 6:6; Rom 15:27; and
Heb 13:16) and of similar expressions circulating in the Hellenistic
Graeco-Roman world.[35] Such an exegetical current appears to be characterised by a reductionist reading of NT passages which deal with the
'community of goods' – in particular those by Luke (for example, the
'main summaries' of Acts 2:41-47; 4:32-35, and the 'narrative diptych'
of 4:36-37 and 5:1-11)[36] – and therefore also of *Did.* 4:8, the content of

35. For the topic of community of goods in Pagan (Graeco-Roman), Israelite-
Jewish and Christian environments, see M. Wacht, s.v. *Gütergemeinschaft*, in *RAC*
XIII (Stuttgart: A. Hierseman, 1984), pp. 1-39, and more punctually H.J. Klauck,
"Gütergemeinschaft in der klassischen Antike, in Qumran und im Neuen Testament",
RdQ 11/42, 1983, pp. 47-79.

36. In an earlier monograph (Del Verme 1977, supra, chap. 1, III.) – which I still
believe to be valid in its substance and which could be further corroborated and
strengthened by the new data furnished by the publication of the fragments of 4Q –
in conclusion to my analysis of the major summaries and of the narrative diptych (pp.
22-41) of the *Acts of the Apostles*, I stated that the problem of the community of goods
in the early community of Jerusalem cannot be considered solved by means of a mere
contrapposition of either reality or idealisation, implying that Luke either describes a
factual reality or invents a situation which has never existed. From an historical point of
view, the truth lies between the two poles: the community of goods in Jerusalem never
became a mass phenomenon but was practised only by a limited number of people (p.
41). Also M. Hengel, *Eigentum und Reichtum in der frühen Kirche. Aspekte einer
frühchristlichen Sozialgeschichte* (Stuttgart: Calwer Verlag, 1973), in chap. 4 – dealing
with the 'communism of love' of the primitive community – referring to E. Bloch (in
particular his work *Das Prinzip Hoffnung*, III [Stuttgart: Akademie Verlag, 1959], pp.
1482-1493) observed that this 'atheistic' philosopher shows more trust in the early
community of Jerusalem than the so-called radical believers. As a matter of fact he
expresses a clearer picture of the historical situation than those of the so-called critical
exegetes. And the supposed contradiction between the statements of Acts 4:32 ("and
no one said that any of the things which he possessed was his own, but they had
everything in common") and 4:36f. ("Thus Joseph who was surnamed by the apostles
Barnabas [which means Son of encouragement], a Levite, a native of Cyprus, sold a
field which belonged to him, and brought the money and laid it at the apostles' feet")
would be only apparent. Hengel points out also that the reference to Barnabas is not a
mere evidence of a single or special case in Jerusalem, but the act of remembering his
actions is motivated by the fact that these were well known to the community of
Antioch, from which Luke derived the information. In the above cited monograph, I
also stated: "Nei sommari si vuole descrivere una situazione generale della comunità
primitiva; perciò Luca si serve della generalizzazione per elevare il singolo avveni-
mento o casi particolari a episodi universali e a una realtà valevole (nel senso che
potrebbe valere) per tutti" (*Comunione e condivisione.*, cit., p. 40).

which is limited to mere charity and to the sphere of economic (and spiritual) solidarity.

The resort to the New Testament (as well as to Hellenistic literature) to expound *Did.* 4:8b-c-d is legitimate,[37] although such an approach encompasses the risk of denying literary autonomy and peculiarity to the passage along with its social and historical-institutional content. I will come back later to some of these aspects. At this stage, however, one must keep in mind that the literary dependence of the *Didache* on the NT still remains problematic, as for the earlier strata of the text it is possible to suppose some sort of autonomy from the NT.[38] In my

---

37.   It appears legitimate (and probably also useful), since the expressions regarding the κοινωνία recurring in the NT are similar to those of *Did.* 4,8b-c-d, although it still persists the historical-literary problem regarding both the genesis of the tradition of the community of goods and its meaning in the different contexts in which it occurs. As to the contents attempts to consolidate the texts on the basis of either literary or lexical similarities should be definitely rejected. In my opinion there is no reason to assume *Did.* 4:8b-c-d- as a mere Biblical inter-text. As is known, the theme of the community of spiritual and material goods was present and active in some Judaisms of the Middle-Judaic period, i.e. among the Essene-Qumranites and among the Therapeutae[?], the Christian Jews of the community of Jerusalem and afterwards among those marginal or 'heretical' groups – such as the Ebionites, the gnostic Carpocratians and the 'apostolic' Encratites, who followed in many respects to the model of the primitive community of Jerusalem (for these groups, see Mimouni 1992; 1998a; 1998b; 2001), and also in the pagan Graeco-Roman environment, i.e. Liparite communism, the social utopia and the myth of the Golden Age, Pythagoreanism, and other political-humanistic philosophies. See Bibliography, supra n. 35. The NT borrowing in the reading of *Did.* 4,8b-c-d can be discarded if one applies to the interpretation of this verse the methodological criteria encompassed in the 'new' terminology of 'Middle Judaism' previously expounded in the Introduction (pp. 113-115).

38.   The problem is extremely complex and consequently is dealt with in many commentaries on the *Didache* and in specific studies of literary criticism, of morpho-critical and editorial history, although with contradictory conclusions. For the moment I refer the reader to Tuckett 1989, pp. 197-230, who suggests the dependence of the *Didache* on the New Testament (or at least from *Matthew*), while Rordorf 1991, pp. 394-423, decidedly denies it. The solution of the problem is, for some respects, closely connected with the selected chronology for the final edition of the *Didache*, a chronology which appears to between the second half of the 1st century and the beginning of the 2nd century CE (or even later, as some scholars have suggested, although this suggestion has very few followers today). In this regard the American scholar C.N. Jefford has been able to identify schematically three schools of thought: French, German and Anglo-American (Id. 1989b, pp. 3-17). Jefford himself suggests the hypothesis of a common source for both the *Didache* and *Matthew*). It must be observed that those scholars who postulate a later edition for the *Didache* – as for instance Kraft

opinion, however, the genesis and meaning of the ethical norms – and therefore of the institutions and/or arrangements they represent – which can be identified in the doctrine of the "Two Ways" of the *Didache* – must be more directly traced in traditions present in the Jewish context. Very few scholars however have moved in this direction to interpret *Did.* 4:8b-c-d. I here refer some of their conclusions to explain better why I would incline to propose a reading of v 8 of the passage 4:5-8 as referring to a factual community of goods.

2.2.1. Jewish Historical Context

Among the modern commentators of the *Didache* the Canadian scholar J.-P. Audet has been without doubt the most convinced supporter of the κοινωνία of *Did.* 4:8b understood as an effective community of goods, different and distinguished from either mere charity or almsgiving described in vv 4:5-8a.[39] Audet interprets the whole section 3:7-4:14 as an "instruction to the poor", characterised by a didactic rather than an imperative style, which has been inserted later in the text – that is after the "sapiential instruction" of 3:1-6 – in the original Jewish treatise regarding the "Two Ways". This treatise, which fundamentally constituted a short "instruction to the gentiles", would present the following structure: following the introduction (1:1-3a), there is a two-part symmetric diptych, that is the "way of life" (2:2-7 with a final clause in 4:14) and the "way of death" (5:1-2); finally the conclusion (6:1) recalling 1:1-2 and following the "instruction" (1:3a)

1965, p. 76, who argues: "...but it would be difficult to argue convincingly that the present form of the Didache is earlier than mid-second century" – must however acknowledge that much of the material of the current text (as that of the DVD of *Did.* 1-6) has reached the didachist "from very early... form of (Jewish-) Christianity" and, above all, that the late chronology assigned to the final edition of the text "is largely irrelevant when particular items in the tradition are discussed" (cit., p. 77). These 'items' must, I believe, include also the community of goods of *Did.* 4:8b-c-d. One must also consider that the date of the final edition of *Acts of the Apostles* (which according to some scholars might have influenced the formulation of *Did.* 4:8b-c-d) cannot be established before the years 80-90 CE. Therefore Giet 1970 could acutely advance the hypothesis that the *Acts* could depend on the *Didache*, with a question: "Dès lors, cet 'enseignement des apôtres': διδαχὴ τῶν ἀποστόλων auquel 's'atta-chaient fermement' les fidèles qui mettaient leurs biens en commun (= Acts 2:42.44), ne serait-il pas notre Duae Viae, déja pourvu du titre de Didachè, ou Doctrina Apostolorum ?" (p. 165). I will come back to this topic in the following chapters.

39. Supra, n. 30. Other motivations, in Id. 1958, pp. 330-335.

referring to the love of God and of one's neighbour. In order to complete the original image of the Jewish "Two Ways" – Audet suggests – one should add that section recovered from *Doctr. Ap.* 6:4-5 (i.e. "Haec in consulendo si cottidie feceris, ...peruenies ad coronam").[40]

The long and complex prehistory of the original Jewish Διδαχὴ τῶν δύο ὁδῶν, hypothesised and reconstructed by Audet, prompted widespread consensus but also a few reservations among some critics. His interpretation of the κοινωνία in 4:8b, also, has been challenged.[41] In my opinion, however, his arguments in support of the general thesis, which claims that the earliest sections of the writing (such as those regarding the "Two Ways" of chaps. 1-6) reveal a strong Jewish character, remain valid. Furthermore the literary and historical motivations he adduces to identify subsequent interpolations or Christian (or what I would define rather as Christian Jewish) readings, which made their way into the original text, remain convincing. I believe that, above all, his methodological perspective remains valid – as well as 'pioneer' – which leads to an interpretation of the *Didache* exclusive of any NT borrowing[42] and to an identification of the possible original *Sitz im Leben* of each section. In this regard, he identifies the context of origin and the recipients of the "instruction to the poor", in which 4:8b is found, among the *'anawim ('aniyyim)*[43]

40. Ed. Schlecht, pp. 308-319 (311-312).

41. For Italian scholars, see Mattioli 1986, pp. 29-35, 60-63, whose arguments appear to be characterised by some sort of 'neo-testamentary (and Hellenistic) pre-comprehension', represented by his frequent rejection of the hypotheses of those scholars who tend to identify Jewish influences in the Didache attributing great value to forms and traditions (*formgeschichtlich* or *traditionsgeschichtlich*) present in the Hebrew-Jewish context.

42. See also his criticism (pp. 330-336 [335]) of the current thesis that the κοινωνία of *Did.* 4:8b reflects Christian ideas and customs such as those documented in the summaries of *Acts* 2:44 and 4:32 and in an allusion in Paul (Rom 15:27). Audet 1958 strongly supports, by contrast, the autonomy of the tradition of the 'community of goods' of the *Didache*.

43. These were – as Audet argues – neither a party nor a sect nor a separated 'community', membership of which was acquired following public adherence and a period of initiation. The *'anawim* were a group of people from Palestinian Judaism – 'Palestinian' must not be considered antithetical to 'Hellenistic' according to Audet – in particular from the lower classes, characterised by a strong hope of renewal despite the continuous political misfortunes and by the trust in God and the coming of His Kingdom which would have restored the balance between the righteous and the wicked (p. 316). A group of 'poor', who cherished prayers and the observance of the Law, and

of Palestinian Judaism, which – for Audet too – must not be contrasted with Hellenistic Judaism.[44]

St. Giet, like Audet and other scholars (for example W. Rordorf) before him, maintains that there is no mutual dependence or correlation among *Did., Doctr.* and *Barn.* As to the common or similar material they share regarding the "Two Ways", the three Christian-Jewish (or simply Christian) writings would depend – although autonomously – from a previous common Jewish source (or sources) regarding the "Two Ways", which in his opinion in the version provided by *Barn.* – notwithstanding the 'clumsy' rewritings and the editing style of the author – would reflect more closely the original Jewish model.[45] The rewritings and the 'seal' of the editing technique of the Pseudo-Barnabas are particularly evident in the "instruction regarding almsgiving", as Giet prefers to refer to *Did.* 4:5-8, if this text is compared with analogous material found in *Barn.* 19:8-11. In *Barn.* the single state-

---

who are well known to us through the canonical *Psalms* and, in my opinion, also through some of the non-canonical texts (eg the *Hodayot* of Qumran [1QHª], the *Psalms of Solomon* and the *Syriac Psalms*), and also through other texts of Qumran (eg 1QM and 1QpHab). "C'est à ces pauvres – writes Audet – que c'est attaché Luc en quelques-uns de ses plus beaux récits, principalement ceux de l'enfance de Jean et de Jésus. C'est à eux qu'est adressée la première béatitude dans Mt. et dans Lc. On sait aussi, par les lettres de Paul et par les Actes, qu'ils ont été à l'origine l'une des composantes majeures de l'église-mère de Jérusalem...", with reference to studies by A. Causse, J. Dupont and J. Van der Ploeg (p. 316). In the light of this information, Mattioli's reservations (p. 35) as to Audet's thesis regarding the identity of the recipients of the "instruction to the poor" (i. e. the *'anawim*) of *Did.* 4:8b appear to be unfounded.

44.　In a comment on the text he wrote: "Il me paraît certain, d'autre part, que cette instruction a été originellement écrite en grec: ce n'est pas une traduction de l'hébreu ni de l' araméen. Mais nous savons qu'à Jérusalem même, au temps de Jésus, il y avait des Juifs «hellénistes» susceptibles de l'entendre (Acts 6:1-6). Le reste de la Palestine n'était pas davantage unilingue. Au reste, au moment où l'instruction aux pauvres a été recueillie par le *Duae viae*, elle devait avoir fourni une bonne partie de sa carrière et s'être acquis un certain prestige dans la διδαχή usuelle des pauvres" (p. 336).

45.　Giet 1970, pp. 73-91. I refer some of his statements: "Tout déformé qu'il soit, le Duae Viae du pseudo-Barnabé reste le plus ancien des trois, et peut, à ce titre, être dans certains cas, le témoin le plus qualifié de la source commune" (p. 88). And he adds: "Ce ne sont pas des certitudes; et l'appreciation à porter sur ses textes est délicate; mais il semble que les *Duae Viae* du pseudo-Barnabé, bien que profondément altéré, reste, ici et là, plus proche de son modèle" (i.e. the Jewish *Vorlage* of the "Duae viae").

ments of *Did.* are clearly distinguished and appear to be greatly altered, although well structured, in relation to contemporary thinking when compared with those of the didachist.[46] Moreover, it appears, at least for this literary unit, that the *Didache* refers to a text prior to *Barnabas*. As to the relations between the New Testament and the *Didache*, I have already mentioned Giet's hypothesis which supposes a probable dependence of the information regarding the κοινωνία of Acts 2:42.44 on the Jewish doctrine of the "Two Ways", which is behind the text of *Did.* 4:8b. The author is conscious of the 'problematic nature' of this hypothesis,[47] and consequently points out that the "Duae viae" of *Didache* could have influenced and inspired the information found in the *Acts of the Apostles* only indirectly, in the sense that the 'Jewish treatise' might have been the 'rule of life' for a primitive Christian community of which Luke could have known. The 'community's adaptation' of the Jewish διδαχὴ τῶν δύο ὁδῶν was, however, an exceptional interpretation by some Judaeo-Christian groups, since in reality it was a specific Jewish moral catechesis intended for the instruction of proselytes.[48]

A year after the publication of St. Giet's book (*L'énigme de la Didachè*, Paris 1970), another French scholar, P. Prigent, in collaboration with the American R.A. Kraft, published in 1971 *L'Epitre de Barnabé* (SC 172). This work, in its general introduction and notes, provides here and there interpretations of *Barnabas*, which could also be useful in the interpretation of the *Didache*. Like J.-P. Audet, St. Giet, W. Rordorf and others, Prigent follows the literary hypothesis[49] of a

---

46.   He writes: "Le pseudo-Barnabé, quoi qu'ont ait pu dire de son originalité litteraire, ne fait pas, en ces chapitres, oeuvre originale: il démarque un enseignement des deux voies, et le fait avec une maladresse insigne. Le décousu des idées, comme la manière dont est formulé le commandement d'aimer le prochain, porte le sceau d'une compilation. And he addes: "Si donc il témoigne d'un état ancien des deux voies, c'est seulement à travers le remaniement qu'il en fait, ou que d'autres en avaient fait avant lui... " (p. 79)

47.   "Cette hypothèse toutefois n'est pas aussi simple qu'elle parait au premier abord", because in Acts 2:42 besides the fraternal community (and the community of material goods) are mentioned "breaking of bread and prayers". What is the relation between these statements and the Jewish *Duae Viae*, which is supposed to be anterior to the *Acts* of Luke? The question is hard to resolve – argues the author – if "la notice des Actes se rapporterait conjointement à la fraction du pain et aux prières des chapitres IX et X de la Didachè " (p. 165).

48.   Ibid., p. 166.

49.   This hypothesis was proposed in 1884 by the British scholar J. Wordsworth ("Christian Life, Ritual and Discipline at the Close of the First Century", in *The*

Jewish treatise regarding the "Two Ways" as a common source for *Barn., Did.* and *Doctr.* The authors of the three works would have had access presumably independently to a Jewish treatise of moral doctrine – already translated into Greek – which they either incorporated into the general outline of their writings (*Did.* and *Barn.*) or merely translated (*Doctr.*).[50] As to the κοινωνία of *Did.* 4:8b, Prigent cautiously evaluates Audet's thesis, which categorically excluded any dependence on Acts 2:44 and 4:32 (as well as on othee NT texts regarding the κοινωνία). By contrast Prigent proposes to interpret the passages regarding the community of goods of the *Acts of the Apostles* as the 'revival' of a community ideal still active in some Jewish circles, as for instance among the Essenes of Qumran.[51] Even if Prigent does not explicitly state it, one may suppose that he is implying an Essene-Qumranic solution for the community of goods referred to in *Did.* 4:8 as well.

Among contemporary scholars of ancient Christianity – as stated above – W. Rordorf appears to be the most attentive in pointing out, probably in the wake of Audet, the Jewish context of the *Didache* by identifying in it a series of ancient (oral and written) traditions, some of

Guardian, London, March 19, 1884) and was followed by other scholars who used it in different ways to determine and define the relations existing between *Did., Barn.* and *Doctr. Ap.* Among Wordsworth's followers I must mention A. Harnack, who modified his previous position (expressed in the *Prolegomena* to *Lehre der Zwölf Apostel nebst Untersuchungen zur ältesten Geschichte der Kirchenfassung und des Kirchenrechts* [Leipzig: J.C. Hinrichs'she Buchhandlung, 1884], pp. 82-83, in which he stated the dependence of *Did.* on *Barn.*) accepting the possible existence of a common source (*Die Apostellehre und die jüdischen Beiden Wege* [Leipzig: J.C. Hinrichs'she Buchhandlung, 1886]) – although maintaining some ambiguities (as Audet observed, ibid., pp. 12-13, n. 1). Harnack's new approach was also contributed to by Taylor's (1886) critical observations. Taylor, in fact, pointing out the affinities between the *Didache* (in particular the doctrine of the "Two Ways" of chaps. 1-6) and Judaism in general, argued against the thesis of a direct dependence of *Did.* on *Barn.* – initially advanced by Harnack – and argued in favour of the presence of a common Jewish source behind the two writings (*Did.* and *Barn.*). This source was intended as an 'ethical manual' for the instruction of proselytes, like that found in the *Didache*.

　　50.　Ibid., pp. 15-20 (20).

　　51.　Ibid., p. 206 n. 1, with the citation of 1QS VI:19 and Flav. Ios., *J.W.* 2.122. In addition a passage from the pseudo-Clementine literature (*Ep. Clem. ad Iac.* 9:3) is quoted confirming the existing correlation between temporal and immortal goods which recurs also in the argument of the κοινωνία in *Did.* 4:8d (parr. *Doctr.* [on agreeing with the conjecture by Schlecht] and *Barn.*).

which could have preceded the final edition of the NT. One can follow the development of Rordorf's line of thought in a series of valid and well documented articles and monographs cited in the annotated bibliography (see the previous chapter).[52]

I will discuss Rordorf's interpretation of *Did.* 4:5-8, and more specifically of the κοινωνία of v 8b. The author agrees with Audet that section 3:7-4:14 constitutes a compact literary bloc, in which the "ideal of the poor" is articulated, although he maintains that it is difficult to identify exactly the addressees of the moral instruction in the originary Jewish source,[53] therefore rejecting the hypothesis that these may have been the '*ănāwîm* of Palestinian Judaism as proposed by Audet. Notwithstanding the reservation he makes, he suggests – on the basis of literary evidence – that the recipients could be traced in that 'ethical treatise' among the married Essenes (cf. Fl. Ios., *J.W..* 2.124-125, 134, 160-161).[54] In that environment – he argues – it is easier to understand texts as *Did.* 4:1-4, 8, 12-14, taking into account also that passages as

---

52.   In particular in two studies the presence of Jewish traditions in the doctrine of the "Two Ways" of *Didache* is re-stated: 1. in the introductory critical notes to the commentary written in collaboration with A. Tuilier (cit., pp. 17-21 [passim]; pp. 22-34; 83-91; 99-101 [passim]); 2. in the article "Un chapitre", cit. (= Rordorf 1972b). Of interest are also some of his more recent contributions: Rordorf 1993 and "Does the Didache Contain Jesus Tradition", cit.

53.   Ibid., 155 n. 6.

54.   *Contra*, Mattioli (p. 61 n. 87 [= p. 91]), who defines Rordorf's hypothesis "discutibile" but fails to provide the reason why it is questionable. As observed (supra, n. 41), the Italian scholar appears to be somehow reluctant to consider the thesis (or hypothesis) of scholars attentive to probable Jewish traditions incorporated into the *Didache*. In this regard, I pointed out his misunderstanding in my earlier monograph *Comunione e condivisione dei beni*, in particular in the Second Part: "La comunione dei beni tra gli Esseni e a Qumran" (pp. 69-131), which he believes is "assai manchevole" referring to the critical annotations by W. Paschen (and Ch. Rabin) regarding the Essene-Qumranic "comunismo" (*sic*). I was at the time well aware of Rabin's conjecture, which I quote and discuss (but which I rejected for textual reasons) in the above mentioned monograph p. 108 n. 44). In fact, my observation could have induced Mattioli to soften Paschen's criticism regarding the Qumranic community of goods. In this regard I observed that among the writings of Qumran one must maintain a distinction between "la posizione di CD favorevole alla proprietà privata (corrispondente ad alcune notizie circa gli Esseni riferite sia da Filone...sia da Flavio Giuseppe...)" and that of 1QS "che esclude la proprietà privata". I finally concluded that it was possible to draw a parallel between the Essenes and CD...and not between CD and 1QS. W. Rordorf (and A. Tuilier) was also described by Mattioli (p. 91 and n. 87 at the end) as "tradizionale, purtroppo..." (but in what sense?), only (or also) because he 'dared' to

3:7-10 and 4:5-7 have some parallels among the Qumran documents. Commenting on 4:8b, Rordorf concludes that the κοινωνία in question (lit. "ce partage sans réserve avec le frère") refers to the community of goods of the Essenes (for example, 1QS VI:18-19; Fl. Ios., *J. W.* 2.122).[55]

The Austrian scholar K. Niederwimmer interpreting *Did.* 4:8b within the passage 4:1-11, which he entitles "Regeln, die das soziale Leben betreffen",[56] points out some vacillations,[57] which in my opinion appear to be in stark contraddiction to what he states in the general presentation of the treatise regarding the "Two Ways" of the *Didache.* In fact, in the *Prolegomena* to his commentary,[58] the author dwells on the hypothesis of a *Vorlage* of a Jewish *Zwei-Wege-Traktat* as a probable source of *Did.* 1-6.[59] Circumstantially and assuming as a point of departure the textual situation of *Did.* 1:3b-2:1 – which is not found in *Barn., Doctr., Can., Epit.* and in other Christian readings of the doctrine of the "Two Ways" – he argues that the *Vorlage*, which made its way into the existing text of the *Didache*, should be connected to an original Jewish text (lit. "ursprünglich mit einem rein jüdischen Text zu rechnen"), probably deriving from the wider context of contemporary religious community codes, as for instance 1QS and 1QSa found at Qumran.[60] More precisely, the author states that the original form of the Jewish treatise followed by the *Didache* functioned as a community code for Jewish groups of renewal, which gathered in the *Lehrhaus* (referring to the thesis by Wengst 1984, p. 67) and practised activities

state, commenting *Did.* 4:8b – as I did as well – that the Essene community of goods (with a reference to 1QS) could cast light on the κοινωνία of the *Didache.*

55.   Ibid., p. 155 n. 6; and p. 161 n. 7. Among the texts quoted there is also *Acts* 2:44 and 4:32, but I believe, in the light of what he previously stated in his *Introduction*, ch. III, 5. (= La Didachè et les écrits néo-testamentaires), pp. 83-91, and in subsequent studies, that the author does not intentionally want to establish a literary dependence of *Did.* on *Acts.*

56.   Niederwimmer 1989, pp. 133-144 (140-141).

57.   Supra, chap. One, pp. 8-9 n. 7.

58.   I refer some of his statements: "Die verschiedenen Versionen des Traktats gehen auf ein ursprünglich jüdisches Grund-Muster zurück, auf einen im Ursprung noch vorchristlichen, jüdischen Traktat über die beiden Wege..." (p. 56). And: " Der jüdische Charakter des ursprünglichen Zwei-Wege-Traktats ist schon früh aufgefallen und hat in neurerer Zeit durch die Entdeckung der Qumran-Texte, nämlich näherhin durch die Analogie 1QS III,18ff. eine zusätzliche Grundlage erhalten" (p. 57).

59.   Ibid., p. 56.

60.   Ibid., pp. 57f., and 87f.

of mutual social assistance. To exemplify such a situation he cites in a note *Did.* 4:8.[61] However in the analysis he proposes of this particular verse within the wider commentary on *Did.* 4:5-8 the exegetical perspective outlined in the *Prolegomena* – somewhat inexplicably! – appears to be devalued.[62] Consequently, in my opinion, Niederwimmer fails to seize the opportunity to advance a more 'stable' hypothesis regarding the original *Sitz im Leben* of both the beneficence and the community of goods referred to in *Did.* 4:5-8a (the former) and in 4:8b-c-d (the latter).

2.2.2. Community of Goods, Didache *and Judaism*

I have devoted particular attention to those scholars who have privileged in their studies the resort to the Jewish context to interpret the κοινωνία of *Did.* 4:8 since I believe that this approach could produce indications useful both to define the meaning of κοινωνία and to determine the historical institutional reality 'concealed' in the problematic verse. In the light of my previous analysis of the text and context of *Did.* 4:5-8 and also considering the solutions proposed by other scholars to the problem regarding the community of goods referred to in this passage (in particular in v 8b-c-d), in this conclusive paragraph I introduce the reader to my interpretation of the problematic passage, although I believe that *Did.* 4:8 will continue to represent one of the many literary and historical 'enigmas' contained in the διδαχὴ τῶν δώδεκα ἀποστόλων.[63]

---

61. Ibid., p. 58 n. 59. Niederwimmer's thesis regarding the 'circle' of "jüdische Erweckter" as the original recipents of the Jewish "Two Ways" is rejected by Schöllgen 1991, p. 39, who believes it to be "weniger wahrscheinlich(e)" in contrast with Rordorf, who hypothesised as possible recipients the "God-Fearers" or proselytes, and subsequently the ethno-Christians in the Jewish environment (Id., *Un chapitre*, p. 118).

62. The author in fact rejects the hypothesis of both Pythagoraean influences (which by contrast Mattioli supports finding "più strette analogie con la cultura e la pratica pitagorico-platonico-ellenistiche", p. 35]) and Essene influences. Consequently he writes: "Eine Beziehung zur Tradition über die (angebliche) Gütergemeinschaft der Pythagoräer bestehet schwerlich". And later adds: "Einen Einfluss essenischer Tradition auf unseren Traktat (i.e., *Did.* 4:5-8) braucht man nicht anzunehmen" (p. 140). Concluding with a final "fall" and alignment with the widespread thesis postulating that *Did.* 4:8b merely invites one to exercise *Gebefreudigkeit* and *Opferbereitschaft* (= generosity and self-denial), which guaranteed the individual social security because of the intensive practice of charity among the members of the community (p. 141).

63. This is the short title of the *Didache*, with the initial small letter according to

The didactic-legalistic tone (supra nn. 11-12) by which both the charity norms (*Did.* 4:5-8a) and the community of goods (4:8b-c-d) are formulated induces one to suppose that the Jewish *Vorlage* of the "Two Ways", on which the didachist depends, developed in the environment-context of the community codes adopted by many religious groups/currents during the period referred to as "Middle Judaism".

In the *Didache* the community of goods among the members of the community is neither conceived nor prescribed in an absolute or radical form. As already observed, it comes to be associated with the practice of charity towards all the needy, including the foreigner and the stranger. As J.-P. Audet already noticed in his comments on the future συγκοινωνήσεις and the plural πάντα of *Did.* 4:8b, these expressions – which at first sight could lead one to suppose the existence of "une règle assez rigide" – should instead be cast and evaluated "dans le style exhortatoire de l'ensemble de l'instruction: il ne faut probablement pas le(s) presser. Il (ils) exprime(nt) un idéal, qui n'est pas un vain mot sans doute, mais qui ne doit pas non plus être une description graphique de la réalité...". Analogously, in fact, in 4:2 one is advised (not ordered!) to look for (lit. ἐκζητήσεις: "You shall seek out", that is a normative-didactic future) "the holy persons every day to find support in their words".[64] Consequently, the author argues, the norms of *Did.* 4:8 (and 4:2) have in reality "un sens relatif". I believe, in fact, that these should be intended as 'advisory norms' which although tying the individual to their observance are applicable only to particular circumstances and obviously only for some members of the community/ies to which the *Didache* was addressed. Audet himself, in conclusion to his observations on συγκοινωνήσεις and πάντα of v 8b, stated: "On ne partage pas tous les jours tous ses biens avec tout le monde. Même dans l'idéal, l'instruction doit donc vouloir dire moins qu'il ne semblerait à première vue. Tout ramener, d'autre part, à de pures dispositions intérieures de détachement serait certainement tomber dans un excès contraire et rester non seulement au-dessous de l'idéal mais au dessous de la réalité".[65]

---

the ms. H54. The long title: Διδαχὴ κυρίου διὰ τῶν δώδεκα ἀποστόλων τοῖς ἔθνεσιν, reported also by the same codex, appears to be a later extension formed in the course of the long literary tradition of *Did.* Cf. Rordorf, in Id.-Tuilier, *La Doctrine*, pp. 13-17 (16).

  64. Tr. by A. Cody, in Jefford 1995a, p. 7.
  65. Audet 1958, p. 334. Furthermore – the author argues – the κοινωνία of 4:8

In my opinion it appears that the economic and charity situation of the community, regulated by and underlying *Did.* 4:8, is very similar to that found in some Essene groups which – in contrast with the Qumranites – lived scattered in the country, that is in villages and cities of the Roman province of Judaea, as reported by Josephus.[66] On the one hand, the Jewish historian describes the admirable community life and the practice of the community of goods of these groups;[67] on the other, he hints at the intensive charity activity of the Essenes both toward those who came from another country[68] and among the members of the community.[69] The charitable activity of these Essenes appears to extend

has to be interpreted in a flexible manner (lit. "avec souplesse"), which does not exempt on any occasion owners from having to share all their goods with their 'brother' of faith in the form and measure their conscience and need require in order to generate an effective fraternal union (ἀδελφότης; cf. Gal 6:6) (pp. 334-335).

66. *J.W.* 2.124: Μία δ'οὐκ ἔστιν αὐτῶν πόλις, ἀλλ' ἐν ἑκάστῃ μετοικοῦσιν πολλοί κτλ. (tr. by H. St. J. Thackeray: "They occupy no one city, but settle in large numbers in every town. On the arrival of any of the sect from elsewhere, all the resources of the community are put at their disposal, just as if they were their own). Cf. also G. Vermes-M. D. Goodman, *The Essenes According to the Classical Sources* [Sheffield: JSOT Press, 1989], pp. 38-39. Josephus (as well as Philo) does not mention the Essenes of the diaspora but rather extols only the Essene communities of Palestine, probably as being more 'heroic'. This text, however, suggests that he probably knew both groups (*sic* Grant 1977, fifth study).

67. *J.W.*, 2.122: Καταφρονηταὶ δὲ πλούτου, καὶ θαυμάσιον [παρ'] αὐτοῖς τὸ κοινωνικόν, οὐδὲ ἔστιν εὑρεῖν κτήσει τινά παρ' αὐτοῖς ὑπερέχοντα ("Riches they despise, and their community of goods is truly admirable; you will not find one among them distinguished by greater opulence than another. They have a law that new members on admission to the sect shall make over their property to the order, with the result that you will nowhere see either abject poverty or inordinate wealth; the individual's possessions join the common stock and all, like brothers, enjoy a single patrimony").

68. *J.W.*, 2.124-125: Καὶ τοῖς ἐθέρωθεν ἥκουσιν αἱρετισταῖς πάντ' ἀναπέπταται τὰ παρ' αὐτοῖς ὁμοίως ὥσπερ ἴδια, καὶ πρὸς οὓς οὐ πρότερον εἶδον εἰσίασιν ὡς συνηθεστάτους κτλ. ("And they enter the houses of men whom they have never seen before as though they were their most intimate friends. Consequently, they carry nothing whatever with them on their journeys, except arms as protection against brigands. In every city there is one of the order expressly appointed to attend to strangers, who provides them with raiment and other necessaries"). Cf. also Vermes-Goodman 1989, pp. 38-39.

69. *J.W.*, 2.127: οὐδέν δ' ἐν ἀλλήλοις οὔτ' ἀγοράζουσιν οὔτε πωλοῦσιν, ἀλλὰ τῷ χρῄζοντι διδοὺς ἕκαστος τὰ παρ' αὐτῷ τὸ [παρ' ἐκείνου] χρήσιμον ἀντικομίζεται· καὶ χωρὶς δὲ τῆς ἀντιδόσεως ἀκώλυτος ἡ μετάληψις αὐτοῖς παρ' ὧν ἂν θέλωσιν ("There is no buying or selling among themselves, but each gives what he has to any in need and receives from him in exchange something useful to himself; they are, moreover,

to foreigners too, that is to people who were not members of their group or movement.[70] These Essene communities described by Josephus (and by Philo) somewhat resemble the Zadokites of *CD*, who appear to be less extremist or radical than the ascetics of Qumran (cf. *1QS*) regarding private property and the practice of charity toward foreigners.[71]

The ethical model (that is the 'coexistence' of the community of goods with the practice of charity) that the didachist proposes to his community as one of the qualifying aspects of the "Way of Life" was therefore already present among some Essenes within the larger Essene movement. If the idea that the *Didache* was compiled in Syria-Palestine is correct, then the norms and modes of the community of goods (and of charity towards all the needy) of 4:8, which I consider to be of Essene origin, could testify to a previous[72] phase of relations (and/or influences) between Essenic Judaism and Christian Judaism.

In fact, religious and social structures and institutions were and remained fundamentally the same among the numerous groups/movements of the Hellenistic Graeco-Roman period, and consequently behavioural 'models' (i.e. 'the ways') of the various Judaisms of the time could coincide; different and distinctive, by contrast, should or could have been the 'motivations' prompting 'their ways'. In the specific case examined in this chapter, the community of material (or perishable) goods of *Did.* 4:8b-c-d is motivated by the consideration that the members of the community already share the more important (or precious) good of immortality.[73] The community of goods among the Essenes,

---

freely permitted to take anything from any of their brothers without making any return"). Cf. also Vermes-Goodman, pp. 38-39.

70.   *J.W.*, 2.134: Βοηθεῖν τε γὰρ τοῖς ἀξίοις, ὁπόταν δέωνται, καί καθ᾽ ἑαυτοὺς ἐφίεται καὶ τροφὰς ἀπορουμένοις ὀρέγειν (Members may of their own motion help the deserving, when in need, and supply food to the destitute). Cf. also Vermes-Goodman 1989, pp. 40-41.

71.   Cf. CD XIII:15-16; XIV:12-16 with comment in Del Verme 1977, pp. 106-108. For a general assessment of the *data* present in CD and its differences with 1QS, see also Klauck, *Gütergemeinschaft*, pp. 64-68.

72.   Probably *still* actual, as I will suggest in 2.2.3. Many studies regarding the Essene influences on early Christianity appeared during the 1950s and 1960s (see Bibliography, chap. 1, III., pp. 21-22). Recently these approaches have been reconsidered by Nodet-Taylor 1998, who reproposed the thesis of the 'proximity' of Early Christianity and Essenism. Cf. also Boccaccini 1998a.

73.   The close connection between material and spiritual goods is re-affirmed also by Paul of Tarsus in regard to the fund-raising that the ethno-Christians of Macedonia and Achaea organised for the poor of the community of Jerusalem. Writing to the

instead, was conceived as an institution which, curbing the immoderate desire for riches of the individual, aimed at promoting a condition of equality and mutual assistance among the members of the group.[74]

2.2.3. *Hellenised Essenism and* Did. *4:8*

Before concluding this chapter I will dwell on some points which I believe need to be further clarified to support some of my previous statements: 1. the concept of 'Essenism' used to interpret the κοινωνία of *Did.* 4:8; 2. the identity of the Essene groups mentioned in order to add new arguments (literary and historical) to the solution of the question regarding the 'co-presence' of charity and community of goods in the same passage: *Did.* 4:5-8 (in particular v 8); and 3. the motivations supporting the hypthesis – or rather the 'conjecture' (supra, p. and n.) – that the Essene model adduced to explain *Did.* 4:8 could have been active in the period after the year 70 CE.[75]

I assume Essenism – as also Pharisaism, Enochism (that is those groups which either lie behind or produced the Enochic-apocalyptic literature) as well as the various groups of Christian Judaism (or Early Christianity) – to be one of the many *species* characterising Middle Judaism: a phenomenon to be understood not in an ideological sense but simply as a chronological delimitation (300 BCE-200 CE). A hi-

Romans he speaks of fund-raising as an obligation, a debt to pay off since the pagans had partaken of the spiritual goods of the people from Jerusalem (Rom 15:26-27). The same perspective can be found in the *Sentences of Sextus*, a collection of Christian and Pythagorean moral sayings (end of the 2nd century CE), where it is stated: "Those who share a common God as their Father but do not share their goods are wicked" (ed. H. Chadwick, *The Sentences of Sextus. A Contribution to the History of Early Christians Ethics* [TaS NS 5; Cambridge: University Press, 1959], n° 228). Also in the pseudepigraphic *Ep. Clem. ad Iac.* 9:3, the necessity of the community of material goods because of an already existing community of immortal goods is once again stated.

74. For these and other motivations, reported in particular by Philo and Josephus, see Del Verme 1977, pp. 78-95.

75. On these three points there exists a vast bibliography, still expanding especially since the end of the deplorable 'embargo' (until 1991) on the numerous fragments – in particular those found in the fourth cave of Qumrân (4Q) – which were known to exist but were not available for study because of their delayed publication. The images of 'mystery story' or of 'embargo' – probably an exaggeration! – are those of G. Vermes ("Qumran Corner. The Present State of Dead Sea Scrolls Research", in *JJS* 45, 1994, pp. 101-110), my former 'supervisor' at the Oriental Institute of Oxford during the academic year 1977-1978 (long ago!), to whom I owe gratitude and appreciation.

story of Middle Judaic thought informs the synchronic study of many active and often competing[76] 'Judaisms' (or ideological systems). The notion of Essenism encompasses the Qumranites also (as known through the Dead Sea Scrolls), although the use of this abstract noun (and of the adjective Essene-Qumranic) aims at nuancing a widespread opinion which postulates a certain equivalence-equation between the community of Qumran and the Essenes recorded by Hellenistic Graeco-Roman sources, in particular by the writings of Philo of Alexandria, Josephus and Pliny the Elder.[77] In this regard, the Austrian scholar Stemberger, in his *Introduction* to the study of the religious currents active in the Palestinian Judaism of NT times, cautions the reader against easy equations, stating that the third group, that is the Essenes (following the Pharisees and Sadducees analysed in his study), although also widely documented by the Qumran texts, cannot be identified *tout court* with the Qumranites.[78] This 'caution' – which is, simultaneously, methodological and historical – explains why I prefer to referr to "*some* Essene groups" and not to "Essenes *in general*": consequently I exclude the Essenes of *1QS*, but not those to whom *1QSa* is directed and neither the Zadokites of *CD* who – like 'our' Essene groups – appear to be less demanding than the ascetics of Qumran (that is those of *1QS*) as to property (and related issues, such as for instance, charity and the community of goods), marriage and the attitude toward the Temple of Jerusalem. Nevertheless all these groups are part of a wider Middle Judaic movement generally referred to as 'Essenism'.

Those Essenes who, as Josephus informs us, lived scattered in towns and villages of Judaea (and, probably, also of the diaspora),[79] in stark

---

76.   Boccaccini 1991; 1993a, pp. 42 and 47-48. The author dwells extensively on Jewish Hellenism, but – at least here – he covers quite rapidly the subject-matter of Essenism. On the contrary, Sacchi 2000 will devote more attention to Essenism, in particular in the *Parte seconda*, where the author will deal with the major themes of the so-called "Middle Judaism".

77.   I already expressed this 'caution' in *Comunione e condivisione* (= Del Verme 1977, pp. 73-74), in particular *Parte seconda* of the book (pp. 69-131).

78.   Stemberger 1991, *Vorwort*; cf. anche Fitzmyer 1992, pp. 100-102 (*question* n° 67).

79.   In my opinion it is not fortuitous that Philo in reporting on the Therapeutae of Egypt (*vit. cont.* 1-20) tends to associate them with the Essenes (*vit. cont.* 1-2) of Syria and Palestine (ἡ Παλαιστίνη Συρία: *omn. prob.* 75). G. Vermes too considered that Philo's Therapeutae could be envisaged as Essenes of the diaspora. For this and other solutions, cf. Ch. Burchard, "Therapeuten", in *Der Kleine Pauly. Lexicon der Antike in*

contrast with the Qumranites who lived segregated in the Judaean Desert on the northwestern shores of the Dead Sea, could have been more exposed than the latter to the influences of Hellenism, active in the Roman province of Judaea during the 1st century CE, as Hengel has shown in a series of convincing studies.[80] Such a (probable) Hellenistic influence on "some Essene groups" lies behind also the more general problem regarding the attitudes of the Jews toward the "gentiles" and the foreigners in general. The conduct of the Jews in the context of Hellenised Judaism – both of Palestine and of the diaspora – appears to be more liberal and open also to non-Jews. This fact could account – always within the boundaries of Essenism – for the differences between the Qumranites upholding a more radical opposition to and separation from the gentiles (Hebr. *gôyîm*; Gr. τὰ ἔθνη), and the (either married or unmarried) Essenes reported by Hellenistic Graeco-Roman sources, whose information often appears to agree with what is stated by the *Damascus Rule* (CD) and by the Appendix of the *Rule of the Congregation* (1QSa). Both these Essene-Qumranic documents, in fact, legislate for the married members of the community, dictating norms regulating the conduct toward internal members, the Jews as well as the

fünf Bänden, Band 5, hrsg. von K. Ziegler, W. Sontheimer und H. Gärtner (Stuttgart: A. Druckenmüller Verlag 1964), cols. 736-738. The existence of Essene groups in environments of the diaspora could be also confirmed by the presence of one or more translations of *1 Enoch*, which – according to Boccaccini 1997; 1998a; 2002a – could be considered a document attributable to some of the phases of the Essene movement: the identification of Essenism with Enochism remains problematic however (cf. J.J. Collins in *ASE* 19, 2002, in particular p. 506), although I believe that for the 1st century CE this could have been valid (recently, S. Goranson, "Essene Polemic in the Apocalypse of John", in M. Bernstein-F.García Martínez-J. Kampern [eds.], *Legal Texts and Legal Issues. -* Proceedings of the Second Meeting of the IOQS [Cambridge, 1995], Published in Honour of Joseph M. Baumgarten [STDJ 23; Leiden-New York-Köln: Brill, 1997], pp. 453-460). Therefore the Greek translation of sections of *1 Enoch* (at least for the *Book of the Watchers* and sections from *the Epistle of Enoch*) could probably be the legacy of some Greek Essenes: cf. Arcari 2003. As to the antiquity of the Greek translation of *1 Enoch*, see also Milik 1976, pp. 70-78, and E.W. Larson, *The Translation of Enoch: From Aramaic to Greek* (New York: University of New York Diss., 1995); "The Relation between the Greek and Aramaic Texts of Enoch", in L.H. Schiffman-E. Tov-J.C. VanderKam (eds.), *The Dead Sea Scrolls: Fifty Years after Their Discovery (1947-1997). -* Proceedings of the Jerusalem Congress (July 20-25, 1997), (Jerusalem: Israel Museum, 2000), pp. 434-444.

80.   See Hengel 1975.1976; in particular, Id. 1988[3], which remains – in my opinion – a 'classic' on Hellenistic Judaism. But on this volume see also Collins 1989.

non-members of the community,[81] with specific references to charity and hospitality which appear to have been practised toward foreigners too. An analogous description occurs in Josephus[82] in regard to the Essenes who live scattered in the towns and the villages of Judaea (probably Josephus was referring to contemporary Essenes).

As to my supposition that after 70 CE Essenism could still continue to influence the *Didache*, which was in the final stages of edition or had been already compiled – besides the hypothesis examined above of a Jewish *Vorlage* of the "Two Ways" behind the ethical material found in *Did.* 1-6 (including therefore the literary unit 4:5-8) – this should be worth considering. It is known, in fact, that after 70 CE any trace of the the Qumranites is lost. Living on the shores of the Dead Sea, were swept away by the material destruction of their settlement by the Romans during the first Jewish war (66-74 CE) – is lost. Fortunately, however, the Qumranites had provided to salvage the scrolls which were to be found centuries later in the eleven caves where they stored them, presumably immediately before or after the destructive invasion of the Qumran settlement in ca. 69 CE. Following the year 70 the settlement (and the Qumranites themselves) ceased to exist, although

81. Stemberger 1991, chap. IV, with exemplifications taken from CD 12:6-11 and reference (n. 22) of Tannaitic parallels studied by L. H. Schiffman. Other texts in Fitzmyer 1992, pp. 93-94 (*question* n° 63).

82. Besides the texts already cited (supra, nn. 66-70), I would draw the reader's attention to *J.W.* 2.132 : "On their return they sup in like manner, and any guests who may have arrived sit down with them." After the morning meal reserved only to the internal members of the community – whom Josephus has previously described in detail (ibid., 129-131) – in the evening the Essenes had another meal in which – as the text examined reports – the guests (Gr. τῶν ξένων) also shared. In my opinion the term 'guests' does not necessarily refer exclusively to 'Essene guests' just passing through, as Vitucci suggests (Flavio Giuseppe. *La Guerra Giudaica* [Scrittori greci e latini – Fondazione L.Valla; Milano: Mondatori, 1974], vol. I, p. 626 n. 10), but could also include 'foreign guests'. In fact if ξένοι were synonymous with 'Essenes passing through', it would be very difficult to explain why these were excluded (in fact they are not mentioned) from the morning meal, while the attribution of a less restricted semantic value to the term ξένοι (= guests in general, to include therefore also those external to the group) could justify their exclusion from the ante-meridiem 'holy meal', since the latter was only for the internal members of the community and included particular rituals and rules (*J.W.* 2.129-131). In my opinion the translation provided by Vermes-Goodman 1989 preserves the general (and original?) meaning of the passage: "Then they return and take their dinner in the same manner, and if guests are passing through they sit at the table" (p. 41).

there is no evidence at this stage as to whether either the Essenes or Essenism *in toto*, or at least the groups of the diaspora (one might think in Syria and in the area surrounding Antioch of Syria), came to an end. It appears that still in the 8th century CE the echo of Essenism was still reverberating, for the appearance of the Karaites, whose positions are akin to those of the Essenes[83] and the Sadducees, shatters the supposed 'idyllic unity' of Rabbinic Judaism, since – as Stemberger observes – that harmony under the Rabbinic direction never really existed, but is only the product of later, and often partisan, readings. The parallels between the Karaites and some of the historical (Middle-) Judaic groups/movements, such as Essenism, cannot be accounted for only by a mere literary transmission (= ancient Qumranic findings) but would imply either a continuity of the Essene movement in that of the Karaites or the dependence of the latter on the former.[84]

3. Conclusion

The *précis* made in the last paragraph (2.2.3.) and the closely connected previous sections (2.2.1. and 2.), do not lead to an unequivocal solution of the problem regarding the community of goods which arises from the analysis of the text and contexts of *Did.* 4:8. They can, however, be considered as *a point of departure toward a solution* of the complex theme of the community of goods in *Did.* 4:8. The *solution*, however, remains unattained.

I would like to describe the 'critical situation', in which both the text and the interpreter of *Did.* 4:8 find themselves immersed, by referring to a verse of *Qohelet*, which also contributes to express my conviction at the end of this chapter: "All things are full of weariness; a man cannot utter it" (1:8). Although the statement is applicable to any research, I believe it clearly reflects the conundrums and dilemmas of historical researches, in particular when examining arguments concealed in ancient texts, which are at the same time problematic and 'enigmatic', as the *Didache* is. I believe that the community of goods of *Did.* 4:8 should be listed among those problematic realities. The problematic is further aggravated by specific difficulties stemming from

83. See H. Bardtke, "Einige Erwägungen zum Problem «Qumran und Karaismus»", *Henoch* 10, 1988, pp. 259-275.
84. Stemberger 1991, chap. V.

the current situation of the studies of Christian origins, which are undergoing an intensive phase of development and renewal, in particular for the increasing attention to the Jewish 'roots' of Jesus, of his movement and of the Palestinian and non-Palestinian communities, which – although adhering to his message and accepting him as the Messiah – continued to remain anchored to some religious and social institutions still active in contemporary Judaism.

The 'roots', which were able to germinate in the soil of Palestinian Essenism (Hellenised and non-Hellenised)[85] as well as of the diaspora, could point students of Christian origins towards a new line of research. I believe, in fact, that these 'roots' deserve greater attention,[86] but without resuming old or obsolete theses, as for instance that of E. Renan (and his followers),[87] who went so far as to interpret Early Christianity (I would prefer 'Christian Judaism') as a successful form of Essenism.

---

85. Cf. Tuilier 1993; Penna 1997; Nodet-Taylor 1998; Boccaccini 1998a; et alii (supra, Chap. I, Part III., pp. 19-21).

86. An example: the *DPAC* – a work by the Italian school highly appreciated abroad – lacks a specific entry for the Essenes, except for some reference under *Encratismo* by F. Bolgiani (vol. I [Casale Monferrato: Marietti, 1983], cols. 1151-1153) which appropriately refers to both the Essenes of Palestine and the Therapeutae of Egypt in order to illustrate different forms of extreme asceticism among groups which soon became suspect to the "Great Church".

87. For E. Renan's thesis (and of Schuré, who maintains that Jesus was an 'initiate' of the secret doctrines of the Essenes), cf. Cullmann 1969, chap. I (at the beginning). As to the problems regarding the relations between Jesus/ Christianity/ Judaeo-Christianity and Essenism before the discovery of the Dead Sea Scrolls, cf. Parente 1962.1964, with a rich bibliography. For a recent discussion, Grappe 2002.

Chapter 3

DEFINING IDENTITIES: WHO ARE THE PEOPLE LABELLED
AS "HYPOCRITES" AND "THE OTHERS" IN *DIDACHE* 8?

1. Introduction

In this chapter I will revisit some arguments that I have explored
extensively elsewhere. I am referring in particular to the tithes and the
fast,[1] two institutions central to the religious and social life of the early
Jewish and Christian communities. I wish herein to focus my attention
again on these institutions in order to search for the presence of particular groups (i.e. the "Hypocrites" and "the Others" of *Did.* 8:1)
within the social world of what may be called "Christian Judaism".[2]
For this reason I have preferred to inquire into the area (i.e. the cultural
and vital context) of Essenism, either Qumranic or non-Qumranic, and/
or Enochian Essenism.

---

1.   Del Verme 1989, pp. 34-94; Id., "I <guai> di Matteo e Luca e le decime dei
farisei (Mt. 23,23; Lc. 11,42)", *RivBib* 32, 1984, pp. 273-314; Id. 1984; "La 'prima
decima' giudaica nella pericope di *Ebrei* 7,1-10", *Henoch* 8, 1986, pp. 339-363; Id.,
"La 'prima' decima nel giudaismo del Secondo Tempio", *Henoch* 9, 1987, pp. 5-38;
Id.,"Les dîmes hébraïques dans l'oeuvre de Josèphe et dans le Nouveau Testament', in
*Rashi 1040-1990. Hommage à Ephraïm E. Urbach. Congrès européen des Etudes
juives,* édité par G. Sed-Rajna (Paris: Cerf, 1993), pp. 121-137; Del Verme 1999.
2.   As I said above (p. 25 n. 32), I would prefer this more neutral terminology to
that of "Judeo-Christians" and/or "Judaising Christians", more common and recurrent
among students of Early Christianity. Actually, the latter is theologically vitiated or, at
least, full of doctrinal preoccupations typical of the Greek, Latin and Syriac works
written by heresiologists (eg Justin Martyr, Origen, Irenaeus, Epiphanius, Jerome, and
Eusebius). By the terms 'Christian Judaism' or 'Christian Jews' I mean the Jews who
believed and confessed Jesus of Nazareth as Messiah, but continued to live within a
Jewish reality. The concept of 'Christian Jews' seems to me an appropriate way to label
such groups, who were (and remained) sympathetic to contemporary Judaism: in fact,
they continued to frequent the synagogues and observed Jewish rites, practices, and
customs. Therefore, the "Great Church" – but only later – was to condemn them as
heretics.

The texts at our disposal are the earliest compositions within Judaism that may be labelled Christian Jewish or proto-Christian writings, starting with the earliest documents in the so-called *New Testament*. Far too often, scholars build a barrier separating the canonical books from other contemporary compositions, labelling the latter, some as "Apostolic Fathers" and others as Apocrypha and/or Pseudepigrapha of the OT and NT, even though the documents in the NT and the other collections belong to or represent the same historical period.[3]

The document of interest to us now, the *Didache*, has been traditionally placed in the category of Apostolic Fathers. Contemporary with these writings are other documents such as *4 Ezra* and *2 Apoc. Baruch,*[4] which are roughly of the same period as the *Apocalypse* of John. Unfortunately, these groups of texts are separated into distinct categories, as if one could distinguish between "Jewish" and "Christian" compositions.[5] A case in point is the Apocalypse of John: many scholars think it is Christian but a few maintain that it is originally Jewish.[6] Such discussions make it clear that alleged Jewish and Christian documents should be discussed together since they represent the same social and historical context in the history of ideas.[7]

In the Introduction to *Giudaismo e Nuovo Testamento*[8] I explored these issues and now propose to expand on them, but limiting my reflections to six points, as follows:

1. One should not limit the research to a general (and generic) presence of Jewish elements in the *Didache*. It is necessary to explore

---

3. For this historical-literary perspective, see Del Verme 1989, pp. 15-20. And more generally, already Charlesworth 1985 (repr. 1987/1988).

4. M. Del Verme, "Sui rapporti tra 2Baruc e 4Ezra. Per un'analisi dell'apocalittica 'danielico-storica' del I sec. e.v.", *Orpheus* N.S. 24/1-2, 2003, pp. 30-54.

5. G. Boccaccini argues against this inappropriate historiographical perspective in Boccaccini 1991.1993.1998b.

6. Eg A. Yarbro Collins, *The Combat Myth in the Book of Revelation* (Missoula, Mont.: University Press, 1976), pp. 101-116, finds Judaic and non-Judaic material. A history of the literary problem posed by the Apocalypse, from the first commentators until the 80s, in U. Vanni, *La struttura letteraria dell'Apocalisse* (Brescia: Queriniana, 1980²), pp. 1-104; 255-311; see also Biguzzi 2004, in particular chap. I, pp. 21-46.

7. A propos, see *Appendix* in Charlesworth 1985. These historiographic and methodological insights, following on the 'svolta' made in the study of Hellenistic-Roman Judaism, to which is directly connected the problem of Christian origins, have exerted a positive influence on scholars, both historians of Early Christianity and NT exegetes, and – to a lesser extent – students of Early Christian Literature.

8. *Premessa*, pp. 15-20, with references *pro* and *contra*.

each element in the *Didache*, searching for specific laws, regulations, doctrines, and institutions active in the many Jewish groups and sects within Second Temple Judaism (esp. the period between 3rd century BCE to ca 135/6 CE).[9]

2. In determining the character of the Christian Judaism preserved within the *Didache* many experts have studied and included only Rabbinic Judaism.[10] This has proved misleading and non-productive. We should explore the clearly earlier forms of communal life, piety and spirituality now becoming evident within pre-70 Judaism, especially in the Apocrypha and/or Pseudepigrapha of the OT and Dead Sea Scrolls. Such clearly Semitic Palestinian sources are rich for exploration as we seek to uncover the religious, social, and intellectual roots of the religious world of the *Didache*.[11] In addition, we must include within our net the Diaspora Jewish literature preserved in Greek; then the net will be filled with early Jewish liturgical, sapiential, moral, apocalyptic, and spiritual concepts and ideas.

3. One must keep in mind that, when the *Didache* was being composed, there was no New Testament and thus, any influence from documents later collected in the NT will appear as influences from one or more documents on the *Didache*.[12] Prior to such so-called influences are sections of the *Didache* which appear to be early and

---

9.   At present, useful and valuable from some respects is the enormous amount of Jewish materials gathered by H. van de Sandt-D. Flusser 2002. Yet, to go further into details, one has to inquire more deeply into 'what kind' of Judaism is meant in the single parts of the whole work.

10.   Beginning with Taylor 1886, on to Alon 1958; more recently, Manns 2000, esp. chap. V (= La Didachê. Traité de halakot judéo-chrétiennes), pp. 335-350; and van de Sandt-Flusser 2002, pp. 172-179 (= Traditional Derekh Erets Materials), and *passim*. For other studies, cf. Draper 1996a, pp. 1-42 (8-10; 14-16), and also chap. 1.

11.   Supra, chap. 1 (= III. Judaism and Christian Origins); Draper 1996a, pp. 13-16; 42, and passim.

12.   The *Didache* cannot be dependent on the NT since the collection (i.e. the NT) was not yet closed, and some compositions included in it had not yet been written. Traditions were still fluid for years after the composition of Matthew and Luke (ca post-70 CE), as Papias and Tatian make clear. Indeed, Papias ca 130 CE wrote five books *Logiôn kyriakôn exêgêseôs* (see Eusebius, *Hist. eccl.* 3:39.1-7, 14-17), of which we have fragments concerning an Asiatic tradition, which will be taken up and reworked by Irenaeus, the defining characteristic of which was millenarianism, widely diffused in ancient Christianity. Tatian, Syrian by birth and a pupil of Justin Martyr, composed the *Diatessaron*, a kind of 'evangelical harmony'. In doing historical work – in my view – one must not separate into isolated 'capsules' the NT, the Apostolic

Jewish: among these are large parts of chaps. 1-6, the so-called document of the "Duae viae" (abbr. DVD).[13] In confronting social issues,
the author of the *Didache* does not show as much dependence on
concepts within the NT documents as upon Jewish concepts which,
before 70 CE, appear to have been paradigmatically important for
various Jewish groups.

4. When in the earlier essays I focused on fasting, tithing and public
prayer I suggested that the *Didache* was not dependent on *Matthew* and
Luke, concluding that the *Didache* – in its earliest *strata*[14] – took shape

Fathers, the ancient traditions posterior to the NT, and the Nag Hammadi Codices (esp.,
The Gospel of Thomas [NHC II, 2]).

13. The bibliography concerning the DVD is immense. Recently, van de Sandt-
Flusser 2002, have devoted four chapters to this topic (see, in particular, chap. 5, pp.
140-190) and all the commentaries treat this topic *in extenso*. To reach a *quasi-con-
sensus* on the antiquity and Jewishness of the DVD, see Rordorf 1972 (Engl. version, in
Draper 1996a, pp. 148-164), and Suggs 1972. Within this current of research Brock
1990 explains with a philological (and historical) perspective the usefulness of the *Pal.
Tgs.* (*Tg. Neof.*, *Tg. Ps.-J.*, and *Frg. Tg.*) to trace/follow the birth of the Jewish tradition
of DVD from the beginning in the text of the OT (in particular Jer 21:8 and Deut
30:15,19 taken together, and other texts esp. from Pss and Prov). To be sure, the
distinguished Oxford scholar was not the first to emphasise the importance of the
OT texts for the origin of the *topos* of the *Duae viae* (before him, J.-P. Audet, G.
Klein, J. Daniélou, Kl. Balzer, A.Orbe, and others), but he was more precise – it seems
to me – than the former researchers in noting the *details of wording* of various sources
in relation to the probable diachronic progression of this ethical motif: beginning from
the OT traditions up to Second Temple (and Rabbinic) Judaism, and on to the NT and
proto-Christian literature (canonical and non-canonical).

14. The *Didache* is a layered and complex work which reasonably has come to be
classified in the genre (Germ., *Gattung*) of 'progressive literature' ("evolved literature" according to Kraft; see also Draper, ibid., 19-22), to mean a writing of an active
and traditional community rather than a book written by a single author. To put it in an
image: the enigmatic work of the *Didache* may be represented as a 'vortex' (in Italian,
'vortice'), a term already used by Steimer 1992, i.e. a whirlpool in which abundant
waters flow together: *in primis*, ancient traditions (especially Jewish ones), which are
taken up (often) or adapted (sometimes) to ethical and cultural requirements of the
community/ies, wherein the Didachist lives or for which he wrote his work. And the
growing process of literary accretion of the Didache ended with the interpolation/
insertion of materials taken up from the synoptic (written?) traditions (viz. 1:3b-2:1;
15:3-4), which carry the work on to its final, redactional phase (ca second half of the 1st
century CE). *Contra*, A. Milavec, "When, Why, and for Whom Was the Didache
Created? An Attempt to Gain Insights into the Social and Historical Setting of the
Didache Communities", who asserts (but too sharply, in my opinion) the unity of the
Didache: "... the Didache has an intentional unity from beginning to end which, up to
this point, has gone unnoticed" (in *Proceedings of the Tilburg Conference on "The*

before the final redaction of *Matthew* and *Luke*. In such earlier *strata* of the work one might find traditions[15] referring to rites and institutions still alive and central in the religio-cultural life of both the Jews and Christian Jews.

5. It follows, then, that one should not refer to a definite parting of the ways,[16] as if shortly before or after the end of the 1st century CE there was a crossroads in the proverbial road, with Judaism taking one route and Christianity another.[17] For example, *Did.* 8:1-2 does not indicate that followers of Jesus were expelled from worship in the synagogue; therefore the mention of "hypocrites" in *Did.* 8 does not lead to the supposition that such individuals are Pharisees or Jews. One might perceive in this chapter and elsewhere in the work too some form of social and religious tension within one large group with factions, perhaps to be comprehended as Christian Jews.

Didache and Matthew" [Assen-Minneapolis: Van Gorcum, forthcoming]). For the Didachist as a redactor of Tradition, cf. Draper 1996a, pp. 22-24, who concludes section 8. by writing: "We do not know what occasion led to this compilation, except that the author wishes to apply old tradition to new circumstances in a time of transition. It is not intended to be comprehensive" (p. 24).

15. I myself keep the word 'tradition' in the sense of the German *"Traditionsgeschichte"*, but not assuming something conveyed and worked out in the final redaction of a given text (in Germ., *Redaktionsgeschichte*). In my opinion, this methodology will help to work out the *Sitz im Leben* and the original meaning either of lemma/sentences or institutions (like tithing and fasting of the "hypocrites" [Matt and *Did.*]), which may refer to the *same* traditions (*traditionsgeschichtlich*) but evoke "two religious systems addressing common problems in divergent ways" (*una cum* A. Milavec, "When, Why, and for Whom Was the Didache Created?", cit.). Such tradition(s) are conveyed at times *quasi verbatim* by both texts (*Matthew* and *Didache*), but they are quite different in time and religious system, as can be seen at point after point in our text.

16. So – yet mistakenly in my opinion – almost all scholars commenting on *Did.* 8:1-3. Among the many, Draper 1992 (but the author seems to have changed his opinion most recently: see his paper in *Proceedings of the Tilburg Conference*). I shall return to this essay (infra, 4., pp. 145ff.) when clarifying some problematic aspects of *Did.* 8:1, to which I will propose solutions sometimes different from Draper's. See also van de Sandt-Flusser 2002, pp. 291-296, who assert: "The whole section (viz. Did. 8:1-3), in sum, reflects an attitude of animosity to Jews and Judaism; the unsubstantiated disparagement of the 'hypocrites' does not seem to leave open any possibilities of reconciliation" (p. 296 quoting [n. 81] Draper 1996a, p. 243). *Contra*, Tomson 2001; Id., "The war against Rome..." in Id. – Lambers-Petry 2003, pp. 8-14.

17. More details about this historical and historiographical problem, supra, chap. 1, but some lines concerning this subject I wrote in *"Didaché e origini cristiane. I."* (see Del Verme 2001a, pp. 21-23, with references to some Italian scholars, in particular Jossa and Troiani.

6. *Did.* 8:1-2 clearly reveals a social situation of two groups in opposition. The proper approach for discerning these groups does not appear to be a comparison of the *Didache* with *Matthew* or *vice versa*. Focus should be shifted, however, to the pre-redactional level of *Matthew* (and *Luke*) with particular attention to the mention of the "hypocrites" referring to tithes and fast. Such an exploration will reveal some novel and challenging insights.

2. The Tithes of the Pharisees (Matt-Luke) Hypocrites (Matt)

The study of tithing in the "woes" against the Pharisees (Matt 23:23 and Luke 11:42) and the significance of the epithet "hypocrites" levelled against the Pharisees (only in Matt) will be the primary subject of this portion of the essay. I should immediately preface that the Matthean and Lucan traditions concerning the Pharisees – with particular respect to tithing, fasting and public prayer – have been studied with the primary goal of exploring the historical reality and religio-social functions of these institutions in Palestinian, Jewish and Christian-Jewish communities. Thus, I do not intend to use this argument to explain the influence of Matthew (and/or Luke) on the *Didache*,[18] which in 8:1 labels those who "fast on Monday and Thursday" as "hypocrites", but to explore the Jesus and/or post-Jesus tradition concerning the hypocrisy of the Pharisees, which might help clarifying what people (and also the redactor of the *Didache*) meant by labelling individuals or groups as "hypocrites" in connection with religio-social institutions like tithes and fast.

2.1. Tithes in the "Woes" of Matthew and Luke[19]

Matt 23:23:   Luke 11:42
Οὐαὶ ὑμῖν, γραμματεῖς καὶ   Ἀλλὰ οὐαὶ ὑμῖν τοῖς Φαρισαίοις,
Φαρισαῖοι ὑποκριταί,
ὅτι ἀποδεκατοῦτε τὸ ἡδύοσμον   ὅτι ἀποδεκατοῦτε τὸ ἡδύοσμον

---

18. See Rordorf-Tuilier 1998, pp. 83-91; 231-232. A good synthesis of the problem and various solutions proposed by scholars can be found also in Visonà 2000, pp. 90-121.

19. Specific studies on the Matthean and Lucan "woes" are quoted in Del Verme 1989, pp. 34-35 n. 39. See also K. Newport, *The Sources and Sitz im Leben of Matthew 23* (DPhil Diss. Oxford University, 1988), Pedersen 1995, and Saldarini 1988.1994.

καὶ τὸ ἄνηθον καὶ τὸ κύμινον,   καὶ τό πήγανον καὶ πᾶν λάχανον,
καὶ ἀφήκατε τὰ βαρύτερα τοῦ   καὶ παρέρχεσθε
νόμου,
τὴν κρίσιν καὶ τὸ ἔλεος   τὴν κρίσιν καὶ τὴν ἀγάπην τοῦ
καὶ τὴν πίστιν·   Θεοῦ·
ταῦτα δὲ ἔδει ποιῆσαι   ταῦτα δὲ ἔδει ποιῆσαι
κἀκεῖνα μὴ ἀφιέναι   κἀκεῖνα μὴ παρεῖσαι

Woe to you, scribes and Pharisees, But woe to you Pharisees!
hypocrites!
For you tithe   For you tithe
mint,   mint,
dill and cummin,   and rue and herbs of all kinds,
and have neglected   and neglected
the weightier of the law:
justice and mercy   justice and love of God:
and faith.
It is these you ought to have   it is these you ought to have
practised   practised
without neglecting the others.   without neglecting the others.

Matt 23:23 and Luke 11:42 are studied side by sid because of close similarities both in their literary composition and their content. This approach thus allows me to mention the delicate problem of sources, oral and written, behind the editing of the *logia* in *Matthew* and *Luke*.[20]

The Problem of Sources

As it is well known, within the literary problem of the origins of the Gospels, the synoptic question remains even today open to many solutions. Nevertheless, for texts within the double tradition (Matt-Luke), which are too similar to justify the combination of terms on pure coincidence – excluding the idea that Matthew and Luke copied one another – the literary hypothesis that these texts depend on a common source remains the most probable explanation. I have adopted this critical solution in the interpretation of the parallel *logia* on tithing

---

20.   It is not my intention to study the literary story of Matt 23:23 and Luke 11:42, but I am interested in their probable dependence on a source prior to the written Gospels.

which do not have a correspondence in Mark. Certainly, one can continue to discuss whether the two versions (the Matthean [23:1-36] and Lucan [11:37-53; 20:45-47]) of the recriminations of Jesus against the Pharisees and scribes[21] are derived from an original document of Q[22], which the specific theologies of Matthew and Luke have rendered in two slightly different forms; or these invectives were already circulating in a double version in the tradition that predates the Gospels.

In any case, it is an undeniable literary fact that Matt 23:23 and Luke 11:42 are the verses with the largest number of verbal similarities[23] in the parallel series of the "woes" (Matt 23:13-36 and Luke 11:42-53). And it appears to be a relatively widespread opinion among scholars of literary criticism that these *logia* derive from a pre-editorial source,[24] one that Matthew and Luke modulated with their own terms but without altering a previous tradition, which stressed the zealousness of the Pharisees (and the scribes?) in the fulfilment of the rules of tithing.

2.2. The "Woe" of Matt 23:23-24

Matt 23:23-24 is the fourth of seven "woes" in a long speech (Matt 23) constructed – according to a method congenial to Matthew – from

---

21. Mark 12:37b-40 shows that even the earliest evangelist is aware of a tradition of denunciation against the scribes, parallel to the more detailed invectives of Jesus against the Pharisees and the scribes in Matt and Luke. Mark has the location of the narrative sequence in common with Matt 23:1-39 – an additional argument in favor of the dependence of Matt on the scheme of Mark – because the denunciation against the scribes of Mark – as was the case in Matt – precedes the eschatological speech (Mark 13 = Matt 24) and comes after the pericope on the messiah, son and father of David (Mark 12:35-37 = Matt 22:41-46; see also Luke 20:41-44). The verbal concordance is very rare: see Mark 12:38b-39 e Matt 23,6-7a. In any case, Mark does not know the form of the "woes".

22. The reconstruction of the original Q source is destined to remain conjectural, and the history of the exegesis offers many examples. The majority of the exegetes, however, point to the text of Luke – in his literary formulation and in the sequencing of the "woes" – as closer to the Q source.

23. Matt 23:23b: ταῦτα [δὲ] ἔδει ποιῆσαι κἀκεῖνα μὴ ἀφιέναι and Luke 11:42b: ταῦτα δὲ ἔδει ποιῆσαι κἀκεῖνα μὴ παρεῖναι The first six words correspond *verbatim*, and as seventh word we read two verbs, both in the infinitive (pres. in Matt, aor. in Luke), of almost the same meaning.

24. Eg, R. Bultmann, *Die Geschichte der synoptischen Tradition* (FRLANT NF 12; Göttingen: Vandenhoeck & Ruprecht, 1967) (VII ed. = II ed. of 1931), compares Luke11:43.46.52.42.(39.)44.47 and Matt 23: (4.6.)13.23.25. 27.29, defending them as *Weherufe* (= invectives), that derived from Q (p. 118).

the fusion of various elements (in general *logia* or short pericopes), interconnected but taken from distinct sources and traditions, which Matthew compacted by placing them in the same literary context. The editorial process, namely the anthological compilation of Matthew shown in chap. 23, is quite similar to that practised elsewhere, eg in chaps. 5-7 and in general in the great speeches (13; 18; 24-25) of his Gospel.

The literary structure of Matt 23 is complex and much debated by critics; but on some points one can arrive at a partial consensus among scholars: vv 1-12 form the first literary section of the speech; the second section is composed of seven woes, beginning with v 13 (= the first woe) and ending with the last woe, of which we know the beginning (v 29) but not the end.

Matt 23:23-24, the fourth invective in the Matthean sequence of "woes", is composed of two parts: v 23 is the first part (par. Luke 11:42, the first invective of the Lucan series), and v 24 is the second part that contains specific material (= *Sondergut*) of Matthew.

The literary structure of Matt 23:23 is almost uniform, occurring in each of the seven woes of chap. 23 with the following elements: 1) an apostrophe, consisting of the interjection οὐαί plus the dative ὑμῖν, followed by the name of the addressee in vocative γραμματεῖς καὶ Φαρισαῖοι; 2) the justification of οὐαί, i.e. the addressees are ὑποκρι-ταί, a central keyword of the literary unit; 3) and a declarative-causal clause introduced by ὅτι, which defines and explains at the same time the previously denounced "hypocrisy".

"Woe to You, Scribes and Pharisees"

The apostrophe οὐαὶ ὑμῖν, γραμματεῖς καὶ Φαρισαῖοι, which re-turns six times – always at the beginning – in the series of seven Matthean invectives (23:13.15.23.25.27.29), raises problems at differ-ent levels (exegetical, historical, and editorial), which are crucial to the understanding of the "woes" in general as well as the literary unit Matt 23:23-24. The difficulties increase in number if the Matthean "woes" are studied with a synoptic attention to the parallel Lucan "woes", which are similar in substance but do not correspond in order and literary composition.

1. The first interpretative difficulty comes from the interjection οὐαί, an exclamation of pain and displeasure as well as a threat. This interjection οὐαί has been interpreted either as a *Septuagintism* which renders with solemn style the Hebrew word *hôy* or *'ôy*, or as a *Latinism*

(i.e. the transcription of Latin *vae*).²⁵ Assuming that the linguistic background of the Matthean οὐαί can be traced to the OT and above all to
the prophetic books where *hôy* appears most frequently, the meaning of
this term is very important because it may unravel the semantic background of Matt 23:23-24. With Garland,²⁶ one might synthesise the
various meanings of the *hôy*-sentences into three categories: 1. *hôy*
indicates a cry of pain, especially in the context of mourning, and
thus can be translated as "alas!'"; 2. *hôy* expresses a cry of grief,
demanding attention or making an appeal to someone, equivalent to
"oh" or "ah!'"; 3. *hôy* introduces a threat or a promise of condemnation and corresponds to "woe!", which not only announces a catastrophe, but positively invokes it: thus, one could read it as a curse.

The speaker in each of the three forms of *hôy* is Jahweh. The
specificity of the prophetic *hôy*, form 3. (= "woe!"), is the stereotypi-
cal condemnation of a group or single person for bad behaviour, which
in turn provokes the prophet to threaten in the name of Jahweh. Reading the Matthean "woes" against this OT (prophetic) background²⁷
allows for a more appropriate contextualisation as well as less repetitive exegesis of the "woes".

For the "woes" of Matt 23, I would contend that they proleptically
represent (= on the historical-editorial level) the final judgement of
Jesus on the false leaders of a recalcitrant people: this interpretation
is in line with the literary structure and judicial tone of Matt 21-25.
Thus, the interjection οὐαί of Matt 23 cannot be read as a simple
expression of pain and commiseration nor a threatening yell mingled
of rage and piety. More precisely, it indicates the threat of a verdict of
condemnation that borders on a curse.

2. A second difficulty rises from the binomial γραμματεῖς καὶ φαρισαῖοι. It is a widespread opinion among exegetes and historians – but
also among scholars of the Q source – that a distinction between
"Pharisees" and "lawyers" (as in Luke 11:42-52) is preferable to

25. Fr. Blass-A. Debrunner, *Grammatik des neutestamentlichen Griechisch*, bear-
beitet von Fr. Rehkopf, 14., völlig neubearbeitete und erweiterte Auflage (Göttingen:
Vandenhoeck & Ruprecht, 1976), §§ 4,2a; 5,1e.
26. D.E. Garland, *The Intention of Matthew 23* (SupplNT 52; Leiden: Brill,
1979), pp. 73ff.
27. The divine 'vendetta' in favor of the righteous is a constant element also in
the "woes" of *1 Enoch*: 94:6-11; 95:4-7; 97:7-8; 98:9-15; 99:1-2, 11-15; 100:7-10, and
generally in the apocalyptic literature.

the pair "scribes and Pharisees" as in the Matthean woes (23:13-32; cf. 23:2). Actually, the Lucan woes – three against the Pharisees (11:42-44) and three against the lawyers (11:46-52) – reflect the religio-historical situation of contemporary Judaism, where the νομικοί (= γραμματεῖς of Matt) were professional exegetes, distinct from the Pharisees, a movement or religious group practising scrupulous observation of the Law (both written and oral).[28] Therefore, the invective of 23:23-24 that Matthew indiscriminately hurls against the scribes and Pharisees – being the parallel of Luke 11:42 where the addresses are the Pharisees – must be interpreted exclusively against the Pharisees (as in the Q source and, presumably, in the public teaching of Jesus).

In any case, it is important to investigate the historical-editorial motive that could have driven the author of Matt 23 to present two distinct groups as a single movement, unless one wants to affirm – simplistically and hastily – that Matthew was misinformed on this important subject in the history of Judaism. First of all, *Matthew* – with respect to *Mark* and *Luke* – shows a tendency to downplay the real distinctions between Jewish parties and religious movements of Jesus'time. Secondly, *Matthew* may reflect the historical situation of Judaism after the catastrophe of 70 CE, when almost all of the scribes came from the class of the Pharisees. Finally, the Pharisaic Judaism of Jamnia constitutes, between the years 70-136 CE, the centre (or one of the centres) of the nascent Rabbinic Judaism that began to move away from the Christian-Jewish communities for whom Matthew wrote his Gospel.

All of this should be considered to explain the hostile image and the pairing of scribes and Pharisees in Matthew: one is confronted with an editorial operation that aims to place (= *Sitz im Leben Jesu*) the hostility that his community was daily experiencing in the difficult relations with Jewish leaders. Indeed, Matthew attempts to present the entire historical process of Israel under the sign of failure, due to the poor leadership of its religious leaders.[29] Thus the "scribes and Pharisees" of Matthew represent – although not exclusively – the *genus* of false leaders in Israel to be condemned to an imminent judgment and punishment (23:33-36).

---

28.   Besides Jeremias 1962³, pp. 265-278 [= *Die Schriftgelehrten*]; pp. 279-303 [= *Anhang: Die Pharisäer*]), see Schürer 1979, II, pp. 322-336; 388-403.

29.   A. Sand, *Das Gesetz und die Propheten. Untersuchungen zur Theologie des Evangeliums nach Matthäus* (BibUnt II; Regensburg: Pustet, 1974), pp. 81-82.

The presence and interpretation of ὑποκριταί raises some rather complex questions because of its centrality in the structural tripartite scheme of Matt 23:23 and other Matthean "woes" (six out of seven times).

Although it is a widespread opinion among scholars of literary criticism[30] that the noun ὑποκριταί (23:13,15, 23,25,27,29) is an author's addition by Matthew the readings still has its difficulties.[31] Therefore, other scholars maintain that ὑποκριταί expresses a 'traditional' reality.[32]

In order to argue for the editorial addition of the term (i.e. that ὑποκριταί is a Matthean invention, an epithet not present in the Q source), the parallel Lucan "woes" (cf. also Mark 12:37-40) are usually cited for the term ὑποκριταί does not occur. In any case, on a general linguistic level, Matthew is among the Synoptics the one that contains the highest frequency (14 times) of words derived from the verb ὑποκρίνομαι (with dropping of the nasal).

In addition, those who maintain the 'originality' of the term ὑποκριταί as a *datum* of tradition (to be traced back to a pre-Matthean source [Q?]), argue that under close examination the accusation of hypocrisy against the Pharisees is known to Luke[33] as well, and that the omission of ὑποκριταί in the series of Lucan woes (11:42-52) is dictated by the context (11:37, a meal) in which Luke has located his threats. This context has necessarily influenced the writer, pushing him to soften his tone of accusation, in order to preserve Jesus from the

---

30. S. Schulz, *Q: Die Spruchquelle der Evangelisten* (Zürich: Theologischer Verlag, 1972), p. 96; F. Heinrichs, *Die Komposition der antipharisäischen und anti-rabbinischen Wehe-Reden bei den Synoptikern*, Licenziaten-Arbeit (München: w.e., 1957), pp. 60-64.

31. If the expression "scribes and Pharisees, hypocrites" is editorial (that is, constructed by Matthew) it does not explain – or at least could seem somewhat singular – why it was omitted from the third woe (Matt 23:16-22), where ὑποκριταί is replaced with ὁδηγοὶ τυφλοί (v 16). And 23:16-22 – which does not have a parallel in Luke – is an evident stylisation on the part of Matthew under the form of "woes" of a traditional saying, which recalls the time when the Temple was still active.

32. R. Banks, *Jesus and the Law in the Synoptic Tradition* (SNTStMon 28; Cambridge: Cambridge University Press, 1975), p. 180; R. Pesch, "Theologische Aussagen der Redaktion von Matthäus 23", in *Orientierung an Jesus. Zur Theologie der Synoptiker*, Fs. für J. Schmid (Freiburg-Basel-Wien: Lang, 1973), p. 291.

33. In fact, Luke 12:1 – immediately after the series of woes of 11:42-52 – refers to the warning of Christ to his disciples: "Beware of the yeast of the Pharisees, that is their hypocrisy", with the iconic image of yeast (Gr. ζύμη) that spoils everything.

social embarrassment of being a 'rude guest'. Indeed, in the introductory portion of the woes, Luke 11:39-41 modifies the 'original' woes (see Matt 23:25-26) in a simple but firm response of Jesus to the marvel of the host, when he does not perform his ablutions before lunch (Luke 11:37-38).

However, the emphasis, the insistence, and the regularity with which Matt 23 stigmatises the hypocrisy of the scribes and Pharisees manifest an emphasis typical of Matthew the author. It thus seems legitimate to speak also of 'author's activity' on Matthew's part when he calls the Pharisees ὑποκριταί, an epithet with the function of a *Leitmotiv*. Certainly, Matthew has not created the tradition on the hypocrisy of the Pharisees,[34] but rather he is the most representative '*tradens-interpres*' of it among the Synoptics.

Ὑποκριτής in the Gospel of Matthew

What is the meaning (or better, the meanings) of ὑποκριτής in *Matthew*? The question is a philological one. But it is also the context of the woes, expressed in Matt 23 by the clause-ὅτι of the tripartite scheme, which qualifies each time an instance of hypocrisy.

The history of the interpretation of ὑποκριτής is complex because the Greek term has assumed multiple meanings in Classical and Hellenistic Greek, in the Jewish literature of the Diaspora, in the *Koinê* of the NT, and the proto-Christian writings.[35]

---

34. This tradition is also referred to by Mark 7:6; 12:15; and by Luke 12:1, 56; 13:15.

35. U. Wilkens, 'Ὑποκρίνομαι κτλ., in *TWNT* VIII, cols. 558-570; E. Zucchelli, *ΥΠΟΚΡΙΤΗΣ. Origine e storia del termine* (Brescia: Paideia, 1962); also J. Barr, "The Hebrew/Aramaic Background of 'Hypocrisy' in the Gospels", in Davies-White 1990, pp. 307-326; M. Gertner, "The Terms Pharisaioi, Gazarenoi, Hypokritai: Their Semantic Complexity and Conceptual Correlation", *BSO(A)S* 26, 1963, pp. 245-268; P. Joüon, "ΥΠΟΚΡΙΤΗΣ dans l'Évangile et l'Hébreu *Hanef*", *RechSR* 20, 1930, pp. 312-316; R. Knierim, "חנף pervertiert sein", in *THAT* I, cols. 597-599; D. Matheson, " 'Actors': Christ's Word of Scorn", *ExpTim* 41, 1929-1930, pp. 333-334; and the dictionaries: H.-G. Liddell-R. Scott-H. Stuart Jones, s.v. ὑποκρίνομαι and ὑπόκρισις; M. Jastrow, *A Dictionary of the Targumim, The Talmud Babli and Yerushalmi, and the Midrashic Literature*, I-II (New York-London: Pardes, 1886-1903), s.v חנף (= I, 484-485); J. Levy, *Neuhebräisches und Chaldäisches Wörterbuch über die Talmudim und Midrashim*, I-IV (Leipzig: Baumgärtner, 1876-1889; repr. Darmstadt: Wissenschaftliche Buchgesellschaft, 1962), s.v. חנף (= II, 83-84); and K. Seybold, s.v. חנף etc., in G.J. Botterweck-H.Ringgren (eds.) in Verbindung mit G.W. Anderson, H. Cazelles,

With respect to *Matthew*, Garland[36] has worked out five categories to include all the meanings of ὑποκριταί identified by the exegetes and philologists, with particular attention to Matt 23:1. ὑποκριταί expresses a conscious deceitfulness, the contrast between appearances and reality, between speaking and doing, between the exterior and interior of a person; 2. ὑποκριταί indicates a state of contradictory objectivity and wickedness as seen by God rather than the conscious deception that one circumvents; 3. ὑποκριταί illustrates a situation of religious error: it is the failure or floundering of faith, the refusal to live the δικαιοσύνη taught by Jesus, in other words the δικαιοσύνη that embodies the will of God; 4. ὑποκριταί alludes to scrupulous attention to the detail of the Law; 5. ὑποκριταί refers to the false teaching and poor interpretation of the Law.

If taken individually, none of these five meanings could properly explain all seven Matthean woes. One needs to rely each time on one or more than one of the afore-mentioned categories in order to translate the complexity of the epithet ὑποκριταί. Indeed, the term ὑποκριτής bears a semantic polychromy, in which specific value (or values) emerge, in each case, from the literary and conceptual structure of the single woe. And thus, the search for a 'comprehensive' or 'universal' significance to explain ὑποκριταί in Matt 23 is impossible.

Ὑποκριταί at Matt 23:23

In Matt 23:23 the Jewish religious leaders ("scribes and Pharisees") are presented under the threat of condemnation ("woe to you"), because their hypocrisy has led them to an ethical and legal failure: in other words, they lack the essential and the secondary principles of the Law, and as a consequence they have betrayed the most important precepts in favour of those less important, such as the precept of tithing.

It seems to me that the significance of ὑποκριταί in this fourth Matthean invective can be found – principally but not exclusively – within the 4th and the 5th of the afore-mentioned semantic categories. Indeed, Matt 23:23-24 explicitly affirms: a- that religious leaders of the people have failed in their role as interpreters of the Law; b- that they are guilty of transgressing the vital commandments of the Law, and

D.N. Freedman, Sh. Talmon und G. Wallis, *Theologisches Wörterbuch zum Alten Testament*, Band III (Stuttgart-Berlin-Köln-Mainz: Kohlhammer, 1982), cols. 41-48.
    36. Ibid., pp. 96-117.

now find themselves in a state of ἀνομία (injustice), as opposed to δικαιοσύνη (justice); c- moreover, the text seems to implicitly contain an historical reference to the halakhic debates among various Jewish schools around the interpretation of the *Torah,* particularly with respect to tithing; d- also – as a 'watermark' – this text reveals the attitude of Jesus and that of the Christian-Jewish communities with regard to observation of certain precepts and institutions of the OT and the position to take regarding Judaism before and after 70 CE.

The vulgar (and widespread) meaning of hypocrite, as a person who externally presents himself as cloaked in honesty but is wicked within; and the meaning of hypocrisy as the equivalent of conscious deceitfulness are only secondary and later in the semantic history of the verb ὑποκρίνομαι and the words derived from it.[37] This is not the meaning of ὑποκριταί in Matt 23:23 as well as in the other woes (eg 23:13 and 23:15) of the Matthean series. An explicit reference to the contrast between the appearance and the reality and to dissimilarities between ἔξωθεν and ἔσωθεν can be found – as far as Matt 23 goes – only in vv 27-28. In fact, Matt 23:23b underscores the ('relative') goodness of Pharisaic acts with the apodeictic affirmation: "It is these (= the payment of tithes) you ought to have practised", even if in the same sentence other wanting aspects are condemned: "without neglecting the others" (i.e. "justice and mercy and faith"). In other words, the ambiguity and deceitfulness of ὑποκριταί is missing in Matt 23:23; rather, it is evident that a denunciation of the attachment to secondary aspects of the Law is to the detriment of the essential ("neglected the weightiest matters of the Law"). Indeed, the hyperbole of v 24 ("You blind guides! You strain out a gnat but swallow a camel!") also recalls a paradoxical and subtly ironic image of the reality enunciated in v 23.

In Matt 23:23-24 there are two images, different in style but expressing the same subject: the "scribes and Pharisees" are poor interpreters of the *Torah,*[38] and are responsible and guilty for having failed to live

---

37. Only in the Byzantine period – and under the influence of Christian use of it – did the group of terms formed by ὑποκρίνομαι acquire in secular Greek the negative significance of "fiction" and "hypocrisy", as these words are commonly meant and used in modern languages. In contrast to the classical environment, ὑποκρίνομαι and its derivatives in Jewish literature of the Diaspora (LXX, Philo, and Josephus) always have a negative connotation.

38. With Garland – who recalls and partially corrects or amplifies the results of other scholars (eg O. Betz, M. Gertner, S.B. Hönig, H. Frankemölle, I. Sonne and Z.

according to the essentials of the Law. Indeed, they have deceived themselves and led astray the people entrusted to their care. Thus, one can read this as a double upbraiding, simultaneously ethical and legal.

2.3. The "Woe" of Luke 11:42

The Lucan *logion* of 11:42 on the tithing of the Pharisees is the first of six invectives: three against the Pharisees (11:42-44) and three against the lawyers (11:46-52). The series of Lucan woes is framed in the context of a meal at which Jesus has been invited by a Pharisee (11:37).

If behind the two accounts of the woes (Matt-Luke) – as seems probable – there is a common source (Q) that largely collected the isolated *logia* and perhaps already homogeneous literary blocks arranged by subject, any attempt to establish whether Luke's or Matthew's text is the closest in style to the supposed original Q source can only be hypothetical. Nevertheless, it is more fruitful to study the *logia* on an editorial level. Such study is possible through the synoptic comparison of the literary and doctrinal peculiarities of Matthew and Luke.

Luke 11:42 which, like the parallel Matt 23:23, is classified *form-geschichtlich* among the "invectives" or "threats" in the NT, occurs within a pericope (11:37-54) framed in a specific editorial structure built to accommodate Luke's literary and theological project (as was formerly seen in Matt 23:13-32), who adapts and rewrites its source (viz. Q) inside the general plan of his Gospel.

Luke 11:37-54 falls in the middle of the so-called "travel journal"

Wacholder) – I would establish a probable parallelism between the expression "all the seekers of flattering things" (Hebr. דורשי חלקת) in the Qumran scrolls (eg CD-A I:18; 1QH X:15, 32; XII:10 ["for flattering things"]; 4QpIs 10; 4QpNah II:2,7; III: 2,4; IV:3,6-7), and the ὑποκριταί of Matt 23. With this result: the Qumranic accusation against the opponents of the community refers to the false doctrine of adversaries (perhaps Pharisees), because it constantly remains in the context of a dispute over the interpretation of the Law, as in Matt 23. The idea of deceit and hypocrisy as 'conscious deceitfulness' remains of secondary significance for ὑποκριταί of Mt 23 and also for דורשי חלקת of the Qumran scrolls. Also elsewhere in the NT and in the proto-Christian literature ὑπόκρισις denotes a certain ambiguity, because the term does not necessarily imply dissimulation but is often used in contexts regarding orthodoxy and teaching (for example, Gal 2:13; 1 Tim 4:1-2; Herm., *Sim.* 8:6, 5; 9:19, 2, 3; Pol., *Phil.* 8:3. See also Matt 15:1-7; 16:5-12; Luke 13:10-17).

or "great Lucan insert" (9:51-18:14): the evangelist places in the fictitious frame of a single voyage to Jerusalem a large number of pericopes, largely presented as isolated scenes. This strategy of Luke as author needs to be taken into account when one wants to raise 'historical' questions or uncover certain 'narrative inconsistencies' in his Gospel.

Literary Frame and the Original *Sitz im Leben*

The accumulation of accusations and threats in Luke 11:37-54 and their cutting tone and content has not passed unnoticed among scholars, who have underlined that the original *Sitz im Leben* can hardly be imagined as a speech made at the table, and agreed on the existing dissonance between the 'frame' and the 'content' of the speech. Luke – and only he – mentions two other times (7:36; 14:1) Jesus' invitation to dinner by a Pharisee; and in such circumstances he recounts a dispute, as in the text we are examining.

The question concerning the original context of the invectives of Jesus against the Pharisees and lawyers, whether it was a *public speech* as in Matt 23 or a *dinner* at the house of a Pharisee as in Luke 11:37-54 has been much debated among scholars. It seems to me, however, that the debate surrounding the original setting of the confrontation remains open. I am inclined to think that the Matthean frame constitutes the best setting (already in the Q source?). Almost certainly, it was the *earliest literary tradition*, considering that Mark – the earliest of the Synoptics – refers to the words of Jesus against the scribes in the context of a public speech (12:38-40) as in Matthew. See, in particular, Mark 12:38a: Καὶ ἐν τῇ διδαχῇ αὐτοῦ ἔλεγεν, Βλέπετε ἀπὸ τῶν γραμματέων κτλ. (the audience is πολύς ὄχλος of v 37).

The distribution of Lucan invectives in two groups and two moments: the first three against the Pharisees (11:42-44) and the latter three against the lawyers (11:46-52) – as opposed to the general pair of scribes and Pharisees in six of the seven invectives of Matt 23:13-32 – seems to reflect an historical reality pertinent to Jewish religious groups in the time of Jesus. This scheme is not, however, exempt from incongruencies and is the product of the literary and artistic expression of Luke. For instance, the conclusion of the pericope (vv 53-54) seems to confirm the artificiality of the setting in which the threats by Luke take place. "When he (= Jesus) went outside, the scribes and the Pharisees began to be very hostile toward him and to cross-examine him about many things" (v 53), an affirmation which is justified if placed at the end of the story told in 11:37-41, but out of context if it is meant as a conclusion for the entire pericope (11:37-52) because Jesus has already said a fair amount (!) with the double series of invectives.

And yet by recalling at the beginning of the following chapter the thousands of people thronging around Jesus, and the presence of the disciples (12:1a) to whom he addresses admonishment to turn from hypocrisy (12:1b), Luke seems almost to remove the previous invectives from the fictitious table scene by setting them in the original or 'traditional' *Sitz im Leben*, which was presumably that of a public speech, as in Mark 12:38a and Matt 23:1 (see also Luke 20:45).

A Convivial Speech. Why?

The significance of the setting of the "woes" of Luke in the context of a dinner will now be considered in a specifically literary-theological context. By accepting the Schweizerian thesis[39] of the trial of the authorities of the Jewish religious leaders that unfolds in Matt 21-25, the pericope of Matt 23:1-32 has been read as a pronouncement of the "verdict of guilt". Unlike Matt 23, the section of Luke 11:37-54, because of its placement inside the "travel journal" which is not yet concluded, does not have the tone of a final conflict between Jesus and the Jewish leaders of Jerusalem that occurs at the end of his public life. On the contrary, the convivial context of the Lucan woes shows that the break between Jesus and his interlocutors had not yet occurred. The hard words of Jesus are thus interpreted more as an appeal to conversion than as a true verdict of condemnation. Thus, the Lucan "woes" seem to recall the second of three categories of the prophetic *hôy* previously discussed. And perhaps they would be better translated as "oh!" or "ah!", that is, as a sorrowful appeal to the conversion of the Pharisees and lawyers, and simultaneously an exhortatory but menacing appeal for those in the Christian-Jewish community of Matthew who practised an executive power (Schweizer).

I have insisted on some editorial aspects of the Lucan invective in order to clear the field of the gratuitous and somewhat widespread conviction among exegetes that Luke is 'historically' preferable to Matthew. Certainly, in the case of the pericope of the "woes", Luke's distinction between the Pharisees and lawyers is credible on historical

---

39. E. Schweizer, "Matthäus 21-25", in *Orientierung an Jesus*, pp. 364-371 (*à propos* of Matt 23:23-24); Del Verme 1989, pp. 39-41.

grounds; even the picture of Jesus at the table with the Pharisees pre-serves 'traditional' *datum* that recalls the style of the real life of Jesus during his public life. But the use of these 'historical *data*' as a frame for the *logia* of Jesus against the Pharisees and lawyers betrays a certain narrative artificiality: while it is consistent with the so-called "travel journal" of Luke, it does not fit with the threatening and judgmental tone of the woes. This narrative dystonia – beyond the literary fact of the earlier and perhaps presynoptic tradition referred to by Mark 12:38-40 (cf. also Luke 20:45-47) – leads me to prefer the *Sitz im Leben* of Matt 23, i.e. a public speech against the Pharisees (and scribes).

The Accusations against the Pharisees

The literary structure of Luke 11:42 is in some respects analogous to the parallel text of Matt 23:23, although less complex in its composi-tion. There is a binary structure: 1. the apostrophe with the interjection οὐαί with the dative pronoun ὑμῖν, followed by the name of the ad-dressees Φαρισαῖοι; 2. the declarative-causal clause with ὅτι, which explains the content of the threat. This second element of the structure could be intended as an antithetical parallelism (ἀποδεκατοῦτε...καὶ παρέρχεσθε) chiastically recalled in the apodeictic affirmation that follows (ταῦτα δὲ... κἀκεῖνα μὴ...). The literary structure of the *logion* highlights the contrast – more accentuated in the first frame of the period – between the punctilious diligence of the Pharisees in the pay-ment of tithes and their transgression of the law and love of God.

Luke's "woes" – unlike the parallel "woes" of Matthew, do not hint at a distinction between "less important" and "very important" aspects of the Law, but the discrepancy in value between the former (tithes) and the latter (justice and love of God) could be inferred from the general tone of the accusation.

The Pharisaic Religiosity and the Duty of Love

The choice of the dyad, justice-love of God, seems dictated by an authorial purpose: Luke intends to place Pharisaic religiosity under scrutiny – tithing in particular – measuring it by the twofold rule of the commandment of love, which Jesus had demonstrated to the lawyer in the preceding chap. (Luke 10:25-28) and here recalled with τὴν κρίσιν and with τὴν ἀγάπην τοῦ Θεοῦ (11:42).

Thus in the first of the six invectives Luke expresses a rather nega-tive opinion on the religiosity of the Pharises, summarised in the pay-ment of tithes "on herbs of all kinds". Such religiosity is not rejected *in toto* (κἀκεῖνα μὴ παρεῖναι of 11:42b) but judged wanting and insufficient, if measured by the 'absolute criterion' of the twofold inseparable precept of love.

Like Luke 11:42, Matt 23:23 also points to the payment of tithes and the transgression of the τὴν κρίσιν καὶ τὸ ἔλεος καὶ τὴν πίστιν, for his partially negative judgment of the religiosity of the Pharisees (and the scribes), but Matthew's terminology more directly recalls OT motives, with the aggravating circumstance that in Matthew the Jewish religious leaders are accused of having failed in their role as interpreters of the Law.

3. Tithing and Fasting of a Praying Pharisee (Luke 18:11-12)

The analysis of Luke 18:11-12 concentrates on two elements in particular: the payment of tithes and the bi-weekly fast, by which Luke sketches an image of Pharisaic religiosity. He does so by means of a parable (exemplary story?) of two antithetical figures, a Pharisee and a publican, praying together in the temple of Jerusalem (18:9-14a).

First, I would like to underline that my hermeneutics in reading the Gospels parables is fundamentally 'traditional' or 'classic'. Along with Jülicher-Dodd-Jeremias and others, I evaluate the 'setting' of the parables, ascribing an historical but not indiscriminate value to concrete socio-cultural details often found in them. For 'concrete details' I mean the so-called *realia*, that is, descriptive details that help to reconstruct the historical situation which constitutes the background of the parables.

The parable of Luke 18:9-14a, with its reference to the concrete details of the tithes and bi-weekly fast of the praying Pharisee (v 11-12) , seems to add new reasons to affirm the importance of turning to the *realia* for the study – in particular to fix the 'focal point' – of evangelical parables; and so indirectly to oppose a historical reading of the parabolic genre.

Luke 18:11-12:
v 11 ὁ Φαρισαῖος σταθεὶς πρὸς ἑαυτὸν ταῦτα προσηύχετο,
 Ὁ Θεός, εὐχαριστῶ σοι ὅτι οὐκ εἰμὶ
 ὥσπερ οἱ λοιποὶ τῶν ἀνθρώπων, ἅρπαγες, ἄδικοι, μοιχοί,
 ἢ καὶ ὡς οὗτος ὁ τελώνης·
v 12 νηστεύω δὶς τοῦ σαββάτου, ἀποδεκατῶ πάντα ὅσα κτῶμαι.

v 11 The Pharisee, standing by himself, was praying thus (literary, on his own),
"God, I thank you that I am not
like other people: thieves, rogues, adulterers,
or even like this tax-collector.[40]
v 12 I fast twice a week; I give a tenth of what I purchase".[41]

Luke 18:11-12 is part of a rather large section (18:9-14a) which scholars have almost unanimously classified under the category of "exemplary stories", along with three other formally identical texts referred to exclusively by Luke (the so-called Lucan *Sondertraditionen*): the Good Samaritan (10:30-37), the Rich Fool (12:16-20 [21]), The Rich Man and Lazarus (16: 19-31).

Luke 18:9-14a: An "Exemplary Story"?
Along with some other scholars, I believe that the definition of "exemplary stories" for these Lucan passages is unsatisfactory because they do not simply present models (positive or negative) of moral behaviour, but rather they offer a judgment on a certain way of thinking and living. In the mind of Luke, the realistic diptych of the two characters praying in the temple of Jerusalem functions as a response to "those who are secure (or confident) in their own righteousness (πρός τινας τοὺς πεποιθότας ἐφ'ἑαυτοῖς ὅτι εἰσὶν δίκαιοι) and regarded others with contempt (καὶ ἐξουθενοῦντας τοὺς λοιπούς)". For this audience, Jesus told this parable (Εἶπεν δὲ καὶ... τὴν παραβολὴν ταύτην) (v 9) to remind them that the judgement as to who is pious and who is a sinner is reserved for God (v 14a).

---

40. Or lessee/revenue officer?, i.e. Latin *publicanus*.
41. NRSV – not correctly in my opinion – says: "I give a tenth *of all my income*" and similarly many other modern translations of the NT (for example, *La Sainte Bible... de Jérusalem* [BJ] and *La Sacra Bibbia* CEI [BCei], but not only these!), because they were perhaps influenced by the Vulgate (*decimas do omnium quae possideo*), erroneously translate ἀποδεκατῶ πάντα ὅσα κτῶμαι (Luke 18:12b) with *je donne la dîme de tous mes revenus* (BJ) or *pago le decime di quanto possiedo* (BCei). On the other hand, Luke uses the verb κτάομαι to underline the diligence of the Pharisee who pays the tithes of *what he purchases* (including that which he already possesses). For this meaning of κτάομαι, F. Zorell, *Lexicon Graecum Novi Testamenti* (Parisiis: Lethielleux, 1961³), s.v. (*comparo mihi*, c. acc. rei *L* 18,12); and M. Zerwick, *Analysis Philologica Novi Testamenti Graeci* (Romae: PIB, 1960²), ad v (κτάομαι, *acquiro, comparo mihi*).

Along with Schnider,[42] I consider Luke 18:11-12 as the first of two segments shaping the central sequence of the parable; the second segment is v 13. In vv 11-13 Luke outlines, in an objective manner, the prayer of two individuals, a Pharisee and a publican, who have already been introduced in the preceding sequence (v 10) in the act of going to the temple to pray. The literary suture between the two sequences is carried out by the verb προσεύχομαι we find again in v 10 (προσεύξασθαι) and v 11 (προσηύχετο). Initially, the two characters move together (ἄνθρωποι δύο ἀνέβησαν) towards the same place (εἰ± τὸ ἱερόν) and for the same purpose (προσεύξασθαι) (v 10); but the style and content of the prayers of one (vv 11-12) and the other (v 13) render the two characters distinct and contrary.

In the final sequence (v 14a) Luke unveils God's view of (λέγω ὑμῖν) the two praying characters: the repentant sinner (ἱλάσθητί μοι τῷ ἁμαρτωλῷ [v 13b]) finds justice, condescension and forgiveness from God (δεδικαιωμένος) in contrast to the Pharisee (παρ'ἐκεῖνον).[43] The Pharisee and the publican had gone (ἀνέβησαν) together to the temple to pray (v 10), but only one of the two, "the sinner", returns (κατέβη) home justified (v 14a). Why? Only through a meticulous examination of the two prayers of the central sequence of the pericope – especially the prayer of the Pharisee (vv 11-12) – can the 'focus' of the parable be rightly clarified and solved.

Two Prayers

The prayer of the Pharisee (vv 11-12) – a text full of asyndetons and other Semitic constructions – is *formgeschichtlich* a *berakhah*, i.e. a laudatory literary genre, private or public, frequently recurrent in the OT (especially Psalms), and also widespread in "intertestamental" writings (Apocrypha and/or Pseudepigrapha of the OT), temple and synagogue liturgy of the time of Jesus, as well as in the later Rabbinic literature.

Luke – like Paul before him[44] – expresses his thanksgivings with the

---

42. "Ausschliessen und ausgeschlossen werden. Beobachtungen zur Struktur des Gleichnisses vom Pharisäer und Zöllner Lk 18,10-14a", *BZ* 24, 1980, pp. 44-45.

43. Παρ'ἐκεῖνον of the codices ℵ B L (less ἢ γὰρ ἐκεῖνος di W Θ 69) is an attempt to reproduce the Aramaci *min* of comparative value, which may most often have – as here (Luke 18:14a) – an exclusive value. The Vulgate translates with a generic *ab illo*.

44. M. Del Verme, *Le formule di ringraziamento postprotocollari nell'epistolario*

verb εὐχαριστεῖν, followed by a causal clause with ὅτι, which clarifies the reasons behind the *berakhah*. The Pharisee thanks God for the guidance and strength that he receives from him, which make him different and better than all other men, labelled as a *massa peccatorum*. The praying Pharisee feels superior[45] to the publican (ἢ καὶ ὡς οὗτος ὁ τελώνης). The latter is located – even structurally – at the end of the first *stichos* of the prayer in a 'polar' position with respect to ὁ Φαρισαῖος, therefore he becomes a *typos* for all sinners.

I want to underline the care of the Pharisee to present himself as different, and perhaps distance himself (σθατεὶς πρὸς ἑαυτόν) from the publican during his prayer. The Pharisee continues his thanks (v 12) to God, for the religious zeal God grants him to observe the bi-weekly fast (νηστεύω δὶς τοῦ σαββάτου) and the payment of tithes on anything purchased (ἀποδεκατῶ πάντα ὅσα κτῶμαι). His prayer[46] does not contain any questions, but only a thanksgiving. The seriousness and genuineness of the *berakhah* of the Pharisee has been widely underestimated by many exegetes to produce moralising, theological or existential readings that do not always reflect – indeed occasionally even distort – the Jewish context in which the parable has been located, and some students reduce the figure of the Pharisee to a mere 'caricature'.[47]

The prayer of the publican (v 13) is essentially a *request*, a cry of a sinner who sincerely asks for the forgiveness of God, aware of his perilous, if not disastrous, religious state. The form of the prayer chosen

---

paolino (Presenza 5; Roma: Edizioni Francescane, 1971). For the semantic value of the Hebrew roots *brk* and *ydh*, see J. Scharbert, s.v. ברך and G. Mayer, s.v. ידה in Botterweck-Ringgren, *TWAT* I, cols. 808-842; III, cols. 455-475.

45. Καί can have a reinforcing value.

46. I would note that also in 1QH[a] similar prayers to the Pharisee of Luke occur: for example, XV:34 reads: "[I give you thanks,] Lord, because you did not /make/ my lot /fall/ in the congregation of deceit (Hebr. גורלי בעדת שו), nor have you placed my regulations in the council of hypocrites (Hebr. נעלמים ובסוד)". Text and transl. by F. García Martínez-E.J.C. Tigchelaar (eds.), *The Dead Sea Scrolls Study Edition*, Vol. One: 1Q1-4Q273 (Leiden-Boston-Köln: Brill, 1997), pp. 180-181. This verse expresses the will of the *orans* to separate himself from the wicked and the awareness of being different from other men, as with the Pharisee of Luke 18:11.

47. Eg L. Schottroff, "Die Erzählung vom Pharisäer und Zöllner als Beispiel für die theologische Kunst des Überredens", in H.D. Betz-L. Schottroff (eds.), *Neues Testament und christliche Existenz*. Fs. für H. Braun zum 70. Geburtstag (Tübingen: Mohr, 1973), esp. pp. 448-452.

by Luke recalls both in content and in literary form the penitential psalms of the OT.

Only in the initial apostrophe (Ὁ Θεός) is the prayer of the publican equal to that of the Pharisee. The prayer of the publican is spare (ἱλάσθητί μοι τῷ ἁμαρτωλῷ) (v 13b), the *berakhah* of the Pharisee continues for almost two verses, 11b-12. On the contrary, the description of the position and gestures of the praying publican (v 13a) is rich in details, whereas the presentation of the Pharisee is succinct (v 11a).

More particularly, the fast and payment of tithes are decisive elements that define the personality and religiosity of the Lucan Pharisee. In fact, the payment of tithes "on all his purchases" and the bi-weekly fast of the Pharisee contrast with the publican, who besides transgressing the precept of tithing also makes a dishonest living from the property of his fellow- men.

Thus, to those "who trusted in themselves that they were righteous and regarded others with contempt" (v 9) Luke opposes God's judgement (v 14a). God does not accept the righteous who discriminate, but rather prefers marginalised but repentant sinners. This is the 'focus' of the parable, which is in line with the teaching and praxis of Jesus of Nazareth.[48]

Tithe and Fast of the Pharisee (חבר?)

The prayer of the Pharisee in Luke 18:11-12 – whether its origins are Palestinian and go back to Jesus (as it seems) or are attributable to Luke – reflects an historical, cultural and religio-institutional situation typical of the Judaism of the Second Temple.

To begin with, the contrast between the Pharisee and the publican realistically documents the situation of unpopularity and contempt with which publicans (or excisemen) (cfr. Mark 2:14; Matt 9:9; Luke 5:27) were generally treated in antiquity, and in Judaism in particular.[49] In this regard, the *halakhic* provisions of the rabbis against publicans testify not only to the disapproval and aversion of the people against

---

48. See Mark 2:13-17 and parr.; Matt 11:16-19; 18:12-14; and Luke 7:31, 35, 36-50; 15:1-32; 19:1-10.

49. O. Michel, s. v. τελώνης, in *TWNT* VIII, cols. 89-94; 94-98. For the social evaluation and (negative) moral judgement on τελῶναι-publicani in antiquity and particularly in Judaism (including the Gospels), ibid., cols. 98-105. In any case, Tertullian's statement that all tax-gatherers were pagans (*De pud.* 9) was already contested by Jerome (*Ep. 21 ad Damasum* 3).

these profiteers but also concern some Jewish groups – as for example the Pharisees – to avoid even physical contact with this despised class: the Rabbinic texts treat publicans and thieves as particularly impure people.[50] Thus the prayer of the Pharisee in Luke 18:11, with its insistence on being different, which in addition creates physical distance from the publican, could mirror a Pharisaic preoccupation with ritual purity. The parable of Jesus attempts to criticise this separatist position of the Pharisees.

It seems to me that the statements of the prayer both about paying tithes on everything he buys (v 12b: ἀποδεκατῶ πάντα ὅσα κτῶμαι) and also about the bi-weekly fast (v 12a)[51] are employed to illustrate the personality of the Pharisee, and by opposition to that of the publican. If my interpretation of Luke 18:12b is correct, one could suppose that this parable of judgement anticipates the (Rabbinic) distinction in Judaism between two types of people, the *ḥaverim* (sing. *ḥaver*, associate) and the *'ammê ha-'areṣ* (sing. *'am ha-'areṣ*, people of the land), according to details of their observance of the commandments of ritual purity and tithing. As is known, the Jewish documentation on this subject is copious but late: the Rabbinic texts date from the 2nd century CE onward, thus later than the synoptic Gospels. But there are good

---

50. Michel, cit., cols. 101-103; Schürer 1973, I, p. 376 n. 108.

51. Although the fast (Hebr. *ta'anith*, and Aram. *ta'anitha*) plays an important part in the religious life of Jews of 1st century CE (S. Safrai, "Religion in Everyday Life", in Safrai-Stern 1974-1976, vol. I/2, pp. 814-816), there are no texts that affirm the existence of a law prescribing the observance of fasting twice a week. One might think that the bi-weekly fast of the Luke's Pharisee (18:12a: νηστεύω δὶς τοῦ σαββά-του) – if taken into serious consideration on the historical level – should allude to the private initiative of a particularly pious person. Certainly Monday and Thursday – market days and synagogal meetings – were preferred days for public and private fasting. But texts that mention fasting on Monday or Thursday are datable only after 70 CE (cf. *m. Ta'an.* 2:9; and *t. Ta'an.* 2:4, 8) with the possible exception of one which could be earlier, such as the *Baraita* to *Meg. Ta'an.* 12 (at the end). For other documentation, see Safrai ("Religion", p. 816). Thus, one could suppose that δὶς τοῦ σαββάτου in Luke 18:12a alludes to the days of Monday and Thursday. Indeed, Epiphanius (died ca 403 CE) remarks that those were the days during which the Pharisees fasted in the time of Jesus: ἐνήστευον δὲ δὶς τοῦ σαββάτου, δευτέραν καὶ πέμπτην (*Haer.* 16.1.5, ed. K. Holl [in GCS 25], p. 211). But long before Epiphanius the *Didache* warns the 'true' members of the community not to imitate the "hypocrites" who fast on the second and fifth days (i.e. Monday and Thursday). On this, vd. infra, point 4. However, one must agree with Safrai that the "custom was confined to certain circles among the Pharisees and their disciples" (p. 816).

reasons[52] to suppose that the contrast mentioned in the Rabbinic sources (*Mishnah, Tosefta, Midrashim* and *Talmud*) was already in existence in NT times.

The Pharisee-*ḥaver* fulfils the serious duty to tithe both on products of the land and on objects that he buys and owns, making sure to honour the duty to tithe even for the original owner or re-seller. On the other hand, the economic fortune of the publican is based on taking from others. Such a contrasting situation reinforces my initial supposition, that the literary and structural analysis of the available *data* in the text of Luke makes it possible to identify the 'focal point' of the parable in the principle that God does not reward those who discriminate but rewards and justifies penitent sinners.

4. The Bi-weekly Fast of the ΥΠΟΚΡΙΤΑΙ (Did. 8:1)

4.1. The Semantic Field of Hypocrisy in the Didache

The lexical field that includes the simple verb ὑποκρίνομαι and the compound συνυποκρίνομαι, the abstract noun ὑπόκρισις[53] the *nomen agentis* ὑποκριτής, and the adjective ἀνυπόκριτος has already been studied and discussed in a series of monographs and articles. "It is truly curious"– noted C. Spicq more than 20 years ago – "the semantic evolution that this group of words has undergone from Homer and Herodotus to the NT".[54] I myself have written about this subject within a monograph on the institution of tithes in the NT and again above with reference to the "woes" of Matt 23 (par. Luke 11:37-53; 20:45-47; see also Mark 12:37b-40), where the term ὑποκριταί frequently recurs with various shades of meaning. Therefore, I can be more succinct on this subject but certainly not hurried.[55]

---

52. A. Oppenheimer, *The 'Am Ha-Aretz, A Study in the Social History of the Jewish People in the Hellenistic-Roman Period* (ArbLGHJ 8; Leiden: Brill, 1977), argues that for the birth of the concept of *'am ha-'aretz le-ma'aserot* - which contrasts the *'am ha-'ares* to a *haver* with respect to tithing – one cannot go before the time of the Hasmonaeans nor after the destruction of the Second Temple (pp. 75-76).

53. Also sporadically ὑποκρισία (in poetry -ίη , eg *Anth. Gr.* 16.289).

54. *Notes de Lexicographie néo-testamentaire*, tome II (Göttingen: Vandenhoeck & Ruprecht, 1978), s.v. ὑποκρίνομαι κτλ.

55. Two important contributions which appeared after my monograph should be mentioned: J. Barr, "The Hebrew/ Aramaic Background of 'Hypocrisy' in the Go-

Besides the NT[56] the *Didache*, like other proto-Christian writings (esp. the so-called "Apostolic Fathers"),[57] uses *lexemes* built from the root ὑποκριν-[58] with various meanings. In fact, this group of terms does not necessarily indicate the difference between being and appearing, hence the fiction in a negative sense of "hypocrisy" as it is vulgarly used in all modern languages. Such meaning is at times present in the texts, but more often hypocrisy recurs in other contexts, such as the interpretation of the Law, teaching and doctrine, religious praxis of a single individual or a group (as we have seen with reference to Matt 23:23 [Luke 11:42; and 18:11-12]).[59] Behind these terms and other

spels", in Davies and White 1990, pp. 307-326; and M. Weinfeld, "The Charge of Hypocrisy in Matthew 23 and in Jewish Sources", *Immanuel* 24/25, 1990, pp. 52-58. One must consider seriously the fragments of 4Q, which have shed new light on the relations and/or tensions within the Essenic-Qumranic movement and outside ("we" and "the others", infra n. 93).

56. Wilckens, ὑποκρίνομαι κτλ., in *TWNT* VIII, cols. 566-571; Spicq and Barr, supra nn. 54-55.

57. H. Kraft, *Clauis Patrum Apostolicorum. Konkordanz zu den Schriften der Apostolischen Väter* (München: Kösel, 1963), s.v. ὑποκρίσις and ὑποκριτής. Particularly, *Barn.* 19:2; 20:1; 21:4; *1 Clem.* 15:1; Herm., *Man.* 2; 8; *Sim.* 8:6; 9:18, 19, 27; *Vis.* 3:6; Ign., *Magn.* 3:2; Pol., *Phil.* 6:3.

58. A. Urbán (ed.), *Concordantia in Patres Apostolicos.* Pars II: *Concordantia in Didachen (Doctrina duodecim Apostolorum)* (Alpha-Omega 64/2; Hildesheim-Zürich-New York: Olms-Weidmann, 1993), pp. 145; 158: ὑποκρίσις 4:12 [*Doctr.: affectatio*]; 5:1 [*Barn.* 20:1]: plur., *idem* [*Doctr.: affectationes*]; ὑποκριτής 2:6 [*Doctr.: adulator*]; 8:1, 2.

59. Indeed, when the LXX with the terms ὑποκριτής or ὁ ὑποκρινόμενος, ἀσεβής, ἄνομος, παράνομος translate Hebraic חָנֵף (= sacrilege, perverse, wicked), the negativity of the term does not lie in the simulation/hypocrisy but in an objective wickedness (discussion of some texts in Del Verme 1989, p. 55 n. 92). Fundamental works in this area remain the studies of P. Dhorme, *Le livre de Job* (Paris: Cerf, 1962); Joüon, "ΥΠΟΚΡΙΤΗΣ", pp. 312-316; and A. W. Argyle, " 'Hypocrites' and the Aramaic Theory", *ExpT* 75, 1964, pp. 113-114. Also Barr, somewhat critical (against Wilckens) but substantially in agreement with Dhorme and Joüon. In my opinion, *data* from the manuscripts of Qumran (Del Verme, cit., p. 54 and n. 91) would merit more consideration in this discussion. One also notes that in the NT (eg Gal 2:13; 1 Tim 1:5; 4:1-2; 2 Tim. 1), in proto-Christian literature (eg Herm., *Sim.* 8:6.5; 9:19.2-3; Pol., *Phil.* 6:3) the *lexemas* in question are used in the context of orthodoxy and teaching. With the term ὑποκριτής and others similar are labelled the opponents (in a religious sense), the dissidents who place themselves outside or in opposition to the true doctrine. Sometimes these terms occur in the context of interpretation of the *Torah* (as in the case of Matt 23:23) as religious practices and institutions are concerned (Del Verme, cit., pp. 51-56). Almost the same problematic is also present in *Did.* 8:1.

similar terms there is frequently a negative *ethical* connotation, in the sense of wickedness/perversion/infidelity, that can refer to the single or a group; but also a *connotation* of confrontation /conflict among subjects.[60]

4.2. Jewish and Christian Practice of Fasting: from Jesus and the Jesus Movement up to the Didache

From Jesus to the *Didache*
Mark relates a dispute on fasting between Jesus and the disciples of John the Baptist and (the disciples of) the Pharisees (2:18-20), that probably collects pre-Marcan traditional material.[61] This dispute is revisited in Matt (9:14-15) and Luke (5:33-35). In *Mark* the discussion of Jesus on fasting is the third of five controversies (2:1-3:6) located in Capernaum. It records a rough change of scene in the public life of Jesus with the appearance of envious characters (Pharisees, scribes, and scribes of the Pharisees) suspicious of his behaviour and activities. The scenes of conflict are described as simple dialogues, all five originating in the praxis of Jesus and of his disciples. The discussion revolves around the ἐξουσία of Jesus, i.e. his "power on earth" bound up with the honorary title of "Son of Man" (2:10).

The fast of Mark 2:18-20:
v 18 Now John's disciples and the Pharisees were fasting; and people came and said to him, 'Why do John's disciples and the disciples of the Pharisees fast, but your disciples do not fast?' v 19 Jesus said to them, 'The wedding-guests cannot fast while the bridegroom is with them, can they? As long as they have the bridegroom with them, they cannot fast. v 20 The days will come when the bridegroom is taken away from them, and then they will fast on that day.

While the disciples of John the Baptist and the disciples of the Pharisees fast, the disciples of Jesus abstain from fasting: this is reason for the scandal both for the group lead by the Baptist and for the circle of the Pharisees. The extended response of Jesus (vv 19-20) justifies the non-fasting of the disciples in the present (v 19) but also anticipates the obligation of the fast for the future, when they (the disciples) will have

---

60.   Audet 1958, p. 170.
61.   R. Pesch, *Das Markusevangelium*. I. Teil (HThK II/1), Zweite, durchgesehene Auflage (Freiburg i. Br.: Herder, 1977), ad locum and passim.

Defining Identities: Who are the People...   171

to fast because their bridegroom (Jesus) will be taken away from them (v 20). The *apophthegma* of Mark on fasting, Semitic in its style and with allegorical tracts, justifies the presence of the guests-disciples (lit. "the sons in the nuptial hall"), the non-fast during the earthly life of Jesus, while the fast of the disciples begins only after the master's death.

The optional and bi-weekly fast of the Pharisees (lacking a specific mandate in the *Torah!*), referred to in Matt 6:16 and Luke 18:12, is not condemned by Jesus, but is welcomed as an expression of interior devotion (ἐν τῷ κρυφαίῳ of Matt 6:18; cf. ἐν τῷ κρυπτῷ 6:6) along with prayers (Luke 2:37). However, vainglorious religiosity (δικαιοσύνη) is condemned: Matt 6,1 Προσέχετε [δὲ] τὴν δικαιοσύνην ὑμῶν μὴ ποιεῖν ἔμπροσθεν τῶν ἀνθρώπων πρὸς τὸ θεαθῆναι αὐτοῖς.

Mark 2:18-20 refers to a real situation that temporarily concerns the disciples of Jesus but not those of John the Baptist and of the Pharisees, because fasting both for Judaism and for Early Christianity was a constant religious practice.[62] In the *logion* of Mark 2:18-20 the fact that the disciples of Jesus did not fast is accounted for but, in addition, the practice of fasting in the Church is justified.[63]

Some exegetes (eg H.W. Kuhn and R. Pesch) interpret "that day" of Mark 2:20b as an explicit reference to the weekly fast of Friday, the day of Christ's death, which is concurrently fixed by the Synoptics and John. This interpretation, in my opinion, is possible but not cogent, because Mark seems to have privileged – in the formulation of the *logion* – ambiguous language, allusive and prophetic, on the part of Christ, and not referred to practices already in use. Perhaps this refer-

62. A. Arbesmann, "Fasten", in *RAC* VII, cols. 447-524; J. Behm, νῆστις κτλ., in *TWNT* IV, cols. 925-936; (H.L. Strack) P. Billerbeck, *Kommentar zum Neuen Testament aus Talmud und Midrasch*, Bd. II (München: Beck, 1924), pp. 241-244; and Bd. IV/1 (München: Beck, 1928), pp. 77-114; F. Cabrol, "Jeûnes", in *DACL* VII, cols. 2481-2501; M. D. Herr and Ed., "Fasting and Fast Days", in *Enc Jud* 6, cols. 1189-1196; J. C. Rylaarsdam, "Feasts and Fasts", in *IDB* II, pp. 260-264; Safrai, "Religion in Everyday Life", pp. 814-816 (793-833); Schürer 1979, pp. 483ff. and *passim*; and L. Ziehen, Νηστεία, in *RECA* XVII/I, cols. 88-107.

63. Anyhow in Mark there is a small 'reservation' around the practice of the fast, on the part of Jesus and the disciples. With Mark – it is probable – a tendency began in the ancient Church: i.e. the refusal of legalistic ritualism that proposed fasting on fixed days and occasions. See, for example, *Barn.* 3:1-5 (SC 172, pp. 88-90) and the commentary of Kraft 1965, p. 164; Herm., *Sim.* 5:1-5 (SC 53, pp. 224 ff.); *Diogn.* 4:1, 5 (SC 33, p. 60), and *Dida. syr.* 21 (CSCO 408, p. 191).

ence to Friday on the part of the afore-mentioned exegetes and others is influenced by the ritual situation that will regulate fasting, but only later, as is documented by the ecclesiastical ordinances[64] and some Patristic sources.[65]

The Fast of *Did.* 8:1

Did. 8:1 is more problematic than Mark 2:18-20, because it was a reference to many of the later ecclesiastical constitutions (specifically, *Didascalia*, *Constitutiones apostolorum* and even earlier *Traditio apostolica* of Ps.-Hippolytus) which attest to fasting on Wednesday and Friday as prescribed in the *Didache*. But unlike these, *Did.* 8:1 does not connote any Christological or pietistic motivations, nor does it offer an historicisation of the days of passion for the bi-weekly fast of Wednesday and Friday.

It seems to me that *Did.* 8:1 could be more usefully located within (Jewish) questions and discussions connected to the form of the calendar (lunar, luni-solar or solar) that also influenced the selection of the days for fasting. As we shall see, *Did* 8:1 can act as an important gauge for recovering the lost identity of some Jewish groups that did not renounce their practices (cultic or ritual), nor their social and moral behaviour, when they converted to Christianity. These Christian-Jewish groups transferred specific Jewish problematics into the new communal (cultic and ethical) context of "Christian Judaism", before the "Great Church", initially looking at them with suspicion, pushed them to the margins – if not entirely outside – of Christian society, essentially branding them as heretics.

---

64. Eg *Dida.* 5.14, 18, 20-21 (ed. F. X. Funk, I, pp. 278-280), which recalls Wednesday and Friday with reference to sufferings (treason and arrest) and the crucifixion of Jesus; and *Const.* 5:14.20 and 7:23.2 (ed. F. X. Funk, I, pp. 279-281 and 408-409; also SC 329, pp. 258-259; ibid. 336, pp. 50-51), with reference to the judgement of condemnation, the treason, the passion and the death of Jesus on the cross. Also, *Canones ap.* 60.

65. Eg Clem. Al., *Strom.* 7.12.75, 2 (GCS 17, p. 54); Orig., *Hom. in Lev.* 10:2 (*C. Cels.* 8.22); Epiph., *Haer.* 51.26.1-4 (GCS 31, pp. 295-297); *Ancoratus* [or *Fides*] 22.1-5 (GCS 37, pp. 522-523); Petrus Alex., *Ep. can. poen.* 15 (PG 18, 508B), with explicit reference to tradition; Aug., *Ep.* 36.13, 30 (CSEL 34, p. 50); Vict. Pet., *De fabrica mundi* 3-4 (CSEL 49, pp. 4-5). Tert., *Ieiun.* 10.6 (CSEL 20, p. 287), on the other hand, records that in his time the fast of the Catholics on Wednesday and Friday was not motivated by the call to the sufferings of Jesus. Other patristic texts in F.G. Cremer, *Die Fastenansage Jesu. Mk. 2,20 und Parallelen in der Sicht der patristischen und scholastischen Exegese* (BBB 23; Bonn: Hanstein, 1965).

4.3. Text and Contexts of Did. 8:1[66]

v 1a Αἱ δὲ νηστεῖαι ὑμῶν μὴ ἔστωσαν μετὰ τῶν ὑποκριτῶν·
v 1b νηστέουσι γάρ δευτέρᾳ σαββάτων καὶ πέμπτη·
v 1c ὑμεῖς δὲ νηστεύσατε τετράδα καὶ παρασκευήν.

v 1a Let your fasts not [coincide] with [those of] the hypocrites.
v.1b They fast on Monday and Thursday;
v.1c you, though, should fast on Wednesday and Friday.

The author of the *Didache* prescribes in 8:1 norms for the bi-weekly fast of the community/ies, fixing it on Wednesday and Friday in contrast to the practice of the "hypocrites" (viz. "dissidents") who fast on Monday and Thursday. This is not a simple piece of advice or recommendation but a command (note the imperative νηστεύσατε of v 1c) that attempts to distinguish[67] the true members of the community from the "hypocrites", otherwise labelled as the dissidents and/or religious errants, perverse/malicious and/or sacrilegious/godless/impious. Ὑποκριταί are here the synonym of ἄνομοι, ἀσεβεῖς, ἄπιστοι.

The compulsory and public fasts[68] of Wednesday and Friday are repeated weekly, and are different and distinct from the prebaptismal fast of the baptizing, the baptized and, if possible, of every single member of the community, in preparation for baptism (*Did.* 7:4). The time of the fast is fixed for baptizing: "one or two days prior" to the baptism with the injunctive form (κελεύεις δὲ νηστεῦσαι) (7:4b).

66. Greek text: Rordorf-Tuilier 1998², p. 172; Engl. tr. by A. Cody, in Jefford 1995a, p. 9.

67. This distinction is underlined by almost all the commentaters on the *Didache*, but as to the interpretation of the subjects and/or group behind the term ὑποκριταί, opinions diverge. See the contribution of Draper 1992 ("Christian Self-Definition"), who has now somewhat changed his position (see his paper "Does the [final?] version of the *Didache* and Matthew reflect an 'irrevocable parting of the Ways' with Judaism?", in the *Proceedings of the Tilburg Conference...*). In any case, my conclusions are different from his of 1992. On the contrary, I would agree with P.J. Tomson ("The halakhic evidence of Didache 8 and Matthew 6 and the Didache community's relationship to Judaism", in *Proceedings of the Tilburg Conference*; Id. 2001, pp. 380-391; and "The wars against Rome, the rise of Rabbinic Judaism and of Apostolic Gentile Christianity, and the Judaeo-Christians: elements for a synthesis", in Tomson – Lambers-Petry 2003, pp. 8-14).

68. These are not explicitly indicated in the text (v 1c) as compulsory, but they were surely so interpreted by the various ecclesiastical ordinances (supra, nn. 65-66) that depend on *Did.* 8:1.

Finally, the *Didache* acknowledges another form of fast different from the compulsory public fasts of Wednesday and Friday and the preparatory fast for baptism. This is the fast devoted to "those who persecute you" (1:3b), an expiatory and optional fast that is a late addition to the *Didache*, together with the interpolation of the synoptic section (1:3b-2:1) missing both in *Barn.* and *Doctr.*

Among the many commentators on the *Didache* in the last 46 years, the less recent Audet[69] along with a few others[70] remains the most interested in the dynamic (i.e. the various layers) of the tradition lying behind the actual text. As has been said, the *Didache* is a many-layered and compound work correctly classified under the genre of progressive literature ("evolved literature" according to Kraft[71]), by which is meant a writing by an active and traditional community rather than by a single author. The image of the *Didache* as a "fluvial vortex" (see Steimer: *Vertex Traditionis*) where many waters meet, clearly describes the text in its final state (ca second half of the 1st cent. CE).[72]

This literary (editorial) and historical (sources/traditions) *status* of the *Didache* makes it easier for me to isolate the 'contexts' of the practice of fasting in *Did.* 8:1 without dwelling solely on the *literal context*, that is, on the ritual and liturgical context (7:1-10:7) in which this verse has been placed.[73] Even hypothetically,[74] this morphocritical reading of *Did.* 8:1(-2) could illuminate the 'conflictual' dynamic between groups or factions[75] present in Christian Judaism, in an historical period that falls shortly after the death of Jesus of Nazareth.

---

69. Audet 1958, pp. 170-173; 367-371 (357-371).

70. Kraft, cit., pp. 59-65; Giet 1970, cit., pp. 197-199 (192-203); Rordorf-Tuilier, cit., pp. 36-38 (34-48); 83-91 (passim); and Niederwimmer 1989b, cit., pp. 64-78 (passim), and 165-167 (158-173); Id., "Der Didachist und seine Quellen", in Jefford 1995a, pp. 15-36 (p. 29).

71. Ibid., pp. 1ff.

72. One cannot be any more precise to the time of the final redaction of the *Didache* (Rordorf-Tuilier, pp 96 n. 2; 232-233); see also Vokes 1993, pp. 209-233 (230-231).

73. So Niederwimmer 1989b, pp. 158ff., who entitles "Die Agende" (i.e. the Ritual) the whole section *Did.* 7:1-10:7.

74. With Kraft, who at the conclusion to § 8. (= The Didache as a Community Tradition), writes: "But for the most part we are left to conjecture if we wish to explain in detail how the various developments (of the traditions derived from the various forms of Did.) came about. Not only is such conjecture legitimate, but occasionally it may also be accurate" (p. 65).

75. For these groups, besides the numerous studies of G. Theissen , I would mention Hellholm-Moxnes-Karlsen Seim 1995.

On the *literal context* of *Did.* 8:1 I will say little, because it has been thoroughly studied in all the commentaries so far cited. I will examine more at length, however, various contexts or vital situations of the bi-weekly fast of the "hypocrites" and "others" and will attempt to clarify who are the people that practice those fasts and at the same time better understand the religious and social function of fasting (and common public prayer) in the community/ies dynamics. *Did.* 8:1 is one of the two additions (the other concerns the 'right' way of praying vv 2-3) that the author of the *Didache* placed in a long liturgical section (7:1-10:7) dedicated to βάπτισμα and εὐχαριστία, two central realities in the cult life of the community. The additions of chap. 8 on the bi-weekly fasts (v 1) and the prayer of the "Pater" three times a day (vv 2-3) break, in some ways, the original continuity of the liturgical source/tradition that the author of the *Didache* transcribed.[76] However, in that *Vorlage*, the two realities (the Baptism and the Eucharist) were introduced with the same formula - περὶ δὲ τοῦ βαπτίσματος (7:1) and περὶ δὲ τῆς εὐχαριστίας (9:1) - that is not found in *Did.* 8 (instead here it returns δέ [v 1] and μηδέ [v 2]).

The *literal context* in which the author of the *Didache* inserts 8:1 (and vv 2-3) confronts the reader with an elaborate text that reflects a late literary (and editorial) situation. In this phase *Did.* 8:1-3 might allow for a comparison with Matt 6:1-18, that is, with the tradition of the "hypocritical Pharisees" who practice almsgiving, prayer and fasts, and an optional and bi-weekly fast (Luke 18:12a) perhaps on Monday and Thursday. Actually, notwithstanding the similarities of wording and content (but in *Did.* 7:1-8:3 there is no reference to almsgiving), the difference between Matt and *Did.* are clear.[77] Thus, we cannot say that the *Didache* derives from *Matthew*.[78]

---

76. Niederwimmer 1989b, p. 158.

77. Draper (pp. 372-373), and before him already Audet (pp. 170-171). On the question of the dependence of the *Didache* on *Matthew*, I turn to A. Tuilier ("La Didaché et le problème synoptique", in Jefford 1995a, pp. 110-130), corroborating the thesis with new arguments. One could think – he writes – of a "common source" (for *Did.* and Matt) that would need to be situated in history (p. 117).

78. *Contra* Massaux 1950, who writes: "Le Didachiste paraît renvoyer ses lecteurs aux hypocrites dont parle l'évangile de Mt.; parlant du jeûne, il a en tête les mots de Mt. prescrivant de ne pas jeûner comme les hypocrites" (p. 616). But Niederwimmer comments thus on the position of Massaux: "Schwerlich richtig". And with reference to the position of H. Köster – who probably sees in ὑποκριταί of *Did.* 8 a reference to a "free tradition" (Germ. "freie Überlieferung") – he concludes:

J.A. Draper, who locates the insertion *Did.* 8 in the final editorial phase of the *Didache*, identifies in 8:1 (and vv 2-3) a strongly accentuated Christian emphasis, which is absent in the parenesis of the preceding chaps. 1-6, where none of the animosity against the Jews or the *Torah* is evident, nor is there a trace of Christian self-definition as against the Jews. And his conclusion that it was "the lack of a clear differentiation from other Judaic groups that caused problems for the (Christian) community, in a later phase, perhaps under the pressure of the Pharisees",[79] seems to me not very convincing, somewhat too general and limited to the literal (and editorial) context of *Did.* 8.

In my opinion, if one pays attention to *other contexts* and examines the historical precedents that contributed to the opposition "hypocrites" *versus* "the others", the fast of *Did.* 8:1 would document a 'peculiar' situation of contrasts among groups within the same Christian-Jewish community. This situation however concerned groups/factions different from those identified by Draper in 1992.

4.4. Ὑποκριταί and "the Others": Trajectory of a Confrontation/Dispute between Groups

Having previously clarified the lexical field of "hypocrites" in the *Didache*, I will now concentrate on the identification of those subjects/groups concerned in the confrontation between the "hypocrites" and "the others" in *Did.* 8:1 (and v 2). Philology and history must be used hand in hand in order to avoid readings of ancient texts through foreign methodologies or otherwise inadequate methods. To some extent, it seems to me that this has happened in the interpretation of *Did.* 8:1.

Indeed, scholars have underestimated the importance of the 'internal dynamic' of the conflict within the community/ies of the *Didache*, and also the reasons for the dispute between the "hypocrites" (the dissidents), and "the others" (the "true" members) of the community. Regarding this conflict, scholars concentrate on the confrontation between the community of the author of the *Didache* and the coeval Judaism (i.e. contemporary Jewish communities). According to others, this conflict concerned some members of the community (Jews and/or

"M(eines) E(rachtens) kann hier Erinnerung an die Jesus-Überlieferung dahinter stehen, muss aber nicht" (p. 165 n. 2).
  79.   Draper 1992, pp. 364-365; 373-374.

pagans converted to Christianity who wanted to imitate the ὑποκριταί that is, the Pharisees, in the practice of the fast, choosing Monday and Thursday) and "the others" (the 'orthodox' members of the community, whom the author of the *Didache* commands to fast on Wednesday and Friday). These readings tend to minimize the contrast present in *Did.* 8:1, reducing it to a generic and *sterile* quarrel on the days of the fast. In my opinion, this text could tell us much more about the actual situation of Christian-Jewish communities of Syria-Palestine in the period immediately before and after 70 CE.

According to some scholars,[80] since the author of the *Didache* aimed at defining the identity of his community in contrast with the Jews of the synagogue, he did not have many choices with regard to the two days for the weekly fast: the remaining pair Tuesday/Friday or Wednesday/Saturday.[81] This interpretative reading is simplistic, if not superficial, because it disregards the essential reason for the selection of Wednesday (rather than Tuesday) and Friday (rather than Saturday). Not only does it not address the important problem of the calendar and of the group identity that adopts it,[82] but it does not address the time when this dispute began, considering that *Did.* 8:1 (and vv 2-3) figures as an addition to the actual literary and editorial context. This addition, however, may have recorded an earlier ethico-ritual-liturgical tradi-

---

80. Knopf 1920, p. 23; Wengst 1984, p. 97 nn. 64-65; and, in part, also J. Blinzler, "Qumran-Kalender und Passionschronologie", *ZNW* 49, 1958, p. 245.

81. Wengst, ibid., n. 65, maintains that Sunday, Monday and Thursday were excluded, because there were days of Judaic fasting, as well as Saturday because of its proximity to Friday and Sunday (Mark 2:20b); thus for the second day of the fast, only Tuesday and Wednesday remained. But one could ask: why not choose Wednesday (instead of Tuesday) and Friday (instead of Saturday) if the determination of Friday and Wednesday – with reference to the chronology of the passion and death of Christ – was an historical (Christian) re-reading which occurred later in the ecclesiastical regulations and in some Church Fathers (supra, nn. 65-66)? On the lateness of these ecclesiatical texts with respect to *Did.* 8:1, see also Blinzler (pp. 241-246).

82. A. Jaubert, "Jésus et le calendrier de Qumrân", *NTS* 7, 1960, p. 27, wrote: "Le texte de la Didaché n'autorise pas à conclure que des jours de jeûne ont été créés uniquement pour s'opposer aux Pharisiens. Il laisse entier le problème d'origine et du choix de ces jours liturgiques. Pour les expliquer il ne suffit pas de dire que le chrétiens désiraient 'changer' et que comme il n'y a que sept jours dans la semaine, il y avait quelque chance de tomber sur le mercredi! Ces vues superficielles ne tiennent aucun compte de la profondeur d'enracinement des usages liturgiques. Il faut expliquer les raisons d'un tel changement". Her conclusion (like mine) is based on the solar calendar (pp. 28ff. and passim).

tion[83] of bi-weekly fasting within some groups or factions of Christian Judaism, formerly belonging – in my opinion – to Jewish (not Pharisaic) circles belonging to Enochian Essenism (whether Qumranic or not), i.e. the so-called Enochians/Apocalyptics.[84]

Group Identity and Solar Calendar

The relationship between the solar calendar and the sectarian self-understanding of the Essenes of Qumran from an ideological and historical point of view has been studied by C. Martone in a paper[85] read at the *IX Convegno di Studi Veterotestamentari* (L'Aquila, September 11-13, 1995). This article – and some others at that Meeting – have illuminated the importance of the calendar and holidays in Israel – in other words, how time is understood and calculated, and its impact on institutions (cult and sacerdotal class), politics (feasts of the temple and feasts of the palace) and on religio-historical events (days of the week with their "qualitative" and not simply "quantitative" or chronologi-

---

83. Audet 1958, p. 368: "son (i.e. the didachist') instruction tient compte d'habitudes déjà prises, auxquelles il se contente d'imprimer la direction qui lui semble convenable"; and Kraft 1965, p. 62): "But it is at least probable that certain smaller components such as 8:1-2a once circulated apart from their present Didache context (Matt. 6:1-5.16-18 is based on similar material)".

84. Infra, n. 93. The supposition that the choice of the days of Wednesday and Friday was or could have been influenced by the Essenic-Qumranic movement or Enochian Essenism (because of the solar calendar) is not a new one, but it seems to lack the attention it merits among scholars. Nor have other studies on the dialectic of Jewish groups, contemporaneous or after Christianity, in the last period of the so-called "Middle Judaism" (Boccaccini) been undertaken. For example, Daniélou 1958, p. 399 and Audet (p. 369) have both simply reviewed the work of A. Jaubert on the Jewish calendars. Idem Kraft (p. 164), as well as J. van Goudoever, *Biblical Calenders* (Leiden: Brill, 1961); Rordorf-Tuilier (p. 37), and Blinzler, "Qumran-Kalender", p. 245, on quoting K. Schubert, *Die Gemeinde vom Toten Meer* (München-Basel: E. Reinhardt, 1958), pp. 127-130. On the contrary, a Qumranic influx on *Did.* 8:1 has been excluded by, among others, H. Braun, *Qumran und das Neue Testament* (Tübingen: Mohr, 1966), II, pp. 155-156); Giet (p. 199 n. 42); and Niederwimmer (p. 167 n. 16).

85. "Molteplicità di calendari e identità di gruppo a Qumran", in G.L. Prato (ed.), *"Un tempo per nascere e un tempo per morire". Cronologie normative e razionalità della storia nell'antico Israele*, RStB IX/1, 1997, pp. 119-138. Anyhow, the importance of the solar calendar for studying the origins of the Qumran community has been pointed out since long time. See in particular Talmon 1965², and after him – but with many others – García Martínez in Id.-Trebolle Barrera 1993; also W. Horowitz (the solar calendar in Mesopotamia and at Qumran), in Bar-Asher - Dimant 2003, pp. 3-26.

cal value). Feasts and holidays are particular periods that give sense to ordinary time; indeed, their significance maps the global timing in which they are inserted.[86]

The solar calendar of the Essenes at Qumran (but, already earlier, of the Enochians we know through *Jubilees* [esp. chaps. 72-82] and *1 Enoch*),[87] with its 364-day year (divided into 12 months of 30 days each with an intercalary day every third month), that is, a year composed of 52 weeks and four seasons (each with 13 weeks and 91 days), starting every year on a Wednesday, which is the day the Lord created the sun, moon and heavens (Gen 1:14-19). This solar year is always the same, repeating itself over and over: it allows every feast to be scheduled on the same day of the week.[88]

86. Ibid., 5-7 (= *Introduzione* by G. L. Prato).

87. See Sacchi 1997b, pp. 127-139.

88. It was Annie Jaubert who almost forty-seven years ago established some specific points in the Jewish calendar system and on the fixity of the liturgical days and holidays of the week in the solar/Sadducean calendar (Ead., "Le Calendrier des Jubilés et les jours liturgiques de la semaine", *VT* 7 [1957], pp. 35-61; and also in other studies here cited). Moving from the intuition of Barthélemy, according to whom the solar calendar of *Jubilees* began on Wednesday, Jaubert confirmed this hypothesis and specified that the Feast of Weeks – based on biblical texts and from information from *Jub.* – fell on Sunday, in other words the 50th day from the presentation of the first sheaf, which fell on "the day after Saturday". Sunday was the best day for departures and new undertakings. Friday, on the other hand, was the day favoured for arrivals and for meetings that precede Saturday. Friday (or Good Friday) derives its importance from the terminal position in the order of the six working days of the week, and from the fact that it was the preparation for Saturday, the day of rest and the liturgical holiday *par excellence* (quotations and discussion of the texts, ibid., pp. 44-46). Jaubert's thesis is based on the fact that *Jubilees*, as the editors of the *Hexateuch*, are using numbered months rather than naming them, such that the dates of both (= *Hexateuch* and *Jubilees*) presuppose the solar calendar of 364 days. Her analysis demonstrates, on one hand, a rigorous observance of the Sabbath on the part of the Patriarchs (who always avoid travelling on this day), and on the other, the particular importance of some days, specifically Wednesday, Friday and Sunday, calculated according to the solar calendar. Besides *Jubilees* and the *Hexateuch*, the later writings of the Chronicler also follow the Sadducean calendar – with respect to the dates according to the number of days and months, esp. *Ezra* and *Nehemiah* (ibid., p. 45). On the importance of Wednesday, Friday and Sunday in the solar/Sadducean calendar, Jaubert returns, taking a cue from the fragments of *Daniel* (10:8-16), found at Qumran (= 6Q 7 [6QDan], ed. M. Baillet, *DJD* III, pp. 114-116, pl. XXIII), which would help her as well to clarify some problematic texts of the Rabbinic tradition ("Fiches de calendrier", in Delcor 1978, pp. 305-311).

The fixedness of the solar calendar reflects the divine perfection and the immutable order that God has created in the world, which – translated into a theological-ideological discourse – resulted in a rigorous determinism that prompted the Essenism of Qumran to negate radically the freedom of man, as one can infer from the "doctrine of the two spirits" (esp. *1QS* III:15-18; I:8-29; cf. also some *Hodayoth*, eg *1QH^a* IV:29-31.37; XIII:16-17).

It was probably the time of Antiochus Epiphanes that saw the transition (ca 175-164 BCE) in the social structure of Israel from the solar calendar (as noted by *Jubilees*, *1 Enoch*, and Qumran) to the new lunar or luni-solar calendar, based – according to Greek use – on the moon (for calculating the months) and on the sun (for calculating the year). The proof that the calendar was changed during this period in Jerusalem comes from *Daniel*, which in 7:25 accuses Antiochus of having changed "time and law" (Aram., *zmnyn wdt*). Such a change is likely to have come about before the break between the Hasmonaeans and the Pharisees, and thus before John Hyrcanus I (134-104 BCE) because if the lunar calendar is also the Pharisaic (and later Rabbinic) calendar it means that he who imposed it was not in conflict with the Pharisees.[89]

The Essenes of Qumran did not accept this change, nor did they appreciate that after the rededication of the temple in 165 BCE the ancient sacerdotal/solar calendar was not re-established. This is one reason why they parted from official Judaism, and perhaps from other Essenes (infra, n. 93: 4QMMT C7), who very probably got used to the innovation. The Qumranites retained the ancient solar calendar (we also find this with the Therapeutics) with all of problems and discussions connected to it.[90] The regulation of the feasts on fixed days, according to the solar calendar of the Enochians/Apocalyptics and the Essenes of Qumran, continued and was extended to some ancient Christian circles[91] and to some Jewish groups not aligned to the luni-solar and Rabbinic calendar,[92] which with some adjustments remains in use today.

89. Sacchi, cit., pp. 137-138.
90. Martone, cit., pp. 137-138; and Fl. García Martínez, "Calendarios en Qumrán, I-II", *EstBib* 54 (1996), pp. 327-348; 523-552.
91. Texts, in Jaubert, cit., pp. 52-59.
92. Ibid., pp. 38-44.

Group Identity, Communion at the Table and "Hypocrisy"

The semantic history of the group of terms ὑποκρίνομαι-ὑποκριτής κτλ. is important because it helps to retrace the identity and dynamics among opposing groups, that is, the ὑποκριταί dissidents and/or perverse and the "others"/true members of the community. This was the sense of the expression "trajectory of a conflict between groups" that I have chosen as the title of paragraph 4.4. Within this trajectory, privileging the semantic area of ὑποκρίνομαι as a translation of Hebraic-Aramaic חנף, other subjects and movements should be analysed together with the Enochians/ Apocalyptics and the Essenes of Qumran.[93]

---

93. The solar calendar (with the liturgical days and holidays) was a nodal point of the conflict between the sectarians of Qumran and "the others", i.e. the "adversaries" of the Esseno-Qumranic community. The question has already been studied the most fully by O. Betz, M. Gertner, S. B. Hönig, H. Frankemölle, I. Sonne, Z. Wacholder and others, but especially by D. Flusser ("Pharisees, Sadducees and Essenes in Pesher Nahum" [Hebr.], in *Essays in Jewish History and Philology. In Memory of Gedaliahu Alon*, Jerusalem, 1970, pp. 133-168) and by Y. Yadin ("Pesher Nahum [4QpNah] Reconsidered", *IEJ* 21 [1971], pp. 1-12), who also refers to Weinfeld. It seems that the community of Qumran accused of "hypocrisy" the group of the Pharisees. Indeed, the latter in the writings of the sectarians of Qumran are defined as "all the seekers of flattering things" (Hebr. דורשי חלקת) in parallel to "mediators of deceit" (Hebr. מליצי כזב) and "all who search after deceit" (Hebr. כל דורשי רמיה) (1QHª X:31.32.34). With Flusser and Yadin I argue that "all who search after deceit" or "those looking for easy interpretation" of 4Q *169* [= 4QpNah] frgs. 3-4: I:7; II:2.4; III:6-7 (critical ed. by J. M. Allegro, *DJD* V, pp. 35-42, pls. XII-XIV; and J. Strugnell, 'Notes', pp. 204-210) and in other Qumranic texts one can probably identify the "hypocritical" Pharisees, in other words "who with their fraudulent teaching and lying tongue and perfidious lip misdirect many" (4Q *169* [4QpNah] frgs. 3-4: II:8-9). More cautious is Stemberger 1991, judging the expression in question as a defamation of adversaries who interpret the *Torah* too lightly, and thus the polemical affirmations of CD must be interpreted in the sense of a break within the Essenic community. I would point out, however, that in the same source (4QpNah frgs. 3-4: I:6-7) they are referred to (= the Pharisees) as having invited the Greek king Demetrius to ally with them against Alexander (lit. "the furious lion"), and that was the reason why Alexander Jannaeus took revenge on the Pharisees and crucified eight hundred of them (Jos., *Ant.* 13.380). I would recall two other texts: 4Q *175* (= 4QTestim): 28 and 1QS IV:10, the only two in Qumranic literature that contain the terms with the root חנף, respectively חנופה and חנף (cf. M.G. Abegg, Jr. with J.E. Bowley and E.M. Cook in consultation with E. Tov, *The Dead Sea Scrolls Concordance*. Vol. One: *The Non-Biblical Texts from Qumran*, s. lemma [Leiden: Brill, 2002]). These terms are translated by "evil" or "abomination" by G. Vermes and E. Lohse (Germ. *Ruchlosigkeit, Gottlosigkeit*); García Martínez-Tigchelaar translate with "profanation" and "insincerity"; Barr (ibid., 310-311, and n. 9) renders the terms as "deceit" and "pretence"; Jastrow, *A*

For example, the opponents/impious/ perverse found in the wisdom books (eg Job, Sir, and Wis) or in the pseudepigraphic texts (eg *PssSol* 4:7), and already in the prophets (eg Isa and Jer),[94] to mention only a few. As for the NT, the so-called "adversaries" mentioned in the pastoral letters and elsewhere should also be analysed.

I will concentrate on the area of Christian Judaism in order to identify the tendencies closest to the *Didache* and to clarify the underlying questions on the conflict/dispute of *Did.* 8:1. I will look at the episode of the dispute between Paul and Peter that took place in Antioch of Syria, in the context of Paul's mission to the Galatians to affirm the freedom of the Gospel with respect to the ordinances of the *Torah* (Gal 2:11-14).

As is well known, the pericope in question raises a series of formalstructural, historical and doctrinal questions.[95] I am interested in the

---

Dictionary of the Targumim, s.v. חֲנַף (= I, 484) frames various meanings: to be insincere, to flatter, to deceive, and hypocrite, flatterer, and faithless. Finally, regarding the very important 'Halakhic Letter' 4QMMT, attested by the paleographic manuscripts datable to the middle of the 2nd and 1st centuries BCE, the work seems located in a period of the formation of the Essenic-Qumranic group, because the text considers the possibility of interlocutors addressed by the writing. Subsequently, however, as is seen in 1QS IX:16-17, contacts with the Qumranites were no longer permitted. In 4Q *398* frags. 14-21 (= 4QMMT C 7-8) one reads: 7 "[And you know that] we have segregated ourselves from the rest of the peop[le...] (Hebr. [...ם]העﬠ מרוב פרשנו[ש...) 8 [and] from mingling in these affairs, and from associating wi[th them] in these things", according to the reconstruction by E. Qimron and J. Strugnell (in *DJD* X, pp. 28-38, pls. VII-VIII). In this passage one can see, on one side "una polemica tra due gruppi che in seguito diverranno i farisei e i sadducei ("noi" e "loro"), on the other side "un'ancora larvata divergenza d'opinione all'interno dello stesso gruppo proto-sadduceo ("noi" e "voi")" (García Martínez 1996, pp. 174-175, and n. 7). The divergence builds up to the internal schism with Essenism, which gave birth to the community of Qumran. All the texts I have quoted so far (along with others) have been interpreted as a reference to the Pharisees before 70 CE by L. H. Schiffman too ("New Light on the Pharisees", in *Understanding the Dead Sea Scrolls. A Reader from the Biblical Archaeology Review*, ed. by H. Shanks [New York: Doubleday, 1992], pp. 217-224, and notes [pp. 308-309]). G. Stemberger, on the contrary, argues that Schiffman has made poor use of linguistics in order to reach an historical conclusion: that is, the essential identity of the Pharisees of the 1st century BCE with the rabbis of the *Mishnah* and *Talmudim* (Id., "I farisei: quadro storico e ideale", *RStB* 9/2 [1999], pp. 17 and 13-16).

94. Wilkens, cit., cols. 562-563.

95. H. D. Betz, *Galatians. A Commentary on Paul's Letter to the Churches in Galatia* (Hermeneia; Philadelphia: Fortress Press, 1979) (repr. 1988[4]), pp. 57-112; B. Corsani, *Lettera ai Galati* (CSANT NT 9; Genova: Marietti, 1990), pp. 147-159; and

Antioch incident for what can be inferred about the dialectic of Christian groups, their tendencies and the relationships or conflicts that occurred amongst them.

Gal 2:11-14:

v 11 But when Cephas came to Antioch, I opposed him to his face, because he stood self-condemned; v 12 for until certain people came from James, he used to eat with the Gentiles. But after they came, he drew back and kept himself separate for fear of the circumcision faction. v 13 And the other Jews joined him in this hypocrisy, so that even Barnabas was led astray by their hypocrisy. v 14 But when I saw that they were not acting consistently with the truth of the gospel, I said to Cephas before them all, 'If you, though a Jew, live like a Gentile and not like a Jew, how can you compel the Gentiles to live like Jews?

Paul does not specify the time nor the reasons for Peter's arrival in Antioch. According to the concise commentary of Act 11:19-22 after the persecution took place at the time of Stephen, some of those who were dispersed – including some "Hellenists" from Jerusalem – had got as far as Antioch, capital of Syria, where they announced the word of God to the Jews of the area (v 19). "But among them were some men of Cyprus and Cyrene who, on coming to Antioch, spoke also to the Greeks, proclaiming the Lord Jesus" (v 20), with great success (v 21). It seems that it was at that time that the church of Jerusalem began to be suspicious, sending Barnabas to Antioch (v 22). Shortly thereafter a large and complex mixed community formed, composed of ex-Jews and ex-pagans. It is thus difficult to establish at what point the cohabitation of Christian Jews and Gentile Christians resulted in a break between the Christian Jews and other Jews, and eventually a departure from the life of the synagogue.

It seems, however, that in the early period of the Christian community of Antioch there was not a particularly tense atmosphere between ex-Jews and ex-pagans, united in their communion at the table. The profound significance attributed to this *koinonia* could have destabilised the relationship if they had not shared the communal meals. This could explain the initial position of Peter referred to in Gal 2:12a. But when some arrived at Antioch sent by James, that is, members of the Jerusalem community, there were those who were scandalised by such a communion with Gentile Christians. Peter then became doubtful and withdrew from the Gentile Christians "for fear of the circumcision faction" (v 12b), and so was rebuked by Paul who "opposed him to his face" (v 11). Paul reminds Galatians of this bitter conflict with Peter because the menacing attitude of the Galatians towards Judaism – provoked by some "zealous" missionaries who had joined them – jeopardised the truth of the Gospel, just as happened in Antioch.

The behaviour of Peter and of the other Christian Jews – including Barnabas – is twice defined by Paul as "hypocrisy" (v 13: καί συνυπεκρίθησαν... τῇ ὑποκρίσει). It refers to their incoherence, their false mien, as they "were not acting consistently with the truth of the Gospel (v 14a). In fact, the Gospel affirms that "there is no longer Jew or Greek" (Gal 3:28), as Paul underlines. Something analogous to the denunciation of "hypocrisy" which can be found elsewhere in the NT (eg 1 Tim 1:15; 4:1-2; 2 Tim 1:5; etc.).[96] In Antioch, then, there were Christian-Jewish groups rigorously tied to the ancient Judaic culinary norms which did not allow the Jew to eat with pagans and imposed a "separation" from them (cf. 3 Macc 3:4; *Jub.* 22:16; *Jos. and As.* 7:1; Acts 10:14), because the food of the pagans was unclean (eg Ezek 4:13; Hos 9:3-4).

4.5. Toward a Conclusion

In this last part of the chapter I have talked of a 'trajectory', of which I have analysed a few examples from Jesus and the Jesus Movement up to the *Didache*. There is much more work to be done in order to reach a conclusion or otherwise more thoroughly documented results. I have, as one might say, removed only some of the clods from the soil in which *Did.* 8:1 is rooted.

The conflict between "the others" and the ὑποκριταί on the question of fasting – the former observing it on Wednesday and Friday, the latter on Monday and Thursday – can be better seen in context if one supposes that in the community/ies of the *Didache* (after 70 CE) there were rival groups simultaneously adhering to the same movement of Jesus. They were probably individuals or groups who had previously lived in a climate of tension among themselves: one group of Pharisaic origins (ὑποκριταί), the "others" with Essene/Enochic offshoots. These two were both searching for their own identity in the

---

96. L. Oberlinger, *Die Pastoralbriefe. Dritte Folge: Kommentar zum Titusbrief* (HThK 11/2.3; Freiburg i. Br.: Herder, 1996), *Excursus* 1; and Gnilka 2000.

new communal situation (i.e. the new 'way') of Christian Judaism. The latter accused the ὑποκριταί of being wicked and dissidents, because by choosing Monday and Thursday as days of fasting they perpetuated the ancient Pharisaic error ("hypocrisy"). The former (i.e. "the others"), who had Essenic tendencies (Enochians/Apocalyptics) – and thus were used to celebrating feasts on specific days, that is, Wednesday and Friday (and Sunday) according to their solar calendar – were opposed to the erroneous choice of Monday and Thursday of the ὑποκριταί.

In short, the choice of Wednesday/Friday in contrast with Monday / Thursday in *Did.* 8:1 would require not simply a 'temporal' reading but a 'qualitative' reading: selected and liturgical days of the Sabbath week, according to the solar calendar, were transposed to the Christian practice of the bi-weekly fast. Other interpretations of *Did.* 8:1 lack the argumentative power of my reading. For example, there are scholars who hold that the ὑποκριταί alludes to pagans converted to Christianity in the Syro-Palestinian region, perhaps in the area of Antioch, where the *Didache* was probably written. These newly converted pagans, without taking into account the 'new situation' (i.e. the Christian "way") would have wanted to follow Christianity while retaining and conserving Jewish (Pharisaic) traditions and practices, such as the days of a bi-weekly fast (Monday and Thursday).[97] As to the reading of ὑποκριταί as a simple, plain reference to the Pharisees (or, more generally, to devout Jews) of Matt 6:16-18, it is an even less supportable[98] interpretation because it is spoiled by an unfounded 'claim' of the NT imposed on the *Didache*.[99]

On the potential of my methodological investigation for discovering the significance of *Did.* 8:1 that privileges Essenism (whether Qumranic or not) and/or Enochic Judaism[100] as the probable source (roots) of the (Jewish) institution referred to in the *Didache* (the bi-weekly fast of

---

97. This is the position – it seems – of Rordorf 1991, p. 422, but in the new edition of the *Didache* (SC 248bis, Paris 1998²) more correctly – in my opinion – he contrasts the thesis of Draper 1992, arguing that the "hypocrites" of *Did.* 8 "désignent principalement certains judéo-chrétiens qui restaient attachés aux pratiques rituelles du judaïsme. Mais ce judaïsme devait être celui des Pharisiens et non celui des Esséniens, puisque la Didachè adopte la discipline de ces derniers pour le jeûne" (p. 224 of the *Annexe*).

98. Milavec 1989, pp. 111-112; Draper 1991b, p. 361.

99. See also Garrow 2003.

100. Boccaccini 1997.1998.

"the others" [8,1c] in opposition to the ὑποκριταί [v 1a-b]), I dare to refer the reader to an earlier paper[101] where I pointed to some methodological procedures to reinforce the legitimacy and importance of reading the *Didache* within a complex and varied historical and literary phenomenon which for some years has been defined as "Middle Judaism" (300 BCE to 200 CE). Apart from this terminology (not universally accepted and by some scholars even vigorously contested) the study of the *Didache* within the rich Judaism (or "Judaisms", including "Christian Judaism") of the Hellenistic Graeco-Roman period remains the most fertile ground to continue research on this enigmatic text without falling into repetition.

5. Conclusion

Did. 8 is fundamentally important for the definition of the identity of the "hypocrites" and "the others", and of the bi-weekly fast of the community/ies for whom the author was writing. The centrality of this chapter has long been recognised by some commentators (beginning with Audet, then to Rordorf-Tuilier, Niederwimmer and others) and in specific studies (such as that of Draper 1992, Del Verme 1999, and Tomson 2001,[102] including many of the pages in the *Proceedings of the Tilburg Conference on "The Didache and Matthew"* (April 7-8, 2003), forthcoming.

The identity of the ὑποκριταί *versus* "the others" of *Did.* 8:1 (and v 2) is relevant for a number of reasons: philological-literary and historical-institutional but above all to define the situation of Christian Judaism within or in contrast to the Judaism of the first cent. CE. Furthermore, *Did.* 8 could be of a certain interest for the study of connections between the Synoptic traditions (in particular the double tradition Matt-Luke [= Q]) that surround the "hypocrisy" of the Pharisees (and the scribes?) and the Didachean tradition of the fast of the "hypocrites". In my opinion, however, to study *Did.* 8 with the intention of discovering the dependence or independence of the *Didache* on *Matthew* will continue to be debated among scholars of literary criticism, with limited results if the exegetes take into account only the literary level of the problem. And the history of the inter-

---

101.   Del Verme 1995, pp. 293-320; and Tuilier 1993.
102.   See also Id. - Lambers-Petry 2003, pp. 8-14.

pretation of the *Didache*, which is well expounded by J.S. Kloppenborg,[103] is evidence of that.

As to the problem of the "hypocrites" in *Did.* 8:1 and the relations to Matt 6:16-18 (but also other sections of Matt 5-7: see K. Syreeni, "The Sermon on the Mount and the Two Ways Teaching of the Didache", in *Proceedings of the Tilburg Conference*), less hypothetical and more useful solutions could be sought for in the historical context of disputes and conflicts among groups within Judaism before or contemporary with the *Didache*. It is thus necessary to concentrate on the study of the birth and development of tradition/s concerning institutions (like fasting, tithing, and public prayer), which are central and vital in the Syria-Palestine communities of the 1st century CE, rather than on literary questions. Institutions, as is well known, are slow to die out and transform themselves in the community dynamics of the groups, especially in the transition from an early community situation to a 'new' one, as was the case in the Didachean community with respect to the Jewish community, from which the new converts came or at which the Gentile Christian neophytes might have looked. The study of traditions and halakhic discussions (see Tomson) regarding these institutions, documented in the Judaism immediately prior and contemporaneous with the *Didache*, could help us to find better solutions to the question of the relationship between the *Didache* and *Matthew*.

In order to explain the significance of "hypocrisy" with respect to fasting in *Did.* 8:1, I have attempted to identify a specific 'trajectory' that beginning with OT traditions continues in the Judaism documented in the Apocrypha/Pseudepigrapha (especially through Enochian literature, whether Qumranic or not), recurring also in the Synoptic traditions (eg Matt 23:23 [par. Luke 11:42], and Luke 18:11-12) as well as in the Pauline Epistles, in the Catholic letters, and finally in the "Apostolic Fathers". This 'trajectory' insists on a close examination of terms constructed from the root upokrivn-. These terms, if their semantic value is traced back to Hebraic-Aramaic חָנֵף, correctly explain the significance of ὑποκριταί of some texts of *Matthew* and of the *Didache*, where a dialectics of opposition between individuals and groups is present: "we" and "you", with reference to the interpretation of the

---

103. "The Use of the Synoptics or Q in *Did.* 1:3b-2:1", in *Proceedings of the Tilburg Conference*.

law. "We" (= the 'true observers'), and "you" (= the 'dissidents/ wicked/perverse', tha is, the "hypocrites").

It seems to me that the study of the ties between the philological value of the term ὑποκριταί and the social-religious context of the institutions *in agenda* (fast and tithes) has been neglected in the attempt to clarify the identity of the individuals and/or groups labelled as "hypocrites". Therefore my reading of *Did.* 8:1 which leads to a philological and historical investigation on to the terrain of Enochic Judaism in order to clarify the conflict between the "hypocrites" and "the others", could merit greater attention.[104]

Finally, if the conflict between the "hypocrites" and "the others" in *Did.* 8 is interpreted as a quarrel within contemporary groups belonging to the same Christian-Jewish community, it is certainly unfounded to speak of the *Didache* as an "irrevocable parting of the ways" with Judaism. Rather, the situation of the Matthean community seems instead to originate from an incipient conflict with contemporary Judaism, a Judaism that if not already Rabbinic is nevertheless destined to become so within a few decades.

104. The next IOQS meeting (July 27-28, 2004) will deal with this very topic: "Defining identities: who is the other? We, you, and the others in the Dead Sea Scrolls". New insights are welcome on this subject.

Chapter 4

THE ΑΠΑΡΧΗ OF THE CHRISTIAN JEWS (*DID.* 13:3-7)
AND SOME ANCIENT ECCLESIASTICAL ORDINANCES

1. Introduction

The legacy of Jewish elements apparent in the *Didache* has long
been examined and analysed by Christian scholars. Recently Jewish
historians too have begun to take an interest in the Jewish traditions
transmitted by the *Didache,* seeing in them evidence for the functioning
of certain Jewish institutions at the end of the Second Temple and in the
Tannaitic period.[1]

In my opinion, the *Didache* can open up new historical perspectives
in the research on the *Fortleben* of Jewish tradition within Christian-
Jewish communities and early Christianity. This does not solely apply
to those Jewish traditions whose sources were anterior to the *Didache,*
which the author inserted into his 'Community Rule' as being applicable to the Christian-Jewish community of around the second half of
the 1st century CE. There are also, in addition, certain passages in the
Didache which seem to reflect an ongoing process of interaction with
Judaism and Jewish institutions, pointing to the existence of a Jewish
Christianity which existed within the bounds of the "Great Church",
and which had not yet manifested any of those traits of belief or
practice which subsequently led to its marginalisation. In order to des-
ignate this distinctive and important element within Early Christianity
it is proposed to use the term 'Syro-Palestinian', seeing that its connections were in particular with the region of Antioch, where its literary
language was primarily Aramaic or an early form of Syriac – but also in
part Greek. At the same time this community evidently retained close

<hr/>

1. For example, S. Safrai, "Religion in Everyday Life", in Safrai-Stern 1974-
1976, vol. I/2, pp. 793-833.

links with the Christian Jewish community in Jerusalem, from which it had originally been evangelised.[2]

In certain respects the *Didache* can be seen as reflecting this Syro-Palestinian Christian Jewish community. In this chapter I shall try to illustrate this, taking the case of the ἀπαρχή in *Did.* 13:3-7 (Point 2.), a text which will also exert its influence on the edition of subsequent normative prescriptions – which can be found in the ecclesiastical rules resuming parts of the *Didache* – when listing the offerings of the *Christifideles* for the ministers of religion and for the poor (Point 3.). The norms of *Did.* 13 as well as those of other Christian texts depending on the *Didache* appear to be modelled on either contemporary or immediately previous Jewish prescriptions informing social welfare practices of the Syrian-Palestinian and/or Diaspora communities.

2. *The ΑΠΑΡΧΗ of* Did. *13:3-7*

In chapters 11-13 the *Didache* provides a series of instructions on Christian hospitality, with reference in particular to itinerant preachers of the Gospel: apostles, prophets and teachers. The passage *Did.* 13:1-7, which forms part of these instructions, is of particular importance in any attempt to identify the *milieu* out of which the document arose - located, in all probability, in western Syria. It also throws light on an archaic feature of this Christian Jewish community, with the active presence still within it of itinerant ministers, who played a charismatic role as apostles, prophets and teachers.[3] In particular, the passage *Did.* 13:3-7 can be seen to imply that the anonymous author, in laying down his prescriptions for the support of a Christian prophet who was settled in the community, gathers together (as indeed he not infrequently does in the course of the work) customs and traditions of the Christian-Jewish communities which had direct personal knowledge of the corresponding practices of the contemporary Jewish communities. This implication is supported by details in the text, which deserve closer examination.

2. Simon-Benoit 1985[2], esp. chap. V; and Simon 1965, pp. 181ff.
3. Rordorf-Tuilier 1998[2], pp. 51-63; also Theissen 1977.1983[2].1988b.2000, who points out the active role of charismatic itinerant ministers within the movement led by Jesus and in the Early Christian communities. An attentive and critical perusal of these and other analogous works has been published by Norelli 1987 and Barbaglio 1988.

After enunciating the general principle that "every true prophet (πᾶς δὲ προφήτης ἀληθινός) who wishes to stay in the community (lit. "among you") is worthy of his keep; likewise a true teacher (ὡσαυτῶς διδάσκαλος ἀληθινός like a labourer, is worth of his keep" (vv 1-2),[4] the author goes on in vv 3-7 to specify the ways in which assistance is to be given. For this purpose he employs a series of concise conditional propositions modelled on legal and future hortatory phraseology in the *Torah,* taking the form ἐάν (reflecting Hebrew construction ם'... יכ), with, in the apodosis, either the future indicative δῶσεις, or the aorist imperative δός or δότε, followed by an aorist participle λαβών with the object ἀπαρχήν, whereupon there follows a list of agricultural products, domestic animals, and other things on which the ἀπαρχή is to be taken for the benefit of the prophets, or (in their absence) the poor.[5]

The literary form is that of a very ancient ordinance, one which was to be drawn upon later by the various Constitutions and Apostolic Canons of East and West, marking the beginning of ecclesiastical legislation concerning the offerings of the *Christifideles* for the clergy and the poor, and in particular by the *Apostolic Tradition* (abbr. *Ap. Trad.*) of Pseudo-Hippolytus (ca. 215 CE), the *Didascalia Apostolorum* (abbr. *Dida.*) (first decades of the third cent.) and the *Apostolic Constitutions* (abbr. *Const.*) (end of the fourth cent.).

We shall return shortly to the semantic problems concerning the term ἀπαρχή. First, however, we should note the presence in this passage of two details which clearly indicate that the author of the *Didache* adheres to the Old Testament legislation and to Jewish institu-

---

4.   Cf. Matt 10:10; Luke 10:7; 1 Cor 9:13-14; 1 Tim 5:18.

5.   A careful analysis of *Did.* 13:1-7 is given by Schille 1966, esp. pp. 89ff.; 99ff., with much attention paid to the form and function of the traditions as set forth in *Did.* 11-13. Nonetheless, Schille's idea that the cases mentioned in *Did.* 13:5-7 refer to forms of private or domestic assistance for itinerant prophets while 13:3-4 refer to a public or community assistance to the prophets who had by now become Church officials, seems to me unconvincing, original though it is. The text, in my opinion, takes up some Jewish forms of aid to priests (and the poor) which the Didachist proposes cumulatively and simultaneously for prophets who have become sedentary and, in their absence, for the poor of the community. Schille's two phases (one private, one public) are entirely conjectural and they take no account of the contemporary Jewish customs which the Didachist (and his community) looked to, nor do they suit the sense of *Did.* 13:1ff., which deal only with prophets (and teachers) who intend to settle down in the community.

tions as providing the basis for the norms of Christian Jewish assistance given to a prophet or to the poor: 1. the equation of 'true (sc. Christian) prophets' with 'the (sc. Jewish) high priests' (v 3b); and 2. the twofold occurrence of the phrase κατὰ τὴν ἐντολήν (vv 5, 7), both in the middle of the passage and at the end.

The transference from Jewish priests to Christian Jewish prophets is made principally, it appears, in order to promote their right to be supported by the community receiving them. Just as the priests of the Old Covenant lived from the offerings of the people, so the ministers of the Gospel ought to be supported by their community. Thus the phrase κατὰ τὴν ἐντολήν raises the concrete forms of assistance recommended to the faithful to the status of a commandment, whether it be sought within the *Torah*,[6] or whether it is an allusion on the Didachist's part to a specific teaching (λόγιον) of Jesus. We cannot exclude the possibility that in laying down the details of the ἀπαρχαί the Didachist was influenced by the Jewish *halakhah* and by contemporary Jewish practice.[7]

2.1. Semantic Values of ἀπαρχή

I would suggest that the key to the passage under examination lies in focusing attention on the semantic value of ἀπαρχή. Philological research on this point has been inadequate. The best and more recent commentators on the *Didache* (e.g. Audet, Giet, Kraft, Niederwimmer, Rordorf-Tuilier and Visonà) concentrate on determining the various levels of composition (that is, traditional material, original material belonging to the Didachist, and successive reworkings and interpolations), with diverse and often contradictory results. They do not give philological notes on the word ἀπαρχή, which is always rendered simply as "firstlings" or "first fruits". Apart from being vague, this

---

6. Also Heb 7:4 and *Did.* 2:1; 4:13.

7. Audet 1958, without denying the probability of substantial references to OT texts, appropriately points out that, in connection with κατὰ τὴν ἐντολήν, the Didachist does not cite any specific text but has in mind Christian customs (eg Acts 20:33ff.). "Sans doute" – he writes – "s'appuie-t-il (= the didachist), de façon immédiate, sur des usages plutôt que sur des textes, en dépit de son insistance sur le κατὰ τὴν ἐντολήν (13:5, 7), que personne ne songera à regarder comme une pure référence à la loi ancienne..." (p. 457). This observation – I would add – is interesting if Paul's behaviour is seen as a refusal to accept financial aids of the kind active in contemporary Jewish communities, a custom taken over in Christian Jewish circles.

rendering sometimes risks making the author's words clumsy or even downright incomprehensible. What, for example, could be meant by "firstlings of money" or "firstlings of clothing"?

We should note that the term ἀπαρχή, even in Classical Greek, could take on many meanings, from 'firstlings' in the strict sense, to 'birth certificate' and 'tax on inherited wealth'; and from 'first sacrificial offering' or 'religious donation' in general (whether to a deity or to his or her servants), to 'first greeting' or 'first word'.[8] To recover what the Didachist meant by ἀπαρχή, we need to look above all[9] at the vocabulary of the Septuagint and at the Hebrew text in question regarding the offerings of the people for the Temple and Temple personnel. We also need to examine what transformations the *Torah* regulations had undergone in the *halakhah* and in Jewish practice of the Didachist's own time and just before.[10]

The term ἀπαρχή in the LXX basically covers two diverse, but related, Hebrew terms, since it renders both ראשית and תרומה. The fact that the same term ἀπαρχή (mostly in the plural, ἀπαρχαί) can represent two separate terms in Hebrew, is itself an indication that the terms ראשית and תרומה were not always strictly differentiated in Hebrew or at least in the way the Hebrew was understood by the translators.

When the Hebrew ראשית refers to a cult offering the LXX normally renders it by ἀπαρχή. The distinctive feature of the ἀπαρχή/ἀπαρχαί = ראשית is its qualitative aspect, pointing to a gift made from the best

---

8.   Cf. P. Stengel, 'Απαρχαί, in *RE. Neue Bearbeitung*, I/2, coll. 2666-2668; H. Beer, 'Απαρχή (Diss. Würzburg: University Press, 1914); J.H. Moulton-G. Milligan, *The Vocabulary of the Greek Testament Illustrated from the Papyri and Other Non-Literary Sources* (London: Hodder & Stoughton, 1949²), s.v. ἀπαρχή.

9.   The use of ἀπαρχαί in the NT and other early Christian texts (eg *Barn.* 1:7; *1 Clem.* 24:1; 29:3; 42:4) does not help my enquiry, because the term in question recurs there either figuratively or transferred to theological contexts (soteriological or eschatological), with the exception perhaps of Rom 8:23. In fact, *Barnabas* and *1 Clement* make use of the term with no reference to offerings of the faithful to the Church or its ministers. See G. Delling, ἄρχω, ἀρχή, ἀπαρχή, κτλ., in *TWNT* I, cols 484-485; and G.W.H. Lampe, *A Patristic Greek Lexicon* (Oxford: Clarendon, 1961 [repr. 1987]), s.v. ἀπαρχή.

10.   Modern commentators have paid altogether too little attention to these changes in Jewish customs. The point is hinted at (but not appreciably developed) by Kraft 1965, who with reference to *Did.* 13:3-7 speaks of "an adapted Jewish *halakic* [sic] tradition based on passages such as Exod 22:29; Num 18:12-30; Deut 18:1-5 (cf. Neh 10:35ff.; Ezek 44:30)" (p. 173).

specimens of a product. Thus we are not necessarily dealing with those fruits which ripened first – for these, the LXX employs the term πρωτο-γεννήματα, which translates Hebrew בכורים (from בכור 'firstborn'), or other such terms which emphasise the element of being first in time.[11]

By using ἀπαρχή for ראשית the LXX translators are specifying the quality: it is 'the best' of the fruits or other products of the soil; or the genuine character of the 'first offering' with respect to the totality of the product – whence we have such expressions as τὰς ἀπαρχάς τῶν πρωτογεννημάτων τῆς γῆς σου εἰσοίσεις εἰς τὸν οἶκον κυρίου τοῦ θεοῦ σου (Exod 23:19), or ἀπαρχάς πρωτογεννημάτων ἐμέρισεν αὐτῷ [= Ααρον] (Sir 45:20b), to indicate either, specifically 'the best of the first fruits of the earth', or simply 'the offering of the first fruits' which had to be brought to the Temple and handed over to the priests. Had ἀπαρχαί just meant 'offering of the first fruits', then the statement in passages like Exod 23:19 or Sir 45:20b would have been tautologous.

In conclusion, as far as the first sense of ἀπαρχή in LXX is concerned, that is when it represents ראשית, the current modern translation of 'firstlings' (Italian 'primizie') can be kept, provided the word is accorded qualitative overtones: it represents 'the best', or 'the first offering' from the produce as a whole. More generally – and this represents the second sense of ἀπαρχή in the LXX – ἀπαρχή can denote any sacred offering or contribution, either to the sanctuary or to cultic personnel.[12] In such cases, ἀπαρχή corresponds to תרומה (lit. 'sacred offering').

Ἀπαρχή = תרומה is synonymous with ἀφαίρεμα which is the other term frequently used to translate תרומה in the LXX. The choice between the two terms, ἀπαρχή and ἀφαίρεμα, seems to have been a

---

11. O. Eissfeldt, *Erstlinge und Zehnten im Alten Testament. Ein Beitrag zur Geschichte des israelitisch-jüdischen Kultus* (BWAT 22; Stuttgart: KB, 1917), p. 108. More generically, M. Tsevat, s.v. בכור (in G.J. Botterweck-H. Ringgren [eds.] in Verbindung mit G.W. Anderson, H. Cazelles, D.N. Freedman, Sh. Talmon und G. Wallis, *Theologisches Wörterbuch zum Alten Testament*, Band I [Stuttgart-Berlin-Köln-Mainz: W. Kohlhammer, 1973]), cols. 643-645. Moreover, I would add that in the writings of the Qumran community too the term ראשית recurs with this meaning of 'first part' of the total produce, with reference to the bread and sweet wine (or must) needed for the communal meals (1QS VI:4-5) and for the Messianic banquet (1QSa II:17-22). The texts concerned read: רשת הלחם והתירוש (1QS VI:5) or [רשית הלחם ו[התירוש (1QSa II:18-19). Cf. also Flav. Ios., *J.W.* 2.131.

12. Eissfeldt, p. 112. This meaning of ἀπαρχή is already present in Classical Greek and in inscriptions from the end of the 6th century BC (supra, n. 8).

matter of indifference to the translators; thus, for example, the offering of materials necessary for the construction of the Tabernacle and for its functioning is rendered as ἀπαρχή by the LXX at Exod 25:2-3; 35:5 and 36:6), but as ἀφαίρεμα at Exod 35:5.21.24 and 36:3, without any apparent difference in semantic value: in every case the underlying Hebrew term is תרומה.[13]

When the biblical text is dealing with תרומות destined for the priests (Lev 22:10-14; Num 18:8, 11-12, 26, 30; and Deut 18:4), in the LXX we normally find ἀπαρχή or ἀπαρχαί. Now on the topic of these תרומות Judaism of the Second Temple period developed a considerable *halakhah*.[14] Of all the offerings to priests discussed in the *Torah,* it was to the תרומות that the Jewish *halakhah* assigned the highest degree of holiness, and the observance of them seems to have caused no particular difficulties for the agricultural population: even after 70 CE the תרומות were regularly made. In any case the economic burden of תרומות – in contrast to the tithes – was not excessive if one fiftieth part of the produce (i.e. two per cent) sufficed to satisfy Biblical and traditional precept.

The principal forms of תרומות in Judaism were twofold: the great *terumah* (תרומה גדולה) levied on all produce of the soil and all fruits of the earth, and the *terumah* of tithes (תרומת מעשר) or 'tithe of tithes'. Both were destined for the priests and were discussed at length in the tractate *Terumoth* of the *Mishnah-Tosephta.*

A third use of ἀπαρχή occurs in some Jewish texts in Greek written in Egypt in the first cent. CE.[15] Here ἀπαρχή means the one-drachma tax which was added to the two-drachma tax, the *Fiscus Judaicus,* which every Jew paid to the Roman state after the destruction of the Temple. This ἀπαρχή of the Alexandrian Jews has been interpreted as a substitute for the תרומות, tithes and other offerings which before 70 CE had been sent by the Diaspora to Judaea. Even Josephus uses the term

---

13. Thus already Eissfeldt, p. 114.
14. *EncJud* XV (1971), s.v. "Terumot" and "Terumot and Ma'aserot", cols. 1023-1028.
15. On these texts, see A. Oppenheimer, *The 'Am Ha-Aretz. A Study in the Social History of the Jewish People in the Hellenistic-Roman Period* (ArbLGHJ 8; Leiden: Brill, 1977), p. 50; to which add *Stud. Pal.* 4.72 (ed. C. Wessely) and other references given by S.L. Wallace, *Taxation in Egypt from Augustus to Diocletian* (New York: Doubleday, 1938 [repr. 1969]), p. 176. To Wallace refers also Grant 1977, Sixth Study, n. 76.

ἀπαρχαί in a general and collective sense to mean the offerings or tribute sent to Jerusalem by the Jews of Asia Minor following ancestral custom (cf. *Ant.* 16.172).

In the light of these various senses of ἀπαρχή in the Bible and in Hellenistic Jewish texts, and given the fact that the Jewish offerings to the priests and the poor (eg the תרומות, the חלה and tithes) were still being made after 70, the complexities of the Jewish Christian ἀπαρχή of *Did.* 13:3-7 become easier to understand. Besides the prescriptions, which are analogous to or in imitation of the Jewish regulations, *Did.* 13:3-7 mentions not only the traditional agricultural products (corn, wine and oil) and animals (sheep and cattle), but also money, clothing and possessions of every kind (v 7). The *Didache* speaks of all these as being κατὰ τὴν ἐντολήν, although the latter categories are not mentioned in the *Torah*. It appears, however, that the custom of paying the priestly offering (ראשית and תרומות) and tithes (מעשרות) on all possessions – although never really widespread and common in the first cent. CE (and even later) – was confined to those who were particularly strict and pious Jews and belonged to religious associations.[16] These associations drew their members (that is the חברים) above all from among the Pharisees, such as the Pharisee of the parable (Luke18:9-14a) who boasts: "I give a tenth of what I purchase" (v 12b).[17] It is probably they who originated the post-Torah expansions and elaborations of tithing and of other offerings.[18] The Jewish Christian ἀπαρχή of *Did.* 13:7, destined for the prophets or (in their absence) the poor, seems to reflect these Jewish practices.

2.2. Text and Translation of Did. 13:3-7

If this interpretation, based on the evidence set out above, is correct, then we can give a more accurate rendering of the *Didache* passage 13:3-7 than the one which modern translations normally provide.

---

16. See also Safrai, p. 825.

17. NRSV – not correctly in my opinion – says: "...of all of my income", and similarly other modern translations of the NT (supra, Chap. Three, p. 141 n. 41). Epiphanius, referring to the Pharisees at the time of Jesus, stresses their zeal in the payment of tithes (ἀπεδεκάτουν δὲ τὴν δεκάτωσιν), of the first fruits (τὰς ἀπαρχὰς ἐδίδουν) and of the *terûmôth* (τριακοντάδας τε καὶ πεντηκοντάδας). Cf. Id., *Haer.* 16.1.5, ed. K. Holl, p. 211; also *PG* 41, 249 n. 4.

18. See Del Verme 1989, pp. 86ff. and passim.

Text of *Did*. 13:3-7: [19]

v 3 Πᾶσαν οὖν ἀπαρχὴν γενημάτων ληνοῦ καὶ ἅλωνος, βοῶν τε καὶ προβάτων λαβὼν δώσεις τὴν ἀπαρχὴν τοῖς προφήταις· αὐτοὶ γάρ εἰσιν οἱ ἀρχιερεῖς ὑμῶν·

v 4 Ἐάν δὲ μὴ ἔξητε προφήτην, δότε τοῖς πτωχοῖς·

v 5 Ἐὰν σιτίαν ποιῇς, τὴν ἀπαρχὴν λαβὼν δὸς κατὰ τὴν ἐντολήν·

v 6 Ὡσαύτως κεράμιον οἴνου ἢ ἐλαίου ἀνοίξας, τὴν ἀπαρχὴν λαβὼν δὸς τοῖς προφήταις·

v 7 ἀργυρίου δὲ καὶ ἱματισμοῦ καὶ παντός κτήματος λαβὼν τὴν ἀπαρχὴν ὡς ἄν σοι δόξῃ, δὸς κατὰ ἐντολήν.

My translation:

v3 Therefore take all the best of the products from the winepress and threshing floor, from the cattle and sheep,[20] and give them to the prophets, because they constitute your high priests.

v 4 But if you have no prophet, give to the poor.

v 5 When you make bread, take the (first) offering,[21] and give it in accordance with the commandment.

v 6 Likewise when you open a jar of wine or oil, take the (first) offering[22] and give it to the prophets.

v 7 In the case of money, clothing, or any other possessions, take from

---

19. Greek text: Rordorf-Tuilier 1998², p. 190.

20. One could also translate: "Therefore thou shalt take all the firstfruits of the products of the wine-press and the threshing floor", with probable allusion to Exod 22:28-29; Num 18:12; Deut 18:4 and Neh 10 [= 2 Esdr 20 LXX]:38a; but 'firstlings' for cattle and sheep is not correct if what is meant is (as seems to be the case) 'the best parts' of the slaughtered animals, i.e. breast, shoulder, hind leg (cf. Exod 29:26-28; Lev 7:28-36; Deut 18:3; Sir 7:31 [LXX]; and *m. Hul*. 10:1. These parts of the animals are called תרומה in the Hebrew Bible, which the LXX translated by ἀφαίρεμα, a synonym of ἀπαρχή.

21. That is a loaf made from the first kneading of dough, ἀπαρχή being the equivalent of ראשׁית alluding to Num 15:20-21 (cf. also Neh 10:38a). In all probability the Didachist is referring to the biblical and Jewish offering known as חלה, the portion which every housewife set aside for the priests when she was kneading dough in the bread-trough. This precept taken up by the Didachist (κατὰ τὴν ἐντολήν) was still in force and generally observed during the period of the Second Temple and even after. For details, see the tractate *Hallah* of the *Mishnah*; and on its obligatory character, cf. Safrai, "Religion in Everyday life", pp. 827-828.

22. Here too ἀπαρχή (= ראשׁית) indicates the 'first offering' taken from the produce in question.

it the offering[23] in whatever way seems best to you, and give it in accordance with the commandment.

The early Church paid a great deal of attention to the matter of ἀπαρχαί offered by the *Christifideles*. It is not by chance that the most ancient ecclesiastical ordinances to come down to us regularly have a paragraph concerning assistance in general to the clergy and to the poor.[24] The forms of assistance prescribed in *Did.* 13:3-7 provide a point of reference for all future Christian ordinances,[25] and these, with their understanding of what was implied by ἀπαρχαί, confirm our view that the term has a wider semantic range than is normally accorded it here, thus including, alongside the first fruits (or the best) of the agricultural products, also any cultic offering (as with תרומה, חלה and, in some respects, the 'first tithe' for the priests) or contribution to the provision for the poor, in line with contemporary Judaism.[26]

It is, in my view, much more questionable to take the ἀπαρχή in *Did.* 13 in the sense of בכורים, or 'first fruits'. It is even less likely to refer to the בכורות (firstborn of animals), for which the LXX employs quite different terms, πρωτογέννημα and πρωτότοκος, which do not appear in the *Didache*. In any case, the offering of both these ceased with the destruction of the Second Temple in 70 CE.

23.　That is the required contribution (here ἀπαρχή = תרומה), or an offering in kind like the תרומות of Exod 25:1ff. and 35:4-36:7, where the LXX translates either by ἀπαρχή or by ἀφαίρεμα.

24.　Cf. L. Vischer, "Die Zehntforderung in der Alten Kirche", *ZKG* 40, 1959, pp. 201-217; T. Natalini, *A Historical Essay on Tithes: A Collection of Sources and Texts* (Washington DC, 1973); and I. Fasiori, "La dîme du début du deuxième siècle jusqu'à l'Édit de Milan (313)", *Lat.* 49, 1983, pp. 5-24. Furthermore, it is known from Origen that the ἀπαρχαί represented an issue debated among pagans and Christians. Of course Celsus would have reprimanded the Christians of his time (the *True Speech* was written by Celsus ca 178 CE) for offering the ἀπαρχαί to God rather than the demons. Origen, in fact, in his reply of ca 264 confutes the neo-Platonic polemist arguing that the ἀπαρχαί must be offered exclusively to God, since He is the creator of the vegetable world (citing Gen 1:11 [LXX]); and that the prayers of intercession must be always directed to God (citing Heb 4:14): 'Ἀλλὰ καὶ ἀπαρχὰς Κέλσος μὲν δαιμονίοις ἀνατιθέναι βούλεται, ἡμεῖς δὲ τῷ εἰπόντι· "Βλαστησάτω ἡ γῆ ... τῆς γῆς. Ω δὲ τὰς ἀπαρχὰς. ἀποδίδομεν, τούτῳ καὶ τὰς εὐχὰς ἀναπέμπομεν, "ἔχοντες ἀρχιερέα μέγαν ... φανερουμένου. (Orig., *C. Cels.* 8.34.1-10, ed. M. Borret [SC 150], p. 248).

25.　For example *Ap. Trad.* 31; *Dida.* 2.25.1-25; 27.1-4; 35.1-4; *Const.* 7.28.3-29.1-3.

26.　Infra, Point 3, passim.

2.3. The ἀπαρχή of Did. 13:3-7 and Residing Prophets at Antioch

According to the *Acts of the Apostles,* the Christian community of Antioch in Syria enjoyed the continual presence of prophets and teachers (Ἦσαν δὲ ἐν ᾿Αντιοχεία κατὰ τὴν οὖσαν ἐκκλησίαν προφῆται καὶ διδάσκαλοι κτλ.) (Acts 13:1). Only five are mentioned by name, but among these are Barnabas and Saul. The community also gave hospitality on a temporary basis to groups of visiting prophets who arrived from other communities (Acts 11:27-28; 15:22, 30-32).[27]

Once the phenomenon of itinerant prophets had given way to that of prophets residing permanently in a particular place, the community needed to find new forms of assistance for them. The ancient norms of ordinary hospitality which had been accorded to itinerant apostles, prophets and teachers for a while, were no longer adequate in the new situation. Our passage in the *Didache* would appear to throw some light on this process of 'sedentarisation' of the prophets (and teachers), and on the new forms of assistance that were organised for their benefit.

The natural and straightforward way in which the Didachist refers to the assistance to be given to the prophets as being "according to the commandment" says something about the way in which the Didachist (and his audience) understood their relationship to the *Torah* ("according to the commandment") and to Judaism (the priests being replaced by prophets). It is in this sense that I spoke of a Syro-Palestinian – Christian Jewish community at the outset of this paper.

The norms, laid down in *Did.* 13:3-7, preserve traditional material of great antiquity. Whether they are understood as being contributed by the Didachist himself, or whether they are considered as interpolations made in the course of the transmission of the text, in both cases the Jewish background to the passage is beyond dispute.[28]

Thus one can perhaps locate the original *Sitz im Leben* of our pas-

---

27. Papa 1974 examines the role of prophets and teachers in the Christian community of Antioch from its origins until the time of the *Didache,* using evidences from *Acts, Matthew* and the *Didache.* Unfortunately in this study too the forms of assistance given to the prophets and teachers of *Did.* 13:3-7 are simply called by the 'generic' term "firstfruits" (in Italian, "primizie") and no consideration is given to contemporary Jewish customs.

28. Giet 1970 writes: "Rien ne prouve qu'elle (= the instruction of *Did.* 13:3ff.) ait été composée pour une communauté chrétienne", and later "...c'est l'équivalence des prophètes et des grands prêtres qui a pu être proposée dans une communauté judéo-chrétienne" (pp. 229-230). Kraft 1965 is more explicit (p. 173).

sage in Christian Jewish circles in Syria such as those which are already attested for Antioch itself, given the presence and important role of prophets (and teachers) in that community which had been the first to be established outside Palestine, at a date even prior to the conversion of Paul.

3. Did. *13:1-7 and Some Ancient Ecclesiastical Ordinances*

If the conclusions derived from my interpretation of the ἀπαρχή in *Did.* 13:3-7 are correct, chap. 13 of the *Didache* represents a precious evidence for the history of the tithes in Tannaitic Judaism too,[29] since the passage in question indicates that the collection of tithes, of either holy or sacerdotal offerings and of the contributions for the poor – besides the contribution from traditional agricultural products prescribed by the *Torah* – could be extended to any form of earnings; and that this practice (at least for some groups or movements) was already in force in the Judaism of the I cent. (or, at the latest, at the beginning of the 2nd century CE). I would like to dwell on this aspect analysing some passages drawn from the ancient ecclesiastical rules, which appear to refer to this chapter of the *Didache*.

Forty-five years ago, Lukas Vischer[30] published an article, brief but rich in references to Christian sources (in particular, the ecclesiastical rules), attempting to clarify the question of the tithes in the early Church. To my mind Vischer's study – along with a few others[31] – still represents the sole specific and relevant study regarding the question of the tithes among the numerous publications which have dealt with the social welfare systems or practices of early Christianity, in the last decades.

In the third part of this chapter I wish to explore a particular aspect of the question which appears to have been neglected by Vischer's analysis: namely the identification of the probable relations between

---

29. For the tithes in Tannaitic Judaism, cf. Del Verme 1989, pp. 176-216.
30. Supra, n. 24.
31. Some references – rather general – regarding charity/benevolence, first fruits and tithes in early Christianity can be found in Grant 1977, Sixth Study, although the parallels with the charitable institutions of coeval Judaism in this study are only sketched out. Also lacking detailed references to contemporary Judaism are the monograph by Natalini and the article by Fasiori (supra, n. 24).

the offerings of the Christian (or Christian-Jewish) communities for the clergy and/or the poor in the ecclesiastical rules and the practice of the offerings (as, for instance, the tithes and the sacred offerings, and those for social welfare and charity purposes) in force in coeval Judaism. I believe that early Christian rules, apart from preserving important data regarding the internal ecclesiastical legislation for the maintenance of the clergy and of other ministers of the community and for the maintenance of the poor, provide us with information useful for identifying the sacerdotal offerings and/or donations for the poor active in both Syrian-Palestinian and diaspora Judaism after 70 CE.

My analysis examines not only some of the normative texts, which, unlike Vischer, will not be examined autonomously – that is, within the early Christian question regarding whether the Biblical and Jewish tithes are still to be considered as binding for the Christian communities after Jesus – but functionally in search of normative details which can enrich the existing scarce historical evidence[32] regarding the reality and modes of Jewish tithes (and of other forms of social welfare), still in force following the catastrophic Jewish war against Rome (66-73 CE) and the destruction of the temple of Jerusalem in 70, episodes which produced the gradual fragmentation of the religious-sacerdotal system centred on such an institution which was central to the Judaism of the periods of the First and Second Temple.

3.1. Apostolic Constitutions

Besides the writings of the NT,[33] the earliest Christian Jewish evidence containing probable historical references to the real situation of the priestly dues and offerings (including the tithes) in the Judaism of the 1st century CE is – as we have seen – the section of *Did.* 13:1-7. This passage of the *Didache* is resumed, almost integrally, by the *Apostolic Constitutions* (7.28.3-29.1-3), which – as is known – for the chaps.1-32 of Book 7 have as their main source the *Didache,* extended and adapted to the changed institutional, liturgical and disciplinary conditions of the Church at the end of the 4th century.[34] The

---

32. Besides the Rabbinical literature *in toto* (from the end of the 2nd century onwards), which poses specific problems as to historical estimation of the traditional and normative *data* contained. See Del Verme 1989, pp.176-216, in particular 182-210.
33. Del Verme 1989, pp. 21-113.
34. A likely date for the edition of the *Apostolic Constitutions* is the year 380 CE (probably a little earlier, but not much later), and its likely place of origin is western

editorial operation that the anonymous Christian author[35] conducted on earlier sources[36] – re-casting them in the framework of a monumental canonical-liturgical work in eight books – could preserve traces of the original meaning of the texts engaged, besides recording the action of extending the texts by the editor and their adaptation to the new ecclesiastical and community situation. In the light of this perspective, I will examine the *Apostolic Constitutions*, a writing which, if considered differently, could be regarded as too late for a historical investigation of the charitable institutions (including the tithes) active in Tannaitic Judaism.

The author of the *Apostolic Constitutions* initially operated a distinction between the ἀπαρχή and δεκάτη, assigning the former (that is the firstfruits) – collected on the same products listed in *Did*. 13:3 – to the priests (Πᾶσαν ἀπαρχὴν γεννημάτων ληνοῦ, ἅλωνος βοῶν τε καὶ προβάτων δώσεις τοῖς ἱερεῦσιν);[37] the latter (that is the tithes) is, by contrast, allocated to the orphan and the widow, to the poor and the proselyte (πᾶσαν δεκάτην δώσεις τῷ ὀρφανῷ καὶ τῇ χήρᾳ, τῷ πτωχῷ καὶ τῷ προσηλύτῳ) (7.29.2). Later in the text, however, the distinction between the two forms of offerings is no longer out, since in *Const*. 7.29.3 – which resumes with some small addition the prescription of *Did*. 13:5-7 – the author appears to indicate by the same term ἀπαρχή (πᾶσαν ἀπαρχὴν) different gifts, of which some are assigned to the priests (ἄρτων θερμῶν, κεραμίου οἴνου ἢ ἐλαίου ἢ μέλιτος ἢ ἀκροδρύων, σταφυλῆς ἢ τῶν ἄλλων τήν ἀπαρχὴν δώσεις τοῖς ἱερεῦσιν) and some to the orphan and the widow (ἀργυρίου δέ καὶ ἱματισμοῦ καὶ παντὸς κτήματος τῷ ὀρφανῷ καὶ τῇ χήρᾳ).

Syria, almost certainly Antioch, that is probably the same area where ca three centuries earlier the *Didache* appeared. For these and other introductory problems, I refer the reader to Metzger 1985 (SC 320), pp. 13-94 (54-62).

35.   Nautin identifies him with a certain Julian, an Arian anomean bishop of Neapolis near Anazarbus, who also wrote a commentary on *Job* edited in 1973 by D. Hagedorn (see P. Nautin, *Costituzioni Apostoliche*, in *DPAC* I [1983], cols. 825-826).

36.   Besides the *Didache, Apostolic Constitutions* 7 report material from the *Apostolic Tradition* by Pseudo-Hippolytus. For the Books 1-6, by contrast, they have as point of reference *Didascalia*. Furthermore, for the Book 7 – apart from the dependence from *Ap. Trad*. (for chaps. 3-46) – the *Apostolic Constitutions* draw some of the norms also from the ecclesiastical canons of previous Councils (eg the 85 canons of chap. 47).

37.   Critical text by Funk 1905, I.

It is likely that the author of this pseudo-epigraphical Christian constitution of the 4th century has interpreted the ἀπαρχή of *Did.* 13 in a comprehensive sense, including both the first fruits (i.e. *primitiae in sensu stricto* [ἀπαρχή = ראשית, namely the best of) and, *in sensu lato*, any offering including the tithes (ἀπαρχή as ἀφαίρεμα = Hebr. תרומה). This would account for the double meaning of the term ἀπαρχή in *Const.* 7.29.1-3, with reference to *Did.* 13. More frequently, however, the *Apostolic Constitutions* intend ἀπαρχή in the specific sense of sacerdotal offering: for example, 8.30.1-2[38] and 8.47 δ'.[39]

Furthermore the *Syntagma doctrinae*,[40] which is one of the sources of indirect evidence for the tradition regarding the text of the *Didache* (esp. for the section of the "Two Ways"), referring to *Did.* 13:3-4 states (and further specifies) that the recipients of the ἀπαρχαί are above all the priests, followed by the widows and the orphans and all the poor of the community.[41] I believe that this norm can be regarded as a precise literary and semantic indication that the ἀπαρχαί of *Did.* 13 in the end provided the model and influence for any form of social welfare system which included the offerings necessary for the maintenance of the clergy and the poor in general: the term ἀπαρχή, therefore, was not used only to indicate sacerdotal offerings.

---

38.   The text presents the simultaneous blessing of the first fruits and of the tithes (v 1); and prescribes that the former should be given to the bishop, priests and deacons for their maintenance, the latter instead are allocated for the maintainance of the remaining clerics, virgins, widows and all those afflicted with poverty (v 2a). It is also stressed that the first fruits are a specifically sacerdotal and ministerial offering: αἱ γὰρ ἀπαρχαὶ τῶν ἱερέων εἰσὶν καὶ τῶν αὐτοῖς ἐξυπηρετουμένων διακόνων (v 2b). For this sacerdotal and episcopal destination of the ἀπαρχαὶ and for the obligation of their blessing the *Apostolic Constitutions* could go back to a custom established in *Ap. Trad.* 31.

39.   This is the fourth of the 85 *Canons of the (Holy) Apostles*. Here the ἀπαρχαί of all the other fruits – that is excluding the first ears, the first bunch of grapes, of oil for lamps and of incense, which must be brought to the altar (7.47 γ' = the third canon) – need not be brought to the altar but can be taken to the house of the bishop and of the presbyters (...εἰς οἶκον ἀποστελλέσθω ἀπαρχὴ τῷ ἐπισκόπῳ καὶ τοῖς πρεσβυτέροις), who will subsequently distribute them to the deacons and the other clerics (Funk 1906, II, p. 564).

40.   This writing (*PG* 28, 836A-845B) has been attributed to Athanasius. Cf. P. Batiffol, *Studia patristica. Études d'ancienne littérature chrétienne* (Paris: Lecoffre, 1880), II, pp. 121-122.

41.   *Synt. doctr.* 6: πρῶτον μὲν τὰς ἀπαρχάς τοῖς ἱερεῦσι πρόσφερε, ἔπειτα θέλε καὶ χήρας ἀναπαύειν, καὶ ὀρφανούς καί λοιπούς... (*PG* 28, 841D).

3.2. Apostolic Tradition

It can be seen that after the *Didache* the writing known by the title of *Apostolic Tradition* of Pseudo-Hippolytus[42] is the earliest and most important[43] among the Christian ecclesiastical constitutions.[44] Originally written in Greek (between ca 215 and 220),[45] this work made its influence felt very soon, in particular in the East (Egypt and Syria), where it inspired many ecclesiastical ordinances (in particular the *Apostolic Constitutions*). It also represents a precious source of information in regard to the offering of the ἀπαρχαί in the Christian (and Jewish) *milieu*.

42. A detailed presentation of the problem of the literary and historical personality of Hippolytus, containing precious cues for further research to unravel the problem of one or two (or even three) Hippolytuses, can be found in E. Norelli (ed.), *Ippolito, L'Anticristo. De Anticristo* (BPat 10; Firenze: Nardini editore, 1987), pp. 9-32. Norelli's presentation, however, reflects a situation of the *quaestio Hippolyti* as it was dealt with in the 1980s and must therefore now be integrated with new studies, for instance those of M. Simonetti (Id. [ed.], *Ippolito. Contro Noeto* [BPat 35; Bologna: EDB, 2000], in particular pp. 70ff.) and E. Prinzivalli (Ead., s.v. "Ippolito, antipapa, santo", in *Enciclopedia dei Papi*, vol. I [Roma: Treccani, 2000], pp. 246-257). Norelli himself, who was inclined to accept the traditional hypothesis (i.e. *Apostolic Traditions* as work written by the Roman Hippolytus), in his recent handbook of the Ancient Christian Graeco-Latin Literature (C. Moreschini-E. Norelli, *Storia della letteratura cristiana antica greca e latina* 1 [Brescia: Morcelliana, 1995], pp. 197ff.) as regards this problem has abandoned the traditional thesis and presents *Apostolic Traditions* as a work external to the *corpus Hippolytaeum*, justly considering it with other writings relating to ecclesiastical discipline. In general, current accredited studies on the works by Hippolytus tend to 'release' the historical and literary personality of Hippolytus from the so-called *Apostolic Tradition*, which is really a work of 'complex' character. Therefore, the original *milieu* of this anonymous canonical-liturgical work remains uncertain as well (cf. M. Simonetti-E. Prinzivalli, *Storia della letteratura cristiana antica* [Casale Monferrato: Piemme, 1999], pp. 38-40). In my opinion the documented diffusion and influence of the work in particular in Egypt and Syria – but also without categorically excluding Rome – represents a good foundation for the observations I attempt to formulate beginning from the norms referred to in *Did.* 13.

43. Thus J. Quasten, *Patrology*, I: *The Beginnings of Patristic Literature* (Utrecht: Spectrum, 1975 [V ed.]). But Quasten's thesis, that the *Apostolic Tradition* was written by the anti-pope and saint, the Roman Hippolytus, who was a strict and fierce opponent of the Bishop of Rome, Calixtus (217-222 CE) as we learn from the *Elenchos*, is refuted by many contemporary scholars.

44. For a concise introduction see Simonetti-Prinzivalli, *Storia della letteratura*, cit., pp. 38-40.

45. Peretto 1996, p. 7, with an updated bibliography in his *Introduzione* (pp. 5-99).

Here I will quote a few passages in their Latin translation (L), which is the earliest (probably dated to the end of the 4th century CE) among the existing versions deriving from the original Greek text.[46] Alongside the Latin version I quote three other versions of Alexandrian origin: in Coptic (S = Sahidic), in Arabic (A), and Ethiopic (E).[47]

46.   The versions and re-elaborations of the *Apostolic Tradition* testify to the interest prompted by this old document, although the reconstruction of the Greek original is difficult if not impossible. The studies by Hauler, Dix, Botte and Tidner, which assumed as a starting point the *Palimpsest of Verona* (a Latin ms. written between 466 and 494 CE although the Latin version of the three text on which it has been composed is dated between 336 and 340. Cf. R.G. Coquin, *Les Canons d'Hippolyte*, PO 31/2, Paris 1966[2], p. 329), have allowed for a reasonable although not definitive reconstruction of *Ap. Trad.* Today, following the discovery of the fragments of the Greek original (Peretto 1996, pp. 27-28 with bibliography) and the detailed clarifications by M. Metzger ("Enquêtes autour de la prétendue «Tradition Apostolique»", EO 9, 1992, pp. 7-36) and Ch. Markschies ("Wer schrieb die sogennante *Traditio Apostolica*?", in W. Kinzig-Ch. Markschies-M. Vinzent [eds.], *Tauffragen und Bekenntnis* [Berlin-New York: W. de Gruyter, 1999], pp. 1-74) we have a more reliable reconstruction of the work (see H.W. Attridge [ed.], *The Apostolic Tradition. A Commentary* by P.F. Bradshaw-M.E. Johnson-L.E. Phillips [Hermeneia; Minneapolis: Fortress Press, 2002]), less approximate than that by Dom Botte. We are however still far away from a final and definitive edition of the *Ap. Trad.* Instead what appears to be definitive is the non-connection of *Ap. Trad.* with Rome and, even more so, with Hippolytus of Rome, so that it would appear convenient to eliminate this point from the discussion regarding the 'historical-literary question' of the existence of either one or two (and, for some, even three!) Hippolytuses. In this regard, Simonetti (*Ippolito. Contro Noeto*, pp. 127-139 [128-130]) states: "Ma, una volta accertato che il personaggio effigiato [nella statua] non era Ippolito, nulla affatto impone di considerare i riferimenti a quelle opere [among which, Περὶ χαρισμάτων ἀποστολικὴ παράδοσις, *Of the charisms of the Apostolic Tradition*] come celebrativi [delle opere del personaggio]: si può invece ipotizzare più plausibilmente (Simonetti, Brent) *una destinazione utilitaria di quei dati, a beneficio della comunità cristiana nel cui ambito era conservata la statua* [emphasis added], e di conseguenza nulla affatto impone di attribuire a un solo autore tutti quegli scritti, dei quali soltanto quello relativo alla Pasqua trova riscontro, e tutt'altro che sicuro (Amore, Bouhot), nell'elenco di opere di Ippolito tramandato da Eusebio" (p. 129).

47.   The *Sinodos*, i.e. the canonical collection of the Patriarchate of Alexandria – which reports as juxtaposed the *Canons of the (Holy) Apostles*, the *Apostolic Tradition* and the Book 7 of the *Apostolic Constitutions* – has not preserved the Greek original but only four versions of the *Apostolic Tradition*: i.e. Sahidic, Bohairic, Arabic and Ethiopic. The versions Bohairic, Arabic and Ethiopic refer to the earlier Sahidic version, which cites the only Greek manuscript (which, as noted above, is lost). Cf. B. Botte, *La Tradition apostolique de Saint Hippolyte. Essai de reconstitution* (LQF 39; Münster: Aschendorff, 1989 [V ed.]), pp. XX-XXIV. I will examine some passages of

Ap. Trad. 31

Reconstruction by Botte:[48]

L	S (A, E)
	Omnes solliciti sint (σπουδάζειν) offerre episcopo in tempore omni
Fructus natos primum quam incipiant	primitias (ἀπαρχή) fructuum (καρπός)
eos omnes festinent offerre episcopo;	prima germina (γέννημα). Episcopus autem accipiat cum gratiarum actione
qui autem offerit benedicat et nominet eum qui optulit dicens:	et benedicat eos et nominet (ὀνομάζειν) nomen eius qui obtulit eos ad se.

L	Barberini Gr. 336
Gratias tibi agimus, d(eu)s,	Εὐχαριστοῦμέν σοι, κύριε ὁ Θεός,
et offerimus tibi primitiuas fructuum,	καὶ προσφέρομεν ἀπαρχὴν καρπῶν
quos dedisti nobis ad percipiendum,	οὓς ἔδωκας ἡμῖν εἰς μετάληψιν
per uerbum tuum enutriens ea,	τελεσφορῆσαι διὰ τοῦ λόγου σου
iubens terrae omnes fructus adferre	καὶ κελεύσας καρποὺς παντοδαποὺς
ad laetitiam et nutrimentum hominum	εἰς εὐφροσύνην καὶ τροφὴν τοῖς ἀνθρώποις
et omnibus animalibus.	καὶ παντὶ ζώῳ.[49]

Ap. Trad. (reconstructions provided by Botte 1984² and by Bradshaw-Johnson-Phillips 2002).
    48. Botte 1984², pp. 110, 112.
    49. "We give thanks to you, Lord God, and we offer the first portion of the fruits that you gave us for sharing, having brought [them] to perfection through your Word and having commanded all kinds of fruits for enjoyment and nourishment for people and every living creature" (tr. by Bradshaw et al., p. 166). The Greek ms. *Barberini* 336, which relates this benediction, is the most ancient Greek euchological text, unfortunately in a very defective form but the versions allow us partially to correct it. This thanksgiving for firstfruits is taken up *quasi verbatim* by *Const.* 8.40.2-4 (ed. Funk, pp.

Reconstruction by Bradshaw-Johnson-Phillips:[50]

L	S	A	E
Let all hasten to offer the bishop the new fruits as soon as they shall begin them;	Let each one hasten (σπουδάζειν) to take in to the bishop (ἐπίσκοπος) on every occasion the firstfruits (ἀπαρχή καρπός) of first grouth (γέννημα).	Let everyone make haste to come to the bishop with the firstfruits of his harvest,	Each one is to give the firstfruits of the grain and be eager to bring it to the bishop;
and let him who offers bless and name him who brought [them], saying:	And (δέ) let the bishop (ἐπίσκοπος) also receive them with thanksgiving, and bless them, and name (ὀνομάζειν) the name of the one who brought them in, saying:	and the bishop will take them and bless them and remember the name of the one who brought them to him, and he will say,	and he is to bring [it] as he blesses and names the one who brought [it], saying:
"We give thanks to you, God. And we offer to you the first of the fruits that you have given to us to eat, [you] nourishing them by your Word, ordering the earth to bear all fruits for the joy and nourishment of human beings and for all animals.	"We give thanks (εὐχαριστεῖν) to you, Lord God, and we bring you the firstfruits (ἀπαρχή καρπός) of wich you gave us to eat, having perfected them by your Word; and you commanded the earth to send forth every fruit (καρπός), for profiting, gladdening, and the nourishment (τροφή) of the human race (= γένος) and all creation.	"We thank you, God, and bring to you the firstfruits that you have given us to eat. You have perfected them according to your Word, and you have commanded the earth to send forth all the fruits for joy and food for the human race and all the animals.	"We thank you, God, and we offer to you the firstfruits that you have given to us for enjoyment, as you have made [the earth] fruitful by your Word. You commanded the earth to be fruitful with every kind [?] for satisfaction-food for people and for animals,

548.550; Engl. tr. in Bradshaw et al., p. 167, in synopsis with *Can. of Hipp.* 36 and *Test. Dom.* 2.14).

50.   Under the title: "Concerning the Fruit That it is Proper to Bring to the Bishop" (ibid., p. 166). *Idem*, Botte, pp. 110-111: "Des fruits qu'il faut offrir à l'évêque"), and Peretto 1996, pp. 133-134: "I frutti da offrire al vescovo", to underline the central role of the Bishop in this canonical-liturgical order.

For all these we praise you, God, and in all things with wich you have helped us, adorning for us the whole creation with varied fruits, etc.

Amen".

We bless you, God, for these things, and all others with which you show kindness (εὐεργε- τεῖν) to us, having adorned (κοσμεῖν) all creation with the various fruits (καρπός), etc. Amen (Αμην)".

We thank you, o God, for this and all the other things you have made for our well-being. You have arranged your creation with va- rious fruits etc.

Amen".

for which we glo- rify you, o God, in all that [by] which you have profited us, all creation [with] its own fruit, etc.

Amen."

Probably because of a confusion between ἀπαρχή (firstfruits or "the best" of the fruits) and ἀπ'ἀρχῆς ("from beginning")[51] – "as soon as they (new fruits or – as it seems – all [i.e. people]?) shall begin them", tr. by Bradshaw-Johnson-Phillips, p. 166) – the reference to the first fruits in the L version with the expression *fructus natos primum quam incipient* appears to be uncertain and obscure, although it is clarified in the following thanksgiving, in which the object of the εὐχαριστία to God[52] is represented by the *primitiuas fructuum* (ἀπαρχὴν καρπῶν in *Barberini* Gr. 336), that is the firstfruits or the best of the fruits.

By contrast, more straightforward in this case – both as to form and construction – are the versions S (A, E) indicating that the author of *Ap. Trad.* with the expression *primitias fructuum prima germina* – which can be translated "the best of the fruits" or simply "the firstfruits of the growth" to offer to the Bishop (both in L and in S, A, E), alludes to the ἀπαρχή. Furthermore the text of L, emphasising the obligation of all the congregation (*omnes festinent*) to offer their produce (*fructus natos*) to the Bishop before using it for themselves (*primum quam incipiant eos*) and to thank God for the *primitiuas fructuum*, uses the term ἀπαρχή with a semantic bi-valency as in the LXX. Actually, it can

---

51. Botte, p. 111 n. 2. The author correctly translates: "Tous s'empresseront d'offrir à l'évêque, *comme prémices des fruits, les premières récoltes*"; analogously, Peretto, p. 133: "Tutti s'affrettino ad offrire al vescovo *le primizie dei frutti delle prime raccolte*" (emphasis added).

52. The thanksgiving to God has a simultaneous 'Christological' tone both in L ("through your Child Jesus Christ our Lord...") and in S ("through your holy Son Jesus Christ our Lord..."), as well as in A and E ("through [or by] your Son Jesus Christ our Lord..."). In the versions S, A, and E the Holy Spirit (πνευμα) is also mentioned with Jesus Christ (Χριστός). Texts in Bradshaw et al., p. 31.

mean either the offering of ripe fruits (ἀπαρχή = תרומה) in general or specifically the firstfruits or the best of the fruits (ἀπαρχή = ראשית). The versions S (A, E), by contrast, interpret the gifts to offer to the Bishop as offering of the firstfruits (*primitias fructuum*) in a temporal sense, that is *prima germina* are tantamount to πρωτογεννήματα in the LXX, when translating the Hebrew term בכורים into Greek.

Consequently one can draw the following conclusion: *Ap. Trad.* 31 – in the L version – presents the ἀπαρχαί of the *Christifideles* analogously to תרומה and to ראשית of the Biblical and Jewish tradition; the versions S (A, E), by contrast, intend ἀπαρχή in the sense of or analogous to בכורים which are collected *also* on several kinds of fruits not expressly mentioned in the written *tôrāh-miqrâ*. In fact, the Hebrew Bible (see, for example, Deut 8:8) – and the *Mishnah* as well (cf. *Bik.* 1:3) – prescribes that the בכורים should be collected only on seven products: wheat, barley, grapes, figs, pomegranates, olives and honey; in *Ap. Trad.* 32, by contrast, the detailed list of the fruits offered to the Bishop and which have to be blessed (by him, i.e. the bishop?) is much longer.

I relate the list below:

Ap. Trad. 32

Reconstruction by Botte:[53]

L	S (A, E)
Benedicuntur quidem fructus, id est uua, ficus, mala grania, oliua, pyrus, malum, sycaminum, persicum, ceraseum, amygdalum, damascena,	Hi sunt fructus (καρπός) qui benedicuntur: uva, ficus, mala grania, oliva, pyrus (ἀπίδιον), malum, persicum (περσικόν), cerasium (κεράσιον), amygdalum (ἀμύγδαλον);

Reconstruction by Bradshaw-Johnson-Phillips:[54]

---

53. Ibid., p. 114.
54. Ibid., p. 170. The list of "the fruits which are blessed" in *Barberini* Gr. 336 numbers only these: "grape, fig, pomegranate, olive, apple, nectarine, peach, plum".

L	S	A	E
Fruits indeed are blessed, that is, grape, fig, pomegranate, olive, pear, apple, mulberry, peach. Cherry, almond, plum,	These are the fruits (καρπός) that shall be blessed: the grape, the fig, the pomegranate, the olive, the pear (ἀπίδιον), the apple, the peach (περσικόν), the cherry (καράσιον), the almond (ἀμύγδαλον).	These are the fruits over which a blessing is said: grapes, figs, pomegranates, olives, peaches, apples, plums.	These fruits are then to be blessed: grapes, figs, pomegranates, the fruit of olive trees, apples, prunes, quinces, cherries, almomds.

In the light of the two passages[55] quoted above, if the ἀπαρχαί of the Christians for the bishop are interpreted either as the specific offering of the firstfruits (ראשית = the best of) or, more generally, as the offerings (=תרומת) of fruits following the L version, it would be possible to conclude that the Christian prescriptions of *Ap. Trad.* 31-32 reflect the *halakhah* and the Jewish practice after 70 CE, when the obligation of the sacerdotal offerings and of the tithes was extended to include all the agricultural products[56] and any kind of fruit. On the contrary, if the Christian ἀπαρχαί were intended as a synonym of בכורים, as it appears to be documented by the other versions S (A, E), the list of fruits does not have a direct antecedent in the *halakhah* and in the practices in force in coeval Judaism. In this case, the author of the *Apostolic Tradition* would be merely reproposing in Christian terms – with slight variations – a Biblical and Jewish institution (that is, the offering of the *bikkûrîm*) which was no longer practised: the בכורים were brought to the Temple of Jerusalem and therefore the practice completely ceased in the period following the destruction of 70 CE.

Furthermore it is necessary to attentively consider the dictation of

---

55. Elsewhere we find also the offering of oil (*Ap. Trad.* 5 [in L and E], in Botte, p. 54), of cheese and of olives (*Ap. Trad.* 6 [only in L], see Botte); but these are elective offerings which recur as a digression within the section dealing specifically with the Eucharistic celebration. However the author takes care not to identify the blessing of these two offerings (very similar to those subsequently listed in chaps. 31-32) with the blessing of bread and wine, which has a different purpose (in Botte, pp. 54-55 nn. 1, 4; and Peretto 1996, p. 112 n. 24).

56. Always in this chapter both L and S, A, E list also the offering of flowers, esp. the rose and the lily but not others, together with a list of prohibited products. The blessing of flowers, esp. the rose and the lily, can be found also in *Test. Dom.* 2.14 (infra, n. 61).

Ap. Trad. 32 in which the blessing of some kinds of fruit (belonging to the family of ther cucurbits) and of vegetables in general is categorically prohibited.the following list, in fact, records:

Ap. Trad. 32

Reconstruction by Botte:[57]

L	S (A, E)
	non autem benedicuntur sycaminum,
non pepon, non melopepon,	nec onio, nec allium,
non cucumeres, non cepa,	nec pepon (πέπων), nec melopepon
non aleus,	(μηλοπέπων),
nec aliut de aliis oleribus.	nec cucumeres,
Sed et aliquotiens et flores	nec aliud de oleribus (λάχανον).
offeruntur.	
Offeratur ergo rosa et lilium,	Si autem offeruntur (προσφέρειν)
et alia uero non.	flores
	(ἄνθος), offerantur rosae et lilia
	(κρίνον),
	alia autem non offerantur.

Reconstruction by Bradshaw-Johnson-Phillips:[58]

L	S	A	E
[but] not pumpkin, not melon, not cucumber, not onion, not garlic, or any of the other vegetables.	But (δέ) neither the sycamore fig, nor (οὐδέ) the onion, nor (οὐδέ) the garlic, nor (οὐδέ) the malon (gourd?) (πέπων), nor (οὐδέ) the pumkin (μηλοπέπων), nor (οὐδέ) the cucumber, nor (οὐδέ) any other ve-	The fruits that are not blessed are sycamore figs, onions, garlic, cucumbers, and all pulses.	And they are not to bless the Egyptian fig, not garlic, not onions, and no kind of gourd, and none of the vegetables, and no other fruits are they to offer

---

57. Ibid., p. 114.
58. Ibid., p. 170.

getable (λάχανον)
shall be blessed.

But sometimes flowers are also offered.	But (δέ) if it will happen that they offer (προσφέρειν) flowers (ἄνθος),	
Therefore let the rose and the lily be offered, but not others.	let them bring the roses and the lily (κρίνον). But (δέ) do not let others be brought.	They may bring roses also, but not other [flowers].
		exept the flower of the rose.

In my opinion the cited list above suggests that the editor of the agricultural and liturgical prescriptions, presenting different kinds of fruits in the same group as the vegetables (*nec aliut de oleribus*, in L; *nec aliud de oleribus*, in S [A, E]), emphasises a preoccupation – I suppose widespread in the author's own Christian community (or in a community which knows and observes the norms[59] derived from an ecclesiastical rule composed originally somewhere else)[60] – with avoiding through the offerings of herbs or vegetables (in Latin, olera; in Greek, λάχανα)[61] those ancient Pharisaic practices which Jesus once criticised and condemned. There would be, therefore, a reference to the *logion* of Luke 11:42: ἀλλὰ οὐαὶ ὑμῖν τοῖς Φαρισαίοις, ὅτι ἀποδεκατοῦτε... καὶ πᾶν λάχανον.[62]

---

59. Supra, n. 46 (at the end).

60. Located – most probably – in Syria although not excluding categorically either Egypt or indeed Rome, without however creating a surreptitious link between Hippolytus of Rome, anti-pope and saint, and the *Apostolic Tradition* by returning to the traditional thesis (now abandoned by the most accredited critics and historians on the basis of philological arguments, such as those proposed by Marckschies, Metzger, and others) that the author was Hippolytus.

61. The prohibition on blessing vegetables can be found also in the *Test. Dom.* 2.14: "Vegetables are not blessed, but fruits of trees, flowers, and the rose and the lily" (in Bradshaw et al., p. 171), while *Can. of Hipp.* 36 appear to assume a more liberal and conciliatory stance: "Every vegetable, all the fruits of the trees, and all the fruits of the cucumber fields are to be blessed, and [also] him who brings them, with a blessing" (in Attridge, p. 171).

62. If my supposition is correct, the 'misunderstanding' of the "woe" in *Luke* (and *Matthew*) in the history of the Christian exegesis of the Gospels would find in this text of the *Ap. Trad.* a venerable precedent. The polemical interpretation and the refusal of Jewish offerings (including the tithes and first fruits) as well as the sacrifices, ritual ablutions and festivities, in order to brand the "justice of the scribes and of the

3.3. Didascalia

Likewise in this pseudo-epigraphical writing, originally composed in Greek[63] in the first decades of the 3rd century CE, the management of the offerings – including the firstfruits and the tithes which the members of the community give to the Church for the maintenance of the clergy and the poor – are listed among the main tasks of the Bishop.

The anonymous author of the *Didascalia* (abbr. *Dida.*), who probably was a Jew converted to Christianity, wrote this ecclesiastical constitution for a community of people converted from paganism and living in northern Syria, presumably around Antioch. The literary model assumed for writing his work appears to have been the *Didache.* The details regarding both the author and the literary genre[64] – as well as the specificity of the offerings recorded in the text – justify my interest in this old Christian order since it appears to provide useful information concerning charitable institutions including tithes, still in force in the Christian *milieu* and coeval Judaism.

The *Didascalia* often refers to the matter of the offerings of *Christifideles* to the Church, in particular in Book 2 (for example, 25.1-25; 27.1-4; 35.1-4);[65] and the centrality of the Bishop is constantly stressed both in receiving and in distributing gifts, on reiterating the importance of the mode of giving and the virtues which must accompany the distribution of offerings. The Bishop is therefore advised to be, above

Pharisees" and be able to extol the evangelical precept: "vende omnia quae habes, et da pauperibus" is evident also in a passage of the *Didascalia* (2.35.1-3), but only in the version S (ed. Funk, pp. 118ff., where it is reported with a diacritical sign). One may note, however, that the anti-Jewish tendency against the tithes, the first fruits and other offerings are not present in *Didascalia*, nor in the *Apostolic Constitutions* in those sections depending on the *Didascalia.*

63.   The writing however has been transmitted integrally in a Syriac version (= S), dated prior to the first half of the 4th century CE, and also – in a fragmentary state – in a Latin version (= L) of the end of the 4th century. In addition, the *Apostolic Constitutions* are useful for the reconstruction of the original text, among which the *Didascalia* represents the main source for Books 1-6.

64.   For these and other introductory notes, see Quasten, *Patrology*, cit., with bibliography. More concisely, P. Nautin, s.v. *Didascalia degli Apostoli,* in *DPAC* I, cols. 948-949.

65.   For the text of *Didascalia* I follow the Latin reconstruction by Funk 1905-1906, I, comparing it with the Greek text of the *Apostolic Constitutions* when necessary.

all, restrained and moderate when taking offerings for himself,[66] while being generous and fair towards all the other recipients of gifts:[67] God, in fact, will ask him to account for his deeds since he must consider himself only as a manager and not the owner of goods offered to the Church.[68]

From a stylistical and literary point of view the norms motivating and regulating the offerings of the community to the Bishop in the *Didascalia* are stated by resorting to several texts borrowed from the Scriptures, both the Old and New Testaments. Paradigmatic in this regard is the section 2.25.1-25, encompassing a lengthy argumentation – more than half of the whole text – the entire chap. 18 of *Numbers* along with other passages from the OT (for example, Deut 25:4; Is 53:2-6, 9, 12; Ezek 34:3) and also from NT,[69] incorporated into the same passage. In my opinion, this section is to be interpreted as a sort of Biblical inter-text within a work of early Christian literature.[70]

The reference to Num 18 in the *Didascalia* is important, since it clearly expresses the Biblical and sacerdotal frame of mind of the author, who constantly transfers the cultic and ministerial functions of the Priests and Levites of the First Alliance to the person and ministry of the Christian Bishop. The right of Priests and Levites to assistance instituted in the Old Alliance, because of their service at the Tabernacle (and Temple), is also reiterated as a *typos* which somehow anticipates or prefigures the main function of the Christian Bishop in the New Alliance, namely the Church, and provides a Biblical foundation for his right to be maintained by the community in which he works. The Tabernacle (and Temple) of the Jews and of the Christian Church are considered by the Christian Jewish author of the work in a relation of 'figure' and 'fulfilment'.[71]

---

66.   For example, *Dida.* 2.25.1-2a, 4, 13a.
67.   Ibid. 2.25.2b, 3, 13b; 27.4.
68.   Ibid. 2.25.2b, 3b; 35.4.
69.   Funk attentively lists them in his critical apparatus.
70.   For these methods, supra, chap. 2, p. 123, n. 33.
71.   I quote some passages: "Scriptum est enim: Non ligabis os bovi trituranti (with reference to Deut 25:4 and 1 Cor 9:9). Quemadmodum igitur bos in area laborans sine capistro edit, nec vero omnia consumit, ita et vos laborantes in area, id est ecclesia Dei, de ecclesia nutrimini, quemadmodum et levitae in tabernaculo testimonii ministrantes, quod erat omni ex parte figura ecclesiae; nam hoc etiam ex eius nomine apparet; tabernaculum enim testimonii ecclesiam praemonstrat" (*Dida.* 2.25.4b-5). An illustration follows: the parallel between the 'service in the Tabernacle' and the

The christianisation and fusion of sacerdotal activity and function of guidance of the OT institutions – for instance, the king and the prophet – are characteristic elements of this Christian pseudo-epigraphical text. These specific traits characterise both the aspect and the ideological-doctrinal perspective of the author: a Jew converted to the 'new' Christian faith. Like the author of the *Didache,* the editor of the *Didascalia* is convinced that the old Jewish institutions contained in the written *Torah* and those still in force in contemporary Judaism can – or rather must – be accepted by the New Israel, namely the Church of God: "Et vos igitur hodie (underlining added), episcopi, populo vestro estis sacerdotes et levitae, ministrantes tabernaculo Dei, sanctae catholicae ecclesiae, et adstantes semper coram Domino Deo nostro; vos igitur populo vestro estis sacerdotes et prophetae et principes et duces et reges et mediatores Dei ac fidelium eius..." *(Dida.* 2.25.7).[72]

There is no contrast but continuity between the Old and New Alliance, that is between Judaism and Christianity, as to the sacerdotal offerings and the provisions for the poor. The sole novelty of the *Didascalia* is to be found in the concentration of the offerings – including the tithes – in the figure of the Bishop, while in the OT and in contemporary Jewish practices the community or people provided for the distribution (to the priests and the poor) of the allocated shares which they were entitled to. As to the receivers of the offerings, there is no distinction between ἀπαρχαί and δεκάται, that is between the 'holy' share for the priest (= ראשית – תרומה – ריאשן מעשר) and

'service in the Church' through the offerings of first fruits and tithes. Furthermore: "Cum eorum (i.e. levitarum) opus esset ministerium tabernaculj solum, propterea terra inter filios Israel sortita eis non obtigit, quia collationes populi erant sors Levi et tribus eius. Et vos igitur hodie, episcopi, populo vestro estis sacerdotes et levitae, ministrantes tabernaculo Dei, sanctae catholicae ecclesiae" (2.25.6b-7a). And in the same chapter: "Nam sicut loco episcopatus deservitis, ita decet vos loco episcopatus nutriri, ut sacerdotes et levitas et ministros ministrantes coram Deo..." (then follows a long citation from Num 18] (2.25.14ff.). Finally: "Sicuti ergo non licebat alienigenam, quinon erat levita, offerre aliquid aut accedere ad altare sine sacerdote (forse con riferimento a 1 Sam = 1 Reg [LXX] 13:13), ita et vos sine episcopo nolite aliquid facere etc." (2.27.1-2). Then follows an exemplification by referring to the *prosphorae,* which in *Apostolic Constitutions* are referred to as either ἀπαρχαί or δεκάται (ed. Funk, p. 107).

72. The text is literally taken up by the *Apostolic Constitutions*, which emphasise the subordination of the Bishop to the sole High Priest Jesus (with a reference to Heb 4:14), who has ascended to heaven and now intercedes on behalf of mankind (with a reference to Heb 4:14) (ed. Funk, pp. 95 and 97).

the 'profane' share for the poor (i.e. the "tithe of the poor" or "third tithe", and other reliefs). The common welfare fund is also concentrated in the hands of the Bishop from which he is entitled to draw *in solido* in order to take care of the material needs of the clergy and the poor.[73]

The concentration and centralisation of the offerings in the hands of the Bishop and the splitting up of the economic fund indistinctly between the clergy and the poor, besides representing a sort of de-sacralisation of the offerings (in fact the distinction between 'sacerdotal' offerings and 'profane' offerings disappears), generates a form of ecclesiastical assistance which – by means of the economic centralisation/ fusion of revenues – favours at the same time a more equitable distribution of goods within the community.[74]

What are the offerings of the *Christifideles* to the Church? The *Didascalia* often lists them in a general form although at times it specifies the contents. In the former case, the following expressions recur: "ea, quae dantur ac conferuntur ecclesiae" or "ea, quae ecclesiae conferuntur" or "res ecclesiae collatae", etc. (cf. 2.25.2, 3, 4); at times some collective nouns, as "oblata, dona, fructus" or "pro-

---

73. *Dida.* 2.25.2-3 prescribes that the bishops dispense to the poor the gifts offered to the Church ("iuxta mandatum bene administrate pupillis et viduis et afflictis et peregrinis") and to use them for themselves at the same time ("sed vos quoque nutrimini et vivite ex eis, quae ecclesiae conferuntur"). The sharing of common gifts establishes a sort of privileged communication between the bishop and the poor in the community: I draw the attention to the repeated use of the verb *communicare* (v 3), either postively (cum egentibus communicantes) or negatively (nec communicant cum pauperibus). The Bishop will have to give an account of eventual abuses to God (Deus enim episcopus vituperat, qui ex avaritia et soli utuntur rebus ecclesiae collatis). Furthermore, in *Dida.* 2.25.8 the *onus omnium* of the Bishop and his *ministerium victus ac vestitus aliarumque rerum necessariarum* recur in tight connection in order to clarify later that the weight and responsability of the Bishop are exercised above all in the distribution of offerings to those entitled: i.e. the deacons, the widows, the orphans, the needy, and the pilgrims. The *Didascalia* often returns to the 'social' and 'charitable' role of the Bishop in order to emphasise the responsibility and care the Bishop must show toward disadvantaged people. Cf. 2.25.13; 27.3; 35.3.

74. Something analogous to what one can hypothesise to be the 'second stage' (namely the 'centralised' stage) in the welfare organisation of the Christian Jewish community of Jerusalem, as referred to in the 'second major summary' of Acts 4:32-35 and in the 'narrative diptych' which follows (4:36-37; 5:1, 11). For these different stages (probably three) of assistance to the poor in the early community of Jerusalem – which must remain hypothetical since there is no 'historical' evidence to prove their existence – see Del Verme 1977 (in particular pp. 42-43).

sphorae" (Greek, προσφοραί) (cf. 2.25.1,8b,13; 2.27.3).⁷⁵ In the latter, one reads: "victus et (or ac) vestitus aliarumque rerum necessariarum" and similar expressions (cf. 2.25.1, 8), or in more detail "muneribus et portionibus et primitiis et decimis et sacrificiis et oblationibus et holocaustis" with reference to the offerings prescribed in Num 18, which are re-interpreted in the light of Christian doctrines and tenets and adapted to the new community situation, in which the role of the Bishop is deemed similar or analogous to that of the Priests and Levites of the Old Alliance (2.25.6-7). Of course the offerings of animal sacrifices are the only ones excluded and forbidden, since it is literally stated that the gift of God's grace in Jesus Christ has made them superfluous for all members of the Christian community (2.35.1).

It is likely, therefore, that the list of offerings provided for in the *Didascalia* – and also in the *Didache* – i.e. including more than agricultural produce or foodstuffs (e.g., clothing and money), reflects or emulates those Jewish customs still in force in post-70 Judaism.⁷⁶ In-

75. In the *Apostolic Constitutions* – for those parts depending from the *Didascalia* – these general offerings are at times interpreted as "tithes" and as "first fruits". I cite only two cases: τὰ διδόμενα κατ' ἐντολὴν θεοῦ τῶν δεκατῶν καὶ τῶν ἀπαρχῶν ὡς θεοῦ ἄνθρωπος ἀναλισκέτω (*Const.* 2.25.2), while in *Didache* one reads "the things offered and brought to the Church"; and προσήκει οὖν καὶ ὑμᾶς, ἀδελφοί, τὰς θυσίας ὑμῶν ἤ τοι προσφοράς τῷ ἐπισκόπῳ προσφέρειν ὡς ἀρχιερεῖ..., οὐ μὴν δὲ ἀλλὰ καὶ τὰς ἀπαρχὰς καὶ τὰς δεκάτας... αὐτῷ προσάγετε (*Const.* 2.27.6a), the *Didascalia* refers only to *prosphoras*.

76. For evidence of this procedure in the Jewish sources, cf. Del Verme 1989, pp. 193-194. I note also two later Christian sources: the first in Epiphanius (*Haer.* 30.11.1-2); the second in Gregory of Nazianzus *(Ep.* 61). The bishop Epiphanius, born in a village near Eleutheropolis in Palestine, tells of the activity of a certain Jew, called Josephus, before he converted to Christianity. Among other things, he writes: καὶ μετ'ἐπιστολῶν οὗτος (= Joseph) ἀποστέλλεται εἰς τὴν Κιλίκων γῆν· ὃς ἀνελθὼν ἐκεῖσε ἀπὸ ἑκάστης πόλεως τῆς Κιλικίας τὰ ἐπιδέκατα καὶ τὰς ἀπαρχὰς παρὰ τῶν ἐν τῇ ἐπαρχίᾳ Ἰουδαίων εἰσέπραττεν (*Haer.* 30.11.2, ed. K. Holl, p. 346). In brief, Josephus held the office of delegate (Gr. ἀπόστολος) of the *Nāśî* (= the head, prince; in Greek, πατριάρχης) of the Jews. We are, therefore, in the period after 70 CE, when the title of Patriarch (or ethnarch) was acknowledged by the Roman authorities to the descendents of Hillel as heads of the Jewish community of Palestine. In his function or office of "apostle" of the *Nāśî* (who?) Josephus was sent to the region of Cilicia to collect the tithes and the early produce in every city (τὰ ἐπιδέκατα καὶ τὰς ἀπαρχὰς). Epiphanius' information suggests that the early produce and the tithes poured into Judaea from the Diaspora too and that the Patriarch of the Jews probably used them for the teachers of the *Torah* (thus Oppenheimer, *The 'Am-ha 'Aretz*, pp. 49-51), since the offerings had lost any priestly and cultic connotation. The passage in Gregory of

deed, the following passage would suggest that the author of *Didascalia* is really considering those Jewish institutions in regulating the distribution of the offerings: "Episcopus enim optime novit eos, qui tribulantur, et unicuique dat secundum dispensationem, ut non unus aut frequenter [et] in ipso die aut in ipsa hebdomada accipiat, alius autem nec semel" (*Dida.* 2.27.4). Here the distribution of gifts to the poor by the Bishop is presented, from a certain point of view, as a reflection of Jewish institutions as the *tamhûy* and the *qûppāh*,[77] the supervision and management of which were the duty of the *parnāsîn* (Hebr. פרנסין), that is the *leaders* or administrators of the local Jewish community, who acted as liaison officers with the district commanding officer,[78] and

Nazianzus suggests that in the Christian *milieu* the offering for the poor was recommended – he refers, in fact, to ἀπαρχαί – not only on agricultural produce but also on inheritance. In a letter sent to his friends Erius and Alipius dated 375 CE (text in *PG* 37, 120-121), rich in warm recommendations regarding the necessity of supporting the poor, the Bishop writes thus: "Ὥσπερ ἀπαρχὰς ἅλωνός τε καὶ ληνοῦ, καὶ τέκνων, τοὺς ἀληθῶς φιλοτέκνους ἀνατιθέναι θεῷ δίκαιόν τε καὶ ὅσιον, ... οὕτω καὶ νέας [sc. ἀπαρχὰς] κληρονομίας, ἵνα τὸ μέρος δοθὲν προθύμως, παράσχῃ τῷ πλείονι τὴν ἀσφάλειαν (*Ep.* 61, in *PG* 37,120). The extension of the collection of the Christian ἀπαρχαί to all goods, including the 'new ones' (= recent inheritance, in Gr. νέας κληρονομίας), completes the list of goods provided for in *Did.* 13:7. In my view it cannot be excluded that analogous customs regarding the ἀπαρχαί and the tithes, as they are documented in the Judaism after 70 CE, could have influenced the Christian practice of extending the offerings (including early produce and tithes) which had to be handed over to the Church for the needs of the clergy and the poor.

77.   As is known – for a general overview Billerbeck, II, pp. 641-647 – the *tamhûy* and the *qûppāh* were two special and completely different forms of assistance to the poor: the former, which took place on a daily basis, was due to poor foreigners or travellers passing through, and consisted of a *dish* of soup (bread, beans, fruit and – at Easter – also wine); the latter, performed weekly, was provided for the poor living in the community and consisted of a *basket* of food sufficient for the whole week and included also clothing and other goods of daily use. In the text of the *Didascalia* the Christian Bishop is sent to supervise the *daily* and *weekly* distribution of offerings, just as the Jewish *parnāsîn* supervised the collection and distribution of the *tamhûy* and of the *qûppāh*. Both the *Mishnah* and the *Tosefta* legislate in detail on these forms of assistance to the poor (cf. *m. Pe'a* 8:7; and *t. Pe'a* 4.9-10 [ed. K.H. Rengstorf, pp. 76-77]), the *Talmud* even more extensively. For probable analogies between Acts 6:1 and these Jewish institutions, cf. Del Verme 1978, pp. 405-427 (in particular, pp. 419-427).

78.   For the activity of the *parnasîn* during the second Jewish revolt against Rome led by Bar Kokhba or Shim'on ben Kosiba' (the Wadi Murabbaʿat texts report the name כוסבה , כוסבא or כסבה) in 132-135 CE, see N. Avigad and Others, "The Expedition to the Judean Desert 1961", *IEJ* 12, 1962, pp. 249-250.

who are already expressly mentioned in the Wadi Murabba'at texts,[79] long before the edition of the *Mishnah* and of other Rabbinical texts.

4. Conclusion

The historical and philological notes of points 2. and 3. lead to draw three plausible conclusions:

1. Firstly, the section *Did.* 13 documents clearly the frame of mind of the Didachist (or of the interpolator of this section of the work), when he (either Didachist or interpolator) prescribes – referring, however, to ancient and traditional materials – the forms of material assistance for the poor residing permanently in the community/ies. If the latter do not reside in the community, the duty of ἀπαρχή does not *ipso facto* cease for the community, which must pass it on to the poor living in the community. The phenomenon of the itinerant prophets (and *didascaloi*) appears in this chapter to have almost died out (cf. *Did.* 15).[80] We can conclude that we are already in that successive phase which can be labelled as the 'sedentarisation' of itinerant charismatic ministers.

2. The second conclusion that can be drawn is that the most likely social context of reference to understand the forms of community assistance, encompassed in the term ἀπαρχή, is to be found in the Judaism of the time, besides the legislation of the *tôrāh-miqra'*. The inter-

---

79. Cf. Mur 42 (in P. Benoit-J.T. Milik-R. De Vaux, eds., *Les Grottes de Murabba'ât* [*DJD* II; Oxford, 1961], p. 156). These are Hebrew texts written on good quality papyrus during the second year of the revolt, that is in 133 or 134 CE., depending on whether the beginning of the war is placed in 131 (as proposed by J.T. Milik, who places the beginning of the Sabbatical cycle in 131/132) or in 132 (as proposed by M.R. Lehmann, for whom the Sabbatical year in question is 138/139 and therefore the first year of the cycle was 132/133 CE). Mur 24 provides, in fact, a precious synchronism – although problematic – between the Sabbatical cycle and the era of liberation inaugurated by the revolt led by Shim'on ben Kosiba'. The tenancy treaties (which include the tithes) were drawn exactly "in the second year of the liberation" and last the five years, that is "until the eve of the remission (= the Sabbatical year)". For further details, see Schürer 1973, I, pp. 542-543 n. 126.

80. *Did.* 15 provides indisputable evidence for the period following the prophetic wanderings. By this time the communities refer to different and 'stable' figures such as the 'Bishop' or the 'Deacon', who "carry out the same ministry as the prophets and teachers" (*Did.* 15:1b: Ὑμῖν γὰρ λειτουργοῦσι καὶ αὐτοὶ τὴν λειτουργίαν τῶν προφητῶν καὶ διδασκάλων).

pretation of ἀπαρχή, as I have explained in point 2., has allowed for the discovery in this complex and difficult term of a semantic polyvalency (since it can refer, depending on the circumstances, to ראשית, תרומה, מעשר ריאשן or מעש עני מעשר עני), polyvalency which is not usually noticed by the commentators on the *Didache*. A confirmation supporting my interpretation of ἀπαρχή can be found also in the resumption and/or reinterpretation of this Didachean passage by some of the early ecclesiastical ordinances (point 3.), in particular the *Apostolic Tradition*, *Didascalia* and *Apostolic Constitutions*.

3. A third conclusion is provided by the value of this chapter (and of the ecclesiastical ordinances dependent on it) in clarifying some points which are obscure or not sufficiently documented by the Jewish literature *in toto* (esp. the Rabbinical literature, which is subsequent to the *Didache*) regarding the history of the welfare structures and charitable institutions/customs active in Judaism after the defeat of the year 70 CE.[81]

Furthermore the analysis made in this chapter confirms the importance of philology and form criticism for suggesting plausible historical conclusions deriving from the *Didache* (including our section *Did.* 13:3-7) if the redaction (and origin) of the work is placed in the Syro-Palestinian *milieu*, probably in the area of Antioch where Christian Judaism coexists and converses with contemporary Judaism. As a matter of fact, in the specific case of the ἀπαρχή, the Christian Jewish community/ies which read and observe the norms prescribed in *Did.* 13 – apart from being in tune with the Jewish procedures and customs of the time – display an internal harmony among the different groups/ factions, a sort of 'regained' harmony which appears to be absent in the earlier dialectics between "the hypocrites" *versus* "the others" (*Did.* 8:1-2), and which could or should have appeared difficult in a short term to attain.

If *Did.* 13 is neither a creation of the Didachist, as I believe, nor a mere interpolation for didactic-social and ministerial purposes, this section is a clear sign that the "the parting of the ways" between Judaism and Christianity is still far away.

---

81. For further details on this last point, see Del Verme 1989, in particular *Parte Seconda*, pp. 115-245.

Chapter 5

ESCHATOLOGY AND/OR APOCALYPSE? *DID.* 16
AND THE SO-CALLED "JEWISH APOCALYPTIC"

1. Introduction

The last chapter of the *Didache* represents an essential field of inquiry for those who want to explore – in the wake of the Hebrew-Jewish 'roots' of the writing – the presence of sources/traditions which could have preceded the edition of the New Testament. Consequently, the new reading of *Did.* 16, if valid, would lend support to those scholars (including the writer) who tend to identify in some *strata* of the *Didache* a sort of 'Jewish prehistory' of the Christian origins.[1]

In *Did.* 16 one can find materials and traditions analogous to those found in the so-called 'eschatological speech' of the synoptic Gospels (Mark 13 parr., in particular Matt 24) and also, to a lesser but not for this negligible degree in John's *Apocalypse*. Here follow some NT passages (which find confirmation in *Did.*), in particular: Rev 1:1// Matt 24:31 (the Son of Man who comes with his angels); Rev 1:7// Matt 24:30 (the pierced Son of Man and the wailing of the tribes, with a reference to Zech 12:10ff.); Rev 1:10//Matt 24:31 (the loud voice); Rev 15:8//Mark 13:26 (the glory and power of God); Rev 16:10//Matt 24:51 (the gnashing of teeth); Rev 16:13//Mark 13:22 (the false prophets); Rev 16:15//Matt 24:43 (the Son of Man who comes as a thief); Rev 18:4/Matt 24:15-20 (the desolation of Judaea; another parallel in Mark 13:14-18); Rev 19:17//Matt 24:28 (the allusion to the birds), and a few others.

If, as is possible, these references which reappear in the *Didache* do not directly depend on the synoptic Gospels (nor on the *Apocalypse*) but are connected to previous Jewish traditions, subsequently incorporated by the editor/author into the text, their presence in the last section

1. Supra, Chap. 1, p. 6.

of the work could represent an important step towards the definition of 'that particular Judaism' recast in the *Didache*.

In my opinion, this acquisition must necessarily stem from an important consideration: if one assumes that the Christian Judaism of the *Didache* is a phenomenon not only organically part and parcel of contemporary Judaism but moreover grafted upon particular traditions of earlier and/or contemporary Judaism, these must be identified and defined. Modern studies on the historical-literary phenomenon of "Middle Judaism" have shown, in fact, that it is insufficient to refer merely to a "generic Judaism" underlying the different *corpora* or writings produced by distinctive middle Judaic movements, but that it is necessary – in order to expound the genesis and facilitate the understanding of the texts of Christian Judaism – to define, if and when possible, which specific Jewish traditions have been resumed, used and rewritten.

For this reason, any analysis of *Did*. 16 would be historically incomplete, if the presumed underlying Jewish *Urtext* was merely referred to as either a nebulous 'Jewish apocalyptic' or a generic 'sapiential-eschatological literature', eschewing questions regarding the many trends and dialectics which these genres either conceal or have been produced by.

Thanks to more recent studies on the apocalyptic genre and to some hypotheses concerning the identity of Jewish groups and/or movements (conventionally referred to as Enochians/Essenes or Enochic Essenism and Qumranites/Essenes or Qumranic Enochism), who appear to be characterised by peculiar traits and whose writings reveal clear evidences of specific apocalyptic traditions, it is possible today to re-examine the final passage of the *Didache* connecting it, more directly than before, to the traditions/tendencies of the above-mentioned groups/movements active in the Judaism of the Hellenistic Graeco –Roman period.

2. Did. *16: a Preliminary Note*

In this paragraph I will examine several general questions, some of which have already been treated in detail by other scholars. The hypotheses and explanations they put forward are different, often antithetical, both as to the 'literary genre' and as to the 'doctrinal content' of the passage. A level of consensus exists, however, regarding the presence of a pre-existing Jewish source which has been later incorporated by the editor-author[2] into the current text of the *Didache*, although scholars still disagree on the evaluation of the modes of inclusion and on the interpretation of the passage as well as on its relation to the pre-existing Jewish text and the *Didache* as a whole.

After explaining the main solutions advanced by other scholars I will introduce my own hypothesis regarding the literary genre and the content of the passage in observance of the methodological criteria listed below:

a. *Did.* 16, from a strictly formal point of view, can be considered an apocalypse: I will explain this point in detail later. Such an observation regarding the literary genre of the passage, which could appear merely formal, inevitably encompasses consequences which could affect the 'setting' of the text which is commonly referred to as "world-view", although this ideological factor should not influence the specifically historical collocation of the text.[3]

The apocalyptic genre, which can certainly be formally defined, is not however a monolithic phenomenon. On the contrary, because of its very formal construction, this genre can represent the vehicle of distinct ideologies and different doctrinal stances. Furthermore, from a strictly formal point of view, it presents numerous internal distinctions.[4]

The inclusion of *Did.* 16 in the final part of the work answers to a literary-structural need, which directs the editor/author in the drafting of the text: this 'eschatological' text, situated at the end of the writing, assumes an axial function in the general structure of the *Didache*. The introduction at 'this' point of the text obviously implies a peculiar re-reading/re-interpretation of the original Jewish text, which could have contained some ideological/doctrinal elements different from those in-tended by the editor/author of the *Did.* This 'selective phenomenon' is understandable in the light of the Scriptural hermeneutical-exegetical

---

2. A careful investigation can be found in Visonà 2000, pp. 229-252.

3. As to the concept of "world-view", see Collins 1998b, pp. 13.21-22.42. The literary genre cannot be regarded as an element documenting the historical existence of a particular 'apocalyptic group' (ibid., pp. 37-38), and Collins 1997, p. 8; Boccaccini 2002a, pp. 169ff.; also Sacchi 2002a.2002b.

4. As to the formal classification of apocalyptic works and their differentiation, Collins 1979, pp. 1ff.; 1998a, pp. 28-31; 1998b, p. 7, and M. Himmelfarb, *Ascent to Heaven in Jewish and Christian Apocalypses* (Oxford-New York: University Press, 1993).

processes,[5] which appear to have characterised the Judaism(s) of the Hellenistic Graeco-Roman period (or "Middle Judaism": 3rd century BCE- 2nd century CE).

2.1. Text and Translation[6] of Did. 16 (with Parr. in Notes)

v 1. Γρηγορεῖτε ὑπὲρ τῆς ζωῆς ὑμῶν· οἱ λύχνοι ὑμῶν μὴ σβεσθήτωσαν, καὶ αἱ ὀσφύες ὑμῶν μὴ ἐκλυέσθωσαν, ἀλλὰ γίνεσθε ἕτοιμοι[7] οὐ γὰρ οἴδατε τὴν ὥραν, ἐν ᾗ ὁ κύριος ἡμῶν ἔρχεται.[8]
v 2. Πυκνῶς δὲ συναχθήσεσθε ζητοῦντες τὰ ἀνήκοντα ταῖς ψυχαῖς ὑμῶν· οὐ γὰρ ὠφελήσει ὑμᾶς ὁ πᾶς χρόνος τῆς πίστεως ὑμῶν, ἐὰν μὴ ἐν τῷ ἐσχάτῳ καιρῷ τελειωθῆτε.
v 3. Ἐν γὰρ ταῖς ἐσχάταις ἡμέραις πληθυνθήσονται οἱ ψευδοπροφῆται[9] καὶ οἱ φθορεῖς, καὶ στραφήσονται τὰ πρόβατα εἰς λύκους,[10] καὶ ἡ ἀγάπη στραφήσεται εἰς μῖσος.[11]
v 4 Αὐξανούσης γὰρ τῆς ἀνομίας μισήσουσιν ἀλλήλους καὶ διώξουσιν καὶ παραδώσουσι.[12] καὶ τότε φανήσεται ὁ κοσμοπλανὴς ὡς υἱός θεοῦ καὶ ποιήσει σημεῖα καὶ τέρατα,[13] καὶ ἡ γῆ παραδοθήσεται εἰς χεῖρας αὐτοῦ, καὶ ποιήσει ἀθέμιτα, ἃ οὐδέποτε γέγονεν ἐξ αἰῶνος.[14]
v 5 Τότε ἥξει ἡ κτίσις τῶν ἀνθρώπων εἰς τὴν πύρωσιν τῆς δοκιμασίας,[15] καὶ σκανδαλισθήσονται[16] πολλοὶ καὶ ἀπολοῦνται, οἱ δὲ ὑπο-

---

5. Vermes 1961 and Brooke 1998.
6. Greek critical text: Rordorf-Tuilier 1998[2], pp. 194-198; Engl. tr. (except for some detail) by A. Cody, in Jefford 1995a, pp.13-14.
7. Luke 12:35; Eph 6:14; 1 Pet 1:13; *Asc. Is.* 4:16.
8. Matt 24:42.44; 1 Thess 5:2-6.
9. Deut 13:2-6; 2 Thess 2-3; Rev 13:11.
10. Is 11:6.
11. Matt 10:21.35-36; 24:10.
12. Matt 24:10.12.
13. Mark 13:22; Matt 24:24; 2 Thess 2:3-4, 9; Rev 12:9; 13:3-4, 8, 12-14; 2 Jo 7; *Jub.* 1:20; *T. Reu.* 2:2; *T. Sim.* 2:7; *T. Levi* 3:3; *T. Jud.* 23:1; *T. Iss.* 6:1; *T. Dan* 5:5; *T. Ash.* 1:8; *Test. Benj.* 6:1, 7; CD IV:12b-19; 1QpHab II:1-6; VIII:10; 1QH[a] X: 10.16-17.21-22; XI:27b-28; *Asc. Is.* (or *Mart. Isa.*) 4:10-12.
14. Joel 2:2; Zeph 1:15; John 8:12; Rev 9:2; *Asc. Is.* 4:5-6; *Apoc. Petr.* 2; *Apoc. Hel.* 2; *Or. Syb.* 2:167; 3:63-67; Iren. *Haer.* 5.28.2; Hipp. *Antichr.* 6; Lact. *Div. inst.* 7,7; Ps.-Hipp., *Cons. mundi* 23; *Dianoia* 45.4-6 (NHC IV.4) and *Paraph. Shem* 44:31-45:8 (NHC VII.1).
15. Is 1:25; 48:10; Zech 13:9.
16. Matt 10:21, 35-36; 24:10

μείναντες ἐν τῇ πίστει αὐτῶν σωθήσονται ὑπ'αὐτοῦ τοῦ καταθέματος.[17]

v 6 Καὶ τότε φανήσεται τὰ σημεῖα τῆς ἀληθείας· πρῶτον σημεῖον ἐκπετάσεως ἐν οὐρανῷ, εἶτα σημεῖον φωνῆς σάλπιγγος, καὶ τὸ τρίτον ἀνάστασις νεκρῶν:[18]

v 7 Οὐ πάντων δέ, ἀλλ'ὡς ἐρρέθη· Ἥξει ὁ κύριος καὶ πάντες οἱ ἅγιοι μετ'αὐτοῦ.[19]

v 8 Τότε ὄψεται ὁ κόσμος τὸν κύριον ἐρχόμενον ἐπάνω τῶν νεφελῶν τοῦ οὐρανοῦ...[20]

v 1 Keep vigil over your life. Let your lamps not go out and let your loins not be ungirded but be ready, for you do not know the hour at which our Lord is coming.

v 2 You shall assemble frequently, seeking what pertains to your souls, for the whole time of your belief will be of no profit to you unless you are perfected at the final hour.

v 3 For in the final days false prophets and corruptors will be multiplied, and the sheep will turn into wolves, and love will turn into hate.

v 4 As lawlessness increases, they will hate and persecute and betray one another, and at that time the one who leads the world astray will appear as a son of God and will work signs and wonders, and the earth will be given unto his hands, and he will do godless things which have never been done since the beginning of time.

v 5 Then human creation will pass into the testing fire and many will fall away and perish, but those who shall have persevered in their belief will be saved by the 'curse' itself (or the 'accursed' himself?).

v 6 And then the signs of truth will appear, first, the sign of an opening out in heaven, next, the signal of the trumpet call, and third, resurrection of the dead –

v 7 not of all, however, but, as it has been said, "The Lord will come and all the holy ones with him".

17. Matt 10:22; 24:13

18. Mark 8:18-9:1; Matt 16:27-28; 24:30; 25:31; Luke 9:26; 1 Cor 15:52; 1 Thess 1:10; 3:13; Phil 3:20-21; 2 Thess 1:5-10; *T. Dan* 5:11-12; *T. Zeb.* 9:8-9; *1 Enoch* 48:10; 53:6-7; 4Q *174* III: 7b-9; *Asc. Is.* 4:14-16a.

19. Deut 33:2-3.5; Zech 14:5; Mark 13:27; Matt 24:28.31; Luke 17:37; 1 Thess 4:17b; 5:10b; *1 Enoch* 39:1; *Const.* 7.32. 4-5; *Asc. Is.* 4:16b.

20. Dan 7:13-14; Zech 12:10-12; Matt 24:30; 26:64; Rev 1:7.

v 8 Then the world will see the Lord coming upon the clouds of heaven...

2.2. Did. *16 "Ethics"?*

Many commentators maintain that the inmost meaning of the final part of the *Didache* should be sought in its ethical character since it can be regarded as a 'short treatise' of moral teachings. On this view *Did.* 16 is no more than the continuation of the previous section dealing with the doctrine of the "Two Ways" (in which the link or *mot-crochet* is provided by the term ζωή of 16:1), in other words that the editor of the *Didache* would have divided into two parts the Jewish original and unitary work (i.e. DVD) so he could include at the end his own argumentations.[21] Eschewing the correctness and usefulness of some of the details – as for instance the relation of *Did.* 16 to the section regarding the "Two Ways" to which I must return later – I believe that this exegetical stance, which tends either to exclude or at least to limit the eschatological motif to the advantage of the ethical teachings, ends by denying that in the apocalyptic genre – where the eschatological element is important although not predominant – the ethical-sapiential theme is also part and parcel.

There is no reason to argue a clear-cut antithesis between ethics and eschatology. Von Rad indeed suggested this,[22] although with a lack of historical sensitivity inasmuch as he assumed that the concept of 'apocalyptic' included both the literary as well as the historical and ideological aspects: the Jewish apocalyptic texts appear to have originated from an encounter (defined negatively by him) between prophecy and sapiential literature. Consequently if one establishes that *Did.* 16 belongs to the apocalyptic 'literary genre', it will be possible to draw a

21.   Bammel 1961, pp. 253-262; Köster 1957, pp. 160, 190, and Kraft 1965, pp. 12-13. Other references in Visonà, pp. 230-233.

22.   *Theologie des Alten Testaments* (München: Kaiser, 1965), p. 328; but, already earlier, H.H. Rowley, *The Revelance of Apocalyptic* (London: Athlone, 1944), pp. 34ff., had pointed out this aspect. More recently and with greater historical awareness, T. Elgvin, "Wisdom with and without Apocalyptic", in D.K. Falk - F. García Martínez - E.M. Schüller (eds.), *Sapiential, Liturgical and Poetical Texts from Qumran –* Proceedings of the 3rd Meeting of the International Organization for Qumran Studies (Oslo, 1998). Publication in Memory of M. Baillet (STDJ 35; Leiden: Brill, 2000), pp. 15-38, and C.J. VanderKam, "The Prophetic-Sapiential Origins of Apocalyptic Thought", in VanderKam 2000, pp. 241-254. Other contributions in Collins 1998a, *passim*.

great number of parallels with other apocalyptic writings in which the ethical-sapiential element is clearly evident. For instance, the *Syriac Apocalypse of Baruch* (abbr. *2 Apoc. Bar.*), *IV Ezra* as well as the *Apocalypse* of John testify to relations with and references to both moral literature and ethical teachings.[23] This view is confirmed by the Qumran literature, which shows that a clear-cut separation between eschatological/ apocalyptic and ethical-sapiential writings would be misleading: in fact it is often possible to find in the texts a juxtaposition of two genres with reciprocal connections (cf. for example *4Q Instructions*,[24] although many other cases could be cited).

The "world-view" (German, *Weltanschauung*) centred on the eschatological expectation of the end, present in the apocalyptic writings in general and also in *Did.* 16, consists in a view of history which encompasses both the past and the present of the community providing a global and unitary image of human history. The historical vicissitudes of the world are believed to be under God's absolute authority (with evident and marked differences in the various apocalyptic writings) and man's fate in the next world depends on his assent or refusal in life to submit to God's will.

2.3. Did. 16: "Apocalyptic" (= Eschatology)?

The preconception which appears to question the validity of the approaches of those scholars who consider *Did.* 16 as 'eschatological' and therefore 'apocalyptic' (a 'leap' in my opinion unjustified), is

---

23.   F.J. Murphy, "Sapiential Elements in the Syriac Apocalypse of Baruch", *JQR* 76, 1986, pp. 311-327; M.A. Knibb, "Apocalyptic and Wisdom in 4Ezra", *JSJ* 13, 1982, pp. 56-74; and U. Vanni, "La riflessione sapienziale come atteggiamento ermeneutico costante nell'Apocalisse", *RivBib* 24, 1976, pp. 285-297.

24.   Cf. T. Elgvin, "Wisdom and Apocalypticism in the Early Second Century BCE. The Evidence of 4Q Instruction", in L.H. Schiffman-E. Tov-J.C. VanderKam (eds.), *The Dead Sea Scrolls: Fifty Years after their Discovery* – Proceedings of the Jerusalem Congress (July 20-25, 1997) (Jerusalem: Jerusalem Museum, 2000), pp. 226-247. The LI Colloquium Biblicum Lovaniense (July 31-August 2, 2002) – the Proceedings of which are forthcoming – had as its central theme "Wisdom and Apocalypticism at Qumran". The outcomes of the debate appear to confirm my line of interpretation. For a detailed and critical presentation of the works of the Colloquium, see C. Marucci, *RivBib* 51/4, 2003, 325-345. On 4QInstructions see Goff 2002 and Jefferies 2002; on the Wisdom at Qumran, Hempel-Lange-Lichtenberger 2002, pp. 445-454; and on the relationships between wisdom and mysteries in Jewish and Paulinian sources see Hempel-Lange-Lichtenberger 2002, pp. 405-432.

derived from the firm belief that the apocalyptic genre (a merely formal reality) should necessarily imply eschatology as an essential doctrinal requisite. Emblematic in this regard is Seeliger's stance who, on the basis of the connection/relation to chap. 11, postulates a prophetic/apocalyptic connotation for the early activity of the community of the *Didache*: *Did*. 16 should be regarded as a sort of *memorandum* of apocalyptic theology - 'notes', as it were, for the apocalyptic preaching of the prophets.[25] With this stance, however, Seeliger fails to clarify the nature of the connection between the apocalyptic genre and its contents: if *Did*. 16 is an apocalyptic memorandum, and not an apocalypse, why did the author use this particular genre? and, secondly, what does "prophetic-apocalyptic connotation" mean? If the connection between prophetism and apocalyptic genre is correct, it still remains unclear in Seeliger's study what is really apocalypticism: is it a literary genre or doctrine/theology deriving from prophetism? It will not suffice to state that the apocalyptic genre can be regarded as the formal expression of a particular eschatological theology. Therefore one could ask: why are there works belonging to the apocalyptic genre which show no interest for eschatology at all (see, in particular, *1 Enoch* and *Jubilees*), and texts which cannot be considered part of the apocalyptic literature in which the eschatological motif appears to be dominant (see for example *1QS* and other texts of Qumran)?

For the definition of the concept of 'apocalyptic' one cannot fail to consider the work by J.J. Collins,[26] in particular for its thorough investigation of the formal dimension, and those by P. Sacchi,[27] who identifies a specific apocalyptic tradition represented, in particular, by *1 Enoch*, which appears to be, all in all, unitary to a point that it is possible to refer to it as 'Enochism' indicating a particular ideology developed within the spiritual and temporal *milieu* of "Middle Judaism".[28] In Enochism the eschatological problem does not constitute

25. Seeliger 1989, pp. 185-192. For other studies, see Visonà 2000, pp. 234-236.

26. Recently, "Apocalypticism and Literary Genre in the Dead Sea Scrolls", in P.W. Flint-J.C. VanderKam (edd.), *The Dead Sea Scrolls after Fifty Years. A Comprehensive Assessment* (Leiden- Köln-Boston: Brill, 1999), II, pp. 403-430.

27. In particular, Sacchi 1997b, who collects several studies on the topic. For a careful critical examination highlighting the risks of reductionism entailed by the author's thesis, see C. Gianotto and Others, "Ancora a proposito di apocalittica", *Henoch* 20, 1998, pp. 89-106.

28. Cf. Boccaccini 1997 and 1998 (rev. by P. Sacchi, "Enochism, Qumranism and Apocalyptic: Some Thoughts on a Recent Book", *Henoch* 20, 1998, pp. 357-365).

a focal point, since the problems regarding the coming of evil in the world and its action in human history appear to constitute the main themes. In this tradition eschatology represents a secondary concern subordinated to protology.[29]

Consequently it appears misleading to argue that *Did.* 16 is 'apocalyptic' only because 'its theology' is of an eschatological character. The

---

VanderKam (1984 and 1996) had already supported the thesis that *1 Enoch* could represent a unitary 'apocalyptic tradition'.

29. P. Sacchi, "L'«attesa» come essenza dell'apocalittica?", *RivBib* 45, 1997, pp. 71-78, including criticisms of the perspective of B. Marconcini, *Profeti e apocalittici* (LOGOS-Corso di studi biblici 3; Torino: LDC, 1995), pp. 193-244, criticisms to which Marconcini replied in "Ancora sull'apocalittica: una luce da non spegnere", *RivBib* 45, 1997, pp. 179-186. Of course, eschatology is an extremely important dimension in the 'apocalyptic world-view' and in particular in texts such as *Dan, 2 Apoc. Bar.* or *IV Ezra*, as well as *T. Levi* and *Apoc. Abr.*; but in texts such as the *Book of the Watchers* and *Astronomical Book*, as well as *Jubilees*, the eschatological dimension is subordinate to the problem regarding the origins of evil (cf. also Collins 1998a, pp. 39-57). Marconcini appears to follow a definition of apocalyptic emphasising the 'literary current', a definition – as Sacchi at p. 72 pointed out – which had already been adopted by J. Carmignac, "Qu'est ce-que l'apocalyptique? Son emploi à Qumrân", *RdQ* 10, 1979, pp. 3-33, and at a lesser degree by Collins himself. In my opinion, however, it appears that the literary aspects force Marconcini to formulate conclusions which, inevitably, lead to considerations regarding the historicity of the 'movement' which could have produced the single apocalypses (cf. "Ancora sull'apocalittica", p. 180). Focusing exclusively on the apocalyptic dimension entails the risk of losing sight of the fact that this is not present only in the writings of the apocalyptic genre but also in many other Jewish *milieux* of the Hellenistic Graeco-Roman period. Consequently, according to this perspective, apocalyptic should be regarded as an 'holistic' container, the chronological and sociological boundaries of which are rather 'extensive', an assumption I find extremely difficult to support. Consequently, the definition of 'apocalyptic' appears to be insufficient if used beyond the formal paradigms and classifications. In this regard see the important statement by Collins 1998a: "Apocalyptic eschatology is most appropriately defined as the kind of eschatology that is typical of apocalypses, although it may also be found elsewhere. The movements most appropriately called apocalyptic are those which either produced apocalypses or were characterized by the beliefs and attitudes typical of the genre. Whether some postexilic prophecy should be called apocalyptic or taken to attest an apocalyptic movement depends on our assessment of the similarities between this material and the literary genre apocalypse. One of the problems that has beset the quest for 'the origin of apocalyptic' is that the apocalypses are not simply uniform but contain diverse sub-genres and motifs that may be traced to different sources. If we wish to arrive at an understanding of the historical development of apocalypticism, it is necessary to differentiate the various apocalyptic texts and the movements that may be inferred from them" (pp. 39-40).

apocalyptic literary genre, because it represents a peculiar formal structure, can include different and, often, conflicting 'theologies'. It is
impossible to demonstrate that the eschatological expectation is at
the centre of different ideologies which have produced distinctive apocalyptic works. This, however, does not rule out the fact that eschatology remains central to the definition of an apocalyptic world-view, as
Collins observed, although this formal aspect differs from the mere
historical-ideological character of the single apocalyptic text as well
as of the group/community/individual producing it.

In my opinion, *Did.* 16 is an apocalypse as to 'literary genre' (following Collins' classification); consequently, its ideology or doctrine
cannot be exclusively intended as eschatological in the traditional sense
of the term. Apocalyptic essentially aims at expanding and universali-
sing the symbolism present in prophetic texts so as to offer a global
vision of human history.[30] In this 'world-view' eschatology plays an
important, though not essential, role in the relationship between God
and man. At the same time, it is impossible to define an 'apocalyptic
group' as unitary and monolithic on the basis of a mere formal classification (as the world-view of eschatology): otherwise one could conclude that, because of the eschatological view of history, substantially
different texts – such as *1QS* or *1QM* and *Rev* – belong to the same
religious group/movement, a conclusion which, in my opinion, is un-
tenable.

2.4. Other Considerations

It is possible to continue the examination of the critical studies of
Did. 16 by referring to other research focusing on the reconstruction of
the liturgical and/or festive, ministerial and sacramental aspects of the
passage. I believe, however, that the 'central history' of the interpretation of this particular passage – as has emerged from most of the studies
surveyed – is well summarised by the two tendencies described above
(1.2. and 1.3).

At this stage, I will introduce my interpretation of the passage in
question, which is based on those methodological assumptions mentio-

---

30. Cf. K. Koch, "Vom profetischen zum apokalyptischen Visionsbericht", in D.
Hellholm (ed.), *Apocalypticism in the Mediterranean World and the Near East* (Tübingen: Mohr, 1983), pp. 387-411; S. Niditch, *The Symbolic Vision in Biblical Tradition* (HSM 30; Chico: Fortress Press, 1983), 177ff., and Arcari 2001.

ned earlier and on the exploration of some of the problems which previously have only been hinted at. My analysis of *Did.* 16 will run along two parallel lines: on the one hand, I will compare the text with the formal/literary structure of 'other Jewish apocalypses' in order to establish whether it belongs or not to the apocalyptic genre; on the other, I will try to establish to which ideology and/or theology of the Middle Judaic period the work refers. Furthermore I will examine the presence and function of the supposed Jewish *Urtext*, which is at the origin or is found in the 'apocalyptic' section of the *Didache*. Finally, I will attempt to identify the recycling techniques applied by the editor/ author of *Didache* to the Jewish *Urtext*.

3. Did. 16 and the Apocalyptic Genre

Did. 16 does not present rigorously all the characteristics of the 'apocalyptic genre' as these have been formulated by Collins in his introductory study published in *Semeia*:[31] it lacks, for example, the 'mediating' element represented by an angelic or super-human figure bringing the revelation and its interpretation. Apart from this omission from Collins's proposed classification – which contains generally valid observations based on the analysis of *all* those modern and ancient texts defined as apocalyptic – many and specific literary stereotypes, which can be found in works of this genre, are however present in our passage.

Following a short introduction of a parenetic character (16:1-2), which constitutes an integral part of the 'apocalyptic section' (as is clear from the connection between τῷ ἐσχάτῳ καιρῷ of v 2 and ἐν γὰρ ταῖς ἐσχάταις of v 3; and also from the connection between sapiential literature and apocalyptic genre, supra, n. 3), there is the future tense of a series of verbs (πληθυνθήσονται, 16:3a; σταφήσονται, 16:3b; μισήσουσιν, διώξουσιν, παραδώσουσι, 16:4a; φανήσεται, ποιήσει, 16:4b, etc.), which constitute a characteristic and important element of the apocalyptic style (cf. Rev 17:1.7; *IV Ezra* 12:3-5 and *2 Apoc. Bar.* 39:1-7; but also *1 Enoch* 61:4-5.12; but more references could be added). In particular the presence of the verb φανήσεται, which is a technical term of apocalyptic literature: Visonà's translation (*apparirà*, p. 355) appears, however, to overlook the form of the verb,

---

31. Entitled *Apocalypse: the Morphology of a Genre*, no. 14, 1979.

which is a passive future perfect. *"Will be revealed"* appears consequently to be the most appropriate translation: that is, the figure of the κοσμοπλανὴς will be revealed by an external act (by God Himself?). The same verbal form also recurs in the following line (16:6: φανήσεται τὰ σημεῖα τῆς ἀληθείας), probably also implying an external revelation.

Another important derivation from and connection with the apocalyptic style and/or genre is the anaphorical repetition of introductory links to the single periods: for example τότε (cf. 16:4b, 5, 6, 8) appears to have in this context the same function as that of the expression καὶ εἶδον in other apocalyptic writings (cf. Rev 14:1, 6, 14; 15:1, 5; 18:1) or καὶ εἶπεν (cf. Rev 17:7; *1 Enoc* 46:1, 3; 48:1; 53:1; 54:1; 56:1; 57:1; 59:1, etc.) or καὶ ἤκουσα (cf. Rev 1:10; 7:4; 16:1, 5; 18:4), always repeated anaphorically. This formal and introductory peculiarity generates a paratactic construction by connecting the sentences by means of a mere conjunction (*Did.* 16:3: ...καὶ οἱ φθορεῖς, καὶ στραφήσονται τὰ πρόβατα εἰς λύκους, καὶ ἡ ἀγάπη...; or 16:4b: ...καὶ τότε φανήσεται ὁ κοσμοπλανὴς...καὶ τέρατα καὶ ἡ γῆ παραδοθήσεται... καὶ ποιήσει ἀθέμιτα...). The paratactic construction clearly expresses and generates a tension towards the ecstatic-revealing element conceiving an ecstatic language. By contrast, the hypotaxis is a formal construction useful and ideal for works of a dialectical and critical character.

Besides these literary figures – found also in oracles and magic texts – *Did.* 16 introduces a form of re-interpretation and universalisation of passages derived from classical prophetism as well as a development of their symbolism to embody new meanings.[32] For instance, in 16:3, by the metaphor of the metamorphosis of the sheep into wolves (καὶ στραφήσονται τὰ πρόβατα εἰς λύκους), in which the editor resorts to the use of a symbolism characteristic of apocalyptic literature, that is the "theriomorphic symbolism" (frequent in the *Book of Dreams,* i.e.

32.   Apart from the studies cited in n. 22, cf. L. Hartman, *Prophecy Interpreted. The Formation of Some Jewish Apocalyptic Texts and of the Eschatological Discourse Mark 13 Par.* (CB.NT Series 1; Uppsala-Lund: Gleerup, 1966). On the "intertextuality" of the Book of Enoch, see P.S. Alexander, "The Enochic Literature and the Bible: Intertextuality and its Implications", in E.D. Herbert-E. Tov (eds.), *The Bible as a Book. The Hebrew Bible and the Judaean Desert Discoveries* (London: The British Library and Oak Knoll Press in association with The Scriptorium: Center for Christian Antiquities, 2002), pp. 57-69.

the fourth volume of *1 Enoch*)[33], the Didachean text expands and universalises the image taken from Is 11:6. Actually *Did.* 16:3 overturns Isaiah's image. In the Biblical text, in fact, the prophet referred to wolves and lambs 'living together' when David's descendant will come, while in the *Didache* the cohabitation ceases and the 'metamorphosis' of the sheep into wolves takes place at the arrival of the Anti-Christ.

Furthermore the allusions of *Did.* 16:5a.7 to Zech 13:9 and 14:5 must be interpreted in the same way, that is as explanation and expansion of meanings concealed in the Scriptures. In fact, both in Christian Judaism and in other currents/movements of "Middle Judaism", there was a tendency to 'discover' in particular Biblical texts 'new meanings' which had been 'concealed' until the moment they were made explicit: the Qumran *Pesharim* and some pericopai of the NT (for example Luke 4:16-21) provide examples which have become paradigmatic. In other cases the Biblical texts are either only vaguely alluded to or hinted at (as in the section *IV Ezra* devotes to the re-interpretation of *Dan* 7: cf. *IV Ezra* 12:10-15), or are left to the free and actualising interpretation of the individual 'user' (as occurs in the *Apocalypse* of John, in which there are more than 800 allusions to prophetic texts for which the author fails to provide any explicit explanation). The 'true' understanding is left to those who are able to grasp the inner meanings of the Scriptures and apply them to their own personal or community history.

As to the references to *Zechariah*, one must distinguish between the re-interpretation of the texts provided by the Jewish community and that by the Didachist. If in the apocalyptic text it is possible to identify the transition from a Messianic meaning (referring to a shepherd-lieutenant of the Lord; the sword striking him will deliver the people to the final test which precedes the time of salvation; the image of the fire is taken from Jer 6:29ff.) to one clearly tied to the wicked action of the enemy of God (in *Zechariah*, the shepherd – who is the main character of the passage – is neither the good one of 11:4-14 nor the wicked one of 11:15-16: he is a sort of headman), certainly the re-interpretation provided by the community of the Didachist could not neglect the Christological implications of the image of the struggle between Jesus and the Anti-Christ. Analogously, the explicit citation of *Zech* 14:5 in

---

33.   I. Frölich, "The Symbolical Language of the Animal Apocalypse of Enoch (1 Enoch 85-90)", *RdQ* 14, 1990, pp. 629-636.

Did. 16,7 is 'slanted' towards doctrinal implications: the national meaning (present in the prophetic text of *Zechariah*: the saints alluded to could be the people of Israel) disappears, and a 'new' meaning appears closely connected to the canons referring to the eschatological expectation.[34] I will need to return later to the ideological and theological implications of this 'peculiar' re-interpretation of the prophetic text of *Zechariah* provided by the *Didache*.

Moreover, the association of a passage from *Zechariah* with one from *Daniel* (*Did.* 16:8: Τότε ὄψεται ὁ κόσμος τὸν κύριον ἐρχόμενον ἐπάνω τῶν νεφελῶν τοῦ οὐρανοῦ...; cf. *Dan* 7:13) can be found not only in the synoptic apocalypse (cf. Matt 24:29-31, including a reference to Zech 12:10), but also in Rev 1:7 (with a reference to *Dan* 7:13 and Zech 12:10ff.):[35] this means that – if the inter-relations among the

---

34. *Did.* 16 cites *Zechariah* not according to the MT but to the LXX. The text, in fact, has πάντες οἱ ἅγιοι μετ᾽ αὐτοῦ (*with him*) and not *with me* (as in MT). This comes as no surprise in a Jewish apocalyptic text. *2 Apoc. Bar.* also uses the LXX (P. Bogaert, *Apocalypse de Baruch. Introduction, traduction du syriaque et commentaire* [SCh 144-145; Paris: Cerf, 1969], I, pp. 361-362), and *Jeremiah* appears to refer to the (Jewish) text of the *Paralipomena of Jeremiah* (as to this work see Sacchi 1999, pp. 265-273). A similar case, namely the citation of the text of *Jeremiah,* which draws on the Jewish source of the *Paralipomena,* can be found also in the Book 10 of the *Jewish Antiquities* by Josephus (cf. P. Piovanelli, "Le texte de Jérémie utilisé par Flavius Josèphe dans le X livre des Antiquités Judaïques", *Henoch* 14, 1992, pp. 11-36).

35. According to the MT of *Daniel* the Son of Man comes "with the clouds of the sky" (*'m 'nnj šmj'*), a generic expression, in which *'m* "caratterizza senza dubbio la coesistenza temporale... Questo costrutto, intenzionalmente impreciso, è preferibile alle versioni dei LXX e della Pešitta, che hanno inteso il Figlio d'uomo veniente sulle nubi del cielo (ἐπὶ, *'al*), traduzione adottata da Matt 24:30; 26:14 e Apoc 14:16. In Mc 14:62 e Apoc 1:7, tuttavia, si legge ‹con le nubi›, in sintonia col TM e Teodozione. Il TM, che è il più problematico, ha di certo evitato l'espressione ‹sulle nubi› onde non sembrare legittimare l'identificazione tra Figlio d'uomo e Jahvé, il quale, nelle teofanie, viene sulle nubi (cf. Is 19:1; Ps 18:11)" (M. Delcor, *Studi sull'apocalittica* [StBi 77; Brescia: Paideia, 1987], p. 149). One can observe that *Did.* 16, in this case too, can be placed in the wake of the LXX (ἐπάνω); and the same transition from *with* to *on* falls perfectly within the spirit of a re-interpretation and adaptation of the prophetic text to apocalyptic literature (the analogous operation by the LXX does not appear to be an oversight, but an intentionally Messianic interpretation): it is not fortuitous, in fact, that the bilingual author of *Rev.* uses simultaneously both forms. For the developments of the "sign of the Son of Man" in Jesus' tradition, see Draper 1993; and, more in general, J.H. Charlesworth, *The Son of Man, Early Judaism, Jesus, and Earliest Christologies,* and P. Sacchi, *Il Messia Figlio dell'Uomo nelle tradizioni giudaiche del Secondo Tempio,* to a public conference during the *Enoch Seminar II,* held in Venice (The University of Michigan's Second Enoch Seminar, Venice, Italy [July 1-5, 2003]).

three texts depend on a pre-existing Jewish tradition – the two prophetic texts were read and interpreted together in a prominently Messianic key. One must also consider that the speculations regarding the "Son of Man" are particularly and conspicuously present in the *Book of Parables*, i.e. in that literary composition found later in the Enoch tradition/ literature (*1 Enoch*).³⁶ In fact, before being a Messianic reality, the Son of man represents a symbol in the wake of that 'apocalyptic symbolism' stretching from *Ezekiel*, in which he constitutes a vocative formula designating the prophet, to *Daniel*, in which he is a collective figure embodying the people of Israel, to the Enochic and synoptic tradition which interprets him as an individual figure or Messianic persona. This 'apocalyptic symbol' of the "Son of man" contributes to prompt a process of universalisation and of 'disclosure' of the prophetic symbolism towards new meanings and perspectives.

The analysis of the literary notes characterising *Did.* 16 appears to have confirmed the assumption that the text belongs to the apocalyptic literature. Of course, the brevity of the passage and the incompleteness of the text render impossible the presence of all the figures of speech characterising the apocalyptic genre: the processes typical of the pseudo-epigraphy and the concessions of the revelation are missing; the angelic mediation is absent along with the pattern of the vision. One must postulate however that the tradition from which the text derives must have been more extensive originally, as the synoptic analysis seems to confirm. Furthermore, what can be defined as the 'reduction

---

As to the position of Rev, see A. Yarbro Collins, "The 'Son of Man Tradition' and the Book of Revelation", in Charlesworth 1992a, pp. 536-568. In Rev 1:13a the sentence ὅμοιον υἱὸν ἀνθρώπου appears to be an allusion to the sentence כבר אנש of *Dan.* 7:13. But while the MT of *Dan.* 7:13 presents the Son of Man as a figure distinguished from that of the 'Ancient of Days', in *Rev* the two figures constitute a sole identity or entity; this, however, already occurred in the version of *Dan* 7:13 of the LXX provided by Papyrus 967: ἤρχετο ὡς υἱὸς ἀνθρώπου καὶ ὡς παλαιός ἡμερῶ(ν) παρῆν καὶ οἱ παρεστηκότες προσήγαγον αὐτῷ (cf. A. Geissen, *Der Septuaginta-Text des Buches Daniel nach dem Kölner Teil des Papyrus 967: Kap. V-XII* [Bonn: Habelt, 1968], p. 108; the reading is similar to that of Papyrus 88: cf. Geissen, ibid., pp. 39-40). It is not certain whether the reading is intentional or the product of a scribal mistake. Yarbro Collins ("The 'Son of Man' Tradition", cit., passim) maintains that ἕως παλαιοῦ ἡμερῶν has been read as ὡς παλαιὸς ἡμερῶν. For a thorough analysis of the question, however, cf. D.E. Aune, *Revelation 1-5* (Dallas, Texas: Word Books Publisher, 1997), pp. 90-93.

36.   S. Chialà, *Libro delle parabole di Enoc. Testo e commento* (StBi 117; Brescia: Paideia, 1997), pp. 303-340.

of tradition' by the editor-author could depend on the liturgical context in which the text was elaborated.[37] The latter aspect could be a further pointer to connect *Did*. 16 to a particular apocalyptic literature, as the style of the writing suggests, which could have originated in the context of liturgical manifestations[38] besides being a personal synthesis of the author-editor of the *Didache*.

4. Did. 16 and the Apocalyptic 'Ideologies'

In this paragraph I will attempt to contextualise *Did*. 16 within a specific ideological or doctrinal tendencies or currents which can be connected, as far as it is possible, with a group or movement within the Judaism of the Hellenistic Graeco-Roman period privileging apocalyptic literary compositions. This is not an easy task and it requires first of all a brief reference to the hypotheses regarding the relationship between Enochism and apocalyptic, since this represents one of the most debated and controversial points in studies regarding Jewish apocalyptic. Scholars have pointed out that the Enochic tradition represents a distinct tradition which has used the apocalyptic genre, although it is not impossible that in the chronological span of the development of

37. Cf. R. Cacitti, *Grande Sabato. Il contesto pasquale quartodecimano nella formazione della teologia del martirio* (SPMed 19; Milano: Vita e pensiero, 1994), p. 63, for the relation between *Did*. and the Easter liturgy.

38. I draw the attention to the relation, for instance, between *IV Ezra* and the penitential liturgy, or the link between *2 Apoc. Bar.* and the liturgy of the synagogue. Furthermore, it appears that Rev was written in the form of a circular letter addressed to different communities, and its liturgical connotation is today beyond dispute among the exegetes. As to the Enochic tradition, it is known that it was held as authoritative by the community of Qumran, although it is not certain whether it was the focus of the group's liturgies. For *IV Ezra* and the penitential liturgy, see D. Boyarin, "Penitential Liturgy in 4 Ezra", *JSJ* 3, 1972-1973, pp. 30-34; Bogaert, vol. I, pp. 157-162, and I. Elbogen, *Der jüdische Gottesdienst in seiner geschichtlichen Entwicklung* (Frankfurt a. M.: Lang, 1931[3]), p. 185, for *2 Apoc. Bar.* and the liturgy of the Synagogue; and L. Mowry, "Revelation 4-5 and Early Christian Liturgical Usage", *JBL* 71, 1952, pp. 75-84; A. Cabaniss, "A Note on the Liturgy of the Apocalypse", *Int.* 7, 1953, pp. 78-86, and U. Vanni, "Un esempio di dialogo liturgico in Apoc. 1,4-8", *Bib.* 57, 1976, 453-467, for Rev and the liturgy of the early Christian communities; and Wacholder 1983, pp. 33-40, for the centrality of *1 Enoc* in the community of Qumran. As to the relations between liturgy and the literary genre (or form) of apocalyptic, cf. D.L. Barr, "The Apocalypse of John as Oral Enactment", *Int.* 40, 1986, pp. 243-256.

apocalyptic tendencies and traditions, often dictated by either polemic or explanatory intentions, other elements could have been incorporated. The 'formal' and 'doctrinal' situation of *Did.* 16 in a broad and variegated *milieu*: it is insufficient merely to state that *Did.* 16 is apocalyptic; rather it is necessary to specify to 'which' apocalyptic the text belongs; and, more in general, one could ask whether the passage in question could be interpretated as a synthesis of various apocalyptic tendencies. A few considerations should follow regarding the possible re-interpretation of previous traditions by the editor-author of *Did.*, re-interpretation which – if it occurred – could be closely connected to the historical and ideological matrix of proto-Christian prophetism. This prophetism, as is known, is well documented by the *Didache* and consequently was active in the community of the Didachist.

4.1. Enochic Judaism

In recent years the debate surrounding the Jewish apocalyptic texts has been characterised, from an ideological perspective, by a renewed interest in the Enochic tradition prompted by the studies of Italian scholars (supra, chap. 1, pp. 27 ff.). As known, the discovery of Aramaic fragments of *1 Enoch* in Qumran has cast new light not only on the antiquity of several sections of the Enochic Pentateuch, in particular the *Book of the Watchers* (the first and earliest book of the work),[39] but

39.   P. Sacchi, "Il «Libro dei Vigilanti» e l'apocalittica", *Henoch* 1, 1979, pp. 42-98 (now in Sacchi 1997b, pp. 32-71). The author examines the chronology of the fragments found at Qumran as reported by Milik 1976 (but see also the previous article: "The Dead Sea Scrolls Fragments of the Book of Enoch", *Bib.* 32, 1951, pp. 393-400): for Sacchi, the *Astronomical Book* is not the earliest section of the text. Furthermore the author maintains that the *Book of the Watchers* should be dated to the year 200 BCE: in reality, the chronology of the first volume should be established earlier, presumably the IV-III cent. BCE (discussion in Sacchi 1981, pp. 438-442; Sacchi 1997b, in particular pp. 47-62; see also J.H. Charlesworth in Boccaccini 2002b, p. 234). The above discussion has remarkable repercussions on the study of the history of Jewish apocalyptic:
      1. *1 Enoch* had the structure of a "Pentateuch" already at an earlier date (except for the *Book of the Parables*, a text added later: cf. J.A. Fitzmyer, "Implications of the New Enoch Literature from Qumran", *TS* 38, 1977, pp. 332-345 and Sacchi 1997b, p. 48);
      2. *1 Enoch* can be regarded as the 'founder' of apocalyptic literature, and its origin is connected with a precise *Sitz im Leben*;
      3. this *Sitz im Leben* must be located in the ideological controversies which broke out during the restoration of the Zadokite Temple following the reforms by Ezra.

also on the ideological context of the tradition from which the work as a whole derives. It is in the wake of this specific tradition that, for instance, the belief in the immortality of the soul appears; but the centrepiece of this tradition (from the *Book of the Watchers* to some of the positions of *2 Enoch*, a later text which takes up again some of the ideas and concepts of the earlier Enoch tradition)[40] is represented by the origin of evil in the world and its repercussions on the life of the individual and of the universe. The fundamental Enochic problems stem, in reality, from a reinterpretation of Gen 6:1-4 (the sexual sin of the angels with the "daughters of men"),[41] while historically it finds its *Sitz im Leben* in the controversy prompted by the reforms introduced by Ezra and the Zadokites (i.e. priestly leaders) once the Jews had returned from the Babylonian exile.

In this context, then, the tradition linked to *1 Enoch* could be defined as a tradition fundamentally aiming at analysing the theme of evil by referring to the ideology of the so-called Jahwist (southern kingdom), which envisaged human history as a progressive decadence of man (and of the universe) from an original state of beatitude.[42] Therefore it is not

Among the 'currents of opposition' to the 'restoration' was also the group/movement which produced the *Book of the Watchers* (Sacchi 1981, pp. 13-50; Sacchi 1997b, pp. 88-108; Sacchi 2000, pp. 174-182). *Contra* the Pentateuch Hypothesis of *1 Enoch* in the Second Temple period, cf. Nickelsburg 2001, pp. 25 and 335-337 (but see the observations of Knibb 2002 [and the review by S. Chialà, *Bibl.* 85, 2004, pp. 143 ff.] on this important commentary).

40. See Sacchi 1989, p. 439.

41. For a recent examination of the passage, see G.L. Prato, "Integrità testuale e coerenza ermeneutica per i tempi primordiali di Gen 6,1-4", in S. Graziani (ed.), with the collaboration of M.C. Casaburi and G. Lacerenza, *Studi sul Vicino Oriente Antico dedicati alla memoria di L. Cagni* (IUO. Dip. di Studi Asiatici. Series Minor 61; Napoli: IUO, 2000), pp. 1991-2016; and H.S. Kvanvig, "The Watchers Story, Genesis and *Atra-Hasis*: A Triangular Reading", in Boccaccini 2002b, pp. 17-21; Id., "Gen 6.3 and the Watcher Story", *Henoch* 25/3, 2003, pp. 277-300.

42. The different perspectives are collected by Boccaccini 2002b: E. Eshel and H. Eshel (pp. 115-129) have analysed the sacerdotal traditions of the *Aramaic Levi* in relation to other contemporary traditions regarding the origins of Zadokism; M. Himmelfarb (pp. 131-135) has presented a partial review of the thesis proposed by D.W. Suter (cf. *HUCA* 50 [1979], pp. 115-135) and G.W.E. Nickelsburg (*JBL* 100 [1981], pp. 575-600): the author admits that a controversy against the Priesthood, in the *Book of the Watchers* (abbr. BW), could derive from the narration of the illicit relationship of the angelical Watchers with earthly women, although she is less inclined to believe that the issue of mixed marriages, in the period following Ezra, constituted a theme of public discussion. It seems that she follows E.J.C. Tigchelaar (*Prophets of Old and the Day of*

fortuitous that this particular protological concept and universal vision of history will later lead to a sort of 'pre-determinism', undermining the possibility and idea of eschatological salvation, as it is shown by the subsequent *Book of Dream Visions* (a work more or less contemporary to *Daniel*), by the book of *Jubilees* and by the doctrinal developments of the community of Qumran.[43]

the End: Zechariah, the Book of Watchers and Apocalyptic [Leiden-New York: Brill, 1996], pp. 198-203) who focuses on the incident of the 'sacerdotal marriage' to establish the *Sitz im Leben* of the anti-sacerdotal controversy of early Enochism. D.W. Suter (pp. 137-142) has reviewed and represented an article he published in 1979, in which he connected the narration of the angelical sin of BW to the controversy against the impurity of the Priesthood; E.J.C. Tigchelaar (pp. 143-145) maintains that the polemics contained in BW 12-16 were not directed against the Priesthood of Jerusalem but against the Samaritan one (moreover, he believes that the author of BW was unaware of the description of the paradise of the righteous ones provided by Gen 2-3, but, independently, followed a tradition *also* found in the story of the *Genesis*).

43.   The relationship between *Jubilees* and the Enochic tradition is demonstrated by the respect by which the author of *Jub.* quotes *1 Enoch*, from the use of the solar calendar and from the reference to the celestial tables in 32:21 (cf. Sacchi 1981, pp. 193-196, and Boccaccini 1998, pp. 86-98). It would be superfluous to refer to the influence exerted by the Enochic tradition on some of the Qumranic conceptions (in this regard, P. Grelot, "L'eschatologie des esséniens et le livre d'Hénoch", *RdQ* 1, 1958-1959, pp. 113-131). The phase of the movement documented by *Jubilees* is revealing for the definitioon of the relation between Enochism and the Mosaic Torah.: for instance, the reinterpretation of the text provided by Gen 1 in chap. 2 (Vanderkam 2000, pp. 500-521, in particular pp. 505-507: the expression רוח אלהים of Gen 1:2 "was the textual trigger for locating creation of the angels on the first day" [*ibid.*, p. 506], although containing a *contaminatio* from Job 38:4-7. The Ethiopic formula by which *Jubilees* introduces the section, *manfās*, reproduces the singular form of רוח of Gen 1:2, but the rest of the text dwells on listing the different angels created on the first day (i.e. the 'angels of the presence', מלאכי הפנים in 4QJubᵃ V:5, or the 'angels of the spirits of fire', ומלאכי רוחות האש in 4QJubᵃ V:6, etc.; cf. J.C. VanderKam-J.T. Milik, "The First Jubilees Manuscript from Qumran Cave 4: A Preliminary Publication", *JBL* 110, 1991, pp. 243-270, in particular p. 257, which one does not find in *Genesis*) or the attention devoted to the so-called 'celestial tables' (cf. J.C. VanderKam, *The Book of Jubilees* [Guides to Apocrypha and Pseudepigrapha; Sheffield: Academic Press, 2001], pp. 91-93; this appears to be an attempt to reconcile the essentially predestined re-interpretation of earlier Enochic ideology with the concept of 'law' of Zadokism) and to problems related with the calendar. "As is well known", writes VanderKam, "the author of *Jubilees* was a strong defender of a solar calendar according to which a year numbered exactly 364 days, no more, no less" (*The Book of Jubilees*, cit., p. 96; also VanderKam 2000, pp. 522-544: in the prologue, on the other hand, the author tries to synthetize when referring to "the divisions of the years of the Law and of the Witness" (1:4), as when he specifies that his theme deals with the "divisions of the times since

The development of the Enoch tradition makes it possible to clarify the ideological and historical origin of other apocalyptic texts: this is the case with *Daniel* and its relationship with the *Book of Dreams*, but also later texts which independently provide a particular response to the fundamental problems stemming from the Enochic concerns (the problem of evil, predestination and justification, predeterminism, eschatological salvation). Thus *IV Ezra* is connected to Adam's sin (cf. 7:116-118), the *2 Apoc. Bar.* recalls the vicissitudes of the guardian angels (cf. 56,10ff.), while *2 Enoch* appears to propose a new reading of the Enochic text, in particular with reference to the anthropological repercussions of protological problems.[44] The case of *Daniel* appears the most emblematic, since some statements can be explained in the light of a controversy with another contemporary text of the Enochic tradition, that is the *Book of Dreams*, a work which attempts to provide an explanation for the vicissitudes following the so-called "abomination of the desolation" assuming as a point of departure the earlier Enochic concerns.[45]

The community of Qumran appears also to have accepted the Enoch ideology (although Enochism must be intended as a wider movement from which the Qumranites later derived),[46] as the numerous fragments of Enoch literature found in Qumran testify, and from other ideas

---

the time when the Law and the Witness were created" (1:29). Part of *Jub.* 1:4 has been preserved by 4QJub[a] I,11-12: [[מ]חלקות ו]העתים ולתעודה לתורנ]ה ולתעודה]]; it is not fortuitous that the text is at the basis of CD XVI:3-4, which defines *Jubilees* ובשבועותהם ספר מחלקות העתים העתים ליובליהם. The *Ethiopic* lexeme *kufālē* is the indirect translation, analogically mediated by the Greek μερισμοῖ, of the Hebrew מחלקות (see VanderKam 2000, pp. 522-523). The means how to understand the calendar conceptions in *Jub.* are almost certainly provided by the *Astronomical Book* and the *Apocalypse of the Weeks*: *Jub.* 4:17, 18, 21 (VanderKam 2000, p. 544; Id., *The Book of Jubilees*, cit., pp. 96-100). On the contacts between *Jubilees* and the Enoch tradition see also VanderKam 1984, pp. 179-188; Id. 1996, pp. 110-121.

44. Sacchi 1989, pp. 479ff.: the points in which *2 Enoch* appears to refer to the earlier Enoch tradition are essentially two, that is the topography of Hell (chap. 10) and the intercession or mediation (chap. 7).

45. Cf. G. Boccaccini, "È Daniele un testo apocalittico? Una (ri)definizione del pensiero del libro di Daniele in rapporto al Libro dei Sogni e all'apocalittica", *Henoch* 9, 1987, pp. 267-299.

46. New light on this point – as well as on many other historical and doctrinal issues regarding Enochism in general – will be cast by the *Proceedings* (in a forthcoming volume: G. Boccaccini [with J.H. Ellens and J. Waddell], ed., *Enoch and Qumran Origins: New Light on a Forgotten Connection* [Grand Rapids Mi.: Eerdmans, 2004) of

stemming from a particular re-interpretation of the Enoch tradition itself. Furthermore John's *Apocalypse* appears to be influenced by certain dialectics which characterise Enoch apocalyptic and, in some cases, re-proposes some of the motifs, although in a reformulated way, as in the case of the juxtaposition angels/stars and mountains/sovereigns.[47]

By clarifying these points I do not aim at narrowing the definition of 'apocalyptic', which I continue to regard as a specific literary genre based on a particular 'vision of the world', but I consider that maintaining that the Enoch tradition represents a term of comparison for later apocalyptic works does not mean *sic et simpliciter* that only those texts which can be directly referred to that tradition are to be considered 'apocalyptic'. It is, in fact, often possible to detect in the texts an 'interlacement' of different traditions. It appears that the book of *Daniel* itself, in controversy with the Enoch tradition, is at the origin of 'other' apocalyptic traditions encompassing *IV Ezra, 2 Apoc. Bar.* and the *Apocalypse* of John,[48] as well as the pseudepigraphic and proto-

---

the Second International Enoch Seminar, held in Venice, July 1-5, 2003. VanderKam 1994, pp. 49-51.

47. Cf. E. Lupieri, "Apocalisse di Giovanni e tradizione enochica", in Penna 1995, pp. 137-149.

48. For the relationships between *Daniel, IV Ezra* and *Revelation,* I refer to some studies by G.K. Beale: *The Use of Daniel in Jewish Apocalyptic Literature and in the Revelation of St. John* (Lanham: University Press of America, 1984); "The Interpretative Problem of Rev 1:19", *NT* 34, 1992, pp. 360-387; "The Old Testament Background of Rev 3.14", *NTS* 42, 1996, pp. 133-152; and *John's Use of the Old Testament in Revelation* (JSNT.S 166; Sheffield: Sheffield Academic Press, 1998). Similar studies, as far as the methodology of inquiry regarding the relationship between *Revelation* and the Hebrew Scriptures is concerned, have been produced by F. Jenkins, *The Old Testament in the Book of Revelation* (Grand Rapids Mi.: Eerdmans, 1972); J. Paulien, *Decoding Revelation's Trumpets: Literary Allusions and Interpretation of Revelation 8:7-12* (Berrien Springs MI: University Press, 1987) (see the observations by G. K. Beale in *JBL* 111, 1992, pp. 358-361); Id., "Elusive Allusions: The Problematic Use of the Old Testament in Revelation", *BibRes* 33, 1988, pp. 37-53; "Dreading the Whirlwind: Intertextuality and the Use of the Old Testament in Revelation", *AUSS* 39, 2001, pp. 5-22. Cf. also J.-P. Ruiz, *Ezekiel in the Apocalypse: The Transformation of Prophetic Language in Revelation 16,7-19,10* (Frankfurt am Mein-Bern-New York-Paris: Lang, 1989); R. Bauckham, *The Climax of Prophecy: Studies in the Book of Revelation* (Edinburgh: T.&T. Clark, 1993); J. Fekkes, *Isaiah and Prophetic Traditions in the Book of Revelation: Visionary Antecedents and Their Development* (JSNT.S 93; Sheffield: Academic Press, 1994); S. Moyise, *The Old Testament in the Book of Revelation* (JSNT.S 115; Sheffield: Academic Press, 1995). The article by A. Vanhoye, "L'utilisation du livre d'Ézéchiel dans l'Apocalypse", *Bibl.* 43, 1962, pp.

242   Marcello Del Verme

Christian apocalypses, as the *Shepherd* of Hermas, the *Apocalypse of Peter* and the *Apocalypse of Paul*.

If the Enoch tradition has found its *Nachleben* in those environments opposing the Zadokite Temple, the 'Daniel-historical' or 'proto-Rabbinical' or Zadokite tradition (as it has been recently defined, see Boccaccini 2002a, pp.164ff.) appears to have occurred in particular in official environments in an attempt to bring the 'apocalyptic genre' back to Zadokite Judaism.

Consequently, to consider as 'apocalyptic' only what can be referred to the Enoch tradition could induce one to deny – or at least neglect – that the controversies which were elaborated by resorting to the use of the same formal tools (as in the case of *Daniel* and of the *Dream Visions*), could cause the rise of either different or more fluid ideological and doctrinal positions.

435-476, can be regarded as the "Founder" of this academic tendency. For the recycling by Rev of some of the Jewish apocalyptic texts, in particular referring to *Daniel*, Beale talks of an "ironic " or "reversed recycling": an emblematic case of this type of recycling is represented by *1 Enoch* 90:12-13, with reference to Dan 7-8 (Beale refers to a "probable allusion with more varied wording", p. 71); the image of the horn, which in Dan 7-8 is an "anti-theocratic" symbol, but in the Book of *Dream Visions* it "represents the saints of Israel (v 9) and, especially, a Messiah-like leader (probably Judas Maccabaeus, vv 9-10, 12-13, 16" (*The Use of Daniel*, p. 72). "It is especially the 'great horn' image in Daniel 7-8 which designates the epitome of anti-theocratic power and its attempt to overcome Israel and Israel's 'prince' in the end-time. By contrast, the 'great horn' metaphor in Enoch is used to emphasize the power of Israel's leader in resisting and ultimately overcoming the eschatological attack of the enemy. However, although the imagery is applied otherwise than in Daniel, the more *general* idea of it in the Enoch context is in harmony with the broad contextual idea of Daniel 7-8 and 11-12, i.e. the final triumph of Israel and its prince" (pp. 72-73). "This different application of the Daniel imagery appears to be intentional and not merely fixed apocalyptic language. If this imagery has been borrowed from Daniel, then the author must have operated according to some rationale in applying it so differently. There is no doubt that the author would have believed that Daniel 7-8 taught the final triumph of Israel and their messianic leader. In light of the observation that Enoch's differently applied imagery is within a contextual framework which is harmonious with Daniel, it may become more understandable to view the writer as developing the Danielic idea of Israel's distress *and* victory according to his own understanding" (p. 73). On the "ironic" reuse, in general, see *The Use of Daniel*, pp. 64-65. For the definition of a further apocalyptic tradition, stemming from *Daniel*, and which could be defined as "historical-Danielic" or "proto-Rabbinic", cf. Arcari 2002, and Boccaccini 2002a, pp. 164ff.

4.2. Did. 16 and Enochism

By what ways can *Did.* 16 be linked to Enochic apocalyptic? My answer to this question calls for a broader approach based on the analysis of the passage in question in the context of the work as a whole.

As a matter of fact, there is a trend among scholars who have thoroughly examined the meaning of *Did.* 16 to read this final section of the *Didache* as if the editor had conceived it in close connection with the initial treatise of the "Two Ways", that is the catechetic-moral section of the work (chaps.1-6).[49] Some scholars – among whom Rordorf-Tuilier[50] – have, however, disagreed with this connection for the following reasons:

a. the first chapters of the *Didache* already encompass passages of an eschatological character, especially in the DVD (for example, *Did.* 3:7; 4:7, 10);

b. the concluding section of the *Didache*, in its current form, does not represent a continuation of the first five sections of the work. The expression Γρηγορεῖτε ὑπὲρ τῆς ζωῆς ὑμῶν (16:1), in fact, could be considered as a mere allusion to the previous sections. Neither does the parallel text of *Barn.* 4:9b, 10 (cf. *Did.* 16:2) help to clarify the connection between the two sections. In reality, the form and content of *Did.* 16 have no bearing whatsoever on the moral and sapiential norms found in the first six chapters of the work.

c. The literary and chronological distance between the two sections (*Did.* 1-6 and *Did.* 16), separated by other sections different as to form and content, reflect the several editorial rewritings which some of the sections underwent. In synthesis, to use their own words, these scholars maintain that the last chapter of the *Didache* represents "une sorte de passage eschatologique" essentially composed "d'éléments tradition-nels".

In my opinion, none of the arguments adduced by Rorforf-Tuilier appear to be decisive enough to settle the controversy:

1. As to point a., it is implausible to separate *Did.* 1-6 from *Did.* 16 on the basis of the observation regarding the presumed presence of 'eschatological' traits already found in the first five chapters of the

49.   Drews 1904; Köster 1957, pp. 160.190; Bammel 1961, pp. 253 ff.; and Kraft 1965, pp. 12 f.
50.   Rordorf-Tuilier 1998, pp. 81 ff. *Contra* also Giet 1970, pp. 254-256.

writing. On the contrary, these very hints – referring to an apocalyptic 'climate' – could have either influenced or compelled the editor-author to complete his argument with further final clarifications and explanations. This 'textual situation' should corroborate rather than weaken the hypothesis (with which I agree) of the connection between the two parts.

2. As to point b., I have already discussed previously the close connections which can exist between apocalyptic and sapiential literatures. Furthermore the textual tenor of *Did.* 16:1should not be underestimated either: the presence of the term ζωη, in fact, contributes to generate, in fact, an effective (and formal) connecting link between the preamble of the "Two Ways" (*Did.* 1,1a: 'Οδοὶ δύο εἰσί, μία τῆς ζωῆς...) and the beginning of the final part of the work. It is not fortuitous that after chapters 1-6, which dwell on describing the prerogatives of both the 'way of life' and the 'way of death', the author-editor decided to introduce the eschatological-apocalyptic section for a further moral advice, although new and different in tone, because of the unpredictability of the time and in view of the coming of the last days. Such advice would be destitute of meaning after the previous disciplinary teachings regarding the modes of brotherly correction (*Did.* 15:3). On the contrary, it states that it is necessary always to be on guard since nobody knows when the Lord will come (cf. 5,2b⟶16,1 ῥυσθείητε, τέκνα, ἀπὸ τούτων ἀπάντων. Γρηγορεῖτε ὑπὲρ τῆς ζωῆς ὑμῶν...). As to the supposed irrelevance of moral instruction for the apocalyptic genre, further clarification appears to be superfluous: I only point out that also in Jewish texts not directly attributable to the apocalyptic genre it is possible to find the combination of ethical instructions regarding the way to follow with eschatological advice regarding the world to come (cf. *T. Sym.* 6:1ff.). The presence of the term τέκνα (vocative plural, "oh sons") in *Did.* 5:2 allows us to establish a parallel with the genre of the "testaments" (as well as with the gnomic and sapiential genre: the "τέκνον-sayings"),[51] in which the father addresses and warns his children by resorting to the use of the appellative "son" or "my son" (cf. *Did.* 4:1), repeated anaphorically: cf. *T. Reu.* 1:1.2.4; *T. Sym.* 2:1; 3:2; and *T. Levi* 10:1).[52]

---

51. Supra, Chap. 1, pp. 115-116, with further references to Niederwimmer 1989, pp. 133-144.

52. As to the final citation from the *Testament of Levi*, it is interesting to observe that the series of prescriptions, which are typical of the genre of the testament (for

3. Point c., touches on a fundamental and central problem of *Did.* 16 regarding the identification of the possible Jewish traditions incorporated into the text of the *Didache*. Of course, any analysis which attempts to dismember the current text – with the intention of tracing the various strata or stages which preceded the final edition often and necessarily remains hypothetical. Anyway, if the prescriptions present in the section of the "Two Ways" (*Did.* 1-6) and the eschatological section of the work (*Did.* 16) represent the 'peculiarity' of the community of the Didachist – although considering also that most commentators maintain that the first six chapters and the final one of the *Did.* are clearly of Jewish origin – the supposition that the two sections in question could originally have circulated in a unitary form it is not groundless. This, however, does not authorize one to suppose that the 'apocalyptic section' was originally a writing connected with the "Two Ways": the connection between, and fusion of, the two traditions could

example, 10:1 ff.), is introduced by a broadly apocalyptic section (see 2:1 ff.). For the *T. 12 Patr.*, it appears that both the *T. Levi* and *T. Reuben* are influenced by Enochism. The *T. Levi*, in particular, appears to derive from a document found at Qumran, the *Aramaic Testamento of Levi* (= 1Q21, 4Q213-214; the fragments of this work are datable to the period between the end of the 2nf century BCE [4Q214 = *T. Levi* 9:11-14] and the first half of the 1st century BCE [cf. J.T. Milik, "Le Testament de Lévi en araméen. Fragments de la Grotte I de Qumrân", *RB* 62, 1955, pp. 398-406; *The Books of Enoch*, cit., pp. 23-24; M.E. Stone-J. Greenfield, "The Prayer of Levi", *JBL* 112, 1993, pp. 247-266]; as to the relation between the fragments of Qumran and the *T. Levi*, cf. R.A. Kugler, *From Patriarch to Priest: The Levy-Priestly Tradition from Aramaic Levi to Testament of Levi* [Atlanta: Scholars Press, 1996]). However, as to the relationship Enochism/*T. 12 Patr.*, a thesis recently proposed (cf. Boccaccini 1998, pp. 138-149), one must keep in mind that the *T. 12 Patr.* is an extremely stratified work or tradition. Sacchi largely followed [see Id. 1981, pp. 319-349] the unitary thesis proposed by R.H. Charles (cf. APOT II, pp. 282-367) and by J. Becker, *Die Testament der zwölf Patriarchen* (Gütersloh: Mohn, 1974); it is, however, important to point out that the thesis of a Christian 'edition' of the work, an hypothesis advanced by De Jonge, does not challenge the 'Jewishness' of the text, but only the possibility of identifying a 'unique' original core: cf. H.J. de Jonge, *The Testaments of Twelve Patriarchs. A Study of Their Text, Composition and Origin* (Assen: Van Gorcum, 1953); "Christian Influence in the Testaments of the Twelve Patriarchs", *NT* 4, 1960, pp. 182-235; "Once More: Christian Influence in the Testaments of the Twelve Patriarchs" *NT* 5, 1962, pp. 311-319; "Die Textüberlieferung der Testament der zwölf Patriarchen", *ZNTW* 63, 1972, pp. 27-64 (on the theory of de Jonge and for a discussion on the *T. 12 Patr.*, cf. Charlesworth 1985, pp. 94-102; further bibliography in Charlesworth 1981, pp. 211-220 [although Charlesworth appears to favour the theory of 'interpolations' and not that of the 'edition').

have been conceived and developed within the community of the Didachist.

This connection could cast light on the ways in which the apocalyptic section was read within the community and/or by the author of the *Didache*: connected with the "Two Ways", chap. 16 appears as eschatological advice coming from an Enochic matrix. The section of the "Two Ways", in fact, expounds ideas treasured by both the Enochic and the Qumran movement, in particular dualism, as is shown by a series of parallels with the *Community Rule* (1QS)[53] and by other writings.[54] This interpretation appears to find further support in the parallel passage on the "Two Ways" in *Barn*. 18:1-2, in which the Didachean terminology is enriched by other details which appear to confirm the connection of the section in question with some of the ideas of the Enochic and Qumran movement. In *Barn*. one reads that "there are two ways of teaching and authority, one of light and one of darkness"; *Doctr*. 1,1 also follows the same tradition, although with further enrichment: "*Viae duae sunt in saeculo, vitae et mortis, lucis et tenebrarum. In his constituti sunt angeli duo, unus aequitatis alter iniquitatis. Distantia autem magna est duarum viarum...*".[55] The terminology

---

53. Cf. Audet 1952. Draper 1983, warns against any parallel only with the Qumran movement (also Rordorf 1972). More interesting, for Draper, are the connections with certain Rabbinical treatises (in particular the *Derek Eretz*, containing an exposition of the commandments of Noah). The question is extremely important: dualism was not a universally accepted belief in the world of Middle Judaism, and it appears to have been a peculiarity of the Essenes and the Qumranites. Such a conception postulates a certain pre-determinism in the sphere of human action, although the individual remains free with respect to divine will. On dualism and its relations with the Essene-Qumranic world, cf. Sacchi 2000, pp. 334-337. On Qumranic dualism, see also J. Duhaime, "Dualistic Reworking in the Scrolls from Qumran", *CBQ* 49, 1987, pp. 32-56; M. Philonenko, "La doctrine qoumrânienne des deux Esprits: ses origines iraniennes et ses prolongements dans le judaïsme essénien et le christianisme antique", in G. Widengren-A. Hultgård-M. Philonenko (eds.), *Apocalyptique iranienne et dualisme qoumrânien*, (Paris: Cerf, 1995), II, pp. 163-211, and D. Dimant, "Dualism at Qumran: New Perspectives", in J.H. Charlesworth (ed.), *Caves of Enlightenment* – Proceedings of the American Schools of Oriental Research DSS Jubilee Symposium (1947-1997) (North Richland Hills: BIBAL Press, 1998), pp. 55-73.

54. See the sapiential fragments referred to as "The Two Ways" (Elgvin 1996, pp. 289ff.).

55. For a synopsis of *Did.*, *Doctr.* and *Barn.*, I refer the reader to Audet 1958, pp. 138-153.There is at the moment a heated debate regarding the relations and interrelations of the three texts (see van de Sandt-Flusser 2002, in particular chaps. 2-4, pp. 55-139): Rordorf-Tuilier 1998, p. 221, confute and reject the thesis proposed by J.S.

of the contrast between light and darkness recalls analogous doctrinal phraseology and concepts present among the Qumranites: cf., in particular, 1QS III:13-IV:26; 1QM XIII:10-16; CD V:18.

As to the Qumranic dualism (and the determinism), many scholars tend to identify in it Stoic influences, similar to those characterising that particular context of Hellenistic Judaism developed in Alexandria of Egypt. For the current of Palestinian Essenism also (and not as the Therapeutae of Egypt) these influences cannot be excluded *a priori*, although "la frammentarietà della documentazione relativa a questa setta (i.e. the Qumran community) rende impossibile una ricostruzione sistematica del pensiero, dal quale però è comunque possibile dedurre la credenza in un ferreo determinismo, ineludibile da parte dell'uomo...(1QS III:15-17; cf. also 1QHᵃ I:8-29). A Qumran ritroviamo dunque una concezione che era caratteristica del pensiero stoico".[56] Of course – after Hengel's studies – it is possible to state that Stoic thought lay behind some of the religious conceptions of Hellenistic-Roman Judaism,[57] including therefore the Essene current; I tend, however, to suppose that Qumranic dualism had its origins *also* in a particular interpretation the community of Qumran provided of the Enoch tradition, in particular of the *Book of the Watchers*. One must not forget that more recent hypotheses maintain that the Qumran community derived

Kloppenborg, "The Transformation of Moral Exhortation in Didache 1-5", in Jefford 1995a, p. 92. In my opinion, by contrast, the tradition underlying *Did., Barn.* and *Doctr.* is more or less unitary, although I tend to reject the supposition that the tradition incorporated into *Barn.* is earlier and original (Kloppenborg) and that the tradition referred by *Barn.* is "more dualistic" than that present in *Did.* (Rordorf-Tuilier 1998, pp. 221ff.). To the theory that the "Two Ways" originally represented a catechetic theme with "multiple reviews", making difficult any classification of the different evidences (thesis by Rordorf-Tuilier), many objections have been raised beginning with Audet, *La Didachè*, p.123, in the wake of J.A. Robinson (*JThS* 35, 1934, pp. 132.142.146). A schema of the 'itinerary' of the *topos* of "Two Ways" in the writings of Early Christianity is provided by Giet 1970, p. 71; and Philonenko ("La doctrine qoumrânienne", *passim*). See also van de Sandt-Flusser 2002, pp. 59ff. and 81-111.

56. C. Martone, *La "Regola della comunità". Edizione critica* (QHenoch 8; Turin: Silvio Zamorani, 1995), pp. 81-82, including a discussion regarding the question 'dualism and Stoicism' in both the wider Essene movement and at Qumran (pp. 81-88).

57. For the influences of Hellenistic culture on the community of Qumran, I refer the reader to M. Hengel, "Qumran und der Hellenismus", in Delcor 1978, pp. 333-372, apart from Hengel 1988³. As to Hengel's work, see the enlightening observations provided by Collins 1989.

from a schism[58] within the wider Enochic-Essene movement or Enochic Essenism.[59] One should not, therefore, be surprised that one of the main points of dissent stemmed from a 'deterministic' interpretation or vision of the world which the Essene-Qumranic group inherited from the Enoch tradition. An analogous operation is implemented by the author of the *Jubilees*. At Qumran, the dualism was considered as a sort of 'radicalisation' of the ideas encompassed in *1 Enoch*. Significant in this regard is the following passage of the *Hodayoth*: " *29*...What creature of clay can do wonders? He is in iniquity *30* from his maternal womb, and in guilt of unfaithfulness right to (sic: better tr. 'until') old age. But I know that justice does not belong to man nor to a son of Adam a perfect *31* path. To God Most High belong all the acts of justice, and the path of man is not secure except by the spirit which God creates for him *32* to perfect the path of the sons of Adam so that all his creatures come to know the strength of his power and the abundance of his compassion with all the sons of *33* his approval..." (1QHª XII, 29-32; tr. by García Martínez-Tigchelaar, vol. One, p.171). This particular theme is rooted in the Enoch tradition and in the re-elaboration it provided of the myth of the fall of the angels of Gen 6:1-4, which the *Book of the Watchers* interprets as the cause of mankind's corruption. The ideology of the *Book of the Watchers* appears to be lie behind a radical shift seen both in the pre-determinism of the subsequent Enoch tradition and in Qumran dualism.

For this reason I believe it is reductive to envisage Qumran dualism as the product of Stoic influences. The same argument can be adduced with regard to the so-called "horoscopes", a genre which finds wide diffusion both at Qumran and in the religious world of Hellenistic civilisation.[60] It appears consequently logical to suppose that the Qumran tendency to identify in each individual parts of 'darkness' and of

---

58. See García Martínez 1987; Id.-Trebolle Barrera 1993; and VanderKam 1994.
59. See Boccaccini 2002b.
60. For horoscopes in the Graeco-Roman world, cf. D. Baccani, *Oroscopi greci. Documentazione papirologica* (Ricerca papirologica 1), Messina 1992. For the Qumran horoscopes, cf. J.M. Allegro, "An Astrological Cryptic Document from Qumran", *JSS* 9, 1964, pp. 291-294; and M. Delcor, "Recherches sur un horoscope en langue hébraïque provenant de Qumrân", *RdQ* 9, 1966, pp. 521-542 (for frg. 4Q186). More in general, see M. Albani, "Horoscopes in the Qumran Scrolls", in Flint-VanderKam, *The Dead Sea Scrolls*, II, pp. 279 ff.; and for the Hebrew or Aramaic texts found at Qumran, see García Martínez-Tigchelaar: 4Q*Horoscope* [4Q *186*] (vol. One, pp. 380-383); 4Q *Brontologion* [4Q *318*/4QBr ar] (vol. Two, pp. 676-679); 4Q *Physiognomy/*

'light' should be connected to a particular interpretation of the Enoch tradition provided by the community.

If the bond between dualism and Enochic apocalyptic tradition is documented – in a phase prior to Christian Judaism – by the Qumran manuscripts (although in a markedly sectarian form), the connection between *Did.* 1-6 and 16 does not appear unlikely. Analysis of the content of the two sections also makes that connection appear possible: the reference to the precepts of the way of light and to the negative remarks regarding the way of darkness find their natural continuation in the warning regarding the end of time. And always in the Scrolls of Qumran it is possible to find several parallels with this connection: for instance frg. 4QTest. (= 4Q *175*) shows that the eschatological expectation of the Qumran community is closely bound up with the 'legalistic' dimension; and one of the Community Rules of the movement (1QS) testifies to the union and tension among the members between obedience to the law and the expectation of the end (1QS V:1-3.7-9.11b-13).

The observance of the precepts of the Law does not exclude but corroborates the expectation of the end of time: to wait for the end means to prepare for its arrival by means of a total acceptance of the Law and the precepts God has entrusted to men.[61] The *Didache* appears to aim at reviving this religious sensitivity, that is a 'spirituality of expectation', which associates the operational element (= human action) in accordance with God's will with the attention (= intention) toward the expectation of the latter days.

Only in this perspective is it possible to understand the reference in *Did.* 16:7b to the "saints" (citation and re-interpretation of Zech 14:5), who only will come with the Lord, along with the final reference to the judgement on the basis of individual retribution (*Did.* 16:7b→*Const.* 7:32.4-5): Ἥξει ὁ κύριος καὶ πάντες οἱ ἅγιοι μετ' αὐτοῦ. Consequently I do not believe it is possible to find in this reference an allusion to a millenarian conception which is not supported by the text.[62] In reality,

---

Horoscope ar [4Q *561*/4Q Hor ar] (ibid., pp. 1116-1119), with an English translation and selected bibliography on a single text.

61.   In order to define the relation between Law and eschatological expectation in the manuscripts of Qumran some scholars refer to a Messianic *halakhah* (among others, García Martínez-Trebolle Barrera 1993, pp. 63-89;165-186).

62.   Visonà 2000, p. 356, n. 14 appears to take a different line, identifying in the text of *Did.* a 'rigorous' millenarian conception (as A.P. O'Hagan).

the "saints" are in this case the "righteous ones", in other words those
who have followed the way of light.[63] This however does not exclude a
retribution in accordance with the merits of each individual: in *1 Enoch*
it is possible to find many passages dealing with the righteous and the
godly ones (cf. 22:9.13; 25:5). Furthermore in 99:10 it is stated: "In
those days, blessed are they all who accept the words of wisdom and
understand them, to follow the path of the Most High; they shall walk
in the path of his righteousness and not become wicked with the wicked; and they shall be saved" [tr. by Charlesworth 1983, p. 80]); and in
91:6-10 the wicked ones are those who break the law, who commit
abuses and violence, who curse and who practise idolatry. The wicked
one is of this kind because he has chosen to disobey the Law, but at the
end, "... the righteous judgment shall be revealed to the whole world.
All the deeds of sinners shall depart from upon the whole earth, and be
written off for eternal destruction; and all people shall direct their sight
to the path of uprightness" (91:14; tr. by Charlesworth 1983, p. 73).
Later the author lists the reasons for observing the way of justice and of
the saints in view of the end of time : "Now listen to me, my children,
and walk in the way of righteousness, and do not walk in the way of
wickedness, for all those who walk in the ways of injustice shall perish" (91:19; tr. by Charlesworth 1983, p. 73).

Such a belief, however, does not exclude an individual retribution,
although this aspect appears to be more marked in the apocalyptic
current deriving from *Daniel* (see in particular, *IV Ezra* 7:104-105

---

63.   For the assimilation saints/righteous ones, see J. Coppens, *La reléve apocalyptique du messianisme royal.* II. *Le fils d'homme vétéro- et intertestamentaire* (Leuven: Peeters, 1983), 93-98. In addition, I refer the reader to *2 Apoc. Bar.* 15:7 and
21:24. As to *Did.* 16:5, Draper 1997a maintains that the text means salvation by means
of the curse itself, in other words that there is a clear reference to the theology of
martyrdom which is present in both Christian and Rabbinic exegeses of Zech 14:5.
Only the righteous saints, who have faithfully faced and suffered death, will rise from
the dead; the wicked will be destroyed, leaving no trace of their existence on earth. This
represents the earliest Christian interpretation and understanding of the resurrection, of
which the *Didache* preserves 'traces' of the lowest stratum 'lying' on the Jewish legacy
(= tradition). Draper argues that the justification of the resurrection of the righteous
one, which appears to be connected with the text of Zech 14:5 and the ideology of the
"cult of the martyrs", had its *Sitz im Leben* in the historical context of the Maccabaean
Revolt. The Jewish ideology/doctrine of the resurrection of the righteous one passed
from the *milieu* of the Maccabaean groups and/or movements to that of Jewish Christianity as documented by the *Didache*.

and also *2 Apoc. Bar.* 13:9-12). In *2 Enoch* 64:4, by contrast, it appears that Enoch is the only one who can intercede in the final day: the final phase of the Enoch tradition radicalises the impossibility of mediation at the time of the Last Judgement.[64]

In the wake of the Enoch apocalyptic tradition God's Last Judgement appears to assume great importance, although this does not exclude a predeterministic interpretation of historical and salvific events: the enthronement of the saved and the righteous ones is decided *ab aeterno*. It must, however, be observed that these texts are not 'treatises of theology' and therefore it would be going to far to try to identify in them a fixed and systematic coherence of thought: in some contexts predeterminism and judgement appear as reconcilable or consistent realities, while in others they remain antithetical or mutually exclusive.

The presence in *Did.* 16:7 of the reference to the "saints/righteous ones" (followed by a probable reference to the Last Judgement with individual retribution[65]), in a literary context (chap.16) which is probably connected with the section regarding the "Two Ways" (chaps. 1-6), lends support the the hypothesis that the original apocalyptic *Urtext*, recycled by the Didachist, may have contained ideas which were somewhat similar to those of Enochic and Qumran Essenism.

4.3. Did. 16 and Other Ideological Motifs of the Judaism of the Hellenistic and Roman Period

A further comparison of the *Didache* with other texts found in the same Syrian area could throw light on how typical ideas of the Enochic movement were present in that environment, as a sort of theological-ideological *pastiche*, which assembled Enochic, Pharisaic and Christian ideas, attributable to different ideological and literary contexts, although always within the same historical-literary phenomenon, the so-called 'Middle Judaism'.[66]

---

64.   In this passage Enoch is defined as "the one who takes away [our] sins". The same peculiarity is attributed – almost *verbatim* - to the celestial Melchizedek in a Qumranic text (11QMelch. [=11Q13] II:6: cf. J.A. Fitzmyer, "Further Light on Melchizedek from Qumran Cave 11", *JBL* 86, 1967, pp. 25-41).

65.   Some literary critics reconstruct the 'lost ending' of *Didache* by recourse to the Georgian version and to the *Apostolic Constitutions* as well. For a concise but clear *status quaestionis*, see Visonà 2000, pp. 236-239.

66.   For this terminological choice, which I believe is useful and functional since it both groups the various literary *corpora* of the period and includes the numerous

To begin with, in the *Ascensio Isaiae* (or *Martyrdom of Isaiah*) (abbr. *Asc. Is.*) one finds accentuated that dualism characteristic of apocalyptic contexts: in 4,1-18 the antagonism between Beliar and the Beloved does not represent a mere 'personal' contrast, but takes on marked cosmological contours, so "l'umanità è chiamata a scegliere tra la fedeltà a Dio e al suo Diletto oppure la sequela di Beliar, e si divide in due gruppi inconciliabilmente opposti".[67] Also in this text scholars identify numerous parallels with the manuscripts of Qumran and the *Testaments of the XII Patriarchs*, and refer to a "dualismo etico-cosmologico apocalittico" (cf. Acerbi, pp. 84-87). The literary and ideological proximity of the *Martyrdom of Isaiah* and the *Didache* finds further confirmation in the same context describing the double *parousia* of Beliar and the Lord, tradition found also in Rev 19:19-20:3; 20:7-10: the deceptive deeds of Beliar – in *Did.* 16:4 emphasised by the lexeme κοσμοπλανής[68] – will lead astray the people faithful to the Lord dispersed over all the land (cf. *Asc. Is.* 4:7-12 and *Did.* 16:4; vd. also *Jub.* 1:20; *T. Reu.* 2:2; *T. Sim.* 2:7; *T. Levi* 3:3; *T. Jud.* 23:1; *T. Iss.* 6:1; *T. Dan* 5:5; *T. Ash.* 1:8; *T. Benj.* 6:1.7; and for Qumran, CD IV:12b-19; 1QpHab. II:1-6; VIII:10; 1QH^a X:10.16-17.21-22; XI:27b-

---

groups/movements which produced the texts, see Boccaccini 1993. *Contra*, M. Pesce as well as other Italian and foreign scholars (supra, Chap. 1, pp. 17-18 and n. 14).

67. Cf. A. Acerbi, *L'Ascensione di Isaia. Cristologia e profetismo in Siria nei primi decenni del II secolo* (SPMed 17; Milano: Vita e pensiero, 1988), p. 84. The interpretation of *Asc. Is.* as a Christianised Jewish writing is today rejected by some scholars, mainly Italian, who have thoroughly examined the text in specific studies. Of course it is possible to suppose a series of sources of different origin, although it has been confirmed that the *Sitz im Leben* of the writing is to be located in a series of internal troubles which several Christian communities experienced during the 2nd century CE: see Norelli 1994. M. Pesce has argued against the possibility that the text of the *Martyrdom of Isaiah* is an originally Jewish work from which the material found in the existing *Asc. Is.* is derived (*Il "Martirio di Isaia" non esiste. L'Ascensione di Isaia e le tradizioni giudaiche sull'uccisione del profeta* [Bologna: EDB, 1984]). This, however, does not exclude the use of 'Jewish' traditions and materials by the author of section II of the work [which represents the earliest phase of the writing] or of section I [the latest phase of the writing in controversy with the author of section I], a possibility that Norelli himself cannot discard (Id. 1994, pp. 93-113).

68. In this regard, Audet 1958 wrote: "Le nom (κοσμοπλανής) est évidemment formé tout exprès pour décrire un mode d'action. Ce n'est pas une simple désignation du personnage. Son intérêt, dans le contexte, est de donner un sens naturel aux «signes de la vérité» (16,6) en regard des signes du séducteur (16,4). L'ἀλήθεια s'oppose à la πλάνη, dont le Séducteur universel est comme la personification..." (p. 472).

28). Beliar's dominance over the world results in the persecution of the righteous and, often, his disguising himself as the Beloved. As to the persecution of the righteous ones see *T. Dan* 5:11-12; 1QHᵃ X:16-17.21-22.31-32 and also 4Q*174* III:7b-9; as to the disguising, cf. *Asc. Is.* 4:6b and *Did.* 16:4.

These traditions, which belong to different middle Judaic environments, are often found combined in the proto-Christian writings: cf., i.e., Rev 19:19-20:3; 20:7-10 for the intervention of Beliar as the final antagonist of God; 2 Thess 2:10-12; Mark 13:22; Matt 24:24; Rev 12:9; 13:3-4.8.12-14; 2 Jo 7; and *Did.* 16:4 for the destructive power of the Anti-Christ; 2 Thess 1:4-5; Mark 13:9.12; Matt 24:29; and Rev 13:7.15-17 for the suffering and the martyrdom which the faithful will have to endure because of the deeds of the devil and his followers.

Furthermore as to the Lord's *parousia*, the Didachean traditions are part and parcel of a variegated and fluid constellation of images: the reference, for instance, to the coming of the Lord with His saints – with the citation of Zech 14:5 in *Did.* 16:7 – is found also in *Asc. Is.* 4:14a, 16b, and the analogous context of glory and triumph. The reference of *Did.* 16:6 to the σημεῖον ἐκπετάσεως ἐν οὐρανῷ (the sign of an opening out in heaven)[69] raises difficulties, but parallel passages can be found both in Matt 24:30 and in the *Didascalia*, although there is no exact match. I believe however that the symbol should not be understood in a Christological sense, that is as a reference to the cross. It is more likely that the text refers to some sort of opening of the sky, a recurring image in apocalyptic texts.

An allusion to the cross would appear to be excluded also by the presence of the lexeme πρῶτον, indicating that the sign of the opening of the sky is the first of a series which is subsequently described: *usually* in apocalyptic literature a progressive series of signs aims at creating an ascending or descending *climax* in order to connect symbols which belong to a more or less unitary sphere (for example, Rev 8:7-9:20). Since the sound of the trumpet and the resurrection of the dead have no bearing on Christology and that the symbol of the cross should accompany the image of the Son of man (in Rev. there is the lamb), it would appear quite hasty to think of it as a first sign/symbol of the latter days. Consequently, a certain degree of vagueness, typical of apoca-

---

69. For an update of the *status quaestionis* regarding the σημεῖον ἐκπετάσεως ἐν οὐρανῷ, see Visonà 2000, pp. 250-252.

lyptic symbolism, appears to characterise the text of the *Didache*, a
vagueness which the readers must constantly attempt to come to terms
with.

5. Did. *16 and the Synoptic "Apocalyptic Discourse" (Mark 13 and Parr.)*

The resumption by *Did.* 16 of some elements present in the apocalyptic discourse of the synoptic Gospels has always attracted the attention of scholars and commentators on the *Didache*.[70] Some see in this
chapter a sort of re-elaboration of Matt 24, while others maintain that
there is no relation between the two texts except for the resort to
common traditions.[71] In my opinion, the latter supposition is preferable
too in view of some precise observations advanced by Köster and
Kloppenborg.[72] It is possible to assert that *Did.* reflects the *Urtext* of
a Jewish apocalypse known and used also by *Mark*: it is not fortuitous,
in my opinion, that the Christian Jewish text of the *Didache* uses only
materials peculiar (= *Sondergut*) to *Matthew* (abbr. "M") and fails to
cite *Matthew* where it is evident that the latter follows *Mark*. I believe
that the *Didache* represents an independent tradition by means of which
also *Matthew* would have altered *Mark*.[73]

It is indisputable in current NT criticism that the 'eschatological
speech' derives from a Jewish source, re-adapted by the distinct communities in which the evangelical texts came to birth. It is possible
then to argue that the understanding of the modes of re-interpretation
adopted by the Didachist of the common Jewish source/tradition
should prove useful for illuminating and defining the prophetic-apocalyptic phenomenon present and active among the first communities
in Syria.[74]

---

70. Cf. Niederwimmer 1989, pp. 250-251; 255-256.

71. Visonà 2000, p. 241, nn. 40-41.

72. Köster 1957, pp. 173-190; and Kloppenborg 1978-1979.

73. Also A. Tuilier, "La Didachè et le problème synoptique", in Jefford 1995a,
pp. 110-130 (for *Did.* 16, pp. 116-117).

74. Visonà writes: "Una triangolazione *Didachè – Ascensione di Isaia – Matteo*
(Norelli), sembra confermare l'esistenza di un alveo comune di tradizione, che punta
all'ambiente antiocheno del I secolo" (p. 353, n. 6).

5.1. The Synoptic Apocalyptic Discourse in Early Christianity

Besides the difficulty of reconstructing the source (or sources) of the so-called 'apocalyptic discourse' in the synoptic Gospels, it must be pointed out that those apocalyptic traditions can be also found in other proto-Christian writings: 2 Thess already recycles specific traditions, which can be found in the synoptic literature (cf. 2 Thess 2:1//Matt 24:31; 2 Thess 2:10//Matt 24:12); and the *Apocalypse of John* appears to include references to Matthew: cf. Rev 1:1//Matt 24:31, that is the Son of man coming with his angels (par. in Mark 13:27); Rev 1:7//Matt 24:30, that is the pierced Son of man and the wailing people, with a reference to Zech 12:10ff.; Rev 1:10//Matt 24:31, the loud voice; Rev 16:10//Matt 24:51, the gnashing of teeth; Rev 16:15//Matt 24:43, the Son of man disguised as a thief; Rev 18:4//Matt 24:15-20, the desolation of Judaea (par. in Mark 13:14-18); Rev 19:17//Matt 24:28,the allusion to the birds; Rev 1:3//Mark 13:20, the proximity of the time; Rev 6:12//Mark 13:24-25, the meteorological and cosmological phenomena of the end of time; Rev 15:8//Mark 13:26, the glory and power of God; Rev 16:13//Mark 13:22, the pseudo-Prophet (with par. in Matt 24:11.24); Rev 21:22//Mark 13:2, the passing away of the Temple.

Since these references are not decisive to establish a system of direct dependency among the various texts, it has been supposed that they are merely the echo of a Jewish apocalyptic source, common both to the Gospels and to 2 Thess as well as to Rev.[75] Such a supposition is able

---

75. According to several exegetes, the Jewish apocalyptic source of Mark 13 and par. is to be found in a work composed following Caligula's attempt (cf. Flav. Ios., *J.W.* 2.10.1-5) to introduce his statue and cult in the Temple. Cf. T.W. Manson, *The Sayings of Jesus* (London: SCM, 1949[2]); W. Marxsen, *Der Evangelist Markus* (Göttingen: Vandenhoeck & Ruprecht, 1959), pp. 101-140, and R. Pesch, *Das Markus-Evangelium*, II (Freiburg i. Br.: Herder, 1980). As to the possibility that also *Revelation* followed this original source, see R. Pesch, "Marcus 13, Tradition-Redaktion. Von der 'Naherwartungen' zu 'Mk II'", in J. Lambrecht (ed.), *L'Apocalypse johannique et l'apocalyptique dans le N.T.* (BEThL 53; Gembloux-Leuven: Duculot, 1980), pp. 355-368 (see the critique by F. Neirynck, "Marc 13. L'interprétation de R. Pesch", ibid., pp. 369-401). R.H. Charles, *A Critical and Exegetical Commentary on the Revelation of St. John*, vol. II (Edinburgh: T. & T. Clark, 1920), also moved in this direction. To account for the presence of these traditions in 2 Thess, several scholars have supposed the possible influence of 1 Thess 4:13-18: for example, B. Corsani, *L'Apocalisse e l'apocalittica del N.T.* (Bologna: EDB, 1997), pp. 99-102. As to the relations among 1-2 Thess and the Synoptic traditions, see A.J. McNicol, *Jesus' Directions for the Future: A Source and Redaction-History Study of the Use of the Eschatological Tradition in*

not only to explain the differences intervening between the edition by Mark and that by Matthew (for instance Matt 24 omits Mark 13:9-13 which has already been included in chap. 10 [vv 17-21] constructing a broad section on the mission; Matt 24 presents, also, interesting additions to vv 10-12 describing the spread of evil and the cooling of brotherly love; another addition by Matthew is the mention of the "sign of the Son of man" appearing in the sky [v 30], an element present also in *Did.* 16, although it fails to account for the relation with the apocalyptic speech of Q (Luke 17:22-37).[76] Notwithstanding the uncertainties and difficulties, the hypothesis of a common tradition still remains the best explanation not only of the inter-relations existing among the texts which appear to be chronologically and environmentally different, but also of the presence of analogous traditions in distinct communities constituting the original *Sitz im Leben* of the writings in question.

Analysing the numerous references to 'eschatological' discourse, disseminated in proto-Christian literature, it appears that the form of speech, as found in *Matthew*, is the one which seems to be more 'developed'. Also in *Did.* 16, as observed for Rev and 2 Thess, the edition by Matthew of such discourse is the one present the most: cf. *Did.* 16:3a//Matt 24:42.44; *Did.* 16:3b//Matt 7:15; 24:10; *Did.* 16,4a// Matt 24:10.12; *Did.* 16:4b//Matt 24:24; *Did.* 16:5a//Matt 24:10; *Did.* 16:5b//Matt 24:13 (cf also 10:22); *Did.* 16:6b//Matt 24:30; *Did.* 16:8a// Matt 24:30; 26:64. This literary (and textual) situation not only leads one to suppose that Matthew has transmitted his source more 'strictly' than others, but it also clarifies how the tendency of the evangelist/ author is characterised by a re-interpretation of and comment on Jewish sources and traditions in order to transmit his message to a particular Jewish community.[77] Consequently, it is possible to assume that the

---

Paul and in the Synoptic Accounts of Jesus' Last Eschatological Discourse (NGS 9; Macon GA: Mercer University Press, 1996), chaps. 2-3, passim (esp. p. 67).

76. On this passage of the so-called Q-Source, see D. Lührmann, *Die Redaktion der Logienquelle* (Neukirchen: Neukirchener, 1969), pp. 37-42; and S. Schulz, *Q: Die Spruchquelle der Evangelisten* (Zürich: Theologischer, 1972), pp. 277-287; 444-446. Discussion regarding the possible relationship between Q and the eschatological discourse in Matt 24, can be found in McNicol, *Jesus' Directions...*, cit., chaps. 4-6, passim.

77. That Matthew refers more closely to the Jewish source of the eschatological discourse, see McNicol, XIff. (and chaps. 4-6, passim). On the relationship between Matthew and the Jewish 'exegetical schools', I refer the reader to the classic study by

recycling of the same apocalyptic traditions by the Didachist can also cast light on the prophetism present in the community for and in which the *Didache* was written.

For the author of the *Apocalypse* it is possible to suppose an exegetical resumption of the tradition which is typical of Matthew's school (i.e. the union of the text of *Daniel* with that of *Zechariah*),[78] in an apocalyptic context with liturgical interests in which a fundamental role is played by the assembly of the Ecclesia[79] called to interpret - in the light of 'new' soteriological events - the past by means of a re-interpretation of its own Scriptural (not in a canonical sense) tradition. For the *Didache*, by contrast, the use and contextualisation of apocalyptic traditions, incorporated into the synoptic Gospels, must be identified in the prophetism active in Syria between the 1st and the 2nd century CE.[80]

5.2. The Re-interpretation of Jewish Traditions and the Syrian Communities between the 1st and 2nd Centuries CE

I have, as I hope, demonstrated the pre-existence of Jewish traditions in some of the Proto-Christian texts (including the *Didache*) and the process of re-interpretation the Jewish traditions underwent at the hands of Christian writers when they were included in 'new' writings – the latter a real process of adjustment of the sources and traditions during what can be called 'kairological' stage of the community. I will now try to clarify the community context of re-adjustment and actualisation of the probable Jewish *Urtext*, devoting particular attention to the community situation of the *Didache*.

I believe that the specific situation of the Didachean community can be highlighted by another work written at the same time and place, i.e.

K. Stendahl, *The School of St. Matthew and its Use of the O.T.* (ASNU 20; Uppsala-Lund-Copenhagen: Gleerup, 1954). For a review of the theory proposed by Stendahl, see F. Parente, "«ΤΟ ΜΥΣΤΗΡΙΟΝ ΤΗΣ ΒΑΣΙΛΕΙΑΣ ΤΟΥ ΘΕΟΥ». Il 'Pesher di Habaqquq' e il problema del cosiddetto 'Segreto messianico' (Mc 4,10-12)", *Aug.* 35, 1995, pp. 17-42 (in particular, pp. 17-20).

78.   Stendahl, p. 214.

79.   U. Vanni, "L'assemblea ecclesiale 'soggetto interpretante' dell'Apocalisse", *RdT* 23, 1982, pp. 497-513. On the eschatological tendencies of the community which produced the *Apocalypse*, cf. S.S. Smalley, "John's Revelation and John's Community", *BJRL* 69, 1986-1987, pp. 549-571.

80.   Supra, n. 74.

the *Ascension of Isaiah*, a work which resumes and follows several Jewish traditions combined with Judaeo-Christian and proto-gnostic concepts.[81] Reading the passage of *Asc. Is.* 3:21-31, it is possible to notice that the editor-author is faced with a grave situation of crisis affecting the community, sharply contrasted with the image of the Church of Apostolic times (vv 13-20): the apostles abandon prophecy (v. 21), there are internal divisions (v 22), the presbyters are corrupted (vv 23-28). These ethical-doctrinal motifs are literarily translated by means of a chiastic reconstruction, which places at the centre the 'problem' of the community: v 21 = v 31; v 22 = vv 29-30; and vv 23-28 (forming the central argument). In place of the Holy Spirit, the false presbyters – as in apostolic times the false prophets – are guided by the "spirit of error, fornication, pride and greed" (cf. 1 John 2:20.27; 3:24, with probable references to Essene and apocalyptic dualistic conceptions).[82] This wrong behaviour causes internal contrasts: the divisions are the 'sign' that the end is near (3:22).

Since the place of origin of the *Ascension of Isaiah* is Antioch and the time of the composition coincides more or less with that of Ignatius of Antioch (beginning II cent. CE) "lo stato di tensione comunitaria che vi (i.e. in *Asc. Is.*) si avverte potrebbe essere stato il medesimo riflesso nelle lettere di Ignazio, visto da una parte che non era quella del vescovo" (M. Simonetti-E. Prinzivalli, *Storia della letteratura cristiana antica* [Casale Monferrato: Piemme, 1999], p. 37). Consequently the study of the letters by Ignatius could be useful in order to identify both the pressing call of the Bishop to unity of the doctrinally divided community – with the condemnation of those who, for instance, denied the veracity of the incarnation (docetism) – and above all to explore the identity of the 'adversaries' among whom – according to some scholars – several 'judaizing' Christian groups, active in the community of Antioch, should be also counted. Excellent results for such an inquiry

---

81. It is debated whether *Asc. Is.* incorporates a Jewish *Martyrdom* in chaps.1-5. M. Pesce (*Il «Martirio di Isaia» non esiste*, cit.) believes it is impossible to refer to a Jewish "text" on martyrdom; further bibliography in Acerbi, *L'Ascensione di Isaia*, cit., pp. 254-268. For the different Christianities in Syria between the 2nd and 4th century, see P. Bettiolo (ed.), *Scritture e cristianesimi nella Siria tra II e IV secolo* (= *CrSt* 3, 1998).

82. *Contra*, Acerbi, p. 220, n. 38. For the relationship between 1 John and *1QS* III:13-IV:26, see A.R.C. Leaney, *The Rule of Qumran and its Meaning. Introduction, translation and commentary* (London: SCM, 1966), pp. 50-53.

should, finally, come from the study of the pseudo-Clementine *corpus* (i.e. *Homiliae* and *Recognitiones*), the work of two different authors both living in the IV cent. and in the Antiochean *milieu* . "La loro (i.e. *Homeliae* and *Recognitiones*) stretta affinità obbliga a postulare una fonte comune, chiamata *Scritto primitivo,* che risalirebbe ai primi decenni del III secolo...e costituirebbe a sua volta compilazione di fonti precedenti, raggiungendo strati antichissimi della tradizione petrina, e, più genericamente, antipaolina" (Simonetti-Prinzivalli, cit., p. 32). The anti-Pauline 'climate' of the *Ps. Clementine* literature (cf. L. Cirillo, "L'antipaolinismo nelle Pseudoclementine. Un riesame della questione", in Filoramo-Gianotto 2001, pp. 280-303) is, in some aspects, anticipated by the earlier *strata* of the *Didache.* For a confirmation of this statement I refer the reader in particular to Draper 1991b, who points out, among other things, how Antioch was at the centre of controversies focusing on the observance of Mosaic Law (*Torah*) and of the dietary norms, and which involve Paul, Peter and the group led by James (Acts 15:1-35; Gal 2:1-14). "In questa dialettica", writes Visonà, commenting Draper's article, "la *Didachè* rappresenterebbe l'ala giudaizzante e antipaolina, schierata a difesa di una fedeltà integrale alla legge e alle sue esigenze" (cit., p. 45). Norelli, by contrast, fails to find in the letters of Ignatius unequivocal traces of controversies between the Bishop of Antioch and 'judaizing' groups present in the community.[83]

The resort to Jewish traditions underlying the synoptic Gospels is illuminating to illustrate this moment of crisis: also in Mark 13:6.22 and par. The contrasts among the faithful are a premonitory sign of the coming end of the world. It is true that the communities, in which the synoptic Gospels have been edited, prefer to connect the apocalyptic speech with the destruction of the Temple of Jerusalem, although I would either hesitate or exclude relating the 'predictions' of the synoptic Gospels regarding the destruction of the Temple to the situation (= preaching) of the historical Jesus. As a matter of fact the connection between the apocalyptic genre and the reflection on the destruction of the Temple is a constant feature – almost a *topos* – of the apocalyptic literature of the 1st century CE. It is more likely, therefore, that one should assume those predictions to be editorial creation of either a

---

83. E. Norelli, "Ignazio di Antiochia combatte veramente dei cristiani giudaizzanti?", in Filoramo-Gianotto 2001, pp. 220-264.

'preamble' or historical 'scenario' in which previous Jewish traditions come to be inserted in order to accomodate them to the current conditions or needs experienced by the community, which evidently were more interesting for the post-70 events.

Asc. Is. 3:22, 29-30 recycles the Jewish sources of the synoptic Gospels in order to describe the internal divisions caused by the foolishness of the presbyters and the pastors: that these divisions were a sign of the coming of the end is a motif which appears to be at the centre of the community's interest. Along with the revival of Jewish traditions the text is also characterised by a process of selection and readaptation of traditions to the particular needs of the community.

Did. 16 appears also to move in the same direction: in 16:3, the contrasts among the faithful are a tangible sign of the imminence of the end; the false prophets and false apostles are guided by the spirit of Satan (16:3ff.); the Anti-Christ himself will appear creating disorder and confusion by disguising himself as the Son of God (16:4). The situation of crisis in the community is projected in an eschatological future (Εν γάρ ταῖς ἐσχάταις), and in the passage it is possible to find the same selective process functioning as in *Asc. Is.*: the particular situation of the Didachean community marks and requires a greater accentuation of those traditions regarding the false prophets and their corrupting activities.

The prophet is entrusted with the task of reading and interpreting the negative experiences of the community and to reproach, in liturgical contexts, those who abandon the way of justice. The final vision, of an apocalyptic nature, comes to fall perfectly within the boundaries of the role taken up by the prophets in the context of the community of Syria, as testified by *Asc. Is.* 3:21-31 and 6-11 and in *Did.* 10:7; 11:1-2.10-11; 13:3: that vision, on the contrary, expresses a sort of reorganisation of the role played by the prophets by means of other figures contesting the visionary principle. It is possible to comment on two passages of *Asc. Is.* 3:21-31 and 6-11 by using Acerbi's words: "...i profeti sono stati costretti a mettere la sordina al principio visionario ed a ricorrere al principio invocato dagli avversari, ribaltando su di essi l'accusa di infedeltà alla dottrina degli apostoli e dei profeti antichi".[84] The reference of *Did.* 16:3 to the false prophets also appears to refer to a period in which visionary-apocalyptic prophetism was envisaged as an 'unau-

---

84. Acerbi, p. 253.

thorised' and disturbing element: to this situation of crisis the editor-author of the *Didache* appears to oppose the image of a final vision from which the processes of audition and unveiling of the revelation are deliberately excluded in order to avoid arousing further suspicion. On the contrary, the vision – dismembered from the original treatise of the "Two Ways " – is placed at the end of a markedly didactic-moral section, in which the characteristic traits of the community are exposed as well as the necessity to adhere to the apostolic dictates.

Evidently, within the different communities of Syria a sort of into-lerance began to spread toward some gnostic attitudes, which will become a peculiarity of later movements and which founded their doctrines on those literary procedures open to the 'vision' of apocalyptic ascendence.

6. Conclusion

In the analysis of the final chapter of the *Didache* some particular aspects have been highlighted which I would like to summarise:

a. From a merely formal point of view *Did.* 16 can be regarded as an apocalypse. The attribution to this literary genre inevitably entails a series of consequences stemming from a specific 'worldview' which can be defined as eschatological (and, therefore, it is possible to con-clude that the use of the apocalyptic genre by the Didachist responds to particular 'ideological' demands), although this cannot lead one to conclude that *Did.* 16 is, either from an 'ideological' or 'historical' point of view, apocalyptic; these associations could derive only from an 'holistic' comparison among different movements, and without jux-taposing a 'literary' concept alongside a sociological and historical one. A more useful approach to contextualising the 'Judaism' of *Did.* 16 appears to be the category of 'Enochism', which is the historical clas-sification of a specific group within Judaism of the Hellenistic and Roman period (and not as the category of 'apocalyptic' which cannot be referred to any 'specific group' within Judaism).

b. The connection of *Did.* 16 with the section of the "Two Ways" (chaps.1-6) better allows one to clarify the ideological context of the apocalypse in question: the importance of dualistic conceptions, which probably derived from Enochic-Essene and Qumranic *milieux*, is a tangible sign indicating where to situate the (ideological) *Sitz im Leben* of the tradition found in the *Didache*.

c. It appears that the Didachist aimed at gathering and amalgamating traditions, which derived from different *milieux* of the Judaism of the Second Temple and from proto-Christian movements. His aim was to provide a sort of 'synthesis' of specific traditions and doctrines, previously active but which were now being re-interpreted in the light of the new community context of which he is a member.

d. The re-interpretation of these traditions – in the light of the problems and vicissitudes affecting the Syrian communities of the 1st-2nd centuries CE – falls perfectly within the hermeneutics of the Scriptures characteristic of the Judaism of the Graeco-Roman period. Obviously, the term 'Scriptures' has to be understood in this context in a very broad sense in order to include not only the texts which will be later referred to as 'canonical' but also other authoritative religious texts. As a matter of fact, it appears that the texts deriving from the Enoch tradition were held in high esteem within the community/ies of the Didachist.

In my analysis of *Did.* 16 – in particular in the final part of this chapter – I have mainly focused on the possible relationship of this chapter to the traditions of Enochic Judaism (or Enochic Essenism) and with Qumranic Essenism, although I believe it would be possible and legitimate (as it has been partially done in section 3.3.) – and probably desirable – to explore also the revival or recycling by the *Didache* of other apocalyptic traditions, as – for instance – the 'historical-Danielic' one. Furthermore, a comparison between *Did.* 16 and other proto-Christian texts, also deriving at least partially from the Jewish apocalyptic tradition, as for instance the *Shepherd* of Hermas, the *Apocalypse of Paul* or the *Apocalypse of Peter*, could yield results capable of widening the horizon of (Jewish) apocalyptic studies regarding Christian origins. Those works, in fact, are bearers of particular ideological elements which would contribute better to document and cast light on the numerous relationships and dialectics existing among the various proto-Christian groups (included the Christian Judaism) and the contemporary, or immediately previous, currents/ideologies/ traditions characterising "Middle Judaism" or Judaism/s of the Graeco-Roman Period.

CONCLUSIONS

The reader who has painstakingly followed the arguments articulated in the five chapters of this *opus parvum* on the *Didache* – after
having perused, at least in part, the numerous titles present on the 'open
shelves' of my imaginary *scriptorium* (to recall the image I presented in
chap. 1), may feel dissatisfied by the meagre results I have reached in
this monograph. Consequently I will not repeat my investigations and
arguments concerning some of the *strata* of the *Didache,* nor do I
believe it necessary to summarise the conclusions of the individual
chapters.

The fundamental lines of my arguments are clear, I believe, and cast
some light on the problems, but patches of shadow remain here and
there where my methods have left uncertainties and mere probabilities.
Firmer and less provisional conclusions are a goal still a fair distance
away. The present monograph aims not to solve problems but only to
clarify some problematic aspects of the enigmatic richness of this ancient Christian-Jewish work in the more general context of the study of
Christian origins *within* or *as part of* Hellenistic Graeco-Roman Ju-
daism/s or the Judaism/s of the Second Temple.

As has been stated, it is difficult to determine in historical and
institutional terms the precise point at which Judaism and Christianity,
which had set out from a common road, reached a crossroads and
parted ways, to become two different religions, often in contrast but
always – at least in the case of some individuals and groups, and in
particular environments – in search of the common source (*v. supra*,
Introduction).

The canonical and non-canonical texts (although, as has been pointed out, that distinction is somewhat irrelevant for a study mainly of an
historical-institutional character) that refer to the Jewish, Christian-Jewish and Christian traditions of the period of the *Didache* and immediately before and after it are not easy to read and can fall victim to the
'interpretative violence' of the scholar who in the course of examining
them may impose his own reading on them. Being aware of these

exegetical pitfalls, I have preferred a 'stratigraphic' reading or a 'reading by sampling', like the archaeologist who starts his exploration of
the whole site by digging individual trenches, in order to produce a
comprehensive and organic reading of the text. Ancient texts, the *Didache* included, in fact reflect in their final edition both the intentions
of the author and community that produced them and the life of the
community or communities that followed the norms prescribed in the
text, particularly when, as in the case of the *Didache*, these were
conceived and produced progressively as ecclesiastical or community
ordinances. Furthermore, the structure of a text includes earlier materials which, like old bricks reused in a new building, preserve and
reveal traces of older traditions. An illustrative analogy might be the
architecture of some Italian buildings (especially of Renaissance Rome)
in which the last stage records the style and techniques of the time but
still preserves visible components of reused older materials.

In a study of the *Didache* such as mine, which has concentrated on
some of the community institutions, rituals and practices (chaps. 1-4)
but without precluding ideological and doctrinal elements (e.g. 'apocalyptic', as in chap. 5), the researcher must ask whether the roots of such
things do not lie in the terrain of a remote or recent past both of the
single individuals and/or of the communities, groups or movements of
contemporary Judaism. In this monograph I have located and identified
those roots in Jewish terrain and I have tried to pinpoit their origin
while avoiding 'blanket' cross-references to the Judaism of the period,
which reveals a plurality and richness of groupings and movements and
of well documented internal ideological and doctrinal positions (chap.
1). Consequently I believe that one must focus on the historical-institutional contents present in the *Didache* in order to collect reliable data
and attain less repetitive exegetical results, since the institutions both of
Judaism, first, and then of ancient Christianity on the whole resisted a
rapid rate of change. This phenomenon has been noticed, for example,
both for the charity and community of goods of *Did.* 4 and for the be-
weekly fasting (and the tithes) of the 'hypocrites' and that of the
'others' of *Did.* 8, for the *aparche* of *Did.* 13 and finally also for the
'apocalyptic' (and eschatological) convictions of *Did.* 16 widespread
among the Jewish, Christian-Jewish and Christian groups and movements.

In the reading of selected passages I have examined in particular the
Enochic traditions, the Essene-Qumranic and Essene-Hellenistic traditions underlying the text of the *Didache*, although other Jewish tradi-

tions and sources should not be excluded (i.e., the gnomic, sapiential and liturgical traditions), for a comprehensive study of the Jewish 'roots' of the *Didache*. By contrast, generalising references to a 'common Judaism' would be unproductive, since this has never existed but appears rather to be a modern invention created for the purpose of affirming everything and nothing at one and the same time.

My interpretation of some of the ethical and institutional passages of the *Didache*, through the application of a morpho-critical method of reading and the history of the tradition(s), does not stem from the mere desire to explore some of the *realia* present in the work but is an attempt to establish a possible independence of the *Didache* from the Synoptic traditions (in particular from Matthew), when the latter refer to realities similar or analogous to those present in the *Didache*. Above all, I have tried to identify the existence of a dialectics among the groups within the community/ies who read and practiced those norms. This dialectic inside the community, which, along with a few others, I like to refer to as 'Christian Judaism' – at least in the passages examined in the present work – records this situation: here we find no reference to an 'irrevocable parting of the ways' from Judaism. On the contrary, the direct institutional dependence on the and from and effective coexistence of the Didachean community with contemporary Judaism(s) is well documented. It follows that the separation of the "Rebecca's children" (in Segal's phrase), that is, Judaism and Christianity or the Synagogue and the Church, is to be deferred to a period following the final edition of the *Didache*. It is possible, however, to find a reference to the incipient separation in the final edition of the Gospel of Matthew.

In conclusion the *Didache* can, as I see it, be included in the list of ancient texts which document the presence of a dialectic among groups and movements in search of an identity ('we', 'you' and 'the others') in the Ancient Near East. Such a dialectic existed within various movements of Hellenistic and Roman Judaism, and then faded out, to reappear in Christian Judaism and later within the various interwoven forms of Christianity up to our own time. It is going on at present day among the peoples and religions of the Mediterranean, being particularly visible in the current Middle East crisis caused by unresolved political-territorial disputes.

Today it is the clash of national and religious identities which seems to have the upper hand but the hope for a re-found unity in the future is still alive, at least in the peoples of monotheistic tradition who trace themselves back to Abraham, the 'father of all believers' (Gen 12 and 15, Heb 11:8 etc.) or to the 'first of the consecrated (*muslim*) to God' (Qur'an 2:131; 3:67; 4:125 etc.).

In this setting the textual and community situation of the *Didache*, which documents the 'cohabitation' of 'Christian Judaism' with contemporary strands of Judaism – in Syria-Palestine and probably in the region of Antioch of the 1st century CE – might offer a model and a sign of hope for a recovery of such coexistence which we too in our own day might be able to achieve.

INDICES

– The Sources Index includes the reference to actual documents, while references to hypothetical (oral and/or written) traditions and documents, eg Q (= Quelle) and DVD (= Duae Viae Document), appear in the Subject Index.
– Page numbers in **bold print** indicate passages which are central to the argument.

I. *Sources*

1. *Miqra' or Hebrew Bible*

2. *Greek and Latin Versions of Miqra'*

2.1. Septuagint

2.2. Theodotion
234-235

2.3. Vulgate

3. *OT Pseudepigrapha*

1. The hypothesis of a Jewish writing underlying *Asc. Is.* has been rejected by several scholars: Norelli, Pesce, Acerbi and others maintain that the text certainly refers to Jewish material but its *Sitz im Leben* must be traced in some of the ongoing disputes or debates within the Christian communities of Syria during the 2nd century CE.

II. *Subjects*

III. *Modern Authors*